THE BLUE HAZE

THE
BLUE HAZE

INCORPORATING THE HISTORY OF 'A' FORCE
GROUPS 3 & 5
BURMA-THAI RAILWAY
1942-1943

LESLIE G. HALL

Kangaroo Press

Cover art by **Richard Cochran**

First published in 1996 by Kangaroo Press Pty Ltd
3 Whitehall Road Kenthurst NSW 2156 Australia
P.O. Box 6125 Dural Delivery Centre NSW 2158
Printed in Singapore through Global-Com Pte Ltd

ISBN 0 86417 786 0

INDEX

DEDICATION

To the memory of my devoted wife, Gladys,
whose faith in my survival and return home never wavered
AND
in memory of the thousands of lads who tried so valiantly to
survive starvation, disease and inhuman treatment, who now rest
eternally in the tranquillity of Thanbyuzayat cemetery, Burma.

LEST WE FORGET

The title of this book was inspired by
a vision a prisoner of war saw during
what was believed to be his last minutes of life

FOREWORD TO THE FIRST EDITION

SURVIVORS OF OVER 15,000 Australians who were POWs of the Japanese have not asked for sympathy, but they have hoped for an understanding of some of the effects, physical and mental, of the three and a half years of their captivity.

This was an experience which could not fail to have changed each of them. In most cases they became better men, more tolerant of others, and grateful for their escape from death. Relatively few, I believe, have remained bitter and resentful—though their scars have never healed.

It is well to consider some of the factors which have prompted these remarks, and some such factors emerge from this book. Individual experiences of POWs varied greatly from man to man, and from place to place, as did individual reactions. So a writer who sets out to tell the story of a group of POWs, is presented with a mass of detail out of which to create a picture truly representative of the group as a whole.

After the fall of Singapore on 15 February 1942, approximately 50,000 British and Australian troops became POWs of the Japanese.

All prisoners were firstly concentrated in the Changi area on the north-east tip of Singapore Island. But the 15,000 Australians were not to remain together for very long. Soon working parties were sent away to camps on or near the island. By 8 March 1942, over 8,750 Australians had been moved away from Changi.

Then in mid-April 1942 the Japanese ordered that a party of 3,000 Australians should leave for an unstated destination overseas, with the promise that there they would find abundant food and good conditions—a promise cruelly false from the beginning. Instead of a place of good food and good conditions, this party was moved north to work on the construction of the Burma-Thailand railway line under conditions as harsh and brutal as any experienced by any Australian POWs anywhere.

This group, being the first of the Australians to leave Singapore, was to be known as 'A Force'. It is the story of A Force, later joined by Australians captured in Java, of which Leslie Hall writes so fully and vividly.

His was a difficult task. He drew firstly on his own experiences, but to his credit he has not given them prominence. Some records and individual diaries were traced and made available to him, but much of what he has written has not previously been made public.

Why now, over fifty years afterwards, should his writings appear in book form?

There is, I believe, good reason. The men of 'A' Force showed a courage of which they, and we, can be proud. But more than courage emerged in Burma and Thailand. Out of hardship and brutality, out of starvation and disease, out of the devastating death toll, there grew up friendships and sacrifices, mateship in its truest form, and inspiring qualities of character, sometimes from the most unexpected sources. When death seemed preferable, these men dared to live.

These are reasons why the story of 'A' Force should be told, why the experiences of these men, and of the other Australians who were forced to work on the Burma-Thailand railway, should be remembered when we sometimes think that we are having a bad time here at home in Australia.

I commend this book not only to those who will read its lines in print, but also to those who will read between the lines, there to learn more of the men of 'A' Force.

Phillip Lyburn Head, MBE, QC
Retired Judge, Major Headquarters
8th Australian Division 1940-45

ACKNOWLEDGMENTS

BUT FOR THE READY assistance and cooperation of the undermentioned, this history might never have been written. Research and preparations have taken many months as decisions as to what should be included or, unfortunately, disregarded were made. I am most grateful to all who provided me with essentials so necessary for the compilation—diaries, letters, memoirs and drawings. They are:

The late Colonel G.E. Ramsay, ED, who, post-war, presented me with copies of reports submitted by him to various Japanese camp commandants. Also, for his friendship—a bond that lasted unto death.

Colonel J.M. Williams, OBE, ED, Commander 2/2 Pioneer Battalion, Corps Troops, and Williams Force, Burma, who permitted me unrestricted use of his personal diary, covering fifteen months of his and his troops' experiences on the infamous Burma-Thailand railway. In addition, I am especially indebted to him for his tireless support and his guidance, encouragement and advice when, at times, I felt I could no longer carry on.

His Honour Phillip Lyburn Head, MBE, QC, retired judge, major, Headquarters 8th Australian Division, who so willingly accepted my invitation to peruse the manuscript and write the Foreword.

J.G. 'Tom' Morris of Canberra (22 Brigade Headquarters) for his untiring efforts to assist me in researching records at the Australian War Memorial—a task that saved me many months of work. Also for his guidance in the selection of photographs.

Former Lieutenants A.I. Farr and J. Kreckler (2/30 Battalion) for their continuing interest in the preparation of the revised edition of *The Blue Haze*.

Max Ramsay, son of Lieutenant Colonel G.E. Ramsay, for his cooperation in providing a copy of *Lust and Vengeance* (history of the Malayan Campaign) and also photographs from his collection.

John Wade (2/15 Field Artillery) for supplying important information on the fate of survivors of the *Rakuyo Maru*.

Alexander Dandie (2/30 Battalion) for his invaluable assistance in the compilation of both editions of *The Blue Haze*. He is affectionately, and accurately, known as the human encyclopaedia.

Linda Goetz Holmes, of Shelter Island, New York, for her much appreciated assistance in procuring copies of official Japanese documents.

Betty Pryde, widow of Captain Alan Pryde, 2/30 Battalion, who provided me with valuable information extracted from her late husband's personal diary.

Tony Clive, Postal Corps, for permission to record valuable information contained in his memoirs and his willingness to assist me in any way possible.

Shirley Maples of Harbord, NSW, for her cooperation in the preparatory stages of committing masses of material to paper. Also for the typing of the Williams Force diary.

Kit Fagan of Frenchs Forest, NSW, who authorised me to include extracts from her late husband's record of his experiences in the Middle East, Java and 'A' Force, Burma.

Margaret Winter of Condell Park, NSW, wife of ex-POW Mark Winter (8th Division Headquarters), a former member of Anderson Force, for her invaluable application to the typing of the complete manuscript, proofreading and advice.

Miss Anne Beatson, of Harbord, and Delyse Hall, Collaroy, for their interest in, and work, on the revised edition of *The Blue Haze*.

Major Reginald Newton, MBE, ED, Editor of *The Grim Glory: History of the 2/19 Battalion AIF*, for permission to use extracts.

The Albert Coates Story, co-edited by the Late Sir Albert Coates and Newman Rosenthal (courtesy Hyland House Publishers, Melbourne).

The Australian War Memorial, Canberra, for authority to use extracts from Lionel Wigmore, *The Japanese Thrust* (Official War History).

The editors and staff, *Men May Smoke: History of the 2/18 Battalion AIF,* for information concerning Ramsay Force.

J.B. Chalker, former POW, Burma-Thailand, renowned artist, for his drawing of the hut at the 55 kilo hospital camp, used extensively by Lieutenant Colonel Coates and Major Alan Hobbs as an ulcer and allied diseases ward. The operating theatre was a lean-to at one end of the bamboo and atap structure.

Dulcie Korsch, widow of John Korsch, corporal, 2/30 Battalion, for permission to reproduce drawings of his impressions of Mergui township and POW huts.

The editor and staff of *Barbed Wire and Bamboo* (journal of the Ex-Prisoners of War Association of Australia) for Australia-wide publicity.

Max Herron, honorary secretary, 2/1-2/2 Pioneer Battalions Association (NSW) and co-editor *Pioneer News* magazine, for publicity. Also, Edward Hansen, president, 2/2 Pioneer Battalion Association, Victoria, in association with George Murphy, honorary secretary and Jack Hocking, treasurer and editor, for their cooperation in publicising the 'A' Force history.

Jock McDougall, editor of *Makan*, official journal of the 2/30 Battalion AIF Association, and his staff, for supportive cooperation and generous assistance with publicity.

The Trustees of the Imperial War Museum, London, for permission to reproduce the Chalker drawings from *The Albert Coates Story*.

R.J. (Dick) Cochran (2/12 Field Company Engineers), Commercial Artist of Mosman, NSW, for the design of the jacket cover.

PREFACE

THE FALL OF SINGAPORE on Sunday, 15 February 1942, was one of the greatest shocks suffered by British and Australian Forces in World War II.

The impossible had incredibly happened! Singapore had been considered an impregnable fortress but this belief proved to be a myth of gigantic proportions. The huge concrete pillboxes existed only in people's minds, as did the belief that any attack would have to come from the sea, but all defence preparations lent weight to that fallacy. The enormous 15-inch naval armament was presented as the rock upon which any aggressor would perish dare they presume to launch an invasion of the Island.

All but one of those huge guns pointed seawards; only one had a traversing base. Eventually, that solitary weapon fired but two rounds and succeeded in blowing up a train standing at Johore Bahru railway station. When the two one-ton shells thudded against their target the fall of the besieged island was a foregone conclusion.

Intelligence forays into the invading force's territory pinpointed the positions of hundreds of watercraft to be used to ferry troops, ammunition and supplies across the Straits of Johore to a planned invasion area.

That plan could have been thwarted if the British and Australian artillery units had been allowed to lay down a bombardment that might have destroyed the boats the enemy had packed together, which were well within gunnery range. Why permission to shell the Johore Bahru foreshores was not given is a mystery that will never be solved. It was not withheld because of shortage of ammunition. That was proved when over twenty 25-pounders arrived at the position held by the 2/30 Battalion in Tanglin Gardens.

A cheery British officer presented himself to Lieutenant Colonel G.E. Ramsay, saying 'Well, here we are, plenty of ammo, where do you want them?'

Ramsay was astounded. A commanding officer's dream come true—guns, no shortage of ammunition, and crews bursting with the opportunity to blast hell out of opposing troops. But with no permissible target to lay down a barrage on, his pleas were ignored and those pieces of a war machine remained silent.

The subsequent order to lay down arms at 8.30 p.m., 15 February, was for humanitarian reasons only. The island's water supply had been cut off by the Nipponese at Johore Bahru. The greatest tragedy throughout the fighting was the carnage inflicted upon the civilian population. That, together with the lack of water, created an impossible situation. Fighting had to cease if a massacre of non-combatants was to be avoided; capitulation was, therefore, an absolute necessity.

When the order to lay down arms was promulgated the defending troops were stunned. 'A fight to the finish' had been General Wavell's command. Every soldier was prepared to carry that out to the letter. Instead they were to become prisoners of war.

Shame and frustration flooded their minds, as a possible surrender was the very last thing on their minds. That they were ordered to do so was unbelievable. They were thunderstruck and dismayed.

What did the future hold for them? They were soon to learn!

⠋ CHANGI

WITHIN WEEKS of their incarceration in the barracks formerly occupied by a British regiment, the Gordon Highlanders, many work parties had been formed and sent into Singapore to labour on the wharves. The go-downs (wharf buildings) were packed with all kinds of cargo destined to be transported to Japan. The spoils of war; tons and tons of it.

The naval stores proved a bonanza; they were packed to the gunwales with clothes, equipment, ammunition and just about everything needed to supply naval vessels of any size or type. The Nipponese were astounded at the vast quantity abandoned by the British.

There was no real scorched earth policy carried out on the island; what was destroyed was the result, in the main, of pattern bombing by Nipponese aircraft. Had the city itself been subjected to the torch, the enormity of the civilian loss could have had horrifying results. Other than blowing up ammunition dumps and rendering artillery pieces unusable, nothing else could have been done. Oil storage tanks had been bombed time and time again, and became torn and twisted metal.

As the sun set on the last day of fighting the island needed no additional lighting; it was ringed with fire from blazing buildings and what was left of oil tanks and vessels burning, wharfside and in the bay.

It was a sad ending for the fighting forces from countries far apart—Britain, Australia and India—who, until the very last moment, expected hand-to-hand fighting to wipe out the stigma of having had to engage in a planned withdrawal, from the beaches of Thailand to the docks of 'mighty' Singapore.

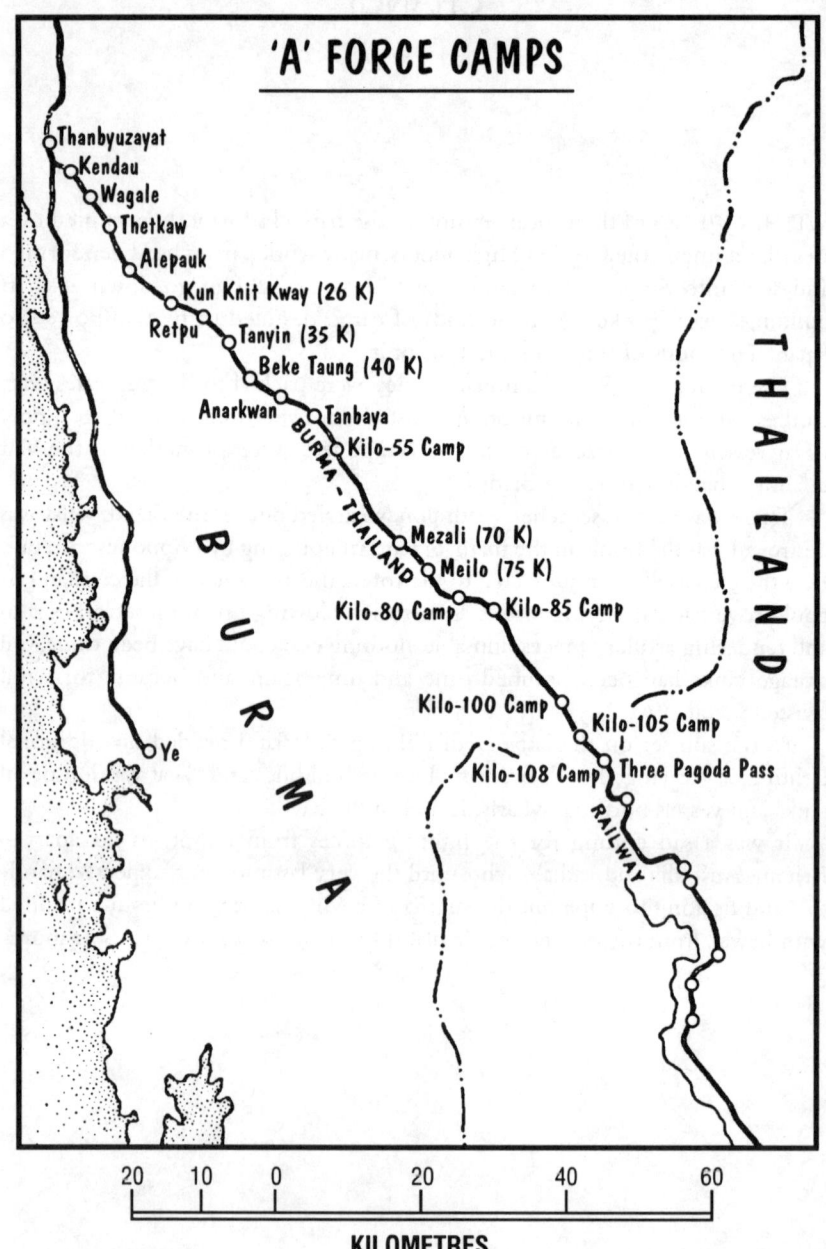

'A' FORCE CAMPS

Thanbyuzayat
Kendau
Wagale
Thetkaw
Alepauk
Kun Knit Kway (26 K)
Retpu   Tanyin (35 K)
Beke Taung (40 K)
Anarkwan   Tanbaya
Kilo-55 Camp

BURMA - THAILAND

Mezali (70 K)
Meilo (75 K)
Kilo-80 Camp   Kilo-85 Camp

Kilo-100 Camp
Kilo-105 Camp
Kilo-108 Camp   Three Pagoda Pass

RAILWAY

BURMA

THAILAND

Ye

20   10   0   20   40   60

KILOMETRES

FORMATION OF 'A' FORCE

IN MID APRIL 1942, orders came from the Japanese Commandant of all POWs on Singapore Island for a group of 6,000 men, irrespective of physical condition, for transfer overseas; destination unknown.

As it was not in the true sense a working party, the inclusion of 'light sick' would not matter. They were destined for an area where good food was to be found in abundance. In addition, medical supplies would be plentiful.

When the Commandant was informed it would be impossible to provide that many AIF personnel unless working parties in Singapore were recalled, the demand was halved.

In reply to the contention that even this reduced figure would necessitate the inclusion of a considerable proportion of men whom our medical officers regarded as being unfit for any hard manual work, AIF Headquarters was advised to the effect that, as stated in the original request, the force would not be required as a working party; the temporary ill-health of a percentage of the troops selected would not constitute any hardship or inconvenience.

Further to this assurance, arrangements were being made for the move to Singapore docks—fifteen miles distant—to be by motor transport, rather than on foot, which appeared to be the original idea.

Organisation

The Force was to be commanded by Brigadier A.L. Varley, MC, Commander of 22 Infantry Brigade, with Lieutenant Colonel C.G.W. Anderson, VC, MC, as senior staff officer.

A CCS detachment under Lieutenant Colonel T. Hamilton, 2/4 CCS, and an Engineer detachment under Major J.A.L. Shaw, 2/12 Field Company RAE; a headquarter staff and three battalions, each of approximately 850, all ranks; No. 1 Battalion under Lieutenant Colonel G.E. Ramsay, 2/18 Battalion; No. 2 Battalion under Major D.R. Kerr, 2/10 Field Regiment, RAA; No. 3 Battalion under Major C.E. Green, 2/4 Machine Gun Battalion.

It was advised by the Japanese that all members of this force would be sent to one destination. Permission to take any tools, medical supplies and/or other equipment was refused and an assurance given that all such facilities would be available on arrival at their new quarters.

This, in fact, proved incorrect in every detail!

Composition of 'A' Force

Unit Quotas	Personnel
22 Brigade Headquarters	53
Records	6
Officers, HQ Staff	7
Brigadier A.L. Varley, OIC	
Lt. Col. C.G.W. Anderson, 2 i/c	
Major J.M. Stringer, 2/26 Bn	
Major J.F. Campbell, AASC	
Captain R.S. Griffin, 2/18 Bn	
Major J. Hordern, 22 Bde HQ	
Captain W. Drower, Official Interpreter	
AIF Pay Corps	5
AIF Postal Corps	11
K and L area	60
RAA	500
RAE	260
8 Div. Signals	160
2/18, 2/19 and 2/20 Battalions	310
2/26, 2/29 and 2/30 Battalions	450
2/4 Machine-Gun Battalions	200
AASC	450
AAOC	300
Provosts Corps	40
AASC (attached to AAMC)	39
Chaplains	5
Red Cross representatives	2

The eventual disposition of all troops, despite assurance given by the Japanese to the contrary, was three areas in Burma, viz:

- Victoria Point under the command of Major C. E. Green
- Mergui, under the command of Lieutenant Colonel G.E. Ramsay
- Tavoy, under the command of Major D. Kerr

On arrival at Tavoy, Lieutenant Colonel C.G.W. Anderson assumed command of the 983 personnel. Major D. Kerr became his 2 i/c. From that point on, the Kerr Force became officially known as Anderson Force—subsequently, in association with Williams Force, No. 1 Mobile Force.

A Memorable Voyage

WHEN THE 3,000 men were assembled on the wharf they expected to see a passenger vessel awaiting their transport. Instead, all they could see were two rusty old cargo craft upon which there was no hope that even half their number could possibly be comfortably accommodated.

One lad, a former wharfie at Fremantle, was startled when he recognised the 'old blue-bottle', as he described it, the *Celebes Maru*.

'Holy Hell,' he exploded, 'if we are to go aboard that thing we'll be in sheep pens. Pre-war, I helped load thousands onto that old bucket and the poor old sheep had barely enough room to stand. Boy, why did I break my resolve never to volunteer for anything in the army?'

It was not too long before the whole group became aware there was to be no 'Queen Mary' liner, or anything like it, for their voyage to God knew where. Imaginations ran riot as they gazed at the hulk that could be their home for days and nights to come. To say many were uneasy would be a mammoth understatement. They were, and had need to be!

Tempers frayed as the hours of waiting grew; parched throats soon emptied water bottles—for those who had them—but then came a greater problem. Jap guards soon made it quite clear that life from that moment was not going to be a bed of roses. The taps were out of bounds, and the first acts of brutality to surface were against those who sought refills for empty bottles.

The sound of closed fists, rifle butts and the thud of boot leather against human bodies told its own tale. One officer, Captain Alan Pryde, No. 1 Battalion Quartermaster (2/30 Battalion) intervened and tasted his first fiendish punishment, a kick aimed at his groin which he expertly avoided, much to the enraged Nip's dislike. What may have followed but for a Japanese NCO, can only be imagined. He pointed to the pips worn by all British and Australian officers, said something no-one could understand unless versed in Japanese, and allowed use of the fresh water tap to whomever needed it.

Two more incidents within minutes again brought home the fact the Changi 'holiday' was over. An Australian caught 'borrowing' a bottle of pickled onions was bashed unmercifully. A short time later another daredevil Digger, who purloined something edible from a go-down, was caught and hung up by his thumbs.

The ferocity of the bashings after some Chinese wharfies committed some 'crime' against Nippon was witnessed by many POWs. They favoured intervention until dissuaded by Major 'Bill' Cousens, who feared such action would only result in frightful repercussions. It was he who had the lad, tied up by the thumbs, released from his intense agony.

Embarkation on the 'sheep ship' was completed at about 0100 hours, after groups of fifty climbed rope ladders with great difficulty due to the gear that had to be carried by each individual. One young boy fell from near top deck level, broke his leg and was sent back to Changi. He was, as it turned out, the luckiest of the 3,000 POWs who had volunteered for the overseas mystery adventure.

As both ships were of similar construction and about 5,000 tons, the allowed space on the *Celebes Maru* was a carbon copy of that allowed in the other rust bucket.

Three holds were provided. The largest, aft end, had to accommodate 640 closely packed bodies in, as forecast by the one time Fremantle wharf worker, sheep pens.

They lay, three in line, hull to centre, and only the shortest could actually sit up. Those above 5 foot 7 inches or thereabouts soon had cricks in their necks as they endeavoured, unsuccessfully, to find some fragment of comfort.

Within minutes the air was fetid; made even worse by those suffering from dysentery. The stench was almost unbearable as the afflicted fouled themselves. Pleas for permission to use the toilets fell on deaf ears. It was only after Lieutenant Colonel G.E. Ramsay made strong representations that the use of the two three-hole 'toilets' was permitted. However, with so many aboard and the necessity for constant use, the area soon overflowed, decking was fouled and the returning users carried back excrement until it lay everywhere in the holds.

Tropical heat, and that generated by body contact, made breathing difficult. To ease that situation, the CO finally convinced the ship's captain that a wind-sock was an absolute necessity to prevent tragedy and burials at sea. With little or no wind whilst hove-to, many suffered.

Fresh water supplies were at a premium; none was available for bathing or washing. After more representations were made, it was finally agreed that a salt-water hose could be used to cleanse bodies.

However, while it was one thing to be hosed down on the top deck of the 'sardine tin'-type craft, Conditions remained appalling in the bowels of the disease-infested ship—much worse than the notorious *Altmark*, and that was an incident that shocked the world. Double or treble the fate of those unfortunates, and some idea of a voyage under Japanese control can be imagined.

Hundreds of men were packed in so tightly that if one moved, a domino effect resulted. They crouched in their own filth. The stench made many retch and that, combined with seasickness, added to the ever-present misery of all below decks.

Constant protests by the force commander (Ramsay) eventually forced the guards to allow batches of fifty men on top deck for a period of twenty golden minutes each. As they stepped onto the decking and inhaled the fresh sea air it was akin to a gift from the gods. But a hose down and a last breath of sweet-smelling ozone were followed by a return to the sickening hold.

How so many survived that frightening voyage is a medical mystery. But fate decreed they would and eventually make a landfall which, for many, would end in a lasting resting place in a foreign country.

Major J.S. Chalmers, Australian Army Medical Corps, was so incensed and horrified at the treatment the below decks troops had to endure that he compiled a report covering the frightful conditions they suffered on that agonising nine-day voyage. It reads, in part:

The conditions on the *Celebes Maru* in which most of the AIF personnel landed at Mergui, South Burma, having travelled from Singapore, were very unhygienic. There were many men aboard who had dysentery, bacillary and amoebic, at Changi. Many of these had residual diarrhoea at time of embarkation, and others had a return of symptoms on the ship.

The latrine accommodation was very poor, one three-hole at the aft and another at midships, 6 per 1,000 men. The absolute minimum army requirements are 5% to 1,000 and 3% over this, i.e. 32 per 1,000.

These latrines were flushed only once per day; hence they rapidly became full and very easily fouled. Men wore boots in the latrines and back to their quarters, infecting those areas where they also ate.

Drinking water was very restricted; no fresh water was available for washing. Eating utensils were washed in a large tub. After the first hundred or so had used them the water was very dirty, but could not be changed until ALL men had used it. Due to the speed which men had to file past the tubs of boiling water (for sterilisation of eating utensils) the actual dipping was more of a pious gesture.

Conditions below deck were insufferably hot, stuffy and crowded. All these factors provided excellent conditions for the outbreak of diseases.

On landing at Mergui (24th May, 1942), South Burma, the AIF detachments were joined by 500 British troops from Sumatra; mixed Army, Navy and Air Force, under the command of Lt. Col. Coates, AAMC.

This Force marched through heavy rain to the school where they were allotted very crowded quarters. They were so crowded it was almost impossible for anyone to move about; the upper verandahs were also packed. Many had to sleep on concrete floors.

*

When the *Celebes Maru* berthed at Medan, Sumatra, 350 Japanese troops came aboard, as a result of which the POWs were forced down into the bowels of the filthy hulk. From that point to Mergui they really did voyage like sheep.

VICTORIA POINT TO THANBYUZAYAT
Extracts from the memoirs of J. G. (Tom) Morris

OUR FIRST PORT of call was Medan, on the north-east coast of Sumatra. We lay at anchor some distance offshore, in considerable discomfort. By now we were occasionally allowed up on deck, and also to use the salt-water hoses there for a quick shower. Later in the day we were joined by three more ships, one of which carried Dutch prisoners of war. The final complement to our convoy was a small Japanese minesweeper as an escort.

Victoria Point

On 20 May, after an uneventful voyage, we anchored some distance off Victoria Point, situated on the southernmost tip of Burma adjacent to Thailand. With the pushing and shoving to which we were now becoming accustomed, accompanied by shouts of abuse, we were bundled down the rope ladders and into the motorised landing craft for the journey to the wharves at Victoria Point. For the rest of the day and well into the night we toiled unloading 44-gallon drums of petrol, bags of rice and salt, as well as other items of equipment from the barges as they arrived from the ships.

A total complement of 1,017 Australian POWs from the *Tohohasi Maru* disembarked here. This group, to be known as Green Force, was under the command of Major Charles Green, 2/4 Machine-Gun Battalion. This meant a further splitting of my unit, as a number of them travelled on to Tavoy further up the coast, as part of Anderson Force, under the command of Lt. Col. Charles Anderson, VC, 2/19 Bn. Some of these I met again at Tamarkan (Thailand) 1944. Some I was never to meet again, as they died during the railway construction in camps throughout Burma.

The following day we were paraded and addressed by the Japanese Commander, Captain Yasuda. He stressed that we were now privileged to work for the Imperial Japanese Emperor; that we were surrounded by sea, Japanese troops and jungle; that any attempts to escape would not only be foolish, but would result in the escapee, when recaptured, being shot.

At this stage, Green Force was split once again. One group of 600 were to work on the aerodrome, whilst the remainder were to be employed in the precincts of the Victoria Point township and wharves. In typical Japanese fashion, the aerodrome party was arbitrarily chosen, simply by counting off according to where he had slept the night before. Although a quartering party had been arranged by Captain White and a Japanese corporal on 20 May, when we tried to implement it, a Japanese corporal refused permission to do so, and forced us to move into groups, in many cases irrespective of rank or unit. A further attempt, on 22 May, to reunite groups and units, was also unsuccessful. Thus, even close friends became separated. For me, however, it was to be the beginning of a lifelong friendship with Eric Bailey, whose care and assistance in desperate times contributed greatly to my eventual safe return to Australia.

On 22 May we set out for the aerodrome, some 8 miles away. Apart from some of the sick, who travelled on a truck with the heavy baggage, we marched, carrying our personal belongings. A truck was sent back at about 3.30 p.m. to pick up our cooks and rations, to enable them to prepare a meal for us on our arrival. When they reached the camp they were given 30 three-gallon and three or four 44-gallon drums for cooking the rice and 'stew'. There was no wood for the fires, and this had to be located and carried some distance before they could begin cooking.

We arrived about 4.30 p.m. tired, hungry and dispirited. First we had to suffer the long tenko, or rollcall, by Japanese armed with the inevitable abacus. Even with this aid it took them ages to arrive at the correct figure. This was to be repeated ad infinitum over the next three years. Quite often, in despair, our own officers took over the counting and the Japanese orderly accepted their figures, which of course were invariably correct.

Finally, somewhere around midnight our meal was ready—rice and 'stew' with a distinct flavour of gasoline from the freshly opened drums. We burped these fumes for days until the drums lost their petrol tang.

The time I spent in this camp was probably the most relaxed and least onerous of any I was to experience over the rest of my captivity. Perhaps the only exception was a short period at Ye in September 1942. Amusement and recreation centred around our concerts—not elaborate affairs—often based on quite bawdy material, circloss, reading for those fortunate enough to possess books, chess and bridge, which were taught to me by Eric Bailey, with whom I now fortuitously shared a two-tiered bunk. Some of the more energetic lads played the occasional game of football or cricket on the aerodrome.

Accommodation in the early stages was somewhat unsatisfactory in the aerodrome camp, with some men sleeping on bare ground underneath an elevated barrack hut. In acknowledging this shortcoming, the Japanese explained that they had only arrived themselves two days previously. To their credit, timber was supplied for flooring and cover provided to act as walls. This at least kept out the monsoon rains.

Work consisted of road repairs, the filling-in of shell holes on the aerodrome, and searching for the mines which the British had laid prior to their departure. The guards caused us no problems and work ceased when it rained, which was almost every afternoon. Morale improved as new friendships were formed, and the need for cooperation, as a means of self-preservation, became apparent. However, we did resent the daily tenkos at which we had to honour the Japanese Emperor, by bowing towards the rising sun. Many rude suggestions were quietly uttered during this procedure.

Lt. Macawley, 2/26 Bn, became our platoon commander. He once again raised our ire by beginning to learn the Japanese language. This meant he had a close association with the Japanese guards—something we frowned upon with deep suspicion. We now bestowed upon him, in addition to his previously earned 'Dice', the epithet, 'White Jap'. How wrong we were! He was a fine officer along the railway line, and his ability to converse with the Japanese often came in handy. He possessed the forethought we so obviously lacked.

Payment for our work commenced in June. The rates were: 15 cents for NCOs and 10 cents for other ranks (daily rate). All Malayan money had been handed to our canteen committee and the amount was credited to each individual's account. The first Japanese pay received was in $10 Japanese rupee notes. As this made individual payment impossible the canteen credit system was again adopted.

A further outbreak of dysentery 'hospitalised' me for about three weeks. This merely meant being segregated in a hut some distance from the others. Food was the normal camp distributed ration served to us in our isolation. The only medicine available was ground charcoal. The open latrine, devoid of any shelter from the elements, was some 50-100 yards away and my 20-30 trips daily to it, often in pouring rain, did nothing to speed my recovery. However, it finally subsided and for the rest of the period at Victoria Point my health was generally good.

Our cooks built ovens and so were able to produce small buns, biscuits and pasties as an occasional treat. In mid-June, our ration scale was increased to 716g of rice and 75g of meat per day. This was supplemented with some vegetables, coconuts and bananas. The meat did give the 'stew' a bit of flavour, although it was a lucky person who saw a small cube of meat or fat floating in his portion. Later, when work on the Burma-Thailand railway commenced, to ensure a fair distribution of 'surplus' food, a system of 'back up' or 'legge' numbers was introduced. Any food left over, after the initial servings, was distributed on a numerical rotation. As there was never much of a surplus, the numbers didn't come up too often.

Our camp was surrounded by a standard wire fence, but night-time 'traders' slipped into the local village to purchase extra food items. The local natives, seeing an unexpected source of business, soon ventured close to the fences in broad daylight. This brought an instant reaction from the Japanese, who quickly dispersed them. We were warned that if we were found outside the wire we would be shot.

We were introduced to two Japanese rules that were to plague us for the rest of our POW days. Firstly, time irrespective of location, was always based on Tokyo time. Thus at one stage the 6.30 a.m. reveille was actually 4.30 a.m.; lights out—our little wick and peanut oil lamp—was 9.30 p.m., but in reality 7.30 p.m. Secondly, we had to supply our own internal guards.

We each experimented with our portion of rice in an endeavour to make it more palatable. With a sheet of iron for a hot plate, we made a sort of patty cake, burnt on each side, with a bit of salt and turmeric for added flavour. The latter certainly did something for the colour, but little for the taste. Coffee was made by burning uncooked rice until it was almost black, and then adding it to boiling water. It at least looked like coffee, and when we were able to add a bit of chintegar—a sort of brown sugar in hard slabs—it even began to taste like coffee! I must add here, that our drinking fluids were always boiled, a fact that was probably responsible for the relatively low incidence of cholera in 'A' Force.

Cigarettes were occasionally issued by the Japanese and, being a non-smoker, I used my issue as barter for extra food. A local tobacco used by the natives was available for purchase through the 'canteen'. It was a vivid red in colour, and the locals smoked it using a minute amount rolled in a slip of paper, narrow at one end and wide at the other. It was extremely pungent and caused spontaneous fits of coughing. In true Aussie style it soon became known as 'hag's bush' or 'mother in law's armpit'.

The most distressing event to occur at Victoria Point was the attempted escape, recapture and execution without trial, of Pte Goulden. On 8 July a report was made to Japanese HQ that Goulden was 'missing' from the camp. Lt Iguchi visited our camp and informed Major Green that the prisoner, when recaptured, would be shot.

On the morning of 12 July he was caught, brought back to camp and taken to the Japanese guardhouse. Major Green protested strongly about the death sentence, but was refused permission to see the Japanese officers. Ten men were sent by truck to dig a grave.

Shortly before noon we were all assembled on the parade ground, and Pte Goulden, under armed guard and with his hands tied behind his back, was marched down to the area. Captain Yasuda, through an interpreter, formally announced the death sentence. In doing so, Yasuda withdrew his sword, and we expected him to behead Goulden there and then. There was a ripple of protest and angry muttering from the assembled prisoners of war, but by resolute command Major Green and our platoon commanders restored calm. Pte Goulden was then marched off towards the hill, accompanied by the firing squad and four of our officers. At 1200 hours he was shot. We then lined the roadside, as his blanket-wrapped body was carried to the main gate, loaded onto a truck, and taken to Victoria Point for burial in the English cemetery.

We were left with a feeling of depression, tinged with a sense of guilt that one of our group had been executed, yet we had been unable to do anything about it. The Japanese, on the other hand, had already shown us another side of their unpredictable nature. We had already suffered two deaths from dysentery. The Japanese attended their funerals, laid wreaths, lit candles, provided a Japanese guard of honour, and donated $10 for additional mourning.

The futility of attempted escape became even more apparent when we learnt that, on 6 June, eight members of 4 Anti-Tank Regiment had been executed at Tavoy, following an unsuccessful attempt. A group of Dutch POWs in the Mergui area—between Victoria Point and Tavoy—met a similar fate. Further executions were to occur at Thanbyuzayat in 1943.

As the Japanese plans for the construction of the Burma-Thailand railway reached the final planning stages—a fact of which we were still totally unaware—the movement north of 'A' Force members, commenced. On 4 August 1942, Major Green received preliminary orders to prepare for a move to Tavoy. On 11 August, we were told to be prepared to move the following day. The cookhouse was to prepare biscuits and buns for six meals. We also were to carry a meal of rice which, in the event, turned sour before we could eat it.

We were transported to Victoria Point by truck, and once again the interminable waiting began. During the afternoon we were given permission to visit the local shops to make whatever purchases we could arrange. Can you imagine a small corner store, with only two attendants, chock-a-block with thieving Australian prisoners of war? There were many genuine buyers, but few of us had money as our last Japanese pay had not been received. In trying to serve customers, give change and protect their stock, they were in a frenzy. By the time we left, the shops were almost totally bare of stock, much of it having disappeared, unpaid for into our haversacks, shorts and other hiding places. I doubt that any group of Aussies would have been welcome there for many a long day.

Towards dusk we boarded a small ship of some 200-300 tons. Our quarters were confined to the deck area and space was extremely limited. There was little room except for standing and sitting. The latrine, once again, was a frame slung over the side of the ship. By now our bread was turning mouldy but we still had to conserve it, as it was to be the only food before reaching Tavoy, some three days away. On the first night it rained heavily. The next morning was fine and the sea smooth, but later showers occurred and, in the heavy seas, many were seasick.

Tavoy

On 15 August we dropped anchor and disembarked into two large steel barges, for the long tow up the inlet from Tavoy Point, then to the township of Tavoy, situated at the mouth of the Tavoy River. Hills rose sharply on each side of this broad stretch of water, and Buddhist temples dotted their slopes. As we marched through the town, the local Burmese population was extremely generous to us, handing out small packages of food as we marched along the streets. (Similar experiences were recounted to us later by POWs who had come via Moulmein and Rangoon). It hadn't taken long for the Japanese to reveal their true colours to the Burmese. Similarly disillusioned were natives of the Philippines, Dutch East Indies and other Pacific areas 'liberated' from their white oppressors by the Japanese.

At Tavoy we had our first contact with Dutch POWs, a mixed group of whites and Eurasians. Many of them had reserves of Dutch currency and considerable trading and buying was effected between us. I swapped one of my khaki shirts for a green Dutch army jacket, which served me well until the end of the war. I was especially appreciative of it on those bitterly cold nights and early mornings which we experienced in Burma during 1943.

We were quartered in an empty mission school. Water was scarce for washing and bathing, the supply being from a deep well in the school grounds. A bucket, on a long rope, was dropped into the well and then hauled on to the top. The kitchen was inadequate, making it difficult to prepare the meals for the constant stream of incoming and outgoing troops. The food did not match the quantity or quality that we had experienced at Victoria Point. One evening Eric Bailey presented me with a dixie of stew, rich and full of meat. Someone had purloined a small goat and put it to good use.

Ye

About 18 August 259 members of Green Force departed for Ye by truck. We were under the command of Capt. Vern Toose, 2/18 Bn. I will always remember this trip, probably the most comfortable I ever experienced under the Japanese. First the stretches of rice and paddy fields across the plains. This was in contrast to the small fields we had seen adjacent to our camp at Victoria Point. There the farmer waited for the monsoon rains to fill his terraced plots. A dozen or so water buffalo were then herded into the water-filled area and, encouraged by mother, father and children shouting and waving sticks at them, were driven round and round, churning the mud and water into a quagmire. Following this the field was ploughed using oxen and an ancient, single furrowed, wooden plough. Finally the rice seedlings were hand-planted into this sloppy mud by the barefooted women and children.

On one occasion the Japanese erected a large marquee in the camp grounds. A day of entertainment was arranged for the local population. We were allowed to have a peep in, but found it pretty meaningless to us, with one exception. This was the boxing, Asian style, using both hands and feet; the first occasion we had seen it.

September 25, 1942

We set out on our march to Thanbyuzayat, 535 troops from Green Force and 248 from Helper's group. We left behind 170 heavy sick. This last group rejoined us in October in Kendau, 4 kilo camp.

In spite of all efforts to repair footwear at Victoria Point, using old motor tyres, 5% of the group were now barefooted. Retreating British troops had blown the two main bridges along the railway line connecting Ye and Thanbyuzayat. Additionally, there was no rolling stock on the Ye side of the railway. Therefore we had a 25-mile march along the rough, metalled line. We did have two small railway trolleys for moving all cooking equipment, some light sick, and all other gear we could possibly load onto the vehicles Then it was a case of push as there were no motors or handles fitted. We had a two-day march in front of us. The first night we camped under the stars. Luckily for us, it did not rain.

Many of the marchers found the going very heavy because of sore feet, in addition to their weakened state of health accentuated by lack of nourishing food, drugs and medicines.

On the second day, after hazardous river crossings in small native boats, we arrived at Lamaign where a train awaited us. We were all tired out and the sight of a real train, two old carriages and cattle trucks, was a very welcome one. (It was a rather unpleasant ride in trucks littered with cow dung, fresh at that, but transportation was much better than walking.) Had we but known it, our journey was into a new way of life that, for a great number, was to be the last in a foreign country. (For some, final horizons!)

Thanbyuzayat

At last we were to learn the purpose of the seemingly inexplicable route we had been following over the past two months. We were to be a part of a railroad construction from this point to the Burma-Thailand border, the Three Pagoda Pass, where we would link up with groups working from the opposite direction. Their task was longer than ours, 294 kilometres as against 127 for 'A' Force.

October 3, 1942

Brigadier A.L. Varley, Commander 'A' Force, arrived at Thanbyuzayat. For the first time since leaving Changi, almost the entire 'A' Force group was to be under his command. To this was to be added a further contingent of 6,000 prisoners of war; Dutch, British, Americans and Australians from Java.

We were to be collectively known as Group 3, Thai POW Branch. The Japanese commander was Lieutenant Colonel Y. Nagatomo (subsequently hanged as a war criminal for his acts of inhumanity against POWs).

Brigadier Varley was to be allowed a headquarters staff as follows:

General Affairs Department	10
Foodstuffs Department	17
Property Department	17
Medical Department	12

The pompous, strutting Nagatomo presented Brigadier Varley with a welcome manifesto signifying instructions to be given to his troops:

It is a great pleasure to me to see you at this place, as I am appointed Chief of War Prisoners' Camp in obedience to the Imperial Command issued by His Majesty the Emperor.

The Great East Asiatic War has broken out due to the rising of the East Asiatic Nations, whose hearts were burnt with the desire to live and preserve their nations on account of the intrusion of the British and Americans for the past many years. There is therefore no other reason for Japan to drive out the Anti-Axis Powers of the arrogant and insolent British and Americans from East Asia in co-operation with our neighbours of China or other East Asiatic nations and to establish the Greater East Asia Co-Prosperity Sphere for the benefit of all human beings and to establish everlasting peace in the World.

During the past few centuries Nippon has made extreme endeavour and made sacrifices to become the leader of the East Asiatic Nations who were mercilessly and pitifully treated by the outside forces of the Americans and the British and Nippon without disgracing anybody has been doing her best up till now for fostering Nippon's real power.

You are all only a few remaining skeletons after the invasion of East Asia for the past few centuries and are pitiful victims. It is not your fault but till your Government do not wake up from dreams and discontinue their resistance all of you will not be released. However I shall not treat you badly for the sake of humanity as you have no fighting power at all. His Majesty the Emperor has been deeply anxious about all the War Prisoners and has ordered us to enable opening of War Prisoners' Camps at almost all the places in the southward countries. The Imperial thoughts are inestimable and the Imperial favours are infinite and as such you should weep with gratitude at the Greatness of them and should correct or mend this misleading and improper Anti-Japanese ideas.

I shall meet with you hereafter and at the beginning of the opening of the office. I require you to observe the four following points:

(1) I heard that you complain about the insufficiency of various items. Although there may be lack of materials it is difficult to meet all of your requirements.

Just turn your eyes towards the present condition of the World. It is entirely different from pre-war times. In all countries and lands all materials are considerably short, and it is not easy to obtain even a small piece of cigarette or a small match stick, and the present position is such that it is not possible even for the needy women and children to get sufficient food.

Needless to say therefore that at such inconvenient place even our respectable Imperial Army is also not able to get mosquito nets, foodstuffs, medicines and cigarettes freely and frequently. As conditions are such, how can you expect me to treat you better than the Imperial Nippon Army. I do not persecute according to my own wish and it is not due to the expense but due to the shortness of materials at such distance places. In spite of my wishes to meet your requirements, I cannot do so with money. I shall however supply you if I can do so with my best efforts and I hope that you will rely upon me and render your lives before me.

(2) I shall strictly manage all of you. Going out, coming back, meeting with friends, communications, possessions of money etc, shall of course be limited. Living manners, deportment, salutation and attitude shall be strict and according to the rules of the Nippon Army because it is only possible to manage you all, who are merely rabbles, by the order of military regulations. By this time I shall issue separate pamphlets of House Rules of War Prisoners and you are required to act strictly in accordance with these Rules and you shall not at all infringe any of them by any means.

(3) My biggest requirement from you is escape. The rules for escape shall naturally be very severe. This rule may be quite useless and only binding to some of the War Prisoners, but it is most important for all of you in the management of the Camp. You should therefore be contented accordingly. If there is a man here who has at least one per cent of chance of escape, we shall

make him to face the extreme penalty. If there is one foolish man who is trying to escape, he shall see big jungles towards the East which are absolutely impossible for communication, towards the West he shall see boundless Oceans and above all, in the main points of South and North, our Nippon Army is staying and guarding. You will easily understand the difficulty of complete escape. A few such cases of ill-omened matters which happened in Singapore shall prove the above and you should not repeat such foolish things although it is a last chance after great embarrassment.

(4) Hereafter I shall require all of you to work, as nobody is permitted to do nothing and eat as at present. In addition, the Imperial Nippons have great work to promote at the places newly occupied by them and this is an essential and important matter. At the time of such shortness of materials, your lives are preserved by the Military and all of you must reward them with your labour. By the hand of the Nippon Army, railway works to connect Thailand and Burma have started, to the great interest of the world. There are deep jungles where no man comes to clear them by cutting the trees. There is also countless difficulties and sufferings but you shall have the honour to join in this great work which was never done before and you should do your best efforts. I shall check and investigate carefully about your non-attendance, so all of you except those who are really unable to work, shall be taken out for labour. At the same time, I shall expect all of you to work earnestly and confidently every day.

In conclusion I say to you 'Work Cheerfully' and from henceforth you shall be guided by this motto

The above instructions have been given to you on the opening of War Prisoners Camp at Thanbyuzayat.

Lt. Col. Y. NAGATOMO
Chief of No. 3 Branch Office of
Thai War Prisoners Camp,
Thanbyuzayat.
Dated this 15th September 1942.

*

The manifesto, as Nagatomo preferred to call it, was, in effect, an insult to the intelligence of the prisoners of war. The words 'you all, who are merely rabbles' stung them into open fury. Prisoners of war they may be, but they had not lost their self-respect; they had not laid down their arms because of a military defeat. They did so by order of High Command, for humanitarian purposes only. They had no intention of degrading themselves by meekly accepting the rules as laid down by the pompous Nagatomo. They were quite determined, as were the men of the Java Party, commanded by Lieutenant Colonel J.M. Williams, to obstruct the railway-building project in every way possible. And they did!

The Japanese engineers sensed the hostility of the workers as did the Nipponese and Korean guards. It infuriated them to such an extent that brutality became their motto.

Several incidents occurred daily with various work parties and they must have been brought to the notice of Nagatomo. Perhaps he had those possibilities in mind when he set out his 'House Rules', which were handed to all force commanders who arrived at Thanbyuzayat after 15 September 1942. They were:

House Rules for War Prisoners
No. 3 Branch Office of Thai War Prisoners Camp at Thanbyuzayat

I have decided to frame the house rules of War Prisoners at No. 3 Branch Office of Thai War Prisoners Camp as contained in the enclosed sheets. All War Prisoners quartered in this camp must adhere strictly according to the rules and must not infringe any of them.

Lieutenant Colonel Y. NAGATOMO
Chief of No. 3 Branch Office of
Thai War Prisoners Camp,
Thanbyuzayat
Dated this 15th September 1942

HOUSE RULES

Article 1: War prisoners should follow the rules of the Nippon Military Army and should obey the order made by the officers. Further, War prisoners should adhere strictly in accordance with these rules and should not infringe any of them at all.

Article 2: War prisoners should never try to escape from either outside or inside of the war office.

Article 3: War prisoners who have no intention to escape should submit a declaration.

Article 4: War prisoners who have not submitted a declaration shall be locked in.

Article 5: In the case of war prisoners who have submitted such declaration and try to escape, they will be punished strictly under the Military Law and if necessary they will be shot dead on the spot.

Article 6: For any action insubordination or violence against an officer or watchman of War Prisoners Camp, the Military Law for punishment shall be very severe.

Article 7: War prisoners, more than two in number, have any such attitude as mentioned in Articles 5 and 6, the leader of them shall be shot to death according to Military Law.

Article 8: For any infringement of law of insubordination against order war prisoners shall be punished according to the ordinance of Military punishment.

Article 9: War prisoners should answer earnest all enquiries made by officers.

Article 10: War prisoners are required not to go out of the compound of war prisoners camp without an order from the office.

Article 11: War prisoner or prisoners should not bring any article from outside into the War Prisoners Camp compound or should not take out any article from the same compound.

Article 12: In spite of being an officer, or NCO, the proper right of command is not recognised except that such a right is only given by an officer of the camp.

Article 13: A meeting of war prisoners is prohibited except by the permission by the Chief of office.

Article 14: Delivery of speech or issue of printed matter is prohibited without the permission of the Chief of the same office.

Article 15: War prisoners should dignify the salutation and its manner and they should march keeping steps.

Article 16: For any Nippon Military Officer, or all other staff of this camp, the war prisoners should give the salute, but while they are working not to salute except Hancho. (section commandant).

Article 17: For Commander of Thai War Prisoners Camp and Chief of Branch office the war prisoners should give STOP salutation, i.e. they must stop and give salute.

Article 18: When Nippon Military Officer approaches a room of the war prisoners or a place where a number of prisoners are gathered, the prisoner who first sights the officer should call 'attention' and all the other prisoners should stand and facing the said officer should respect him with the salutation.

Article 19: For inspection purposes, if previous notice has already been given to war prisoners, they should stand in front of their bedsteads in a row and should call the attention and give the salutation at the call of the KUMICHO (Head Warden or senior).

Article 20: Symbols given by the office should always be attached to the uniform as instructed.

Article 21: Serial numbers shall be given to all war prisoners instead of their real names.

Article 22: The number given to each of the respective war prisoners should be marked and affixed at the front part of the body.

Article 23: War prisoners should live in the house allotted for them and should also sleep there.

Article 24: About 50 war prisoners should live in one house. One KUMICHO (Head Warden) shall be selected from one of the NCOs by the Chief of Office. In the case of the commissioned officers, one of them shall be appointed KUMICHO.

Article 25: KUMICHO should be responsible for conveying orders or instructions and should carry them into practice. Consequently KUMICHO should manage all the affairs; the Wardens shall also take up a petition.

Article 26: KUMICHO should mention the everyday working of the war prisoners in a Report Book in which the work of war prisoners, their diligence or idleness etc. should be recorded.

Article 27: Some of the war prisoners shall be required to report for duty to service the commissioned or NC officers of the highest rank.

Article 28: The number of persons for duty as mentioned in the previous article, shall be the rate of one for four Officers. These persons shall be appointed by the Chief of the Office according to the recommendations made by SHOMU KAKARI (General Affairs Department).

Article 29: Time table of daily work is as follows:

TIME

7.30	Getting up.
8.30	Breakfast.
9.00	Replace service of day. Muster roll call. Start of work.
10.00	Diagnosis.
14.00	Luncheon.
19.30	Dinner.
20.00	Muster roll call in evening.
22.00	Putting out light.

Article 30: Time of daily work shall be signalled by blowing of the trumpet or by sound of the alarm. Chief of Office can alter time of work if necessary.

Article 31: For checking of the numbers of war prisoners, the muster roll call will take place at the fixed hours in the morning and evening.

Article 32: All the war prisoners should stand in a row for muster rollcall at the signal and each KUMICHO should check the number of war prisoners respectively and should receive the checking of Nippon Officers or NCOs. If it is impossible for a sick man to get up from the bed answering the muster rollcall, the muster rollcall can be made at the bed.

Article 33: In case of rain, the muster roll call can be taken in the rooms according to the directions of the daily attendant of the Nippon army; in such case war prisoners should stand in front of their own bedstead.

Article 34: Time in the office shall be fixed according to Nippon standard time (24 hours system).

Article 35: War prisoners are prohibited to enter into the office of the Nippon officers, compound of isolated houses of war prisoners or any other place where they are not required to work.

Article 36: War prisoners are permitted to take off or remove clothes except the special case. In this case the symbol attached to the left arm should be removed to the left side of the loin.

Article 37: War prisoners are permitted to read books which are passed by the censorship of Japanese officer.

Article 38: Beddings, clothing and all other articles should be used economically as are being used now. If it is absolutely necessary for a fresh supply, articles shall be supplied when obtainable.

Article 39: War prisoners are prohibited to sing or talk loud.

Article 40: Smoking should be done at the places where ashtrays are placed.

Article 41: Fire is prohibited at places near combustible materials.

Article 42: In each house at least one bucket should be arranged and it should always be kept full of water.

Article 43: At each house the light should be put out at the fixed hour but one light at the centre of each house should always be remained and it is the duty of the nightwatchman to keep it on.

Article 44: Putting out of the fire at the cooking house should be done when all work is finished for the day. Every possible attention should be paid to avoid blowing up of fire.

Article 45: War prisoners should work willing for their duties that is orders.

Article 46: Commissioned Officers or NCOs should also work positively.

Article 47: War prisoners, except those who are ordered on special duty cannot be absent or stop the work, without obtaining the permission from Nippon doctor.

Article 48: War prisoner shall be given a standard armband (two violet lines on white cloth) when he is permitted by the doctor to stop work or rest.

Article 49: Compulsory work shall be organised under the control of Nippon commissioned Officer. The KUMI shall be one of the units of the working company and two KUMI shall make one HAN.

Article 50: The HANCHO (Head of Han) shall be selected from commissioned officers of war prisoners, who shall be appointed by Chief of the Office according to the recommendation of the Chief of General Affairs (SHOMU KAKARICHO).

Article 51: HANCHO should command two KUMI for the working and shall have an arm badge one red line on yellow cloth.

Article 52: War prisoners should obey the order of KUMICHO (Head of Kumi) or his senior and execute the respective duties positively.

Article 53: War prisoners should not speak, smoke or rest on the ground during the working hours, excluding interval time.

Article 54: War prisoners who are diligent to their duties, and whose diligence is enable to show the good example to others, shall be praised by the Chief of Office.

Article 55: Holidays of the Nippon Army shall also be the holidays for the war prisoners.

Article 56: Wages shall be paid to war prisoners on the 5th of every month, at the rate of 25 sen to commissioned officers and NCOs of the highest rank and 10 sen for common soldiers.

Article 57: This can be increased sometime to war prisoners by 35 sen at the highest.

Article 58: For receiving wages, a letter of attorney shall be presented by KUMICHO to the General Affairs Department, SHOMU KAKARI mentioning all the names of each KUMI separately.

Article 59: If anybody wants to receive new Diagnosis, he should report to KUMICHO and KUMICHO shall report to the daily attendant of NCO who shall take him to the war prisoners' hospital between 1000 and 1200 hours.

Article 60: War prisoners should keep the cleanliness always washing their bodies by means of cold water bath.

Article 61: War prisoners shall be vaccinated once every year, and shall be injected for cholera and pest once every four months. Sometimes medicines shall be given for protection of malaria.

Article 62: War prisoners shall receive bodily examination in every month and if there is any defect in their health they shall be given an armband (one violet line on white cloth).

Article 63: Communication to families is permitted once in every month for commissioned officers and NCOs of highest rank, once in every six weeks for NCOs and once every two months for common soldiers. Time of communication and form of letter shall be instructed every time by the chief.

Article 64: War prisoners cannot be allowed to dispatch postage of letters or baggage without the censorship of the Nippon Officers

Article 65: War prisoners are allowed to have cash not exceeding Yen 50 commissioned officers, Yen 40 for NCOs of highest rank, Yen 30 for NCOs and Yen 20 for common soldiers.

Article 66: The rolling list in which is written the cash exceeding the amount mentioned in above article, should be made by KUMICHO and the cash should be deposited in the accounts department, through SHOMU KAKARI.

Article 67: On consideration of actual circumstances at the spot, daily use of articles, such as papers and washing soaps shall be supplied.

Article 68: For selling of foodstuffs or daily use articles, Sales Depot (SHUHO), shall be opened. Time of selling or system shall be fixed separately.

Article 69: War prisoners shall be permitted to offer religious prayers but it should not interfere with their daily work or order.

Article 70: The war prisoners shall be permitted sport or intelligence games but it should not interfere with their work or order.

Article 71: The war prisoners should try to learn the Nippon language and to know real feature of Nippon.

Article 72: Daily attendance of commissioned officers and NCOs shall be appointed. The number shall be one commissioned officer and two NCOs from 1,000 war prisoners. The symbol of the former will be arm badge with one white line on red cloth and the symbol of the latter will be arm badge all red.

Article 73: Daily attendant commissioned officer of war prisoners shall obey the orders of the Nippon daily attendant commissioned officer and should prevent escape of war prisoners and keep them in order, and should try to adhere to house rules. Furthermore they should look after cleanliness arrangements, fire protection, night watchman's duty.

Article 74: The daily attendant commissioned officer of war prisoners should make a daily record in the report book to be given by Nippon army.

Article 75: The daily attendant NCO of war prisoners should help the commissioned officer of war prisoners and attend specially for minor points such as the duty for sending patients to the war prisoners' hospital and mentioning the condition of patients on the list and reporting the result in this concern to KUMICHO.

Article 76: KUMICHO shall appoint one night watchman for each KUMI. The nightwatchman should be changed every one hour and they shall have the symbol of white armband.

Article 77: Night watchman should cooperate with the members living in the same house, especially looking after the number of war prisoners at night, the protection of fire. They are not permitted to act freely.

Article 78: Among the members of war prisoners five each of the commissioned officers and NCOs shall form SHOMU KAKARI (General Affairs Department). The head of the SHOMU KAKARI shall be selected from Senior Commissioned Officers and others shall be appointed by the recommendation by the SHOMU KAKARI and ordered by the Chief. In the members of SHOMU KAKARI persons to work as interpreter shall be included, Symbol of SHOMU KAKARI members shall have arm badge (one blue line on yellow cloth).

Article 79: SHOMU KAKARI should transfer the order of requirements from office or to work for investigation which may be instructed by office. Further, shall take steps to send petitions that may be presented by war prisoners for mutual understanding.

Article 80: Food Stuff Department (RYOSHOKU KAKARI) and Property Department (BUPPIN KAKARI) shall be formed and the head of both depots shall be appointed from commissioned officers of war prisoners with one assistant of NCO. Also will include representatives who is recommended by each KUMICHO. Symbol of RYOSHOKU KAKARI is blue armband and BUPPIN KAKARI is one white line on blue cloth.

Article 81: RYOSHOKU KAKARI is required to attend for receiving foodstuffs, cooking, distribution, preparing of menu, transportation of tablewares, also keeping the cooking room clean and tidy, maintenance of cooking utensils and water supply and discharge arrangements.

Article 82: BUPPIN KAKARI is for keeping good arrangements of books, literature, taking out or bringing back of properties and requiring and maintaining them.

Article 83: For the health and physical attendance, a Health attendant (EISEI KIMMU SHA) shall be appointed from among war prisoners, who shall preferably be appointed from war prisoners with medical knowledge or profession. The number of EISEI KIMMU SHA shall be fixed according to the number of war prisoners. The symbol of EISEI KIMMU SHA shall be arm badge with a red cross and two lines for commissioned officer and a red cross and one line for a NCO.

Article 84: The EISEI KIMMU SHA should be on duty and getting along at the war prisoners' hospital under instruction from Nippon doctor. Rest of the duties with the regard to the admittance into the hospital should be decided by the Nippon doctor.

Article 85: Once in each week during holidays, house inspection of war prisoners shall be done by Nippon Officers. Particulars shall be decided and suggested separately.

Article 86: Petitions from war prisoners shall be accepted through KUMICHO
which should be presented to SHOMU KAKARI (General Affairs Department)
and SHOMU KAKARI should offer to the Chief Officer.

Article 87: These house rules shall be translated in English and Dutch languages
and each one copy shall be kept at each KUMI for the better understanding
of all war prisoners.

*

The situation developing at the 26 kilo camp, and others, was a cause for alarm.
Men engaged on the railroad construction were constantly dropping from sheer
exhaustion, due to the lack of food and the hard work. Bashings were daily
occurrences; the Koreans were especially sadistic, taking their example from
their Jap superiors.

Perhaps the most brutal of the guards were BB (Boy Bastard), his mate BBC
(Boy Bastard's Cobber), the Snipe or Pinhead, Dillinger and Jungle Jim.

By their cruelty—bestiality is the better word—they earned, and justly so,
the hatred and contempt of every POW who had the misfortune to suffer at
their hands at some time or other. Rifle butts, bamboo waddies or, if handy, a
pick handle, became their 'tools of trade'.

If the guards were too short to reach the head of a worker they would stand
on a heap of rubble and lash out in a display of sadistic fury. Screams of 'currah
currah' forewarned men of an impending punishment for some unfortunate
lad, probably ill or totally exhausted, who would end up receiving the thrashing
of a lifetime.

However, there were many occasions when the infuriated and despised guards
thought they had severely hurt an alleged offender when the person on the
receiving end of the 'tool' had in fact learned a trick or two and 'rode' the
blows.

Jungle Jim, a 6 foot 2 inch Korean, recognised the Australians' adeptness in
thwarting injury by 'riding' or swaying with the blows. He acquired the art of
changing direction in mid air, and succeeded in breaking many arms. Along
with many of his colleagues, he paid the ultimate penalty post-war.

The health of all working troops by February 1943, was such that force
commanders were making submissions to Lieutenant Colonel Nagamoto via
Brigadier Varley, in respect of lack of rations, medicines and drugs. Nagatomo
acknowledged these with deadly silence.

'A' Force commander never let up in his insistence for clemency in all matters
concerning his troops. He was aghast at the work they were being forced to do
whilst underfed and in such weakened condition as to become prone to serious
illnesses.

RAMSAY FORCE
Mergui, Burma

IN THE AFTERNOON of 24 May 1942, the convoy anchored off the township of Mergui, south Burma, and Lieutenant Colonel G.E. Ramsay was ordered to prepare the 1,000 troops under his command to disembark immediately.

The majority of the men were in a very weakened condition due to the rigours of the nine-day voyage. They suffered from lack of food, dehydration and multiple diseases. Dysentery was rife and the medical officers feared a possible outbreak of beri-beri.

Nonetheless the men were forced to unload supplies, such as they were, including bags of rice weighing 250 pounds each. According to the Japanese— 'one mans to one bag', an utterly impossible task even for able-bodied, well fed men. After many bashings with rifle butts, fists and waddies, the Japs finally agreed to allow four men to each bag. Tools and other equipment had to be manhandled from ship to shore by men hardly able to carry their own pitiful possessions.

When the unloading had been completed the troops were ordered to collect their gear and march to the Mergui National School. By this time many of the local population had gathered to witness an unexpected spectacle; white men working like 'coolies' under the iron heel of the Japanese.

Some appeared to be somewhat nervous, but many took little notice of the Nipponese and passed food and money to the prisoners of war. Hostile guards put an end to that and even ground some of the provisions underfoot.

Lieutenant Tokoro, Camp Commandant, informed Ramsay that, as he had been unaware POWs were arriving, no preparations had been made for their reception or housing. He also informed Ramsay that he would be responsible for the 500 British prisoners of war already in residence at the school in addition to his own 1,000 troops, their behaviour and discipline.

A formidable task confronted Ramsay in allotting billets. He and his staff had to make prompt decisions as he did not want companies broken up. At the very best, the premises would have been acutely strained to house 600 adults, let alone 1,500. Conditions on land were obviously going to be almost as cramped as they had been on *Celebes Maru*. (Brigadier Varley and his troops had found a similar condition existing at Tavoy, 150 miles further north, when they arrived. Very primitive housing was provided for his 1,000 troops.)

Major Chalmers was very concerned by the unhygienic conditions and feared an outbreak of disease if proper arrangements were not speedily made. On inspection, he found one long concrete latrine which was divided into twenty small cubicles suitable only for children, and three small latrines containing six cubicles suitable for adults. There were twenty-four pans to serve these, many of which were leaking; two of those were reserved for use for the regimental aid post. As the result, several cubicles had no pans and it was difficult to block these adequately. The pans were emptied only once every twenty-four hours, during the night, by private contractors for the school.

There were only four urinals in the main latrine, but these emptied on to channels in the floor. The urine, plus the washings from the latrine floors, flowed out in an open drain which emptied near a shallow well which was used for washing, and on to a swamp area at the bottom of the school grounds.

The British troops had already used the latrines—including cubicles without pans—and were washing and cleaning their teeth in the swamp water. In spite of another well being made available for washing water and the other one being placed out of bounds, it was very difficult to prevent this practice from being continued.

The latrines were not lit and at night it was impossible to see them. This, combined with the small size of the holes in the cubicles, led to fouling of the floor and of footwear. The pans, which were emptied each evening, were always overflowing by the early hours of the morning due to the large number of men afflicted with bowel complaints. From the very first hours of occupation of the school, many men found it necessary to station themselves as near as possible to the latrines. Their maladies had so weakened them they felt it was tempting fate to risk a return to their quarters.

The desire for food was of tremendous importance to all personnel. Hunger was a driving force and everything edible was soon scrounged. The first meal in the school was served very late, but the kitchen staff excelled themselves in its preparation under the most trying conditions. The ration was a small serving of saltless rice, unaccompanied by meat or any vegetable matter. But it was a meal, that was important.

On the day after arrival an attempt by Lieutenant Colonel Ramsay, Major Chalmers, Medical Officer, and Captain Hence, Adjutant, to make suitable medical arrangements resulted—after a certain amount of opposition on the part of the Nipponese 'medical officer'—in one room on the ground floor being set aside for use as a hospital. They were told there was no hospital in the town. By that evening the room was packed to capacity. The next day a second room was taken over and it was soon filled.

A second latrine—two pans only available—was set up near the hospital but great difficulty was experienced in keeping other than ill men from using it. In any case, it was totally inadequate for the number of very sick men.

There were no beds and many patients lacked even a groundsheet or blanket. The British troops had practically no bedding or mosquito nets and very few clothes. Eventually, the hospital conditions worsened to such an extent the Japanese commandant made other arrangements.

On Wednesday, 27 May, the grand gesture was made—a 'house' some distance from the camp. It turned out to be one building of the incomplete civil hospital, the existence of which the Nipponese had earlier denied. They were to be permitted the full use of one large ward, a smaller one for the staff and a kitchen which was nothing more than a roofless framework.

That afternoon Major Chalmers, plus six other ranks, cooks and orderlies, took up residence with sixteen very ill patients. A few days later the admissions became so great that four wards were packed with men suffering from dysentery, malaria, malnutrition and allied ailments.

The kitchen staff were supplied with one kwali and two buckets. Later a second kwali, cracked and useless, arrived, plus one trench stove and three buckets. All cooking utensils were made from scrap iron found near the building and the kitchen roof was built by the engineers.

There was a marked lack of hospital supplies, with only two washbasins and bedpans. Water had to be obtained from a well some distance away from the hospital. The civil hospital authorities provided twenty beds and the inventive engineers were able to make an additional twelve from materials scrounged. They did a remarkable job.

Many patients had to lie on bare mattresses, but the majority were on the floor without groundsheets or bedding of any description. The Japs eventually delivered seventy torn, dirty and bloodied blankets (obviously from a battle area). With no sterilising facilities, it was weeks before any of these could be used.

From petrol tins supplied by the Nipponese the engineers made basins and bed pans. Some of the scroungers came up with eight old chairs. It took the 'ginger beers' but a few days to turn them into commodes.

The drugs promised by the Japanese at Changi were merely wisps of imagination. Nothing, absolutely nothing, in the line of medical supplies ever eventuated, except a small quantity of magnesium sulphate.

The 'Grand Utopia' never in any sense became a reality, and the dark clouds were just beginning to emerge. The cemetery was soon mute evidence of that!

The civil hospital operating theatre was out of bounds to POW personnel and when a tracheotomy became necessary; it was performed on the kitchen table. Later, Tokoro relented and use of the theatre was granted, but only on condition the POW medical staff used their own instruments. That provision was, of course, another negation of the promises made in Changi. Lieutenant Colonel Coates and Major Chalmers had only a meagre supply of instruments with which they had to make do. They were first put to use a few days later when a strangulated hernia had to be repaired. The operation was a success and the patient recovered.

As always in cases of desperation, a way out of any situation will be found. Whilst working on the landing strip a resourceful POW managed to contact a native who, hating and despising the Japanese for what they were doing to young females in the town, and the punishment suffered by parents who objected to such use being made of their daughters, was ready and willing to assist in any way he could.

He was set a task to find the drugs so badly needed for the many lying near death in the improvised hospital. Some days later he handed over a large package. He refused any reward despite the great risk he had run searching through Nipponese supplies.

Of tremendous importance was the 'Spiroside', a drug invaluable in the treatment of amoebic dysentery. Other drugs of lesser value, but just as important, were also in the package. Later, more medical supplies came 'over the fence', despite the presence of Nipponese guards. The handover was in daylight, well organised and resulted in many lives being saved. Fortunately, no searches were made on the delivery days, and the 'courier'—unnamed—evaded apprehension.

The lack of emetine and anti-diphtheria serum did, however, result in loss of life. So much so that the civil hospital surgeon suggested that Major Chalmers use pulped mangosteen skins to alleviate suffering and possible deaths. Whilst the delicious-tasting fruit was in season, it became an important remedy for the seemingly ever-present dysentery and diarrhoea. Unfortunately the season was too short and another lifesaver was soon denied the medical staff.

Lieutenant Colonel Ramsay and Lieutenant Colonel Coates made almost daily requests to Lieutenant Tokoro for drugs. At times they were met with bland refusal; on other occasions Tokoro told them shipping was the problem. However, he did allow Ramsay to go shopping in the town, believing he was on a hopeless pilgrimage. The venture was partially successful and Ramsay was able to procure a small quantity of disinfectant, iron compounds, etc., which were a boon to the medical staff.

Unknown to the Nipponese, the local surgeon found 4 ounces of 'Pulv Ipecac co' and nearly 4 ounces of 'Pulv Bism Sulnitrate' which he handed over to Major Chalmers. Small as the supply was, it was put to good use.

MERGUI LABOUR CAMP

ON 26 MAY 1942, all prisoners of war able to stand were ordered to parade for an inspection by Lieutenant Tokoro. As he surveyed the assembled troops, his attitude could be construed as that of the cynical victor over the vanquished. Dressed in ceremonial uniform, sword dangling from his left side, he gave the impression he was totally in command. And indeed, he was!

Only those in his immediate vicinity heard what he said—he spoke good English—but that mattered little; his actions, arms waving, the occasional grasping of the sword hilt in his right hand, were significant in themselves.

There was no question that he expected, required and demanded absolute discipline. Any transgression would incur his and the Great Japanese Nation's displeasure.

Any offence against the Imperial Nipponese army guards would result in serious consequences for the offender or offenders. Any attempt to escape would bring down his wrath, as would being caught outside the boundary of the camp without permission or escort, and repercussions would fall upon all in the camp; even the sick would suffer.

Responsibility for the good conduct of the prisoners would be that of company or kumi—Japanese for platoon—commanders. Should any of their men misbehave the commander would also have to accept punishment.

He warned that all should work hard, diligently and be thankful to the kind Nipponese for their good treatment. They would be well fed, the best workers to receive bigger rations. Payment for all work would be on the basis of rank and diligence. The sick to be well cared for, but 'as sick mans do not work', they could not expect to be fed.

Guards must be mounted each night by the prisoners; change-over after one hour. House rules would be laid down and strictly adhered to. No contact of any kind would be permitted with local townspeople. Any prisoners attempting to attract the attention of the natives would, if detected, be placed in the guardroom for punishment.

As the strutting Tokoro walked away from the parade murmurs of anger were quite audible in the ranks. Momentarily, it appeared he would turn and vent his fury upon the POWs, but cool heads prevailed and they returned to their quarters in splendid parade-ground style. Back in their quarters, groups formed and many plans were made. Three men who were quite determined POW life was not for them made up their minds to seek succour from the locals.

The welcome given by the villagers no doubt triggered their belief that, if apprehended by Japanese guards, at worst they would be incarcerated in the guardroom and suffer some type of physical punishment, as well as being forced to live on drastically reduced rations.

The more they discussed the proposition the more they believed its possibilities outweighed those of remaining under the iron hand of the Nipponese. Despite protests from many of their mates who thought the trio were just dreamers, the boys said there was to be no turning back; they were going to break out that very night. However, there was a change of plan when heavy rain commenced to fall and they decided to await a more favourable opportunity.

After the long voyage from Singapore and the frightfulness of the hold, actual physical labour was, to some extent, something to look forward to. Not for one moment did the POWs imagine that they would be worse off. Hard work, as anyone knew, never hurt anyone. And in this instance they were to be paid for their labour; the money could buy food!

On the fifth day, the first of the work parties headed out for the landing strip they were to build. The sun shone brilliantly and as they marched along many gathered wild fruits, including the sweet mangosteens. However, there was no jubilance or singing; they just hoped for the best, and soon copped the worst.

No-one had the slightest idea what they would be employed on. It did not matter; at least it would be only of a light nature. The Japanese were aware that the majority were too weak for any hard labour.

On arrival at the aerodrome site they were issued with picks, shovels and chunkels (a type of large hoe), bamboo poles and rice bags which were open at each end. They were puzzled; rice bags and poles! What were they supposed to do with those? The answer soon came.

Gangs were formed and led out onto what looked like a rough outline of a landing strip or, maybe, a roadway. The engineers pegged out areas that had to be dug up. The spoil to be carried many yards away and dumped. How? Open-ended rice bags slung between the poles.

A chorus of, 'We can't do that, we're not blasted coolies' met with an immediate response, 'Carry or be punished'.

For a moment or two it looked ugly as guards menaced them with waddies. An officer, fearing trouble, advised the men to get on with the work as they had no other choice.

'Like hell we will. They should have bulldozers and trucks for a big job like this. You tell that bloke in charge we don't work that way; get machinery.'

Major Charles ('Bill') Cousens (2/19 Battalion) sized up the situation very quickly and prevented the near-frenzied guards from bashing up the unwilling workers, whose dignity was such they resented the Nipponese expecting white men to labour as coloured coolies had been doing for years. He ordered the POW ringleaders to do as they were ordered by the Japanese guards. Otherwise the whole party would be penalised.

'It is obvious,' he said, 'they have no machinery; manpower only, and they have plenty of that in us. At the moment, we are their prisoners—I don't like it any more than you lads—but we are under their control. We will just have to make the best of it and save many problems.'

His military tones apparently soothed the guards' tempers and the undignified work proceeded. One to dig, one to shovel and two to carry. After a couple of hours a yasumi (rest period) was called and the still angry men sat, squatted or lay down on the ground.

The guards, all naval, appeared a bit bewildered at the turn of events and stood in a group watching the weary prisoners of war resting in all kinds of postures. They chattered away rapidly in their own language, some pointed, not actually at their charges, but apparently at the little that had been achieved in the two hours since the first sod had been turned.

When the work resumed it was obvious the guards were determined it was to be at a faster rate and 'currah currah' was frequently heard. A few of the men felt the weight of a waddy if they rested without permission.

As the hours wore on the weight in the rice bags became heavier, the picks harder to swing and the shovels filled with earth more difficult to raise. But yasumis became less frequent and physical weakness was obvious.

A meal of plain unsalted rice was served and the tired workers, many now suffering from diarrhoea, the onset of a malaria attack, and from under-nourishment, looked a sorry sight. After a forty minute break they were at it again, digging, shovelling, plodding like people in a daze.

The only measure of relief was to call out 'benjo', a request for permission to relieve themselves. The calls became so frequent the guards became a bit suspicious and watched a few men to see whether or not they were shamming.

Fortunately nature provided the answer for those who were under observation, and no trouble was experienced, despite the frequency of men, genuinely affected or not, seeking permission to retire for a few minutes. However, the break, short as it was, only added to their weariness when they returned to the job.

Approximately nine hours after they had set out from the camp a halt for the day was called; then tenko, return of the tools, poles and bags. Everything was counted time and time again. The guards lacked the ability to get it right first count. The waiting made the workers feel bitter and frustrated; they wanted back to camp, a wash, a meal and sleep!

If the first day's work on the drome was a disaster, the subsequent period was much worse. The Nipponese saw the landing strip as a vital link and its construction as a major priority. They demanded large number of POW labourers, regardless of their state of health. Lieutenant Colonel Ramsay never acceded to their demands and only provided a minimum number, claiming quite truthfully that the troops were too weak to work, due to the lack of nourishing food.

Meanwhile, the POWs were praying for the beginning of the rainy season, believing all work on the landing strip would be postponed. No-one, they argued, could possibly be expected to carry mud in rice sacks, not even their gaolers.

Food was of the utmost importance for all personnel in the camp or hospital; there was never enough rice, no salt (and that necessitated carrying salt water from the bay for all cooking purposes), vegetables or any other additives.

The local inhabitants, recognising the near starvation the prisoners were undergoing, offered to supply all the foodstuffs required by the imprisoned troops—an offer Tokoro bluntly refused. In addition to such refusal, he gave warning to the townspeople they would be flogged and gaoled, should they even attempt to trade with the prisoners of war. Many subsequently suffered both penalties.

Despite the dire warnings, work parties passing through the village were more often than not given dried fish, boiled eggs, fruit and money. Camp-gate searches were always feared and, at such times, ingenuity was necessary to prevent confiscation of what they may have gathered. When anything was found a bashing resulted, while the others were allowed to go on their way. It was a risk run; if successful, a change of diet for the sickies resulted.

On some occasions Tokoro would permit Lieutenant Colonel Ramsay or Captain Pryde, Quartermaster, to purchase foodstuffs in the town marketplace with an accompanying guard to ensure that no illegal transactions or overbuying took place. On those rare pilgrimages both officers were able to procure much-needed nutrients for the very ill patients.

However, whilst the rice ration issued to the POWs by the Japanese varied from one day to another as the sick list grew or, in some ways, diminished (by death for instance), it was never the weight claimed by them. When disputed by Captain Pryde, he would be told a certain number of bags had to be delivered and were, despite the fact some of the bags contained only a few pounds of rice and were not full bag weight. To the Japs, bags were bags, half-full or otherwise and no argument would be entered into. Invariably the prisoners of war missed out.

The incredible overcrowding at the school camp was of great concern to Ramsay. Hardly a day passed when he failed to bring that fact home to the Japanese camp commandant, who would blandly outspread his hands as if it was out of his control.

Daily, the spread of disease, the legacy of undernourishment and cramped conditions of the living quarters in the school and hospital areas, increased. The incidence of dysentery was so disturbing that Lieutenant Colonel Coates and Major Chalmers, in association with Ramsay, made impassioned appeals to Tokoro for immediate relief. Eventually, he agreed to forward their complaints to his commander, Captain Itsui, at Tenassirum, near Tavoy.

Discipline within the school camp precincts was not made any easier as diseases spread. Always present, too, was the gnawing desire for food. It was a subject no one could ignore. The men argued that the officers were not pressing the requirements on the Japanese, as the situation demanded. They threatened to take things into their own hands if the situation did not soon improve.

One group reasoned they had sufficient strength to disarm the guards, take over the town, and, in some way, contact Allied forces to come to their aid. Wild ideas! Not exactly; they could easily have overpowered the Japanese personnel, but obtaining military support was another matter, one that presented great problems.

If Tokoro had complete signalling equipment it would be easy for the signallers within Ramsay Force to find a frequency on which the navy or aircraft—Allied, of course—could be contacted. But Mergui was no Dunkirk, and India was hundreds of miles away, not a mere twenty.

Fierce arguments developed amongst quite a few members of the company commanded by Major Charles Cousens. The six ringleaders were quite determined in their plan to wipe out the Japanese Garrison, secure their arms and depend upon the RAAF wireless operator, one of their members, to call for immediate aid from the nearest Allied forces. To many, their argument was a sound one. Freedom, they reasoned, was near at hand.

A senior NCO whom they approached was astounded at the proposition, and warned them that the plan, should they make the attempt, was doomed from the start. No matter how fast they moved, there was not the slightest doubt the Nipponese would flash news of the attack to their headquarters.

No-one actually knew where the Japanese had their signals office, how it was guarded, or how strong their transmitter was. If it was only short-range, it might be worse than useless as a signalling device to attract Allied forces. In any case, hardly a day passed without an enemy vessel at anchor in the bay. The moment the crew heard small arms fire ashore, they would immediately call for assistance. Within minutes planes would be overhead, bombs would rain down and the townspeople would suffer more than the POWs.

When the NCO told them he felt duty bound to acquaint Lieutenant Colonel Ramsay of their intentions, they called him a coward and a Nipponese collaborator. Whilst the taunts might have stung, as indeed they did, he stuck to his intentions and was on his way when he met Major Cousens. He told him what was being planned and suggested the two of them seek audience with Ramsay Force commander.

'No,' he replied. 'I'll deal with those concerned. There is no way in the world they can do what they think. Sheer stupidity on anyone's part to even contemplate such a thing. All they would accomplish would be disaster for the whole camp, and the inhabitants of the township. If they had any hope of succeeding, I would be right behind them, but there's less hope of escape from here than there was at Changi.'

(Major Cousens, the NCO concerned, plus an RAAF sergeant pilot and four others, had planned to escape from Changi in a Japanese DC3 plane. The aircraft was always refuelled at dusk and made ready for dawn take-off. The Australian pilot had actually been aboard one of them but found it impossible to start the engines; the Nipponese pilots removed the auxiliary starting motor from the plane each evening; no elastic bands were available to swing propellers.

So the escape bid ended before it started. The same thing applied to a seaplane anchored in Changi Straits.)

After a lengthy discussion with the lads whose hopes had been so inflated, the idea was totally abandoned on a whole-force scale, but not so individually, as later events indicate. Major Cousens, however, was not a party to what subsequently occurred. He had been taken to Tavoy, en route to Japan where he was forced under threat of facing a firing squad if he refused, to broadcast on their behalf.

At midnight, 16 June, there was an uproar throughout the school; all occupants were ordered to parade. No one knew what for until Ramsay and his staff, quartered in a house outside the school area, arrived.

The Japanese claimed they had apprehended two escapees and they were tethered to a tree near the guardroom. They demanded to know from what company they came, and the name of their commander or commanders.

In the pale moonlight it was impossible to tell whether the two men were from the camp or Burmese—the late tenko was another of the irritating tactics the Nipponese often adopted. Each commander was ordered to account for every man under his control. If anyone was missing and was reported as being present, the commander concerned would suffer a fate similar to that awaiting the escapees.

One Australian senior NCO, shocked to discover his company was two men short, found himself in a quandary. What was the right thing to do? Telling his men he would make no decision on his own initiative, but would abide by the majority vote, he gave them fifteen minutes to decide. In the meantime he told Ramsay of his dilemma but made no request for guidance. That, he said, was up to the troops for whom he was personally responsible.

For a few moments Ramsay just looked, then said 'You must be aware, sergeant, whatever you report may have serious repercussions not only on the two at the gate—they are Australians, I saw them as I came in—but on you and every man in the force, sick or otherwise. As your commanding officer, I should order you to carry out your duty in accordance with Army rules. In this case, I make no such order. It is up to you and your men. Go back now, Tokoro is waiting'.

On his return to his assembled charges he felt as if his feet were made of lead. He would not shirk the responsibility the three chevrons he wore gave him, nor in any way directly cause harm to the two men now in Japanese custody.

One man spoke up, 'It's a unanimous decision, Sarge, report them as missing. We can only hope our captors observe The Hague Convention.'

Minutes later the sergeant was marched into the tent where Lieutenant Tokoro sat awaiting his report. Lieutenant Colonel Ramsay was allowed to accompany him. After due ceremony the Japanese camp commander, speaking in perfect English, demanded to know why the two men had been permitted to leave the precincts of the school without permission or under guard. 'You may', he said, 'be subject to punishment for failing to do your duty as commander-sentry. What have you to say?'

'The men are quartered in very cramped conditions and on two floors. As far as I was aware, they had gone to the latrine. I fell asleep when they walked out, but as they passed me one wanted to know if I had any scran.'

'Scran, scran. Whatever is that?'

'Food, sir, they were hungry and I am sure that is why they went beyond the school fence. They wanted something to eat. They took no belongings and that, to me, is proof they went out because of their extreme hunger.'

'Are you hungry, too?'

'Yes, sir, very much so.'

'But you did not attempt to accompany them on their excursion, did you?'

'No, as far as I was concerned they had requested permission to go to the latrine.'

'At that hour of the night?'

'Yes, they both have diarrhoea. I had no reason to think otherwise.'

'You did not ask them?'

For what seemed an eternity Tokoro remained silent. He just looked at the two standing erect in front of him. Then, like a pistol shot—'What time did they go out . . . quickly, what time?'

'I have no idea. I do not own a watch nor does anyone in the company.'

'No excuse. Were they away a long time. If so, why did you not go to check on them?'

'To the first question, I have no idea, I fell asleep. To the second, quite a few who have bowel complaints lay near the latrine all night long. And, sir, I too must sleep. I cannot keep awake twenty-four hours per day.'

'Then you should not be a commander. However, I will not punish you now. I must report to Captain Itsui. I will do as he orders. You may go, both of you.'

At 0900 hours the next day Tokoro demanded Ramsay report to him concerning the two men now in the guardroom. From that hour on and for almost every day, Ramsay pleaded clemency for his two imprisoned men. Japan had been a signatory to The Hague Convention and Ramsay demanded the right of protection for the unjustly charged men.

Tokoro, a little taken aback, jumped to his feet, glared at the Australian officer and appeared as if he was about to exact physical punishment on his opponent. Instead, he said—'The Imperial Japanese Government never ratified the signature. Nippon has its own laws. However, I will pass on your petition to Captain Itsui who will decide the punishments to be inflicted.'

Some days were to pass before Ramsay was summoned and Tokoro gave him the text of Itsui's report. It was a bone-chilling sentence—'EXECUTE WITHOUT DELAY'.

Ramsay fought against the inhuman decision so strenuously that it appeared Tokoro might disregard his superior officer's order. However, despite his personal feelings, he was a Japanese officer, charged with the responsibility to act in accordance with the Emperor's military rule.

The two Australians, were driven to an undisclosed area and forced to dig their own graves. Although bound hands and feet, they stood as straight as a gun barrel as the firing squad pressed triggers.

Lieutenant Tokoro failed to inform Ramsay of the impending executions until they had been carried out. He did, however, pay tribute to their bravery.

The shocking news of the useless killings angered every POW in the camp. So obvious were their feelings, Tokoro sensed some possibility of retaliation and he doubled the guards. The prisoners of war guessed why.

Overcrowding of the school camp was a source of great worry to Lieutenant Colonel Ramsay, and he continued to hammer this aspect to the touchy Tokoro. In the end, Ramsay's determined approaches succeeded. Permission was granted to move the force to a new campsite, one that had been built to house the Nipponese troops who were to garrison the township.

For the very first time since sailing out of Singapore harbour the men of Ramsay Force had room to accommodate themselves. The huts were of bamboo construction, atap-roofed and contained two floors. Open sides allowed for plenty of ventilation and fresh air. At last, freedom of movement and a measure of comfort, except for bamboo slat bed-spaces.

Captain Alan Pryde was allowed at various intervals to visit the local market—escorted by a guard—to buy what was on offer. Unfortunately Tokoro was not generous enough to permit regular shopping and supplies were soon exhausted. Other than the Burmese bounty-hunting police, the townspeople of Mergui did their utmost to augment the rice diet—the little there was—of the prisoners of war. At times, baskets of eggs found their way under the fence. They were invariably fed to the sick personnel. One problem did arise at Mergui camp. It was the relationship between officers and men—normally referred to as Other Ranks. It became so obvious Lieutenant Colonel Ramsay felt it incumbent on him to enlighten those concerned as to their respective responsibilities. He promulgated the following:

Message to all Ranks of British and Australian Forces, Mergui Camp. 2.8.'42

My aim ever since arrival here has been to spare no effort to improve conditions with a view to helping you, bodily and mentally, so that as many of you as possible will benefit, either to take your place again in the fighting services or to return to your homes in health and strength, whichever fate may have in store for you (us). In order to accomplish this, I have adopted the policy of deferring to Japanese authority in minor things and concentrating in making a definite stand on more vital cases such as when men's lives or health are at stake.

I do not claim to have been 100% successful, but I am convinced that this has resulted in providing many amenities for the benefit of the majority in the difficult circumstances in which we at present find ourselves, which would not have been available to us had any other course been adopted.

There are many things I do not like, of course, any more than you do, such as having to use Japanese words of command, etc., but I regard these as more in the nature of pin-pricks and not sufficiently vital to make an issue of at the risk of endangering our other concessions, as after all, we are not yet in a position to dictate terms.

The Japanese commander has now informed me that he has received instructions from his headquarters in Tavoy;

(1) That any prisoners of war found outside the camp area *for any purpose whatsoever*, without authority will be treated as an escapee and shot, as has already happened a few days ago.

(2) That no excuse will be accepted and that any representations made by myself or staff will be useless.

As a result of much persistent effort on the part of myself, with the able assistance of my Adjutant, Captain A. Hence, Battalion commanders and other officers, who are constantly making suggestions for your comfort, a number of concessions of real benefit have been obtained.

Every effort is still being made to increase the available supplies of fruit and eggs, but even as its stands, this has been of tremendous advantage and there is little excuse now for a man risking his life for a few extras.

If some of you pride yourself on the belief that you are too smart to be caught, then I say that it is grossly unfair to your people at home for any of you to risk your life and the happiness of your people for so little.

Each further offence also endangers such benefits as we have been able to obtain for the majority and hampers our efforts towards trying to obtain more.

We also have a duty to local inhabitants. The Burmese Police have considerably increased their vigilance and tightened their restrictions, thus increasing the risk; and I am informed that a native, only a day or two ago, was placarded and beaten in the streets with sticks, and others have been arrested, for handing cheroots to some of you fellows; while I was informed that, at Tavoy, a native caught giving food to a POW was thrashed and then sentenced to five years gaol.

It has been thought by some [that] two or three men, who were put in your own guardroom, were placed under Japanese sentries voluntarily by my orders. Nothing is further from the truth.

The Japanese sentries took control because your own NCOs and men on guard failed to do their job. The Japanese themselves found these men, who should have been in the room roaming about the grounds. Our own guards, through a misguided sense of comradeship, instead of rendering these offenders a service, rendered not only them, but the rest of you, a great disservice by failing to realise their responsibility to me and what I am trying to do.

Some of the offenders in the guardroom were found guilty of stealing from their comrades; and nobody has been sentenced for detention there, without my hearing the whole of the evidence personally and being satisfied in my own mind that the punishment I awarded was deserved.

Discipline is essential in any phase of life you care to mention. If you were to start out to form a club of any sort, sporting or otherwise, you would immediately start drafting a set of rules and regulations for the guidance and control of members. In service units, as we are still, even though POWs, it is not practicable for decisions to be made by popular vote.

I have been given the responsibility by Malaya Command and AIF headquarters for the welfare and the safety of the troops here, and no-one can relieve me of that responsibility; therefore within the limitations imposed by the Japanese, the final decisions must be mine; but where a matter arises, on which I have an open mind, and which affects you all personally I have invited your representatives on two occasions to a conference, in order that I may hear your views and suggestions, to which I have given the fullest consideration; and I must say that I have appreciated the cooperation adopted by your representatives on these occasions.

I hate orderly rooms, and there are few things I dislike more than having to sentence a man for some offence against rules which are framed for the good of the force as a whole, but in some cases I have been forced to take this action. I deplore the dissemination of exaggerated or unfounded stories.

On one occasion, on it being reported to me, that one of the men in the guardroom was being beaten by the Japanese, my Adjutant and myself were in the guardroom within two minutes of hearing this report, prepared, if necessary to immediately see the Japanese commander; only to find there was no truth whatever in the allegations made.

With the invaluable assistance of my Adjutant, I have been able to save five men in this camp from being shot. So long as I felt it was within my power to save you from such extreme penalty, I have always been reluctant to deny you any privileges which you are able to obtain for yourselves; provided that in doing so you did not endanger the privileges of the remainder, or act in such a manner as would bring discredit upon your own self-respect and the prestige we have enjoyed as Britishers.

Now that I feel that any representations I make to save a man's life would meet with little, if any success, I would be failing in my duty to you, and to those at home who care for you, who are eagerly awaiting your return, and who perhaps are dependent on you, did I not take some definite action.

Even should the British or Australian Governments take some future action, that would be of no use to the man who had been shot, and would afford little consolation to his family.

I have decided, therefore, that strong disciplinary action will be taken against any man found attempting to leave this area, or the hospital area, without proper authority. And, also, against any member of a guard who fails to do his duty in this respect. I feel that this decision is quite consistent with my original aim mentioned earlier, and I always prefer to make an appeal to men's decency, rather than to threaten them.

To my mind this matter is so vital and affects all, I do appeal, therefore, to those appointed for guard duty from time to time, to do your job conscientiously; and to the remainder of you to cooperate by not making any more difficult than it is the job of your officers or of the guards appointed by me, for the good of all.'

*

The letter was promulgated in order to explain to the members of Ramsay Force that, although they were now under Japanese control, they were still servicemen and considered as soldiers of the line in all respects.

It was intended, therefore, to maintain normal military discipline as applied prior to becoming prisoners of war. It was to offset, too, the belief that, since they were commanded by another authority, all ranks were now equal, and neither badges or rank, or even chevrons, divided then in any way.

Many were resentful of their own officers assuming control when it was, in the opinion of the other ranks, shameful enough to have to subject themselves to Nipponese commanders.

With the advent of the rainy season the prisoners of war had reasoned the camp commandant would not expect them to work under such extreme circumstances. Such an idea was soon dispelled; Tokoro issued an astounding order—'ALL MEN WILL WORK IN RAIN'.

The building of the aerodrome was by manpower only, with the 'white coolies' trudging back and forth from daylight until dark. This was bad and monotonous enough in dry weather but in teeming rain it became an absolute misery. The bags were heavy enough with dry earth, but when that turned to mud it was sheer purgatory. Very few prisoners had groundsheets, and most were sopping wet from the moment they stepped out onto the muster area at dawn until they returned to camp as darkness set in.

When Tokoro reduced the rice ration, because of the large number of sick POWs—'sick mans don't eat'—the ravages of hunger began to take their toll. The ever-present yearning for hot, roast meals and piles of delicious home-cooked food nearly drove men frantic. So much so one, Bill, was determined to risk apprehension by the Burmese bounty hunters, and set course for the village for food. To accomplish his task he studied every inch of the fence, found a convenient way out under the wire and made plans to slither the ten yards to the jungle growth.

For a few nights he watched the prowling police, noticed they paid regular visits to the Jap guardhouse, noted the approximate times and formulated his plan. The few he confided in warned him of the danger and advised him to suffer his hunger rather than end up with a bullet.

'No,' he replied, 'I'm after eggs and bananas for the sickies as well as getting a good feed at the same time. The villagers won't put me in; the police I can dodge.'

Few really believed he was in earnest until one night bedlam broke loose in the guardroom. Yelling, and screams of someone in pain or frenzy, it was hard to tell which, indicated some poor wretch, POW or Burmese, was receiving savage treatment. A quick check of the huts revealed one man missing.

Whilst all were discussing what action to take the bloodied frame of the missing POW emerged from the darkness. He had been properly done over. His hairy chest was a red blob, his face almost a pulp. As his mates crowded around him he told them of his capture by the Burmese police, how the guards bashed him with rifle butts, boots and bamboo waddies before throwing him into the bamboo prison cell.

'How come they let you out, Bill?'

'They didn't,' he said, 'I climbed out through the bamboo. They think I am still there.'

'Holy hell, what is going to happen when they find you've escaped?'

'Search for me, I suppose.'

Within minutes his mates had the blood cleaned from his body and advised him to lie on his bed space and pretend he was asleep, just in case a search was slapped on.

It was not very long before guards began rushing through the huts. There was a problem. Bill was easy to identify; only two in the whole camp were endowed with such hairsute growth on their chest, and the Nips knew. Many a time they had plucked at the hair in anger or just for spite.

When this fact hit Bill he realised he had to surrender himself, or place his mates in a dangerous situation. Others almost pleaded with him to sit tight and await results, but it was of no use. A yell from an adjoining hut indicated the guards had picked the wrong man.

Bill sprang from his bedspace and almost ran to where all the noise came from. As he entered the hut a bewildered guard looked at the prisoner he was prodding with a rifle and then at the new arrival; he was quite puzzled and, momentarily, did nothing. Suddenly he emitted a yell and within moments other guards came and the 'escapee' was taken away.

Tokoro, who had been advised of the happening, called for Captain Arthur Hence, Adjutant of Ramsay Force, and demanded to know why one of the prisoners of war had attempted to escape.

Before any explanation could be offered Lieutenant Colonel Ramsay interceded and stressed that no-one had tried to get away. He, Tokoro too, knew why the lad had gone out under the wire. He was a captive of hunger, desperate for food and survival.

No matter how the two Australian officers pleaded for a lesser charge than attempted escape, Tokoro was adamant. However he did say he would submit their defence of the prisoner to his commanding officer, Captain Itsui. The sentence, if any, would be issued by him. Whatever that may be, Tokoro assured them, he would carry it out.

For some days the battle of words continued and at one point it did appear that Tokoro was relenting. However, his determination to obey Itsui prevailed.

The first intimation Ramsay had of Itsui's decision came when the illegally convicted POW was bundled into a truck, tied up under heavy guard, and taken away to an undisclosed area.

As the vehicle passed a group working around the camp grounds, they saw 'Bill', and heard him say, 'Tell the Colonel they are going to shoot me. God bless you.'

This third killing stunned everyone, and threats of a reprisal were made. But, angered as they were, any unwise action would only result in blood-spilling. The logical, cool minds of Colonel Ramsay and Captain Hence, in addition to many others, prevented what could have been a very nasty situation.

Work party guards were obviously jittery and fear could be seen in the eyes of many. It was noticed that the heavy bashings had eased off and the frequent yelling of 'currah currah' diminished to a marked extent.

Tokoro was well aware of the simmering hatred he had engendered and he endeavoured to ingratiate himself with the white-hot group by permitting an early finish to the day's work, then addressing them en masse.

He made no apology for what had happened, nor did he make any promises he had no intention of keeping. But he did *suggest* there *could* be a change of diet and went so far as to imply that the POWs could have steak or bacon and eggs for the morning meal, instead of water 'pap'. Laughter and derision were the response, for everyone knew he was trying to 'con' them into the belief he had their welfare at heart. Tokoro's deception failed in its intent to present the Japanese rule as a merciful one, instead of the iron-fist so far demonstrated.

The meagre rations and hard work, made the harder by the continuous monsoon rain, had taken their toll. An outbreak of the feared amoebic dysentery and other allied illnesses caused the sounding of the Last Post on twenty-five occasions. Even the life of the CMO, Lieutenant Colonel Coates, was at risk. It was sheer willpower and dedication to his profession that eventually brought him back from the very edge of the grave. In later months those two attributes played a major part in the salvaging of lives that may have otherwise been lost.

The Mergui saga, as far as Ramsay Force was concerned, came to an end on 16 August 1942, when the order came to move to Tavoy, 150 miles further north, the very heart of the Itsui domain.

As harsh as the voyage from Singapore had been, it bore no resemblance to the misery and horror the prisoners of war had to endure on vessels smaller than a Manly ferry. To sit with oustretched legs was impossible; those who did try soon found they had to huddle, knees to chin, for as long as humanly possible, then alternate with a 'stander'.

In the bowels of the wallowing hulk men gasped for breath, so heavy was the atmosphere. Many, unable to control their bodily functions, fouled themselves and those near them. Finally, a 'bosun's chair' was rigged on both sides of the vessel and the men were allowed to relieve themselves as they hung dangerously close to the hull. When the swell increased, as it did from time to time, it was a miracle some of the weak and emaciated did not plunge into the waters below. Had anyone done so, it is doubtful the skipper of the coaster would have hove-to in order to save the unfortunate man.

The crush of human bodies on the upper deck had but one consolation. At least they had fresh, though very hot, air to breathe and they had easy access to the 'toilets'.

At various intervals, the 'below-deckers' rotated with the upper-deck passengers for very obvious reasons. Had they not done so, there is no question death would have made its presence felt in the 'black hole' of the hold. No windsock was provided and in the heat of the day, hell itself could not have been hotter.

At dawn on 18 August 1942, the vessel dropped anchor some miles from Tavoy township. The prisoners of war were offloaded on to barges and, after some delay, towed up the river, disembarked and marched to a school, the pre-war Tavoy High School.

The remainder of Ramsay Force, comprising administration and medical personnel, embarked on another small coastal vessel in Mergui Bay, en route to Tavoy. That voyage was anything but pleasant, and was described by Major Chalmers, AAMC:

On the afternoon of the 18th August, after two false starts previously, the 'new' hospital cases and personnel embarked. There were 95 patients and about 70 medical and camp troops on a vessel of about 500 tons. Some difficulty was experienced transferring the stretcher cases to the ship—the stretchers were made up from bamboo poles and rice bags, and some old wire bed frames Those cases were accommodated on the hatch cover, with a tarpaulin above them. The commodes from the hospital were taken aboard for the convenience of dysentery cases.

Great difficulty was experienced in nursing the stretcher cases, and rain beat in under the overhead cover during the night. Even though all were aboard at 1800 hours the voyage did not commence until 0540 hours on the 19th.

On arrival at Tavoy River all cases were transhipped to an old barge, *all* ordered down into the hold. The area was extremely crowded; many patients were exhausted by the trip. And, at night, without lights, it was absolutely impossible to care for the very sick, particularly when stretcher cases needed commodes or bed pans. After an hour or so the atmosphere was terrible. Worse still, the crew refused to permit even the walking patients up on deck.

Due to heavy rain a cover had to be kept over the hold throughout the five hours trip to the Tavoy wharf. It was only after some great difficulty that another barge was obtained for other than sick personnel. The latter, the Japanese demanded, be forced down upon the very sick.

We arrived at Tavoy wharf at 0500 hours, only the stretcher cases and five attendants remained on the barge, all walking patients, bar twenty, had to march to the Tavoy High School camp. The majority of the marchers were totally unfit to do so.

Five hours later the stretcher cases were taken ashore and transported to their quarters They were all in a bad way, having had no food whatsoever since the previous evening, a small piece of 'bread', two eggs and a little soup since leaving Mergui.

The trip was an undue hardship to the patients and the death of one the day after arrival must, to some extent, be attributed to the trip.

Deaths, due to illness at Mergui, reached a total of 5 Australians and 12 British troops. Other losses, three, execution by the Japanese.

Mergui hospital admissions, 24th May 1942 to 16th August, same year:

(1) Australian, throughout the period = 519

(2) British throughout the period = 367

Grand total throughout the period = 886, 59% of Ramsay Force.

Illness included dysentery (Bacillary and Amoebic), cerebral tumour, cirrhosis of the liver (one of each, plus dysentery), cardiac beri-beri, laryngeal diphtheria, malnutrition, tinea, scabies and malaria.

IMPRESSIONS OF MERGUI CAMP

IN THE HISTORY of the 2/18 Battalion, *Men May Smoke*, Lieutenant Colonel G.E. Ramsay wrote the following account of the Mergui camp:

In order to obtain a proper perspective of conditions in Mergui, it is necessary first to consider the composition and origin of the AIF Force which left Singapore on May 15th, 1942, and the instructions received concerning it by HQ, AIF, as these have a bearing on subsequent events.

An Australian force, the strength of which was amended several times, but finally fixed at 3,000, all ranks, was ordered to be ready to leave Singapore for an unknown destination on or about 14th May, 1942.

The Nipponese authorities were informed that, to provide 3,000 troops for this expedition, it would necessitate the inclusion of a large proportion of men who had recently come out of hospital, and who were otherwise not fully fit physically, and would be unable to do the long march to Singapore. Most of the fit men from units, with the exception of a nucleus administrative staff in each case, were unavailable, as they were already engaged with various working parties required by the Nipponese in and around Singapore.

I was given to understand that a reply had been given to HQ, AIF, that this would not be any disadvantage, as it was not intended that the force be used as a working party; and that the troops would be moved to Singapore from Changi by motor trucks.

The impressions gained by they HQ, AIF, in regard to the requirements of the Nipponese in connection with this force were, among other things, as under:

(i) That the whole force would move to one destination.

(ii) That there would be no necessity to carry any medical supplies, other than what may be required during the voyage, covering a period up to about one (1) week or ten (10) days; as there would be adequate supplies available at the appointed destination.

(iii) For the same reason, a ban was placed on the inclusion of any engineer's tools, cooking utensils, accessories, or any other equipment of a like nature.

With the above requirements as a basis, the details of the proposed organisation of the force were submitted and approved by Nipponese HQ The approved organisation was as under:

Commander (Brigadier)
HQ Staff of Force (including Padres and Red Cross representatives)
3 Battalions each of 860, all ranks (approximately)
Engineers' detachments of 200, all ranks (approximately)

Medical and Dental Detachment of 120, all ranks (approximately)

– making a total of 3,000, all ranks, comprising most of the troops from all units left at Changi.

On arrival at the wharf, it was realised that some division would have to be made for the voyage, as the Brigadier was informed that there were two (2) ships, one to carry 2,000, and the other 1,000; but it was not expected that apart from this contingency, the organisation approved by the Nipponese HQ at Changi would be further changed. In regard, however, to the 1,000 troops placed under my command for the voyage, consisting of one battalion and the medical and dental detachment, a Japanese sub-officer, who appeared to be in charge of the embarkation on the *Celebes Maru*, entirely ignored the company and platoon organisation, and arbitrarily divided my whole contingent into parties of fifty (50) and himself selected the first officer that came under his notice to command each party; and later, more senior officers, to command groups of parties. They could easily have been so arranged for counting and checking purposes as required, but the changing of commanders, and the identity of my sub-units, considerably hampered both administration and control.

When it became known that it was intended to land 1,000 troops at each of three (3) different points on the coast of Lower Burma, the Brigadier, on the other ship, was apparently allowed to make the necessary allocations; as, although I was not able to get personal contact with him since before leaving the wharf at Singapore, I received a message that I was to land at Mergui with my battalion, with portion only of the medical and dental detachments from the *Celebes Maru*, together with portion of the Engineer detachment from the other ship.

On the arrival of the 500 British POWs from Sumatra, I was informed by the commander of the Nipponese garrison at Mergui that a further reorganisation under my command would be required. The method adopted in this instance, however, differed considerably from my earlier experience.

At a conference of myself and my senior officers and the Nipponese commander and staff on the evening of our arrival, I was handed a typewritten list of instructions setting out in full the Nipponese requirements in regard to control, discipline, procedure, penalties for offences, etc. From my point of view, this was eminently satisfactory, added to which I was allowed to prepare and submit the proposed details of reorganisation of my force into a HQ, with two (2) AIF battalions and one (1) British battalion within certain set limitations which still allowed me sufficient margin to use my own discretion to quite an extent; my suggested organisation, when completed, being accepted in its entirety.

Some criticism has been offered by some of my officers in their reports regarding the lack of preparation for our accommodation on our arrival. In this regard, I was of the opinion that, for some reason unknown to me, an unforeseen change had been made in the original plans made by the Nipponese authorities at Changi, probably at short notice, and that, as a result, it had not been possible for any arrangements to have been made earlier at what was probably an unexpected destination.

This was further evident from the fact that we were landed at three (3) different points instead of at one place, and subsequently of the serious shortage of medical supplies and cooking facilities, despite the earlier assurances, and also later, by the demand for working parties. On the position being explained, however, I greatly appreciated the fact that the numbers of men demanded were very reasonable in the circumstances, and that no attempt was made to enforce men who were marked as 'Unfit for Duty' by our own medical officers. I am of the opinion, too, that this work had a beneficial effect on the health and physical fitness of my troops, and helped to relieve the monotony of camp life as a POW, and also enable men to earn some pay, although small, by means of which they were able to take advantage of the very real and welcome concessions allowed to us in the form of vendors being permitted to sell fruit and tobacco, and later, eggs, within the camp area.

This proved of further assistance in helping to maintain the health of the troops, as the rations issued by the Nipponese were insufficient, lacked variety, and were not balanced enough, according to our own standard, either to keep up their strength for any manual work, or to prevent beri-beri, of which there were a number of cases.

The rice generally was of poor quality, but on the completion of the baker's ovens, erected by our own troops with the permission of the Nipponese, better use was made of the flour, which made possible an issue of a small bun per man for one meal daily.

The high incidence of sickness among the troops during the first weeks after our arrival, I am of the opinion, was due in part to the state of health in which the troops were previously, aided by the extremely trying conditions on the voyage; but these conditions were very considerably provided in the first four (4) weeks in our camp at the Mergui School.

The establishment of a separate hospital materially assisted the attention which could be given to the sick, but even there, the efforts of my medical staff were seriously handicapped, not only by the unhealthy conditions then still existing at the camp, but also by the lack of beds, blankets and other hospital facilities; and my senior medical officer is of the opinion that some at least of the deaths resulting from such diseases as amoebic dysentery could have been prevented had the necessary drugs been available here; or had permission been granted at Changi to bring a supply with us.

With the move to the splendid new quarters, which proved to be airy, hygienic, comfortable, and ideally suitable for the climate, an improvement in the general health commenced, and was maintained. The one disadvantage, in my opinion, at the new quarters, was the Nipponese decision that all junior officers must sleep in the huts with the men.

Unpleasant incidents on the working parties were rare and, in many cases, where my soldiers had been struck by Japanese sentries without sufficient justification, I appreciate the prompt action taken by Japanese officers to prevent any recurrence. The work which the troops were called upon to do was not unduly arduous, except on one or two occasions where some parties were compelled to unload heavy bags of cement for long periods with very little rest, which in some instances caused neck and shoulder abrasions. The additional wear and tear on boots caused by the continued working parties required, made replacements a pressing problem.

The most regrettable incident during our whole stay at Mergui was the shooting of the two (2) members of the AIF for allegedly attempting to escape. While such penalty was included in the list of instructions handed to men on arrival, I still have very grave doubts that this action was in accordance with accepted International practice.

TAVOY, BURMA

THE TOWNSHIP of Tavoy was, in many ways similar to that of Mergui. Rumour had it this port was one of the main rice-exporting areas of Burma. The sight of the small wharves and store-houses soon dispelled that belief.

When the prisoners of war were all ashore the usual tiresome tenko commenced. When the count was finally agreed upon the guard in charge informed Lieutenant Colonel Ramsay the group had a thirty-seven-kilometre march to their destination. That information proved to be entirely incorrect. In reality it was only a couple of kilometres to the American Baptist School (Tavoy High School) where Major Lloyd (2/29 Battalion) awaited their arrival.

Due to his administrative ability the billeting arrangements were simplified. The ORs were housed in the main (stone) building; the officers in the house formerly occupied by the school administration staff.

Hygiene: Latrines had been made ready by the former occupants, a Dutch group.

Cooking: A large kitchen had been prepared for instant use, except it was considered as entirely suitable by Australian standards. Under the supervision of Captain Arthur Hence, Adjutant, Ramsay Force, a meal (rice only and a meagre issue at that) was speedily prepared. It was the first food tasted since early morning when the POWs had been issued with a very small, and mouldy, rice bun.

Bed spaces: Approximately twenty four inches per man, sufficient to permit each occupant room to stretch out. All belongings—what few they had—were stowed at the head of the space allotted.

Being acutely aware of a probable lightning search by the guards, hiding places for any valuables, photographs, etc. were soon established, hopefully well out of sight of Nipponese eyes.

The camp commandant, Corporal Kumada, forbade any further communication with the party that had arrived at Tavoy on 26 May, on board the *Tohohasi Maru*. Brigadier Varley and his force were encamped in the vicinity of the aerodrome. All troops considered fit were engaged as construction labour on the damaged areas. To augment workers on the drome, a group to be known as 'J' Company, taken from Ramsay Force, was detailed and moved to that site.

The remainder of Ramsay Force was engaged in work in and around town clearing out offices and factories to house Japanese troops. Those jobs were all sought after as many opportunities presented themselves for the acquisition of additional foodstuffs. The townspeople were only too willing to outwit the truculent guards and present prisoners of war with many gifts that eased hunger pains.

Those fortunate enough to be on the village marketplace details and receive dried fish and other food, did their utmost to get back through the gate without the guards discovering their 'booty'. Some were caught and punished on the spot. The 'illegal'—as far as the Nipponese were concerned—possessions were confiscated and no doubt ultimately consumed by the guardians of the 'liberty'.

The most abhorred tasks at Tavoy were the wood parties. No-one wanted to be called upon to undertake the three-mile march, fell, cut and split rubber trees, load them onto pre-war, British owned mule limbers to which six workers were 'hitched', and haul the heavy loads over hills back to camp. No opportunity existed to contact Burmese traders for the purpose of obtaining additions to the meagre rice diet.

In pouring rain, the timber men did it hard. The limbers or, to the uninitiated, drays, bogged down in ankle deep mud, at times knee deep, and the task of pulling them—even for the strongest—was an appalling strain on their strength. When possible, parties were alternated on a daily basis.

The drome, or Brigadier Varley's, force had the worst introduction to Tavoy. When they arrived—by sea—they were force marched the twenty five miles from the mouth of the river, to be quartered in large hangars with stone-littered floors. For the first night they hardly noticed the intense discomfort, being too tired to bother about wobbly stones for mattresses.

It took many days for those exhausted men to recover from two fiendish experiences: the long voyage under the most primitive conditions, then the agony of marching such a great distance without even a drink of water, or a meal!

Small wonder escape plans were in the minds of many. They all feared these experiences prefaced a future of near starvation, illness and probably death as their only salvation. Only too well they recalled the treatment the Japanese had handed out to the Chinese in the rape of Nanking, and other battle and concentration areas.

Eight boys from the 2/4 Anti-Tank Regiment decided such an existence was not for them. They made plans. Their ill-fated attempt at liberation highlighted the impossibility of man overcoming dense jungle while lacking food, medicine and professional guides. They not only had to surmount these problems, but also another—bounty hunters!

Their subsequent apprehension, mockery of a trial and execution put a pall over the whole force. Brigadier Varley paid tribute to their great bravery as they faced the firing squad. They stood tall and straight; true soldiers of their country, far-away Australia.

Despite the fact the Japanese subsequently permitted canteen-type trading within the camp, only those who had money had access to this unexpected luxury. However, the pittance paid for work by the Nipponese restricted purchasing power and so a system of barter developed, much to the delight of the Burmese whose accepted any trinket, clothing or bits thereof. This meant mates were in a position to assist their ailing friends who were not only penniless but, in some cases, dying from the lack of quality and quantity in the rations provided.

In countless instances, true mateship surfaced in prisoner of war camps. Without a genuine mate and with illness taxing one's ability to overcome debilitation, death obtruded.

Representations were made to the Japanese camp commandant by Lieutenant Colonel Ramsay, his Adjutant, Captain Hence and later, when he arrived at the camp, Lieutenant Colonel Coates, Chief Medical Officer 'A' Force, for the right to visit the village market for the purpose of purchasing foodstuffs and consequently improve the prisoners' welfare.

The obvious presence of malnutrition, dysentery, malaria, beri-beri and allied illnesses, was eventually the reason the commandant, a corporal, relented and granted the requests. Additionally, he took no action when a trader blatantly entered the camp with his horse-drawn gharry (cart) and proceeded to sell his wares. It was not long before rice cakes, fruits and ghular (a type of sweetener) were sold from the vehicle. The smiling Burmese was quite happy, even though he received little cash. He preferred to barter, Japanese currency being worthless as far as he was concerned.

Tavoy, like Mergui, was not to be a holiday or rest camp. Far from it. The POWs were to work and an aerodrome had to be completed. The demand for a maximum number of fit men far exceeded those physically able to even lift a tool.

At no time did Ramsay or Hence agree to supply the number of workers the Nipponese considered minimum. Despite the fact the rations were slightly better by virtue of the allowable purchases, the workload increased, offsetting the advantage gained. Long hours and slave-driving tactics by the guards at the drome site soon took their toll.

Daily the sick parades grew, while many others, unable to attend, were bedridden. The resultant fall-off of work numbers delayed the planned drome completion date by weeks.

This state of affairs infuriated the Nipponese engineers and camp commandants. Captain Itsui, their commanding officer, insisted on a larger number of workers from the Brigadier Varley and Ramsay camps.

There were ravings and threats of reduced rations and of privileges relating to outside camp purchases. These were often prevented anyway, then reconsidered, with hints that permission may be granted, subject to very stringent conditions. With the full weight of Lieutenant Colonels Ramsay and Coates, plus the persuasive efforts of Captain Arthur Hence, the Japanese commandant would relent and allow the Chief Medical Officer (Coates) to visit the marketplace to purchase eggs and bananas. But the visits were few and far between.

The commandant was an enigma. On some days he was, as many said, almost human. However, where sex was concerned he was responsible for a vicious murder of a Burmese woman who had refused to hand over her twelve-year-old daughter to the Japanese personnel.

Whilst he did not actually commit the crime, he saw one of his guards kick her to death just outside his office door. Prisoners of war who tried to intervene were bashed and taken away from the scene. A sickening and revolting sight, it was a cruel sadistic lesson directed at the parents of young girls in the township.

As had happened at Mergui, the rice ration to all POW camps in every area of Burma, and subsequently Thailand, was reduced, when the number of fit men fell below the numbers required by the Nipponese engineers. The old cry of 'sick mans do not eat' resulted in a reduction so great as to promote more illness.

The guards argued that their 'generosity' in allowing Coates to purchase fruit and eggs from the township (though always in minimal numbers, if any were available) more than adequately made up for any reductions in the rice rations. That of course was a spurious justification of withholding food from the prisoners. But it was one the Nips adhered to, despite strong objections from the Australian officers.

One incident occurred in the Ramsay Force encampment which had a tinge of humour, as well as providing much-needed protein for the many lying seriously ill in the hospital area.

The Nipponese camp commandant had a well-fed goat he was fattening for a feast. However he made one great error. No-one was placed in charge of the valuable animal and one night it suddenly disappeared.

Lieutenant Colonel Ramsay was concerned at the health of his troops at Tavoy and, after a long discussion with his Chief Medical Officer, he decided to place on permanent record an analysis of the various ailments treated by the medical staff, up to that particular period in 1942. It reads:

An arbitrary distinction was made by the Nipponese between diarrhoea and dysentery. Cases with frequent motions, but no blood or mucus, were classed as diarrhoea, all with mucus and or blood as dysentery. Of the 886 patients admitted to hospital, approximately 700 came under these two headings.

The dysentery was of a severe variety, with fifteen deaths. Although most cases commenced as typical bacillary dysentery, approximately 30 were shown to have *Entamoeba histolytica* in the stools. These cases were the bulk of the cases which lasted for long periods, and due to the lack of Emetine could not be satisfactorily treated. Seven deaths occurred amongst this group. They were diagnosed as Amoebic by the pathologists at Mergui civil hospital. The greater number of the slides were seen by Captain Brereton or myself and there was no doubt in our minds that the organism was *E. histolytica*, in spite of criticism which has been made since arrival at Tavoy. Further, the stools of these cases often showed the typical 'anchovy paste' appearance.

The treatment of both types of dysentery was rendered difficult by the irregular supply of mag-sulphate and the lack of Emetine, except for enough for two cases who improved rapidly under this treatment. The therapeutic effect also confirmed the amoebic diagnosis (as in Lieutenant Colonel Coates' case).

The majority of the amoebic dysentery cases gave a history of previous attacks.

• *Diphtheria*—No facilities were available for culturing swabs from throats, but there were at least three definite cases of the disease. Gunner Davis had a very extensive laryngeal diphtheria which finally lead to obstruction and, in spite of a tracheotomy (by Lt. Col. Coates), death. Two other cases of faucal and pharyngeal diphtheria cleared up, in each case with a residual laryngeal parasite. There were five cases of suspicious faucal and tonsillar infections.

• *Malaria*—Both new and relapse cases of malaria occurred, but drug supplies were adequate and no difficulty was experienced with treatment.

• *Scabies and Lice*—There was a brisk outbreak of scabies and lice; the latter commencing in the British lines. No suitable arrangements for disinfestation of clothes could be made in the main camp, so these patients were admitted to hospital for a couple of days as an efficient stream disinfestor had been built there. The move to Tavoy was commenced before the lice could be properly cleared up and some have been carried here.

• *Skin Disease*—A moderate amount of tinea occurred among the troops, but skin disease, on the whole, was much less than experienced in Malaya.

• *Nephritis*—One very severe case subacute nephritis occurred and several cases of pyelitis. Citrates and other alkalis were practically unprocurable; though a small amount of hexamine was available there was no acid phosphate to combine with it.

• *Pneumonia*—One case of severe broncho-pneumonia occurred.

• *Operations*—Two operations only were performed, a tracheotomy and a strangulated inguinal hernia with undescended testis (both by Lieutenant Colonel Coates).

• *Vitamin B Deficiency*—There was a good deal of oedema of the extremities, but this appeared to be protein deficiency rather than beri-beri However, there were many cases with signs of peripheral neuritis with paresis and some sensory changes. Several of the chronic cases of dysentery died from sudden collapse and suggested cardial beri-beri.

• *Hookworm*—Three proven cases, ankylostomia, occurred.

Conclusions:

(1) There was a high incidence of sickness at Mergui, but this can be attributed to several factors—

   (a) The presence of many dysentery carriers, from Changi and Sumatra.

   (b) The conditions on the ship coming to Mergui as several (dysentery) cases commenced on the ship.

   (c) The extremely bad conditions at the Mergui school, and to obstruction to bettering them.

   (d) The extremely unhygienic habits of the British troops.

(2) The drug supplies were always inadequate.

*

Green Force, it was subsequently learned, had been force-marched from Ye to Thanbyuzayat, a distance of well over forty kilometres and thence to the 4 kilo camp where they and other forces to follow were to commence the construction of the infamous Burma-Thailand railway line.

Ramsay Force was to remain at Tavoy until 15 December 1942, when it was ordered to close camp and to follow Green and Anderson Forces. The POWs were transported to the Ye railhead and rested for two days. Then came the gruelling march that sapped the failing strength of the so-called fit, unfit and very ill. Other than a small hand truck, loaded with kitchen and other gear, no arrangements had been made for the sick. The Japs did provide two Burmese to man the truck.

On that debilitating cross-country grind the spectre of death faced them all, as it had with Green and Anderson Forces. Many carried not only their own gear but that of mates barely able to walk a step at a time. Truly, on 18 December, fate watched over a great but emaciated body of men. The real courage of the majority was something to marvel at; bodies clinging one to the other as they trudged in a seemingly endless line. How they made it to Thanbyuzayat, the huge staging camp, will forever remain a mystery.

One galling act committed by the guards on that march was to deny the salt-hungry men the right to gather even a pannikin full as they passed a pan. Acres of gleaming white crystals! And men would cheerfully have died for the privilege of filling billy cans, eating utensils or anything with a cavity. Those who attempted it ran that risk and those caught in the act were severely bashed.

Whilst 'currah currah' could be heard up and down the line of cursing men and arguments ensued, many pounds of the precious alkali did fill many vessels. It was later used for two purposes; to add taste to the life-giving rice and by the medical staff to make saline.

Smoke over Singapore immediately prior to the surrender (Australian War Memorial Negative No. 012447)

Lieutenant Colonel C.M. Black, CO 2/3 Reserve Motor Transport Company and Commander Black Force (Australian War Memorial Negative No. 30391/12)

Lieutenant Colonel C.G.W. Anderson, VC, MC, CO 2/19 Battalion and
Commander of Anderson Force.
(Photo coutesy Major Reg Newton. Australian War Memorial Negative No.73661)

Sergeant Leslie G. Hall

Crowded dysentery ward, Mergui hospital (Sketch by Wilson Mills)

Hospital cookhouse, Mergui (Sketch by Wilson Mills)

Ramsay Force Commander, Lieutenant Colonel G.E. Ramsay

Major Charles Green

Lieutenant Colonel Albert Coates, Chief Medical Officer, 'A' Force
(Australian War Memorial Negative No. 103286)

Major Alan Hobbs, 2i/c to Lieutenant Colonel Coates

POWs aboard salt wagons. Photo by George Aspinall, the unofficial Changi
photographer (Australian War Memorial Negative No. 157866)

POWs being transported by train along the Burma-Thailand railway
(Australian War Memorial Negative No. P0406/40/10)

Typical huts provided for POWs in Burma and Thailand
(Australian War Memorial Negative No. 157871)

Interior of a typical hundred-metre atap-roofed hut. Sleeping space
for each man measured approximately 2 feet 6 inches in width
(Australian War Memorial Negative No. 157878)

WILLIAMS FORCE

LIEUTENANT COLONEL J.M. Williams commanded the 2/2 Pioneer Battalion, Corps Troops, which had been in action in various theatres of war with the 6th, 7th and 9th Australian Divisions in the Middle East.

When the 8th Australian Division was fighting a withdrawal action down the Malayan Peninsula, the 2/2 Pioneer Battalion (and attached troops) was aboard the British liner *Orcades*, en route, they thought and hoped, for Australia. But the unexpected fall of Singapore resulted in a change of plans and they disembarked in Java. Their role was a defensive one in support of the Dutch military forces.

The Commander of the Java Force, renamed Black Force, was Brigadier A.S. Blackburn VC, and the force consisted of 2/2 Pioneer Battalion, 2/3 Machine-Gun Battalion, 2/6 Field Company RAE, 105 General Transport Company, 2/2 Casualty Clearing Station, 'B' Company Headquarter Guard Battalion (less two platoons), personnel of Line and Communication, Pay, Postal and Records, plus the 2/3 Reserve Motor Transport Unit commanded by Lieutenant Colonel C. Black.

As history records, the Netherlands armed forces surrendered to the invading Japanese troops, thus depriving the Australian fighting unit of the opportunity of consolidating its battle line. The end to the Java campaign, which the support troops had expected to last for a longer period, was a complete let-down. They were prepared to continue fighting; despite the lack of air cover and over-whelming odds. Hostilities ceased 10 March 1942.

Shattered and bewildered by the sudden cessation of a war that had hardly begun, the men became prisoners of war. It was the beginning of a type of life they never envisaged.

The Bicycle camp, Batavia, where the main body of POWs was quartered, contained Black Force personnel of No. 1 Squadron, RAAF Lockheed-Hudson Bomber Reconnaissance Group (which had dealt the Japanese a stinging blow when attempting their initial landing at Khota Baru, north Malaya, 8 December 1941), survivors from HMAS *Perth* and 131 Battalion Field Regiment, United States Army.

One of the most upsetting incidents at the Bicycle camp occurred when the Japanese escorted officers to Koenigplein gaol for interrogation purposes. No-one knew or could guess what would happen to them if they failed to cooperate.

Three Australians, Lieutenant Colonel J.M. Williams and Captains Ross and Handasyde, 2/2 Pioneer Battalion, were taken early in May. They suffered unbelievable torture during the four weeks they were held. When they refused to divulge information of any kind, military or otherwise, the Japanese began their 'inducement' tactics.

These officers, like others before them, were strapped to chairs and bashed unmercifully with any weapon, be it wood or metal, the interrogating staff had to hand.

Hour after hour the treatment went on. At times, a merciful fate intervened and they became oblivious to everything, unaware of darkness or light, days, hours or even meal times—of which there precious few.

There was hardly any let-up, even after cigarette lighter flames burned and blistered their swollen hands. The pain suffered then was maddening, but not enough to exact any information from the determined officers.

In the case of Lieutenant Colonel Williams, and probably others as well, they subjected him to the end-all (water) treatment, pouring water into his body via the nostrils. However, and apparently to the amazement of his tormentors, he divulged nothing.

In *4000 Bowls of Rice* Linda Goetz Holmes writes:

No doubt the Japanese couldn't believe their luck at capturing a whole battalion of rugged Australians—and an engineering unit at that. So it is not surprising that Williams Force became the core of No. 1 Mobile Force, and mobile it was; on the move constantly under worsening weather, supply and jungle conditions. The heavy monsoon rains became incessant, as did the screams of the guards. 'Speedo! Speedo!' They would shout in broken English, all the time pelting the POWs with rocks as the prisoners tried to complete their impossible quotas of work with primitive or worn-out tools.

TOM FAGAN POW DIARY
Java to Moulmein

IN JULY the Nipponese have been taking Other Ranks to interrogation areas. As the officers, bashed almost to death, revealed nothing, do they expect men of lower rank to break under similar treatment? They don't and won't; officers or privates, all men, and loyal to their country of origin.

On our daily work parties bashings are received for the most frivolous reasons. Rations are low, mainly plain boiled rice at that. How can we continue to live like this? What lies ahead for us? Rumours are flying around that parties are to be sent overseas within weeks.

This time they were not baseless rumours and in October, 1942, a group numbering 1,500 boarded a rusty looking 5,000-ton Nipponese freighter that had seen better days. Just how and where the troops could be 'stowed' was a matter of serious conjecture.

From dock-side, it looked an utter impossibility in view of the enormous amount of cargo being loaded. However, after being paraded and counted, then forced to scramble up narrow, swinging, steps to the deck, they soon realised the Japanese knew how to squeeze humans into the narrowest possible space.

The excited guards were yelling and screaming as if all the demons in hell were scrambling up the side of the rust bucket. To get rid of them with all speed they directed them down almost vertical ladders into the very bowels of the rodent-infested hulk.

Like all other vessels that prisoners of war voyaged in, it was shoulder-to-shoulder accommodation, no room to stand up; little fresh air and to make matters worse, hundreds were forced to find room under and around Bren gun carriers. No-one was allowed to get into them; those who tried were bashed.

Those unsecured machines boded ill if the ship ran into a violent storm, an event quite common in those waters. If they were unfortunate enough to steam into rough weather those pieces-of-war would be tossed around like corks. The possible result had frightening aspects.

In No. 2 hold 744 troops were jammed in so tightly sleep was impossible unless literally lying one upon the other. For the following thirty-six hours the ship (if it could be called that) remained at the wharf. The heat at the bottom of the hold was almost intolerable; it was an effort to breathe, the stench from sweating bodies, urine and those suffering from dysentery, was indescribable. Toilet arrangements were the same as applied on other prisoner ships, a box-like affair slung over the side of the vessel.

Rations, one and a half pints of tea per man per day plus a meagre issue of rice and soya soup with a hint of radish floating in the liquid. Some boys still had tinned food that had been on issue at Batavia and ignored the rice. However, due to the oppressive heat and loss of body liquid, water was what they needed, but could not get.

Not one drop of water was available for drinking or bathing and acute thirst began to raise its ugly head. Men dreamed of luscious, gushing, clear mountain springs. Visions of waterfalls were with them every moment.

Up on the decks, yells of delight could be heard as the guards played around the large hoses, probably salt water, but they were permitted as much fresh water as they wanted. Thirst to them was just a word.

Every effort was made to induce the Japanese to allow the suffering men access to the upper deck for additional water, if only for drinking purposes. All requests refused.

The voyage to Singapore, approximately seventy-two hours in fetid conditions, was nothing but a frightful nightmare. It was so bad, one Australian soldier passed away.

When the order came for disembarkation it was as if the war had come to an end and they were homeward bound. But it was not to be. Their stay at the 'country club', Changi, was like a breath of heaven.

The prisoners of war there did not know the real horrors of a concentration camp, not a Japanese guard in sight. Men roamed the grass swards at will; they were all clothed, food was not a scarce commodity, morale was high and brutality was an unknown factor, except for the occasional bashing by the Indian guards.

To the troops from Java the sight and experience was unbelievable, but true. Now they were here, here is where they hoped to stay for the duration. Unfortunately, their wild dreams were soon to be shattered. Just three days later they were again aboard a hell-ship, en route to no one knew where. A total of 1799 crammed into two holds of the *Mayebassi Maru*, in addition to Japanese troops who were to voyage in apparent comfort, just below upper deck.

Seventeen days after the Java Party had lined up in Batavia they arrived at Moulmein, Burma, after a most horrifying trip wherein they were forced to suffer inhumanity of the very worst kind. The run up from Singapore was beset with bashings, lack of food and water, illness of a kind that brought many close to the very edge of a watery grave.

BLACK FORCE

ON 30 OCTOBER 1942, Lieutenant Colonel Chris Black led his 593 Australian and 190 American servicemen onto trucks that were to transport them to the 35 kilometre point from Thanbyuzayat, where they disembarked. They faced a five-kilometre march to the most forward jungle camp, Beke Taung.

This encampment was to be their first taste of native-built, atap-roofed huts. They were filthy but, for a wonder, waterproof. The two buildings were long, open on one side and contained a platform of bamboo slats (split poles) about thirty inches above floor level, which formed their bed and living space.

A fairly large kitchen contained six kwalis over prepared fireplaces. Whilst the rest of the force personnel cleaned the hutments the cooks hurried to prepare their first meal—plain rice, washed down with weak vegetable soup.

Water came from a native well some 500 yards from the living area. There was also a small stream about the same distance away in the jungle. Additional help was readily forthcoming for water haulage; everyone was hungry and willing to help the 'babbling brooks' in any way possible.

For that day at least all was more or less peace and quiet—quite a new experience. The tranquillity of the cleared jungle compound belied what lay in the near future. Not one man dreamed they were about to face the great trial of their lives. Many were to succumb, and the survivors were never to be the same men again.

Ahead of them lay nothing but pestilence, disease, starvation, unimaginable brutality and work far beyond their capacities. In a way, it was well no-one could foresee the future.

The following morning, other than the cooks who had risen one hour earlier, a bugle call awakened the troops to a new way of life. They breakfasted on plain boiled rice and then lined up for their first task on the Burma-Thailand railway, soon to be named the 'Railway of Death', for that it surely was to be. Their first job was to build an embankment. Their antiquated tools—chunkels and well-worn shovels.

The first shock to their systems came when they discovered they were to work as 'coolies'. They had witnessed natives carrying materials in baskets suspended on bamboo poles. Perhaps they had laughed at the sight. Today, they were the ones who could be made merry of, white men actually carrying baskets of earth to a spot approximately 100 yards away, just like the maligned natives.

The Japanese were very easy the first day and everyone was on his way back to camp and a rest by 2.00 p.m. This, the POWs thought, is going to be a breeze. Nothing very hard in what they had done in the few hours out on the job. Time left over to enjoy a swim.

But, unaware of the cunning of their captors, they were, to coin a phrase, led up the garden path. Even the next few days were comparatively easy—back to quarters early, a meal, wander in the jungle unhindered by their guards, a leisurely swim then gather wild berries to add taste to the rice they would have to eat. Unfortunately there were no villagers in the vicinity and no opportunity to trade or buy foodstuffs.

The ration issue soon became very poor and the Japanese decided on search parties for what looked like lily root. Large quantities were collected and used under the watchful eyes of the medical officers. Stomach upsets and diarrhoea outbreaks soon became evident and diagnosed as due to the consumption of the horrible tasting lily root. The doctors ordered its immediate disposal and had supplies of it buried.

The attitude of the fit men at work was also beginning to concern the medical staff. They were playing right into the hands of the Japanese by going flat to the boards so as to enjoy free time in camp.

Advice to ease up went unheeded and within a week up went the daily quota to 1.2 metres to be cleared per man per day. This was the first of many increases until the day came when quotas were completely forgotten as the 'speedo' tactics which dictated, not soil removal, but hours—more and more, and still more.

Linda Goetz Holmes gives some insight into the Japanese attitudes to the POWs they worked so cruelly:

Even the continuing brutality of relentlessly driving the POWs to work on the railway far into the night appears to have a precedent in Japanese military training. A British colonel who was allowed to observe Japanese training methods in 1934–35 once questioned the captain in charge of some recruits why he was driving the soldiers to a new task after three days and two nights without sleep. Why not let them rest up and be fresh for the next day, he asked. 'They already know how to sleep,' the captain replied. 'They need training in how to stay awake.'

*

Time and time again the shifts extended to twenty four hours, and sometimes even longer. The work demands became utterly unreasonable and real brutality became a daily occurrence. Men were bashed, kicked and knocked unconscious for the least infringement of the guards' sadistic rules.

Black Force was not denied news of the outside world as Arch Caswell and his friend, Brian Breillat, had built a radio set. They had hidden the various components in their kit when they sailed away from Java, as did Bill Gibb.

Distribution of the news from the broadcasts was entrusted to one officer, Flight Lieutenant Ken Smith. He did it casually and modestly, but with conviction. Those privileged to receive it knew it was the truth he was dispensing, not just the 'latrine-o-grams' which abounded in every camp.

Via that secret radio many of the prisoners of war received cheerio calls from home. Such unexpected greetings were a tremendous boost to those who had the good fortune to have it conveyed to them. Somehow they felt as if the folks at home knew they were at least alive and living in hope of an early release.

It did not take long for the Japanese to realise that someone in the camp had a radio. A loose word here and there, however innocently expressed, fostered suspicion. But that was all they had. Searches failed, so the guards decided one way of silencing the 'bird' was to strip every piece of wire they could find in and near the huts.

Eventually the radio was hidden in a stool, one upon which many a Nipponese sat when camp was moved. In some camps a water bottle from which water could actually be poured was a favoured hiding place.

By November it was evident that the water supply was becoming critical. The dry season had set in, streams no longer existed and the well was just a soak.

At the end of that month Black Force went back to the 26 kilo camp where Ramsay Force was already in residence. From that point the two forces were closely associated and were together at the 75 and 105 kilo camps.

The combined forces were to suffer the same problems, short rations, hard work, long hours, disease, absence of medical supplies and resultant deaths.

WILLIAMS FORCE
October 1942—January 1943

BY COURTESY of Colonel J. M. Williams, OBE, ED, formerly Commander 2/ 2 Pioneer Battalion, extracts from his personal diary are used. They describe in graphic detail, the history of the force that bore his name throughout the construction of the Burma-Thailand railway, 1942-43.

*

The Unit marched out of Moulmein gaol, Burma, on Monday, 26 October 1942. The 599 officers and other ranks faced a three-mile march through the centre of the town, to the railway station where they were to board a train; 30 personnel to each cattle truck.

The townspeople gave the marchers an unexpected welcome in contrast to the Javanese, who had become pro-Japanese the moment fortunes changed. Instead of derision, they received gifts of food and smokes, the Nipponese guards were disregarded as the populace patted the Australians on the back, smiled and some were heard to say, 'We feel sorry for you, Australia'.

The train departed at 1100 hours and arrived at Thanbyuzayat Japanese Base Camp, No. 3 Prisoners of War Group (whose headquarters were in Bangkok, Thailand) at 1500 hours. They were met on arrival by Brigadier A.L. Varley, Commander 'A' Force.

As soon as quarters had been allotted, Lieutenant Colonel Y. Nagatomo, Camp Commandant, ordered a conference of all Commanders.

After lengthy discussion Nagatomo agreed to the formation of two units, Williams Force comprising the 2/2 Pioneer Battalion, survivors of the HMAS *Perth*, and odd personnel ex-Java, a total of 884 officers and other ranks.

Black Force to be made up of all members of the 2/3 Reserve Motor Transport Unit, RAAF personnel and the 2/6 Field Company Engineers, plus unattached Motor Transport troops. A total of 600, less 90 who were apparently to be assigned to Base Camp duties.

At the conclusion of the conference the two Force Commanders were ordered to have eight (8) copies of the nominal rolls ready for submission to Base Headquarters staff the following morning, after which there was to be a full parade before the Japanese Camp Commander, Lt. Col. Y. Nagatomo. It was eventually held at 1800 hours.

In his address of welcome he told the assembled troops, in part, 'You are only a few remaining skeletons after the invasion of East Asia for the past few centuries and are pitiful victims. It is not your fault but till your Government do not wake up from the dreams and discontinue their resistance all of you will not be released.'

He also assured them 'they were the remnants of a rabble army, did not know how to dress'; forgetting, quite conveniently, the Great Imperial Japanese army had failed to provide clothing of any sort for any one prisoner.

As he walked away from his Improvised rostrum a ripple of laughter followed his progress, the seat was out of his pants. Exposed was a red patch, whether a cloth repair or a feature of his oriental posterior, no one could tell.

Organisation—The word platoon, as expressed in the British and Australian armies, did not apply in Nipponese terminology. Instead, and from that day on, the Japanese word was to be used. A KUMI comprised 50 soldiers, 100 became a Han. Commanders were to be known as KUMICHO and HANCHO, respectively. Special armbands would be issued and had to be worn by all commanders.

'A' Force Disposition—All distances quoted would be in kilometres as from Thanbyuzayat to the Burma-Thailand Border at the Three Pagoda Pass. Conversely, Bampong to the same point, Thailand side.

4 kilo camp	Green Force
18 kilo camp	Anderson Force
26 kilo camp	Ramsay Force (as from 20.12.42)
35 kilo camp	Williams Force
40 kilo camp	Black Force (moved back to the 26 kilo camp, 29.11.42—water supply failed)

[*Thursday 29.11.42*] Transported by motor lorries to the 35 kilo camp, known as Tanyin. The first task was to clear enough of the jungle growth to prepare a parade ground.

Only four (4) huts, weather-worn at that, available for the whole force; 200 men crowded into each one. Their first meal was not allowed to be served until after the interminable tenko. The men had to eat in the dark.

The cooking gear, what little there was, was of very poor quality and the food ration, as usual, was on the low scale. One small yak provided an additive that was hardly recognisable in the small issue of rice in each dixie. At least, minute as it may have been, it was a meal for the tired and ravishingly hungry men.

For the Williams Force troops, their first day on the railway job was anything but a happy one; perhaps an indication of what was to come. Hard work, meagre meals and shortage of cooking gear; Korean guards, the latter a bitter pill to swallow!

[*30.11.42*] Three men in the work party bitten by snakes; fortunately, not fatally. A ration group delivered five yaks but three escaped due to the lack of ropes to hold them. Their recovery was impossible as, poor in condition as they were, they certainly knew how to melt away into the jungle growth.

For the next two days, Saturday and Sunday, the men worked from daylight until dark clearing the area in preparation for the eventual building of the rail line. Two hundred men inoculated against tropical diseases.

[2.11.42] Of great concern was the unexpected influx of 200 natives for whom accommodation had to be provided. Their presence completely wrecked the orderliness the camp had acquired in the three-day occupation. Hygiene was not one of their specialities and the Australians were not very happy to have possible disease-carrying workmen associated with them. They were soon brought into line.

The following day was spent on camp duties, preparing bamboo bed-spaces, making tables, washing what clothes they had and generally cleaning up.

[4.11.42] Many of the troops thought Christmas had come early; a herd of 20 yaks arrived. At first glance, the food on the hoof looked good. However, on close inspection, it was soon evident that there was more bone than meat on the weakened animals. As one observed, 'they were worn down to their feet'.

In order to supplement the meagre rice ration on issue a request was made to the Camp Commander for the provision of a canteen. In addition, more drums for the kitchen as cooks were experiencing great difficulty in preparing the food for the large number of men.

Also stressed the plight of the men in regards to clothing, footwear in particular. Many of them were barefooted and the hard work they were involved in necessitated strong boots. Huge clumps of bamboo and other jungle growth had to be cleared.

To do this work it would be tough on well-fed and booted workers, but working like slaves as required by the railway engineers and their cohorts, the guards, on practically empty stomachs (watery pap for breakfast) and without feet protection, it became a mammoth task.

[6.11.42 – 7.11.42] Orders received to enclose the camp area with a fence. As usual, no supplies of necessary materials; the jungle had to be attacked to obtain same.

Quite a stir of excitement when the men were told goods had been received for sale in the permitted canteen. Many were disappointed when they were only offered, in the main, Burmese cigars the size of normal cigarettes.

A feeling of sadness pervaded the camp on Sunday; news of the death of Private Burrows, 40 kilo camp, was most disheartening.

Out of sheer necessity every effort was made to better the welfare of the troops; we were successful in two of our requests for improved conditions. The first, the actual implementation of a camp controlled canteen, and secondly, and very importantly, three extra wooden tubs for use by the kitchen staff.

However, strong approaches for increased rations resulted in being told to add more water to the so-called soup concoction. When even stronger representations were made for an increase in the rations, the Camp Commander (Yamada) was told additional staff was also required to assist kitchen men.

His bland reply—'Work the cooks 24 hours per day.'

'Which,' he was told, 'is exactly what they are doing now.'

In truth, the overworked lads in the kitchen were doing a truly great job under extreme difficulties. But, they carried on without a grumble as they knew their mates were being worked into the ground from daylight to sunset. And, food was their basic necessity; each man had to move 1.2 metres of earth per shift.

[9.11.42] Foreshadowing the future was the demand for more work by each man daily. The moment the normal day's work had been completed, the engineers added extra tasks. The physical strain was so great four men collapsed on the job.

This necessitated a very strong protest at the unfairness of the engineers in imposing extra work on the wearied, hungry men. The fact that some, irrespective of the number, had fallen and were incapable of carrying on, was sufficient evidence to prove the workers were at the very end of their endurance.

The following day 51 men were diagnosed as unfit for duty and kept in the camp. The Camp Commander was so incensed he decided on an immediate inspection to determine their fitness or otherwise. After his visual examination, he agreed they were, in fact, too ill to go to work

Perhaps as a result of the strong approaches by all concerned, some attempt to increase the rations was made on Wednesday, 11 November, when a root vegetable was added. It was so unpalatable quite a few men became ill after its consumption.

The effect of the root vegetable was so great on so many, a Dutchman recognising it for what it was, told many of the men it was so bad, not even the Indonesian natives would attempt to eat it.

At work on the following day, the engineers relaxed on their demands as to extra tasks after completion of the daily quota. As a result, men were back in camp at sunset.

Based on the fact the Camp Commander had satisfied himself as to the inability of 51 sick men to work, and the cessation of demand for additional tasks on the job by the engineers, the protests in both instances had unquestionably been upheld.

On Thursday, November 12, word was received from Black Force at the 40 kilo camp, concerning the shortness of rations and alarm at the dwindling water supplies. Out of a complement of 600 troops, 200 were unfit for duties.

Lt. Col. Eadie, Medical Officer, 35 kilo camp, was very concerned when he was more or less forced into unpleasant decisions, when he sent some very sick men out to work. However, not without voicing disapproval and they were later returned to camp. Two were so ill they had to be admitted to hospital.

When a container of oil (5 gallons) was delivered to the camp it was received very cheerfully by the kitchen staff, who proceeded to use it for frying rice. It lasted for five days, but over that period few were aware it was possibly an extract, or was castor oil. It did not worry anyone. At least, it was change from plain boiled rice.

Commissioned officers were told all batmen were to carry out nightwatch duties as from Friday, 13 November. Unknown to the Nipponese, the officers had been sending their batmen out on work parties to give some relief to overworked, unfit and undernourished workers.

In subsequent consultation the Camp Commander agreed to officers sharing equally on nightwatch duties with the men concerned.

However, he disagreed as to the previously arranged yasumi [day off] for the following day, Saturday. Despite all protests he demanded and insisted all fit men be sent out to work.

Dysentery is rife in the camp as the Japanese consistently refuse medical supplies. Everyone is adhering strictly to the necessity for hygiene perfection. The menace of flies is a problem, but other than to exterminate as many as possible by internal camp staff, little else can be done. Three men were admitted to hospital, in a critical condition, today, 13th.

The Camp Commander issued orders today [14.11.42] for the immediate construction of a hut. It is to be used as a guardhouse. All indications suggest Japanese guards will soon augment the number already in residence.

All troops given the third injection (1.5cc) today. Pleasant surprise, Camp Commandant authorised church services and a concert tonight. (Lieutenant Yamada is regarded as the most lenient CC.)

[16.11.42] Allowed to build a canteen today. Excellent news if it was not for one important factor—NO STOCK. Bad news, cholera has broken out in the village close by. Ban placed on the use of unboiled water. Two containers delivered. One will go to the kitchen and the other one reserved for washing.

Over the last three days supplies have arrived for sale in the canteen. Just on 700 eggs (not all fresh) and 100 bundles of chindegar (native sugar) now in stock. However, the Japanese decided they needed some and confiscated quite a lot. The balance, equal to a bit of an egg and one-eighth bundle of sweetener for each man in the camp. Supplies quickly exhausted. The change in diet very much welcomed.

One unpleasant aspect of today was the unwarranted vandalism by the Nipponese of timber which had been sent to the camp for latrine structuring, when they commandeered the lot to build tables, chairs, shelving and sundry boxes. What was left over, they used for their latrine area.

Everyone reacted angrily to the theft but protestations fell on deaf ears. Yamada was, on this occasion, acting, in a way, out of character.

*

Actually, the living conditions at Tanyin, 35 kilo, were the best on the line, due in the main to the insistence of all Australians for perfection in all matters concerning the health and welfare of troops. Yamada undoubtedly respected the forthright Australian attitude and, as far as was in his province, acceded to many requests.

In the other camps, such as found by Lieutenant Colonel Anderson at Thanbyuzayat, Major Kerr at Kendau, 4.8 kilo, the Dutch group at Wagale, 8 kilo, and Lieutenant Colonel Black at Beke Taung, 40 kilo, the Japanese Camp Commanders were not only truculent, but uncooperative and sadistic.

When Anderson Force moved from their initial camp to the 18 kilo area, Alepauk, they found the going very unpleasant. The force commander had a tough time in his endeavours to improve on the primitive facilities confronting them. Worse still was the constant demand for increasing the workforce, irrespective of the health of the troops who were suffering the ravages of dysentery, malaria and allied illnesses.

The arrival of 200 Korean guards in November did not augur well for any prisoner of war. As later events were to prove, they practised unbelievable acts of bestiality, glorying and wallowing in the new-found power, particularly when it came to the 'White Slaves of the Sons of Heaven'.

Brigadier Varley fought Lieutenant Colonel Nagatomo every inch of the way in his endeavours to better the lot of the 'A' Force personnel who were his responsibility. He consistently made representations for a Red Cross ship to be allowed to transport supplies for his troops. At all times Nagatomo listened to his requests, then apparently disregarded them. In subsequent conversations with the various 'A' Force Commanders, he told them any approaches to Nagatomo were similar to hitting one's head against a brick wall. Williams' diary continues:

*

[Friday, 20.11.42] More canteen goods arrived—20,000 Burmese cigars; all smokers happy, but would have been more pleased had the supply been of foodstuffs rather than just smokes.

A local cholera scare has caused the rapid evacuation of all the natives. Noted in diary, 'I wish we could all go with them'. Fate, of course, decreed otherwise.

The following day brought bad news, five more dysentery cases reported and one lad going blind due to malnutrition and neuralgia; 33 now hospitalised, 94 men unfit for any duties.

Sickness is on the increase, many now afflicted with beri-beri, some relief afforded when a bottle of vitamin B tablets was donated by the Camp Commander, Yamada. 'They,' he said, 'are used by the staff as a preventative against beri-beri.'

With medicine and drugs aplenty for them, no wonder few, if any, of the Nipponese or Koreans suffer illnesses in any way approaching that prevalent amongst the prisoners of war under their jurisdiction.

[Sunday, 22.11.42] Much noise and movement in the Japanese quarters when the additional guards arrived. A lot of speechmaking but no trouble, as yet, for the POWs (Obviously Yamada had them under control.) Heat oppressive today. Three more men admitted to hospital.

Advised by Camp Commander, Yamada, to proceed to Thanbyuzayat to attend a conference of all 'A' Force commanders, supposed to commence at 1900 hours, 24th.

Brigadier Varley discussed, in the main, matters of pay affecting officers. It was decided that if officers were to be in receipt of payment, they would receive a maximum of 20 rupees (10/-) per month, the balance to go to the Red Cross representative to purchase what goods—food, medicine or drugs—might be available for use in the various hospitals.

The following day *[25.11.42]* Nagatomo held a conference at 1400 hours (actually commenced at 1650 hours) and officers' rates of pay were fixed at—

Major General	416 rupees per month
Colonel	310 rupees per month
Lt. Colonel	220 rupees per month
Major	170 rupees per month
Captain	122½ rupees per month
Lieutenant	85 rupees per month
2nd Lieutenant	70 to 83 rupees per month

The shock announcement was a deduction of pay monthly for lodging, clothes, etc. When clarification was requested the assembled officers were informed, 'They may receives clothes later, plus soap, sanitary paper, rice, vegetables' or in other words meals as provided currently, based on Japanese currency, at a cost of 10 cents per day.

Under no circumstances are officers to have more than 70 rupees in their possession at any one time. If they have any money left over after the last payment, the equivalent sum to be deducted from the next pay. That balance to be paid into the local bank, the interest earned to be used by the Brigadier to provide extra food for hospitals.

Interest payment at 2¾ per cent, payable each year subject to six months notice of intent to withdraw. On that basis outlook for increment of foodstuffs seems bleak and the hospitals in for a long wait. Question is—how long do the Japs think the war will last?

All commanders made complaints in respect of the quality of rice being supplied. Samples of grain containing weevils, grubs, etc were produced. Additionally, written complaints of a general nature were submitted.

[26.11.42] Departed Thanbyuzayat at 0900 hours, arrived back at the camp at 1300 hours. Whilst at Base, was able to procure 110 eggs, plus 8 bundles of sweetener for the sick personnel.

Results of Conference
1. Protest against prices charged for canteen goods.
   Reply: Prices charged us were the same as charged by the Burmese merchant. (We accidentally saw the invoice held by the Burmese merchant and we estimate that the CO of the POW camp has made 1,000 rupees out of us already).
2. Request that 17 rupees for Australian hospital, 13 rupees for Dutch hospital to be made available to purchase goods urgently required.
   Reply: No funds available, buy it yourselves out of your next pay.
3. Request that coolies in our camp lines be given another camp.
   Reply: Lieutenant Colonel Nagatomo will make enquiries.
4. Request that older men be employed in making a garden and supply vegetables to troops.

Reply: No money available to buy seeds. Men over 50 to be used if started; some vegetables to go to the Japs. (In Timor this scheme was in operation and war prisoners received one out of each 7 lorries of vegetables produced. Japs garnered the rest.)

5. Request for permission to write home.

Reply: Higher authority to advise when this can be done. Indications show little chance of this privilege. The Jap orders say we can write home every month.

6. Request for rest one in seven days instead of one in 10-12 as now in use.

Reply: IF commander in charge of railway works agrees. Indication, no change.

7. Reference my protest of Jap soldiers striking one of our men.

Reply: Japanese are used to inflicting this kind of punishment and said he had taken this matter up with me. Up until now, he has not spoken to me at all.

8. Request for drums to boil water.

Reply: Drums not available except for Railway Japanese troops.

9. Request for medical conference.

Reply: As usual, 'later' so we received nothing, as expected.

Prior to the conclusion of the conference, Lt. Col. Nagatomo warned us again that when the three Dutch officers and the one man—presumably an OR—who had escaped from the 8 kilo camp were recaptured, they would face execution.

Lieut. Yamada, our Camp Commander, ordered all officers to sleep in the same hut as those under their command. Also stated they must not assemble. Pointed out to him that officers and men always lived in separate huts and that the men worked much better if allowed to get away from officers now and again. He said he would think it over and let us know.

Health state of troops obviously worsening. Had 180 on the sick parade today. Construction of the canteen hut completed today *[27.11.42]*. Although we were not told or given any information, it does appear some of the guards must have kicked their toes during the hours of darkness. Yamada has ordered the removal of all tree stumps, or bamboo clumps, from the grounds as soon as possible.

Lieut. Summers reported he was hit from behind by a guard, reason unknown. Made a complaint to Yamada. He sent for the guard concerned and ticked him off properly.

Lieut. Yamada, educated in England, is a reasonable Japanese officer; the only one recognised as such on the whole railway project. As far as the POWs at 35 kilo are concerned, he has given them as fair a deal as in his province to do.

The day he is replaced, leniency, if there is such a thing in a POW camp, will go by the board. Every officer, and the whole of the troops, will regret his departure.

Illness was so bad from 28 November two sick parades each day were held; one at 5 p.m. for old patients, the second at 7.30 p.m. for new ones.

On that day Lieut. Summers was again struck in the face by an angry Japanese engineer. When the act was brought to the notice of Yamada he had the offending Nipponese paraded to him. There was question, the tone of his voice (Yamada's) indicated the offending engineer was thoroughly told off.

That same afternoon Yamada visited the working site and asked many questions. For the rest of the day, punishment was non-existent and the work proceeded peacefully.

[29.11.42] Black Force, due to water shortage, were moved from the 40 kilo camp to the 26 kilo, where they will link up with Ramsay Force when they arrive on 20 December.

Trouble again erupted on the line; this time demands by the engineer for increased tasks. He endeavoured to force the men well beyond the agreed metreage and clearly resented their failure to obey his order. The intervention of Yamada again solved, what could have been a very nasty situation or confrontation.

The problem of men contracting 'happy feet' is one of considerable concern to all Camp Commanders and Medical staff. Neither drugs nor medicine of any kind provided to combat the frightful torment. For those unlucky enough to fall victims to it, sleep is almost an impossibility. All they can do to obtain relief of any kind, is to keep on the move. The application of cold or hot water on any part of lower extremities only induces greater pain.

Some raw rice issued today. It was used to vary the liquid intake of plain boiled water. Some of it was ground, burned then added to hot water. On the menu, a new coffee blend.

[30.2.42] To enable the staff to complete the pay sheets after dark, the Nipponese graciously issued a bundle of birthday cake type candles. For a few moments the minds of all swept back into the past—those tiny pieces of illumination! Such memories they evoked. Smiling faces, a gaily decorated cake—happiness abounding; then back to earth with realisation of the present situation.

*

It was hard to sweep away memories of joyful fragments of time. However, the hard facts of POW life was quickly borne home to them. The workers were to get 25 cents per day! Williams' diary continues:

*

The vexed question of insufficient rations for workers and sick alike is of the greatest concern. To correct this situation Yamada was approached for permission to visit the local village in order to purchase foodstuffs. Surprisingly, he agreed; on one condition—the purchasers were to be accompanied by guards.

The sight of armed guards with potential customers frightened the villagers and only salt, not too much of that, and a few paw-paws were offered for sale. Had they been unguarded, it is possible much more would have been made available. As it was, little was gained from the excursion, except slightly more nourishment for the very ill.

[1.12.42] Not a very good day for the men manning the pile-driver; a back-breaking job accompanied by guards yelling and bashing all and sundry. It was a problem that had to be tackled. When Yamada arrived on site it appeared obvious there were about six yelling 'bosses' trying to run approximately 90 men, and one pile.

It was a chaotic scene, guards and engineers differing one with the other, the workers on the receiving end from both groups. Yamada restored some sort of order in deference to urgings from the Hancho (work party commander).

Major Meagher left for the Base camp to present pay sheets. He was permitted to take six very ill men with him to where some sort of treatment might be accorded them. At least, some drugs unavailable in work camps could possibly be provided at Thanbyuzayat.

[2.12.42] Lieutenant Colonel Nagatomo had issued an open invitation to attend a Nipponese cinema at the Base camp. A party of seven departed 1630 hours with wonder in their minds as to what awaited them at, of all things, a picture show in a POW camp.

At the 25 kilo the vehicle decided to call it a day. After some delay they commenced to walk. Some thirty minutes later they were overtaken and arrived at Base, hot, covered in dust and with just about every bone in their bodies aching from the rough and tumble, hair-raising lorry ride.

Before they were allowed into the camp they were sprayed with disinfectant which, in turn, created mud on bodies and clothing. They felt and knew they must look filthy dirty.

Their seats were mats, anything but clean, flat on the ground. The following two hours was an unforgettable experience watching boring Burmese drama. That was followed by a Japanese newsreel, two cartoons and a fifteen-reel feature film of the Jap-China war. The show ended at 0030 hours.

The ride back to camp in a three-ton truck bouncing over the bush tracks was, to say the least, a horror trip. There were no seats. All the passengers stood up and hung on for dear life. At 0230 hours they debussed, at last. It was a relief to be back.

Had there been sound equipment to stimulate the boring films, perhaps the discomfort suffered may have been accepted, but to put up with hours of anything but entertainment was just too much.

The news of the late finish of the pile-driving crews was an additional upset after suffering the indignities of what was supposed to be a pleasant outing. It is an infuriating state of affairs and about time Yamada takes action. Men are being driven into the ground by the insatiable demands of the engineers; they lack good food, are overtired and have little resistance to illness.

[3.12.42] Had long discussion with Camp Commandant, Lieut. Yamada on all matters concerning camp, rations, work requirements beyond initial agreements, failure to receive canteen supplies and the halving of rations to the sick troops.

As the pile-driving crew was back in camp at 1730 hours today there is no question Yamada has had his say with the railway engineers. He has carried out his stated intention to discuss the problem with those concerned.

But there was some dispute as concerned another kumi. They had completed their task but instead of returning to camp, were given extra work. They objected; sat down. It was well after 7.00 p.m. when they were dismissed for the day.

Learning of this happening, influenced a decision. Accompany the kumi on the job tomorrow. Observed the activities of the three kumis and how hard they actually worked. After the completion of the allotted work was astounded to hear the engineers demand additional tasks. Strongly objected and pointed out to the engineer the fact the men had laboured long and hard. Obviously, they were overtired and unfit to be expected to continue.

Whilst in discussion with the obdurate Nipponese instructed the kumi to rest. Argument ensued as both sides adamant in respective attitudes.

Ultimately, in the words of the Hancho, some extra work had to be done or they would have to remain on the job for many more hours. He said to try and reason with the stubborn Japanese was a sheer impossibility. It was tantamount to speaking to a block of wood!

From observation it was quite obvious, if the work requirements remain as at present, it will not be long before few, if any, men would be physically able to do any work at all.

It is not known whether or not Yamada received orders to report to Base Headquarters or, in fact, whether he intended to lodge the complaints made to him with Lieutenant Colonel Nagatomo to save face.

Yamada was unquestionably against cruelty to prisoners of war; he signified his feelings by his sympathetic hearings, lack of antagonism and the support he gave when genuine problems arose.

But, he had many hurdles to overcome before he could obtain any clemency for railroad workers from the pompous Nagatomo. As Commander No. 3 Thai Prisoners of War camps in Burma, he behaved like a 'Supremo'.

The following day was a great relief to all, no work! Many hours spent procuring wood for the kitchen and other fires, cleaning clothes and, for a few, against the rules, a visit to the nearby village; they wanted to buy or barter for food. The unfortunate aspect about it was the fact some of the guards caught up with the indiscreet lads who bought into trouble.

The goods they purchased were immediately confiscated by the guards and then, surprisingly, handed over to the canteen staff for sale within the camp. But the matter of illegal wheeling and dealing was something quite against Nipponese orders. Actually, in other camps, the unauthorised trading would have been considered as attempts to escape, and the penalty would have been death.

Once again, Yamada allowed his sympathies to override strict, laid-down Japanese rules, wherein any prisoner caught outside the camp area could be charged with the most alarming offence. [See Scanlon case in chapter 15.]

In this instance, perhaps without the knowledge of Yamada or his guards, the culprits suffered no penalties except being ticked off for allowing themselves to be caught. For the latter a lesson learned; if you do it, don't get 'Nipped'.

That night a concert was staged. It was actually a talent quest. Even the

Nipponese faced the judging panel. They sang in both languages, their own and English. [Lieutenant Colonel Williams' notes do not record who or if any contestant was given an award—Author.] The show went on for 2½ hours.

During the day Yamada had sent one of his soldiers into 'town', probably Base or a close-by trading post, and he returned with 97 rupees worth of goods. They soon disappeared from the canteen shelves.

On 6 December, 237 very ill men lined up—those who could stand—on sick parade. They were in addition to the 26 in the camp hospital and 37 in Base hospital, Thanbyuzayat. Due to the paucity of the ration issue and the very hard work the men are forced to perform on a long-day basis, their immunity to disease of any kind is diminishing at a fast rate. What few supplies come into the canteen in no way compensate for the reduced rice ration.

Yamada's return from the Base camp has brought quite unexpected results, an ultimatum—'From this day [6.12.42] all orders are to be given in Japanese and only that language is to be used when referring to any of the departments!'

Permission to visit the local village, even in the company of guards, is strictly forbidden. However, church services may continue to be held.

The following day [7.12.42] the new Commander No. 3 Prisoner of War Camp, Burma, accompanied by Brigadier Varley and Lieutenant Colonel Hamilton, visited the camp. He expressed his satisfaction with the condition of the whole area. Prior to the group returning to Base at 1300 hours (they had spent 45 minutes on the inspection) the promises made for the future were very heartening; if carried out. They were—'Increase in ration supplies within four days and continuity in canteen goods.'

On that same day, however, came word of more problems associated with work demands by the railroad engineers. Again, intervention was necessary and certainly obtained results. There's no question; persistence in efforts on behalf of the men was paying off. The guards and engineers now appeared to accept the fact that what was said was meant. Result, came an easing of extra task demands.

[8.12.42]—anniversary of Japanese invasion in the Pacific Region. A Burmese trader arrived with a dray load of valued goods, such as sugar, eggs, cigars, dried fish, biscuits and beans.

One snag, no one had enough money to make a purchase. A request for an advance on pay was granted. The 132 rupees was enough to buy all the sugar and cigars. As no credit was permitted, the trader wandered off, despite the pleading looks of his potential customers.

The following day, and in keeping with the new commander's promise, 18 days supply of oil and salt arrived. Although only two items, they were urgently needed and very helpful.

The constant lack of nourishing food is having effect on the health of everyone in the camp. A total of 64 new patients in the Base hospital, 30 in the camp infirmary and another 300 on sick parade.

The bodies of many of the troops are covered in sores, quite a few suffering from beri-beri and two have lost their sight.

*

The fact that so many of his soldiers were contracting serious illnesses weighed heavily on the shoulders of their commander. Lieutenant Colonel Williams, a man of great compassion, fought the Nipponese every inch of the way in his endeavours to better the impoverished life of his men.

However, no matter what the protests, demands or requests, the Japanese obeyed (with just a few possible exceptions) the so-called orders of their Emperor to the letter! Hence the sudden change in the demeanour of Yamada. For the time being at least, he had become different.

*

[10.12.42] A Japanese doctor and the commander of the railroad project paid a surprise visit to the camp today. Their obvious mission, to check over the huge number of sick, unfit men.

They moved among and viewed the stricken skin and bone hulks; men, nine months ago in prime health, now after nine months of POW life, reduced to a pitiful physical state, but still mentally determined to outwit their captors who had no interest in whether they lived or died.

The Japanese only concern was, whether they were fit to work, or worth feeding.

Apparently, but no-one could tell from their Oriental expressions, they were satisfied few, if any, could be diagnosed as fit to work. They made no comment, one way or the other.

The work late programme is on again; all kumis out until 7.00 p.m. A lot of hours of back-breaking labour all for (in Australian currency) 2/2 per day, seven days a week. Sometimes, graciously allowed one day rest in ten.

Pay day for the workers on issue today [12.12.42], all in 5 rupee notes, nothing smaller. A difficult problem to overcome as no one, legally, with any notes of smaller denomination.

Lieutenant Mitchell, a Kumicho, was severely beaten up today, almost to death. He has suffered injuries to his chest. No X-ray facilities, extent of bone damage not really known.

A very strong protest was lodged with Yamada but it is doubtful if anything will come of it. The railroad engineers are becoming a law unto themselves.

[13.12.42] Very good news today, informed by the camp commander of an increase in the rice ration. The large quantity received gave credence to the statement.

The bad news was—the execution of the Dutch officers who had been recaptured after an attempted escape.

[14.12.42] Hard to believe but it has actually happened, canteen supplies comprising—700 eggs for 850 hungry men, 250 blocks of sugar, one bag of onions, some curry powder, cigars (Burmese) and some soap. The shelves were again completely bare before sunset.

It is possible the protest so strongly directed to Yamada in respect of the cruel bashing of Lieutenant Mitchell, may have had some result after all. The railroad engineers have lessened their demands; a decrease in the punishment rate. A rest day promised for tomorrow.

[15.12.42] A promise kept, yasumi today and more supplies for the canteen. Not much, but a little is better than nothing at all. Base commander paid an official visit. Made no comment.

[16.12.42] Winds of change! Petty Officers Bilshaw and Clark badly bashed up by the same Jap who attacked and injured Lieut. Mitchell four days ago. A further protest to Yamada only elicited the fact the Nipponese engineer concerned was 'a problem child'. Little satisfaction for those frightfully beaten up by him.

As the result of increased ration and canteen supplies the sick parade was down by 100 today. A very noticeable improvement in just two days with much better food available. An example, if the Nipponese understood it, of how to get men fit for heavy work.

[17.12.42] The present health state of troops, 290 sick with various ailments, plus 33 in camp hospital and 77 in Base hospital.

Experiencing great difficulty in persuading the Japanese to decrease the working hours for the bridge-building kumi. Not making much progress. The engineers take little notice of Yamada.

Ramsay Force arrived at Thanbyuzayat today *[18.12.42]* and word has it they will be at the same camp as Black Force, the 26 kilo camp.

The whole of 'A' Force is now to be fully engaged in the construction of the Burma-Thailand railway. The disposition being:

Thanbyuzayat to Beke Taung (40 kilo) camp
(40 kilo camp closed 29 November 1942, lack of water)

4.8 kilo camp	Green Force, Kendau.
8 kilo camp	Dutch Force, Wagale.
18 kilo camp	Anderson Force, Alepauk.
26 kilo camp	Black and Ramsay Forces, Kun Knit Way.
35 kilo camp	Williams Force, Tanyin.

One great loss Williams Force suffered, occurred on 22 December 1942. The Camp Commander, whether under instructions or on his own initiative no one knew, ordered the surrender of all yak hides. Until then, they had been dried, semi-cured and used to repair what boots a few of the troops still managed to keep in one piece. The pieces of hide, tied to the upper, afforded some foot protection, if only for a short time.

Yamada, or some of his minions, must have found a market for them and decided on financial gain. The Nipponese are never backward at coming forward where money is concerned. The fact that at least 200 prisoners of war were barefooted meant little, or nothing, to any of them; money did.

*

Although quite ill with dysentery, Williams lodged a strong protest at the unwarranted acquisition. But it was all to no avail. The hides had to go and did.

*

The following day began with the usual hard work for the men; the Nip quartermaster, possibly blessed with some Christian thought, gave the Australian Force Commander a gift—three eggs. Maybe he believed the 'children' of a chook could be a cure for a very dangerous, debilitating ailment. At least, if not as he thought, they certainly helped to fill a void.

The same day three pigs arrived at the camp, for sale at 90 cents per kilo. The officers had a tarpaulin muster and raised sufficient funds to make the purchase and the squealing porkers passed into Australian possession just two days from Christmas, an appropriate time. One which foreshadowed a welcome change in diet for the sick, as well as all the lads sweating their hearts out on the bridge-building job, the one task that created so much bitterness, bashing and injury.

[24.12.42] Christmas Eve and it's ten times worse than being in a workhouse. Cleaning camp, with the sick, to receive the three Nippon officers. The men finished work at 5 p.m. All in early. The band arrived at 1915 hours. We gave them a meal and they put on a good performance. It was good to hear a band again. About 50 Nipponese and 80 Burmese listened as well. Yamada returned with the band; he had organised the show. Finished at 2130 hours and band stayed the night.

[25.12.42] Christmas Day at Tanyin, Burma. And what a Christmas! Three pigs boiled up for dinner. We had nothing in which to bake them. Trays for ovens are like so much gold sheet here. We cannot get metal to make egg slices much less frying pans. The Japs gave us a small orange each for Christmas. The band left at 0900 hours with Yamada. The concert at night was good. Turned cold later in the evening.

[26.12.42] Perhaps, in a way, from the sublime to the ridiculous. As from this day 'smoko' breaks to be reduced by half. The midday meal to be of only 30 minutes and all work tasks to be increased by 50%. Shock tactics perhaps, but the workers give it another name.

A new but welcome resident, Padre Smith. He arrived this morning.

[27.12.42] Lieutenant Yamada, who had been called to Base camp, returned with some very unexpected material. Printed cards for all prisoners of war to complete. This was news to be sent home, and normally, something all men would want desperately, IF allowed to use their own wording, entirely.

But these were different and would not give the information in its true form. They read . . .

> 'I am interned at the war prisoners camp at Moulmein in Burma.
> My health is good . . . poor . . . bad.
> I have not had any illness.
> I am—have been—in hospital.
> I am—am not—working (pay at . . . per day).
> I am with friends.'

Three lines were left to write a message of approximately fourteen words, plus the signature of the sender.

Yamada being something of an enigma, it was impossible to tell whether he was motivated enough to really want to help the hard-driven POW workers or not, when he requested information as to hat and boot sizes worn by all men in the camp.

*

At about this time Yamada announced that work demands on the railway would be increased from 1.2 metres per day per man to 1.7 metres. The harsh demands facing the workforce infuriated Williams and he immediately lodged an official protest. His diary continues:

*

The following day Yamada authorised a church service to be celebrated by Padre Smith, Roman Catholic faith.

Seven men returned from Base hospital today, 28th.

As it appeared the railway engineers were taking no notice of the strongly worded protest made to Lieutenant Yamada, further approaches were made. No official reply given, but Yamada did visit the work site the following morning.

The next day brought unexpected supplies for the canteen, 900 eggs, 90 bundles of sugar and 6,000 Burmese cigars. The prices were very high; you could say blackmarket rate! But they were needed, price or no price. The buyers went into hock, more or less, to procure them.

*

As the pile-driving crew were having one hell of a bad time, the force commander went out to the bridge to endeavour to get a fair go for his men. Due, perhaps in the main, to the language difficulty, tempers frayed and heated words were exchanged, but his visit had the effect of calming the Nipponese engineers and guards.

Lieutenant Colonel Williams' stern countenance never relaxed in front of the tormentors. And even though he spoke little Japanese, he had a way with him that left no doubt in anyone's mind that he meant what he said.

*

The Nipponese were seeking tradesmen in the following categories—bootmakers, electricians, welders, temperers and finishers. Luckily Williams Force had no one with any of the qualifications required.

Hopes were high on New Year's Eve for an early finish to work to permit the men to prepare for some sort of celebration to farewell a hate-filled Old Year, and to welcome a 'hopeful' New Year. No one believed for one moment they would ever see another Old Year out as prisoners of war and they wanted to make this something to be remembered.

At 1330 hours work was over for the day and wood parties went out in all directions to gather fuel for the evening fires. One group 'found' a yak bull and a calf. Their taste buds worked overtime anticipating beef stew for every inmate of the camp. Alas, the Japanese had different thoughts. The bull was to fill their overfed stomachs, the tiny toddler was all the POWs were allowed as an additive to the meagre rice ration.

To obtain some sort of hint of home, the calf, small though it was, was roasted on a 'spit'. For the majority, it was just the aroma that touched their innards. But they did not mind that; the undernourished ailing boys had gratitude in their eyes as pieces of hot meat were placed in their dixies as the midnight hour sounded.

[1.1.43] New Year's day—no work!

In true style the Japanese turned on the liquor—for themselves! They spent the whole day imbibing whisky and brandy until their senses were dulled; resulting in a quiet day for the prisoners of war without any incident of brutality.

As the hours of night drifted in, so did the voices of the camp artists in song and revelry. The whole camp, even many of the sick, joined in the lyrics with memories of home and happiness. So inspired were the singers, one only had to close eyes and allow imagination to transport them momentarily to happier surroundings.

[2.1.43] Two men returned from Base; a surprise visit of three from the 26 kilo camp conveying good wishes to all of Williams Force.

Half holiday as from 1400 hours today, hard to believe, but true. The workers deserved and had a bit of a spell; some spine-bashed, others paid visits to those in poorer health in an endeavour to cheer them a little. A word here, a smile— some made jokes—it all helped and the patients were grateful.

However, as far as the Nipponese were concerned it was a case of give with one hand and take with the other. The railroad engineers put away their waddies for the day, but demanded fifteen rupees for the calf they had 'exchanged' the previous day for the bull the POWs had found grazing in the jungle.

For sheer hypocrisy, this 'took the cake'. It was outright robbery, a type even Ned Kelly would have abhorred.

[3.1.43] Forthcoming events cast their shadows before them—one hardly needs a crystal ball to perceive what may happen in the very near future. The well, our only source of supply, is down to a depth of 12 inches. Totally insufficient to provide for all needs in the camp.

We were taken by surprise at 2000 hours last night when an advance party of Anderson Force arrived. Their most disturbing news was to the effect another 900 men, all from 18 kilo camp, would be arriving within hours.

Rapid preparations had to be made for their kitchen facilities and accommodation. To do this, two huts had to be evacuated and the 280 occupants crowded into already closely packed huts. Men slept anywhere and everywhere; they had to, space was such a scarce commodity.

At 1200 hours today the first group arrived and from then on more and more came. Fortunately, as darkness set in the last of the tired, worn-out men limped into camp.

At muster rollcall a total of 1,700 men are resident. The all-important matter now, is water! The 12-inch supply in the well cannot possibly provide for such a large number. Luckily, due to soakage, perhaps, we have managed for this day.

[4.1.43] Today, 4th, a new wash tub was installed. Anderson Force has fitted out two kitchens. One for Australian troops' use (600 men) and a separate one for the British group of 300. To facilitate camp arrangements there was no call for railroad workers today. Yamada, who had made an inspection at 1200 hours did not leave until 1600 hours. He was made aware of the all-important water scarcity and authorised the sinking of another well.

As from this day, Lt. Col. Anderson (promoted to that rank 1.8.41) as senior officer, assumes command of the camp.

More trouble on the railroad job; the engineers are demanding greater tasks of all workers. The result, a very late return to camp.

As was normal, as far as the Australians were concerned, despite the hard work, long hours and insufficient food, some found refuge in song after lights-out.

*

This annoyed a guard, who had come in with Anderson Force, and he awakened Williams and ordered him to stop the melodies many were enjoying. When asked the reason for his objection the guard intimated that the less sleep the workers had, the less work they would or could perform the next day.

*

Tuesday, 5.1.43: The well is now dry. To enable possible soakage it would be necessary to deepen it by at least 10 feet. But permission to do so has to be obtained from Yamada and this is not immediately forthcoming; only an order to conserve all water in the well, if any, for Nipponese use.

However, all things are possible, and by practising ingenuity—another word for pilfering—drinking water was found for the prisoners of war. There was none available for ablution or laundering. Authorisation to deepen the well by the suggested 10 feet was eventually given. A stage was erected and willing hands soon sunk the soak-hole to the permitted depth. Unfortunately, there was no instant gushing of the precious liquid and many waited and watched for the signs that would indicate a possible plentiful supply.

[6.1.43] A visit to the work site by the two force commanders (Anderson and Williams) may have had some effect on the engineers when Anderson gave an assurance of a good day's work by all men, providing some revisions were made. It was agreed that from that point the men would have a ten minutes break each hour and a meal at noon.

Whilst no guarantees were offered by the Nipponese it was hoped they would honour the verbal undertaking. However, as a passing shot, the engineers told the two Australian officers they could, if they wanted to, force the prisoners of war to work a twelve-hour day.

*

Later happenings were to prove that was no idle threat!

*

This morning the well was deepened by another two feet; they hit a gusher. Everyone had a bath. Condition of the soak will be improved once it is properly timbered.

With 1,700 men now in the camp it is necessary to extend the perimeter by an additional ten feet to enlarge the parade ground.

Misfortune struck the camp today; one of our very thin yaks passed on. It, too, proved life cannot continue unless there is food intake; the distressed animal expired from starvation. The meat ration, flesh from one cow, is approximately 70 pounds. Just how far will that go to meet the needs of all the prisoners of war encamped here!

Well timber arrived today and the walls are now three-quarters timbered. The depth has been further increased by an additional three feet. It is now fifteen feet deeper than when we took up occupation. However, until a pump has been installed, the drawing of water for all requirements is a very laborious undertaking.

The revised work schedule appears to have been shot to pieces very quickly. Williams Force kumi in late, Anderson Force kumi later still.

The meat situation very grim today *[8.1.43]*; another yak found dead and unfit for human consumption. Until further deliveries are made the rations are depleted by the animal losses. Protein is essential for the men engaged in hard physical labour, as it is for the sick personnel. Whilst few are aware of it, there is sometimes a meat and vegetable additive in the rice they consume; the amount is so minimal for the quantity and the taste denies it.

The sound of the Last Post was heard today as the body of a lad from Anderson Force was laid to rest. The service was conducted by Padre Kellow.

Good report as to the water supply; the inflow to the well is too fast to permit of any further deepening. If the present indications mean anything, our water worries are over for the time being.

[10.1.43] 'Moo' noises heralded the arrival of 20 yaks so thin that four walked abreast in one wheel track. How much meat content is in them is anyone's guess. As far as the butcher boys are concerned, very little. As there is no time to fatten them, and in any case there's no feed available for that purpose, the whole 20 beasts would hardly make one meal for 1699 men.

Lt. Col. Black (26 kilo camp) called in today for an examination by Lt. Col. Eadie, RAAMC. He reported conditions at his camp were as reasonable as anyone could expect under Japanese jurisdiction. Certainly no better or worse than here (Tanyin).

Great to-do by the Nipponese; distribution of 265 very thin, worn blankets. Only redeeming feature, they're better than nothing.

Tomorrow, we have been told, rubber slippers will be supplied to workers without footwear. True, they arrived, but the whole 195 pairs were just plain rubbish. The rubber perished. In the words of one 'lucky' recipient, drew the soles of his feet 'sumpin' orful'. The only benefit, they keep the wearer's feet off the ground. Hard to say which would be worst, drawn or sore feet.

[12.1.43] Pay day, but nothing to spend it on. The canteen completely bare. No guarantee when supplies will arrive. More rubber shoes on issue, left foot only, size 6½. A few galvanised iron plates made available to men who had no mess gear.

FORMATION OF NO. 1 MOBILE FORCE

IN EARLY 1943 Anderson and Williams forces were amalgamated. The following is a report of the combined force's activities and conditions prepared by Lieutenant Colonel C.G.W. Anderson, VC, MC (Australian War Memorial File No. AWM 54 554/2/4).

(A) *ANDERSON FORCE:* The Force of 710 moved by day march from Thanbyuzayat to the 18k camp at Alepauk, on 10.10.42. On 2 January 1943, it moved by motor transport to 35k camp at Tanyin, where Williams Force was camped.

(B) *WILLIAMS FORCE:* The Force of 875 moved by Motor Transport from Thanbyuzayat to 35k, Tanyin on 28.10.42.

(C) The combined forces moved by night march from Tanyin 35k to Kunknitway 26k camp on 30 March 1943. Up to this date the tasks set the PWs were earthworks for railway formation, but early in April, when the rail laying reached 26k, the main task became sleeper and rail laying, with bridge building, draining and revetting as subsidiary tasks. Thereafter, Anderson and Williams Force moved together.

In May 1943, the Japanese designed the PW groups then in construction camp at Taunzan 60k, as Mobile Camp No. 1, to be employed on sleeper and railway laying, and that it was to move stage by stage, as the railhead was pushed towards Siam. This intention was carried out over the period May to December 1943.

The composition of Mobile Camp No. I was:
ANDERSON FORCE: Approx. 500
WILLIAMS FORCE: Approx. 600

MOVEMENT DETAILS

DATE	FROM	TO	METHOD
24.4.43	26k Kunknitway	45k Anarkan	Rail motor train Evening.
9.5.43	45k Anarkan	60k Taunzan	Rail motor train Day.
13.7.43	60k Taunzan	70k Mezalie	(1) Rail motor train and and day march. (2) Other group marched from work.
30.7.43	70k Mezalie	80k Apparon	Rail motor and march by day for sick and camp details. March from work for remainder.

1.9.43	80k	95k	Night march except for sick, and some
	Apparon		camp details by rail motor.
11.9.43	95k	108k	Night march except for sick, kitchen
			and R.A.P. staff.
17.9.43	108k	116k	Rail motor and 4k march for sick and
		Siam	camp details. Rest marched from work.
21.9.43	116k	122k	Day march for all. Some baggage and
		Siam	camp gear by rail motor.
26.9.43	122k	131k	Rail motor for 80, and baggage. Day
		Little Nieke	march for remainder.
26.12.43	131k	133k	Day march for all. Sick carried on
		Nieke	stretchers, also kitchen, office gear,
			baggage and medical stores.
11.01.44	133k	55k	Steam train for 24 hours.
		Kanburi	
		(Siam)	
13.01.44	Kanburi	Tamarkan	4½ day march. Baggage by truck.

(Burma-Siam border at 112k from Thanbyuzayat)

Camp Accommodation: The hutments in all camps were of the same type. Long bamboo and atap sheds with central or side aisles between or along raised bamboo platforms. The aisle floors were earthen, always damp and frequently flooded because of lack of drainage. Despite protests sufficient men were never held back from railway work to repair huts, and to carry out hygiene and drainage.

Kitchens were usually just atap roofs over filthy ground often found to have been used as native cattle shelters.

Sick bays or so called 'hospital' sections were never provided, but had to be established in the ordinary huts, except when cholera or smallpox was present. Then the Japanese would allow isolation huts to be built without allowing fit men off work to do the building.

No lighting was provided except for a few oil lamps for the office, so that the men had to buy expensive candles and coconut oil.

Accommodation on hut platforms steadily decreased from the original one metre width per body and baggage, to one half metre. In the camps from 60 kilo eastwards, the Japanese made no pretence of allocating any scale, but simply ordered the force to get into so many huts, and these varied in size from camp to camp.

Often 25 men had to be fitted into a space 4 x 5 metres. This was done by men building bamboo and rice-bag bunks 3 to 4 tiers high, and so close that any one man moving at night disturbed all. The Japanese and Koreans allowed no time or materials for building bunks or for humpies outside the huts, when it was impossible to get all men in.

At the 131 kilo camp the advance party found only two small huts, new but without roofs, to accommodate 900 men. The Japanese i/c of POWs pointed out the sites where a kitchen and other huts could be built, and the Japanese railway officer merely laughed.

Roofing was provided in a few days and the framework for another put up for the POW camp details. The sick to roof with banana and other foliage.

Except in the 113 kilo camp, all huts had been occupied prior to the entry of Mobile No. I personnel, by Burmese and or Tamil coolies, and on several occasions the POW advance party had to clear a hut or huts of stray, sick or dying natives, without assistance from the Japanese or Koreans.

Often the POWs arrived in camp too late in the evening to clear other than the crudest masses of filth, verminous rags, etc., from the sleeping platforms. No time from railway work was allowed subsequently to carry out effective cleaning, burying or burning and the overworked camp staff was unable to achieve a proper standard of hygiene, before the next move was made.

In several camps coolies were housed in the same huts as the POWs, despite protests and request for proper control of hut sanitation. Common for coolies to be housed adjacent to POW huts, and in 116 kilo camp the native cholera hut was adjacent to, and on the higher side of the POW hut, so that all liquid filth washed into the POW hut.

Movement: All movement from camp to camp was made irrespective of time and weather conditions, and after the 160 kilo all moves were made in the monsoon period.

From the 45 kilo onwards, movement of a camp was not allowed to interfere with railway work, so that the working parties would move out in the morning, march to work carrying tools and, sometimes, a portion of their personal gear.

The Japanese railway battalion ordered the moves, and were supposed to provide the accommodation ahead. There was always friction between the railway battalion and guards, and there was rarely any evidence of coordinated pre-planned movement. Orders to move often were given at short notice, without details being supplied until the last moment.

Requests for transport for kitchen, office and RAP gear, heavy baggage and for those unable to walk, always met with a first refusal. There was usually some form of motor transport or bullock cart transport readily produced for the carriage of Japanese guard equipment, furniture and personal gear. If any space remained POWs might be allowed on.

Where transport by rail motor was ordered, all gear, including that of the Japanese guards, had to be manhandled to the boarding point, which in some cases was 500m or more from camp. Beyond 60k the railway journey was always stopped short of the new camp (except 131k) by 1 to 4k, necessitating manhandling by repeated trips, of all gear, made under pressure of Japanese 'speedo' tactics.

Where the move was made by march, with some motor transport, heavy strain was imposed upon the camp details, officers and light sick, in loading, and marching inadequately fed and clothed in bad weather. Often transport was so limited or in such bad condition that the workers' sleeping kits, clothing, etc,

could not be brought up to them until the day following the move, and in the
case of the very bad move from 108k to 116k, it was three days before all the
gear could be brought from the railway siding at 112k.

As to the transport of the sick, who could not be left behind or transferred
by rail to the 'hospital' camps at Thanbyuzayat, 30k or 55k, the PW camp
commander had to make the best arrangements he could, using rail motor or
carrying by improvised stretchers. The Japanese and Koreans always suggested
the 'light' sick and the few RAP orderlies should carry the stretcher cases. In the
move from 60k to 70k, some of the heavy sick (cardiac beri-beri, tropical ulcers,
chronic malaria and convalescing cholera) were ordered to be sent back to 55k.

RAMSAY FORCE
Thanbyuzayat

RAMSAY FORCE arrived at the vast Thanbyuzayat staging camp in the late afternoon of 18 December, 1942, to be met by the Commandant, Lieutenant Colonel Y. Nagatomo, a strutting, pompous Nipponese, small of stature, loud of mouth and full of scathing sarcasm.

As he mounted the rostrum from which he was to deliver his tirade of vituperation, many wisecracks could be heard that paid few compliments to the power-crazy Japanese officer.

He, however, gave the impression the attentive troops were greeting him, as he construed suppressed laughter as beaming smiles. They were anything but!

Nagatomo's first words became imprinted on the brains of now straight-standing POWs. Even those so feeble they could hardly bear the weight on their feet, did so to prove they considered themselves as 'soldiers of the line' and not, as he put it, despised prisoners of war.

'You are', he began, 'the remnants of a rabble army. Why, you don't even know how to dress properly' He conveniently forgot to mention they had had no uniform issues since 1941, or that what they did have since then had been worn to near nothing in the tropical climate.

Many of the G-stringed lads made audible remarks which, if he heard and understood, would have brought the wrath of the guards upon them in many unpleasant ways. Just as well he did not really understand.

He went on, 'Until such time as the stupid British and American Governments see eye to eye with the Great Imperial Nippon Government, you will be kept here to work for Nippon. We intend to build this railway *even if it has to go over your dead bodies.*'

The moment Nagatomo was out of the way, quarters were made available for the almost exhausted men; old bamboo huts, atap halfway up the sides, same on the roof, except there was less there and the sky was quite visible.

The normal bamboo-slatted platforms which served as sleeping quarters had millions of other occupants as well. Bed bugs swarmed everywhere. The men cared little; at last they had a resting place, humble as it may be, for their weary bodies.

A meal of plain rice and nothing else was served at dusk. Many of the sick heaved at the sight and smell. No question, the grains had been swept from the floor. The pungent odour drew their memories back to the first taste of the dreadful gluey mess at Changi.

At the very mention of their first habitation in a POW camp, comparisons were drawn.

Selarang Barracks! A dream-place, or as many said, the real country club they had so foolishly volunteered to leave.

Then, the embarkation in a veritable rust-bucket not even fit for the sheep it had previously transported. They had suffered nine days of horror on that frightful voyage that ended at Mergui. There, at least, they had enjoyed fresh air, even if rations were on the light side. However, there had been times when eggs and bananas supplemented the meagre rice servings.

A few weeks of crowded conditions there changed when Tokoro agreed, under pressure from Lieutenant Colonels Ramsay and Coates, to allow his 'guests' to occupy the new huts built especially to house Japanese troops. They proved to be spacious, two-tiered, and free of bed bugs.

The work on the drome site was hard, particularly in the monsoonal period. The guards, formerly naval men, whilst happy to dish out punishment, had some leniency.

From the very outset, the atmosphere at Tavoy had changed dramatically and woe betide anyone who committed the slightest transgression. Gone were the front-line soldier guards. Now they came under the vicious control of the most inhumane personnel ever to wear a uniform.

Just as dawn broke on 20 December 1942, Ramsay force was ordered to prepare to move to Kun Knit Way some 26 kilometres from the staging camp. Transport was provided and the sufferings the very sick experienced on the forced march from Ye, were not repeated. Again came the promise of better things for 'all mans'; plenty of good food, medical supplies and very little work.

This time, however, Lieutenant Colonel Ramsay and his staff, were well aware of the specious 'promises' of the 'kindly disposed' Nipponese authorities. Nagatomo's assurances fell on deaf ears. Not one man fell for the blarney of 'good camp, very plenty room and little, if any, hard work'.

Still, it all sounded so very nice until the camp was sighted. Perhaps Nagatomo and his guards had been comic actors in civil life. If not, they missed their true vocation.

The huts at Thanbyuzayat were bad enough, but the housing now presented was only fit for the vermin domiciled there: filthy, smelly bed bugs, rats, lice and other unknown 'creepy-crawlies'. A clean-up was the first consideration, even before the alleged kitchen could be put into use.

Hygiene? The former occupants, Burmese labourers, had not concerned themselves with that and their droppings were evident everywhere. Temporary latrines were quickly arranged, pending a supply of borehole equipment, which never came.

Black Force, Java Party, were encamped across the site of the proposed railway and had been there for some days. Contact with them was forbidden, but few took notice of the order and many new friendships were formed.

At about this time real news of happenings in the outside world were being revealed to Ramsay force by the famous, and illicit, 'nightingale', the radio whose construction was recalled by former Lieutenant Johnny Kreckler (2/30 Battalion) in June 1995, as a second edition of *The Blue Haze* was being prepared.

*

My old friend Les Hall rang me, very pleased with himself. *The Blue Haze* is to be reprinted. It was first published in 1985. However, a part of the manuscript was lost. Now with a re-print due I would like to begin my contributions with a tribute to the author.

Sergeant Leslie Hall, Signal Sergeant: his distinguished service during training and more particularly in action, where he was granted the MID, balanced well with his leadership qualities. Les was on top of things even under the most difficult circumstances. He was liked and respected by all.

Colonel Ramsay gave him the job of building and operating a secret radio in the prison camp, a deadly assignment if discovered by our captors. Les did as directed and did it well. Ramsay force was made up of 1,000 officers and men and like any similar grouping of men there is always a small number that stand out. Les was a member of that group.

*

It was to this night-singing bird, immortalised in song as recently as 1940, that 'Gentleman George' Ramsay referred in his Christmas Eve address to members of Ramsay and Black forces at the POW railway construction camp at Kun Knit Way (26 kilo peg).

Although the Japanese interpreter was present as Ramsay Force commander spoke, he was apparently too naive to interpret his subtle remarks. From time to time he nodded his head as if in agreement, or perhaps, being human after all, he was thinking along the lines of the Australian officer's sentiments.

Ramsay, always a man of eloquence, was superb that evening as he comforted his homesick 'boys'. His voice was deep in sincerity, touching in his reference to home and loved ones, counselling one and all to take the greatest care of themselves in the rough period he forecast, quite correctly as it turned out, in the near future.

Interlaced with his words of cheer he told the assembled POWs they would, from time to time, hear of world events via their platoon (kumi) commanders. But no one, and he stressed this, must endeavour to find the location of the beautiful singing bird. If someone inadvertently mentioned its existence and the Nips found out, the Last Post would, in all probability, have to be sounded. Lieutenant Colonel Ramsay told the assembled POWs:

I have assembled you here this evening to give you a message of good cheer despite the conditions in which we find ourselves, but first of all I want to give you a message of a different sort which closely affects every one of you. In this season of the year it is quite fitting I should talk to you in the form of a parable, but there is one more potent factor which makes this necessary, and that is the presence amongst us this evening of guests of a type and race not normally included in our list of invitations to our festive gatherings.

I understand that you have been in the habit of hearing a little bird singing in this camp, but that, coinciding with my arrival to take command here, its song was no longer heard. I am given to understand that this is attributed to me, but I can assure you that is not the case. I do not think our friends would recognise in me one who has any particular influence with our little feathered friends, but I think in this instance I may be able to assist the bird of whom you are so fond to sing once more.

This, however is dependent upon certain conditions, the first of which is that this bird, which sings with a clear, true note, is very timid, and any attempt on the part of any one of you to locate its nest may cause it to cease singing altogether. Any discussion of the tune it sings may also have the same result.

The bird I refer to is a nightingale, and must not be confused with the note of another bird which is of Australian origin named the lyre-bird. This may not be spelt the same way but it is the same meaning. As you know, it is a mimic and reproduces anything it might hear, whether there is any foundation for it or not. If there is any doubt in your mind at any time as to whether the song you hear is from the nightingale or the lyre-bird, any one of your officers—who are all keen bird-lovers—will be able to set you right. If you observe these conditions rigidly, and do not go on any bird-nesting expeditions, I feel confident that the results will be to everyone's satisfaction.

Upon an evening such as this Christmas Eve our hearts go out to our dear ones at home, and we can only hope and trust that this will be the last Christmas in which we find ourselves in such a position. I know that your spirit is such that it does not sound so ludicrous as it might appear when I wish you all a Merry Christmas.

*

It was a grim warning and everyone took heed of it. It was the only sombre note in the forty-minute address and subsequent carol singing.

As the listeners filed away to their respective bed spaces many had moisture in their eyes. A sudden silence settled over both camps. In that time, the thoughts of every man, irrespective of rank or origin, were of those who were waiting so patiently for their return; mothers, wives, sweethearts and families.

To the men of Ramsay Force, the construction of a railway to Thailand sounded like a pipe-dream. Those of an engineering bent said it was an impossibility. They had reason to espouse that belief as some years prior to the war, British engineers and surveyors had studied the terrain and reported against the proposal. Mountains, jungle and rivers presented too great a challenge.

The Japanese thought differently; they wanted and needed it for a supply line to their armies fighting desperately in northern Burma. To them, the word impossible meant a task took just a little longer than normal. To overcome the gigantic problem they poured manpower, and women too, in many thousands to build what some of the world's leading engineers said could not be done.

At daybreak on 22 December 1942, the men of Ramsay Force shouldered their issue of picks, shovels and chunkels and set off for their first task on a project that wouldn't end until some frightening eighteen months later.

At first glance it appeared a somewhat easy job; a metre of earth to be moved per man per day. But the sly engineers had a plan. In a way it was simple, such as some confidence tricks are. They told the workers, 'You finish your metre, then go back to camp' Just like that!

The Aussies responded in the very way the Nips apparently expected; they turned the sods as if it was child's play and by noon they were on their way back to do, as many stated, a bit of spine-bashing. Others accepted the unexpected free hours as an opportunity to catch up on the cleansing of what few possessions they had, or to give extra care to their sick mates. This, they thought, is going to be a cinch.

Christmas Day. 'All mans have a yasumi'; rest day, on this day when any thought of working would be considered a travesty. No one, except the cooks, would expect to have to perform even the lightest task.

The cooks! What a magnificent bunch of men they were. From almost nothing, out of rice alone came mouth-watering delicacies, 'doovers' they were called. No-one cared what they contained; it was a dinner to be remembered. The recipe was a close secret known only to the sometimes maligned 'babbling brooks'. It was not a meal the men would normally enjoy in the comfort of home, but it was, well, somehow different. The warm-hearted smiling toilers in the kitchen were justifiably proud of their culinary art. They accepted the plaudits of their cobbers with the very best of modesty and grace.

Nonetheless, some considered the kitchen staff had the cushiest jobs of any in the camp. They had more to eat, so it was erroneously thought. At times, those who slaved over the fierce fires gave their ration to the needy, ill and malnourished.

Whenever a move was made from one camp to another, be it day or night, the first to commence work were the cooks. Within hours, rice being available, those lads had a meal ready for everyone. No one worked longer on behalf of their mates than the seemingly tireless 'babbling brooks'. What they could do with rice, grass, leaves, meat—on very rare occasions—was unbelievable.

As far as meat was concerned, whenever a yak was supplied the Japanese and Koreans demanded, and most times got, the largest portion. If luck was really in and more than one yak was supplied, the guards commandeered the greater number for their own consumption.

In proof of that, not one Japanese or Korean guard died from malnutrition, beri-beri or any disease or illness resulting from lack of nutritious food; few suffered any type of illness. If they did, it was something few POWs were aware of.

By New Year's Day the real duplicity of the sadistic engineers and Korean guards unfolded. The days of one cubic metre of earth to one man had become just a memory.

The gradual increases commenced on Boxing Day, two metres per man; still the Aussies failed to realise they were making rods for their own backs. It was not long before the task was *four* metres per day!

With increased tasks there were also constant bashings from the hated Koreans, who now wielded power they never dreamed would be theirs (they had been downtrodden by their arch-enemy, the Japanese, all their lives; and learnt well from their oppressors). They gloried in the authority now vested in them; and they used it!

One of the most sadistic of the group was the 'Boy Bastard' a short man in stature, a vicious brute by nature, who belaboured anyone who dared to raise his head from the ground he was digging.

By mid January with the yells and screams of the Jap engineers, 'currah currah' and 'speedo' from the waddy-wielding guards, the building of the hated railway was really on. It was now a dawn-to-dusk work day and all pretence of fewer hours had gone by the boards. Day after day men crashed to the ground from sheer exhaustion, illness and, on many occasions, from the crash of rifle buts against skin-and-bone bodies.

There was no question the Japanese engineers were now in a frenzy and the guards near crazy, as Nagatomo demanded more and more work from every POW who could walk.

As far as 'A' Force was concerned, 1943 was to be the blackest of years.

At the end of 1942, Lieutenant Colonel Ramsay had submitted a report on the conditions and the health of his men. It read:

Handed to the Nipponese Engineer
31.12.42

I submit the following points and respectfully ask that they be given very earnest consideration as every effort is being made by my officers and myself to supply as many men as possible who are able physically to do hard work required of them.

1. HEALTH POSITION ON ARRIVAL IN BURMA

(a) Detachment from Singapore Island (Changi).
After the capitulation of Singapore, Australian troops were taken to Changi on Singapore Island, about sixteen miles from Singapore township. A few weeks later the Nipponese authorities there commenced calling for large working parties which were taken and quartered in Singapore and suburbs and engaged on various jobs required by the Nipponese. These were specially selected for their physical fitness as ordered by the Nipponese.

Early in May, 1942, a force of 3,000 troops were ordered to prepare to move from Changi to proceed by sea to an unknown destination. By this time the great majority of Australian troops, comprising several thousands of fit men were already working in and around Singapore; those left at Changi consisting of those not considered fit enough to have been sent on those earlier parties, and even including some who had been sent back from those working parties as being unable to stand up to continuous work; also sick men and men suffering from war wounds recently discharged from hospital, plus a number above normal military age.

The Changi troops under my command are a portion of this force and mostly comprise what was left at Changi from six separate infantry battalions.

This position was explained to the Nipponese authorities at Changi and permission sought to recall some of the fit men from Singapore for inclusion in the force to move overseas. I understand that this request was refused, the Nipponese officer stating that it would not be necessary, as the fact that most of the men available at Changi were not physically fit would not constitute any real disadvantage, as this party, which was to proceed overseas, would *not* be required as a working party.

(b) Detachment from Java

The troops from Java include a large number of members of a Motor Transport Unit, who, apart from being well above normal military age, were subjected to far less stringent medical examination than other soldiers, by reason of the nature of their services as drivers, being considered much less arduous. Many of them were therefore considerably below the normal physical standard, even before undergoing the strain of the last year.

2. CONDITIONS SINCE ARRIVAL IN BURMA

(a) Changi Detachment

On arrival at Mergui the POW accommodation for the first few weeks was extremely overcrowded and shared with 500 British troops from Sumatra, many of whom had dysentery when they arrived. As a result, despite the efforts of the Nipponese officers with the very limited resources at their disposal, a severe epidemic of dysentery broke out amongst my troops causing several deaths and further adversely affecting the health of the remainder.

(b) Java Detachment

The extremely trying conditions of the sea voyage severely taxed the strength of the great majority and imposed such a severe strain on some that the effects are still being felt. In many cases, this was further aggravated by a subsequent outbreak of dysentery with several deaths, later followed by the strain of the march from Babe Toung to the present camp.

3. MEDICAL SUPPLIES

I understand that medical supplies are expected to be available very soon, in fact some have now arrived. These should be of great assistance towards restoring the health of my men who have curable ailments and should, in fact, improve the position generally; but I would respectfully point out that, while every effort will be made to restore as many men as possible to full physical fitness, it might please be realised that due to the prolonged lack of drugs, medicines, etc., during the past few months, many ailments have become deep-seated and the improvement in these cases must naturally be slower than had it been possible to treat them earlier.

Further, my Medical Officers are at present conducting thorough medical examinations of all doubtful cases, and are compiling a list of those who are physically incapable of doing the hard work required on the railroad, or to whom the risk of permanent injury to heart, etc., would be too great.

4. CAMP DUTIES

The number of men on camp duties are being reduced to a minimum and (except for certain duties the nature of which in themselves is heavy work and which requires men to be physically fit) are drawn from men only fit for lighter work and include batmen and even some of the cooks.

I respectfully submit that in view of the importance of meals that the number of cooks required to cook them, whether cooking in one kitchen or in two separate kitchens as at present, could not be reduced without adversely affecting these meals, and I would ask that there be no alteration for the present, at least, in regard to the kitchen.

5. FOOD RATION AND CANTEEN

It would be of considerable assistance in maintaining the daily quota of working men required if the canteen facilities could be improved so that men could purchase eggs and other items to augment the present issue ration, which is a diet to which Australians are unaccustomed. A regular canteen service would also provide a further incentive to the men to earn as much money as possible.

6. CONCLUSION

The arduous nature of the work, the dust, shortage of boots and clothing, and the tendency for all skin afflictions to be aggravated by the climate, are further difficulties and I would like to say that I feel that more men could be provided daily, if the working periods were reduced to six consecutive work days.

I would like to take this opportunity to thank the Nipponese Engineer Officer and his staff for allowing my troops to adopt the alternative method of excavating in hard shale, this making it somewhat easier for the men when working in this hard type of ground

(i) Troops above normal age

	35–40	41 and above	Total
Singapore Island	131	74	205
Java	197	155	352
Total	328	229	557

(ii) Personnel shown by Medical Officer as for Light Duty only.
PERMANENT = 129

(iii) Copy of one day's sick report (30.12.42), excluding light duty as shown above, certified by Medical Officer as being unfit for full duty:

Dysentery	95	Alimentary	22
Malaria	19	Uro Genital	3
Influenza	3	Eye trouble	8
Beri Beri	63	Ear trouble	6
Nervous Disorders	4	Skin Diseases	141
Respiratory	45	Bone and Joint Injuries	62
Circulatory	6	Injuries	24
Pyrexia of unknown origin			12
		Total	*513*

(signed) G.E. RAMSAY, Lieutenant Colonel, commanding POW Camp, Kun Knit Way.

*

As there was no reply to the foregoing letter, Lieutenant Colonel G.E. Ramsay submitted a follow-up on 10th January, 1943. It read:

Nipponese Engineer Officer in charge,
Kun Knit Way Railroad Construction.

My officers and myself are still trying to supply the full number of men required on the railway, but it is impossible to find enough who are fit and strong enough to do such hard work for more than a few days together.

I respectfully ask and would be very thankful if you could reduce the number asked for each day to the number which could be supplied regularly say 650 to 700 per day, as this would also save a lot of trouble to the Nipponese guards each day in trying to obtain extra men. Although the number of men in this camp may appear to be large, the reasons that so many are unable to perform continuous hard work are:

(1) Nearly all men here who came from Singapore are those who were regarded by Nipponese as unfit for working parties.

(2) Most of the fit Australian soldiers were taken earlier by Nipponese on their working parties at Singapore.

(3) Most of my soldiers who came from Singapore are those that were left from six separate infantry battalions after the fit had been taken by the Nipponese.

(4) The Nipponese authorities at Singapore said that the men leaving (Singapore) with me need not be fit as they would not be required for working parties.

(5) Many of the soldiers from Java (and some from Singapore) are above normal military age and by reason of their employment as Motor Transport Drivers, were not required to be nearly as fit as ordinary soldiers.

(6) Dysentery and the strain of the past year has further affected all.

(7) It is very difficult for Australians to work hard on their present diet. They are unaccustomed to it. They are used to more meat, butter, eggs and other things, containing more of the necessary vitamins.

During the past two days the vegetable supply has increased greatly, but I am informed that the meat supply for the next week or more is to be reduced, as it was reported that 30 animals intended for POW camps had escaped from Thanbyuzayat and that this camp's share of the loss would be six animals, which is a very serious shortage.

The attached schedule shows that out of 1,550 men in this camp there are less than 1,200 available for railroad work, before making any allowance for the large number of sick daily. The men attending the daily sick parade include a large number of men with sore feet, ulcers on legs and feet, and tinea of the crutch makes it impossible for them to work or even walk for any distance. This number is increasing.

The number on daily sick parade is high for the further reason (apart from the reason shown in paragraph 1 above) that there are about 180 men aged 40 years and above who are not included in the figure of 172 (shown on schedule as permanently unfit) but who are unable to do heavy work for more than 2 or 3 days consecutively. The total number of these men aged 40 and above equals 257.

The additional medical supplies which helped temporarily are now almost used. A list of all ailments from which the men are suffering is forwarded daily to Nipponese headquarters.

(Signed) C.E. RAMSAY, Lieutenant Colonel, commanding POW Camp, Kun Knit Way.

In January 1943, a second group of prisoners, Group 5, became part of the Burma-Thailand railroad-building project. The largest number were ex-Java and included Americans, Australians and Dutch. They were to work independently of Group 3. Shortly after they arrived Brigadier A.L. Varley made a submission to Lieutenant Colonel Nagatomo suggesting the desirability of segregating the three nationalities and placing them in different camps.

Additionally, and for obvious reasons, submitted it would be in the best interest of the Nipponese if the Dutch personnel in Group 3 could be exchanged—on an equal number basis—for Americans and Australians in Group 5.

Nagatomo agreed to study the submission. In the meantime some of the Dutch had to go to the 26 kilo camp (Kun Knit Way) where many of Group 5 were already established.

That was the very opposite to what Varley had in mind, remembering the Dutch were not as keen on the implementation of strict hygiene procedures as the Australian troops.

In fact, Brigadier Varley warned Nagatomo that such disposition would hinder rather than assist the railroad project. An outbreak of dysentery could possibly result, and that would more than considerably reduce the workforce.

It was at that period Anderson Force, at the 18 kilo camp, had an influx of 200 British troops. Very shortly after their arrival the sickness rate began to escalate and only one man in three was capable of working.

The ailments in the main were abdominal troubles and/or leg ulcers. The brigadier, on a visit to all camps, considered Green Force camp, 4.8 kilo, was the best on the line; the 18 kilo the worst. Many huts at the 18 kilo camp were so weather-worn that portions of the huts had lost roofing.

The medical fraternity of 'A' Force comprised, in part, Lieutenant Colonel Hamilton, Senior Medical Officer, Majors W.E. Fisher, A. Hobbs and S. Krantz and Captain Gordon Cumming, all of whom in association with Lieutenant Colonel Albert Coates and Major Chalmers, made impassioned appeals to the various camp commandants for a continued supply of medical essentials.

In the main, appeals fell on deaf ears. But despite the never-ending setbacks, not one of them ever gave up trying to force the Japanese to provide even the barest of basic medical supplies. At Mergui and Tavoy a limited amount of life-saving medication was provided, but in such minute quantities it was insufficient to arrest the spread of disease.

The mentality of Nipponese camp commanders varied to a great extent, depending, perhaps, on rank. Commissioned officers brutalised lower ranks, and there commenced a domino effect, with the prisoners of war the ultimate sufferers.

The diversity of their character was exemplified at Tavoy on the first Tuesday in November, 1942. Corporal Kumada, knowing of the great Australian racing interest, especially the Melbourne Cup, concurred in a suggestion the famous race be simulated by the prisoners of war. His excitement was stimulated and he offered to donate a 'Cup'.

He did, too; a highly polished coconut shell, fitted with two shining brass handles!

At first many of the POWs considered it was just a furphy and nothing would come of it. However, fever pitch grew as the great day approached and the actual cup was displayed. Under the circumstances, it seemed incredulous the Nipponese would even consider such an event, let alone participate to such an extent a public holiday was granted! For an emotion-lacking Oriental, a 'yasumi' for an imaginary horse race was something right out of character.

A track was laid out on the soccer field, entries were invited and a large field was apparent. When acceptances were declared, the field, due to illness, was reduced to about nineteen starters.

As forecast by the 'weather bureau' the sun shone brilliantly, a moderate northerly breeze blew up and some of the 'horses' (pre-race nerves probably) began to perspire as 2.55 p.m. approached. Pedigrees of the runners included the names of many very famous equines of former years.

Appropriately attired 'bookmakers' laid some amazing wagers; the currency in the main being cheroots. The wealthy bet in cash (if Nipponese money could be so termed), urgers abounded and the 'course constabulary' had quite a busy time preventing 'nobbling' and a possible rigging of the great event.

'Snack' stalls were set up and rice-coffee sellers did a roaring trade at ten cents a mug.

Prior to the parade of starters, and before 'horses' were mounted, the 'Governor General' (Lieutenant Colonel G.E. Ramsay) and his 'aide' (CPO Tucker, formerly of HMS *Repulse*) arrived in a gaily decorated conveyance, a bullock dray, drawn by six 'brawny' bay or black 'horses'. The brass band played a fitting welcome.

'Lachie Melville', the race caller, was superb in his description and he had the crowd on its toes as the favourite raced clear, lost his footing and fell just before the finishing post. A rank outsider, 'Walla Walla', starting at 100:1, won by the narrowest of margins—a toe!

A jubilant 'Alibaba', the camp canteen representative (Burmese), had been authorised to attend the meeting and donated real money for trophies for the minor races.

The 'Governor General' made a very fitting speech at the presentation ceremony and congratulated the POW 'MRC' committee on its outstanding organisation. He apologised to the 'jockey' for failing to present the normal miniature cup, it had gone astray, so he was informed, in a 'navel' engagement, the type all punters had an affinity for. The day ended with a 'mock' trial of an 'owner, trainer and jockey' for failing to allow their well-fancied horse to run on its merits.

The annual 'Cup Ball' was held in the reception hall of the main building that evening. The Guest of Honour, Lieutenant Colonel Ramsay, then happily donated all profits from the meeting to the hospital fund.

Below is a medical report prepared by Captain Gordon Cumming at the end of January 1943:

1. *Personnel of the Camp.*
These comprise:
(a) Australian troops ex-Singapore (No. 1 Bn 'A' Force). Most of these soldiers are those left from 6 separate infantry Battalions after the fit men had been taken by Nipponese for Singapore working parties.
(b) Australian troops ex-Java. Many of these soldiers are above normal military age and by reason of their employment as Motor Transport Drivers, were not required to be nearly as fit as ordinary soldiers.
(c) American troops ex-Java.
(d) British troops ex-Sumatra.
(e) Dutch troops ex-Java (Newly arrived)

Dysentery and strain of the past year has affected many of the above troops.

2. *Sick Personnel.*
(a) Attending Regimental Aid Post.
(b) In the camp hospital.
The following figures are self-explanatory and represent a daily average. It is pointed out there have been numerous Malaria relapses, cases of sore throats, avitaminosis and general debility.

SUMMARY OF AVERAGE DAILY SICK PARADE

Total attending 591

Dysentery and diarrhoea	84	
Malaria (NYD/P)	58	
Avitaminosis	65	
Nervous	2	(A large percentage of
Respiratory (URTI)	87	these cases attending sick
Circulatory	5	parade are suitable after
Alimentary	29	examination, to perform
Urogenital	4	light and other camp duties.)
Eye	21	

Ear	1
Skin	141
Sore feet, arthritis, etc.	73
Minor injuries	17
Dental	4

INMATES OF CAMP HOSPITAL

Diarrhoea	9
NYD/P	19
Scabies	30
Tinea	1
Infected sores	7
Total	66

3. Medical Supplies

The medical supplies have been far from adequate. It is no exaggeration to state that even when Medical Supplies are received at the camp, which is on rare occasions, there is gross insufficiency; the supply, as a rule, is exhausted at the end of a week.

This state of affairs renders simple treatments impossible and is a contributory reason why so many men are unfit to carry out the daily work as is expected of them by the Nipponese. It would appear that the Nipponese consider that the smallest amount of a drug, say 1 oz is sufficient to achieve the same results as would be obtained using 3 lbs as judged by our standards.

The matter is regarded as urgent and it would be appreciated if something could be done to alleviate the position.

4. Food

The food at present supplied is regarded as insufficient in calorific values and vitamins. A conference of the Commanding Officer, Lt. Col. C. Black, the Medical Officers and Red Cross Representative, was held on the 29th instant, to discuss ways and means of supplementing the present rations for the whole Camp, with special regard to a relatively small number of men who require special diets.

In view of the fact that it is impossible at the moment to evacuate any of these latter cases to Base Hospital, it is the intention to utilise a certain proportion of the Red Cross Grant in purchasing such items as eggs, fruit, etc.

It is hoped to use the greater portion of the grant in supplementing the diet for the whole camp.

5. Medical Boards.

During the month a Medical Board consisting of the three Medical Officers was held with a view to classifying various cases and their suitability or otherwise to work. This has proved satisfactory and is of assistance to those responsible for the supplying of working parties.

6. Evacuation of cases to Base Hospital.

The question of evacuation of cases to Base Hospital, Thanbyuzayat, has already been submitted to the Senior Medical Officer and is mentioned here merely for completeness It is realised that there are numerous difficulties to be surmounted.

7. Working Parties.

Several incidents have occurred recently over the matter of working parties. Although the Medical Officers make detailed examinations of men and state that they are unfit to perform railroad work, the Nipponese Engineer Officer has demanded that these men go to work on the railroad.

It is pointed out that many of these men have tried railroad work, but are unable, owing to past illnesses, etc., to stand up to the arduous nature of the work. Nevertheless, the Nipponese will not accept our rulings and keep asking each day for more men. This state of affairs still continues, despite the fact that the Commanding Officer, Lt. Col. C.E. Ramsay, submitted a full report of the whole matter to the said Nipponese Officer. Also, on two occasions, the Nipponese Medical Officer has inspected men in camp (after the remainder had left for railroad duty) and on the last occasion admitted that the men remaining in camp were sick men. It might be remarked that the Engineer Officer, although protesting on many occasions, has never actually sent sick men to work.

8. Camp Hygiene.

The camp hygiene, as a whole, is highly satisfactory. The latrine system adopted is of the long, shallow slit-trench type. The excreta is covered immediately after defecation and the fly menace from this source is reduced to a minimum. Nevertheless, the fly menace is serious and all possible measures are being taken to safeguard the health. Disinfectants for use around the kitchen, hospital, etc., are badly needed.

Lice—Most Kumis are affected and although a disinfector has been installed to cope with the situation, it is rendered impossible owing to the fact that the buildings themselves are 'alive' The buildings, prior to the occupation of our troops, were occupied by natives.

9. Buildings.

These are worthy of special mention. It is considered that the construction of the billets is far from ideal, inasmuch as the occupants are exposed to draughts, thereby contracting colds and chills. Particular reference is made to flooring which is composed of bamboo poles each separated on an average of one inch apart.

Overcrowding—Owing to an influx of a further 209 Dutchmen, overcrowding is unavoidable. This means that men are lying almost side by side and in view of the numerous sore throats occurring, the whole thing is deprecated. It is impossible to take prophylactic measures to prevent spread of any epidemic

(Scabies as a present example) under these conditions. the only solution is the construction of additional buildings.

(signed) D.C. Cumming, RMO, Captain.

*

The frustration suffered by Ramsay as to the conditions under which his troops had to work and eat was never more evident than when he submitted letters to Nagatomo. He pulled no punches in this regard and, though careful in his phrasing, went straight to the point.

When it was reported to him the loss of cattle destined for POW camps resulting from the escape of a large number, he reacted swiftly. However, his only course of action was to contact Nagatomo as speedily as possible. The letter he wrote reads:

I desire to bring under your notice the position in regard to the number of animals received for killing being less than the Nipponese scale of 3 animals per day. The reason given for this shortage is that the other animals escaped before reaching this camp. This shortage of meat seriously affects the health and also adversely affects the number of men available for Railroad work.

For period 8th January, 1943, to 23rd January 1943 (16 days) . . .

3 animals available for each of 12 days.

2 animals only available for each of four days.

Plus 2 extra animals caught locally.

Total for period—46 animals (including the 2 caught) for 16 days. Average 2.87 per day.

For period 24th January, 1943, to 1st February, 1943, (9 days) 18 animals available. Average 2 per day.

It would be greatly appreciated if it is possible for some adjustment to be made.

(signed) G.E. Ramsay Lt. Col., Commanding POW Camp, Kun Knit Way.

*

There was no acknowledgment from Nagatomo, nor any additional animals to make up for the losses sustained. The Nipponese had very bad memories where supplies of anything required failed to arrive. Letters of protest received scant attention despite follow-up verbal requests via the interpreter.

On 31 January Ramsay again sought action from Nagatomo concerning rations; this time with reference to vegetables:

I have to draw attention that vegetables due on the 30th January for consumption on the 31st January (2 meals) were not received. On the 31st a supply was received which I am informed is to last to 2nd February, being the evening meal for 31st January and midday and evening meals for each of the 1st and 2nd February, a total of 5 meals; no provision being made at all for the meal missed on 31st January.

Further, the quantity today is invoiced at 2,486 Kgs but the amount actually received is 827 Kgs only, representing about one third of our entitlement. Another 400 odd Kgs more received on 1st February but this increases it only to approximately half our entitlements

I might also mention that salt received weighed 70 Kgs only instead of 80 Kgs.

I would respectfully ask that this matter receive urgent consideration, please, as it constitutes a very serious shortage in the meals of men, particularly those required to do hard manual work.

(signed) G.E. Ramsay, Lt. Col. Commanding POW Camp, Kun Knit Way. 2nd February, 1943.

*

With all attempts by the Japanese to exhibit some sign of compassion completely cast aside, work demands became greater and greater. The degree of illness made no difference whatever. They were in the process of building a railway, sickness or deaths notwithstanding. They had thousands of prisoners of war to supply the labour, and supply it they must.

Submissions by all camp commanders, Lieutenant Colonels Ramsay and Black, Majors Green and Kerr, as to rations, living conditions and their troops state of health, resulted in a 'manifesto' from Nagatomo. It reads:

REPORT AND INSTRUCTIONS BY LIEUTENANT NAGATOMO AFTER FORMATION OF No 3 BRANCH THAI PRISONER OF WAR CAMPS, BURMA

On the 14th August of the 17th year of Showa (1942), I received the order to open the 3rd Branch of the Thai POW organisation in Bangkok. On the 15th September the first draft of prisoners, namely about 1,200 Dutch arrived at Thanbyuzayat.

After this date I received eleven more drafts, the latest being on the 21st January of the 18th year of Showa (1943), so that I now have 9,440 POW in my camps. On the 25th January when the 5th Branch was opened my work as far as receiving POW was completed.

In the beginning we had practically no supplies of materials with which to work. But I began to collect all that was necessary, and I worked day and night in the interests of POWs and in the carrying out of the great work on the railway.

My aims were to have an efficient organisation with a high percentage of prisoners working. During this period I received great support from the military units which were in my neighbourhood. In addition, my office staff has given me great assistance although my staff at the inception was very small, but I had given the motto . . . 'Any work ordered today must be completed today'. Therefore we worked day and night to build up the POW organisation. I offer my sincere thanks for your help to all of you.

Now I will explain to you the task which lies before us, for my own staff as well as for POWs.

(1) Duties and Cooperation of Camp Commanders.
Eight camps are now in operation, in which there are an average of between 1,200 and 1,800 POWs, and although I believe that the staffs of the Camp

Commanders are too small this cannot be helped, as it is ordered by the Head Office. Therefore, I hope that the Camp Commanders (Japanese) will work as hard as possible, and I expect that the staff of Headquarters and of each camp will do their best in order to ensure smooth working. I hope that mistakes will be avoided and that a good cooperation will be the result. The Camp Commanders must be fully conversant with the general conditions of the POWs and as Camp Commanders they should exercise justice to all those under their command.

(2) Cooperation for less Sickness and a larger percentage of workers.
Everything possible is being done for the POWs but there is still 3800 sick which is 40 per cent of the total number, I regret this fact, and we must increase the number working on the railroad. It is also my wish that we now adopt the mottos—'Decrease the sick' and 'Increase the number of Workers'. The Head of all POWs in Thailand has said that his aim is to have only 7 per cent of sick and that the workers should move 1.7 metres of earth per day. We must work hard to achieve this objective.

Heading	Percentage *of Total*	*Total*
Sick in Thanbyuzayat Hospital	10%	940
No duties in camps	10%	940
Members of the various Kakaris	7%	658
Special duties	3%	282
Railway workers	70%	6,580
		9,400

The eight camps mentioned in the 'manifesto' were:
1. Ramsay Force;
2. Black Force, including RAN and RAAF;
3. Green Force;
4. Anderson Force. (Lieutenant Colonel Anderson was Chief Staff Officer, 'A' Force);
5. Williams Force; Java Party, 2/2 Pioneer Battalion, plus survivors of HMAS *Perth*;
6. Other AIF forces;
7 & 8. British, American and Dutch.

*

But nothing really changed. Nagatomo blamed transportation problems for the scarcity of everything. However, despite the shortages there was to be no let-up in the railway-building project. He had his orders, the labour to carry them out, and he would.

The Japanese engineers demanded speed and drove the workers unmercifully. Lack of food for the prisoners of war was none of their concern. They had a railway to build and nothing else, as far as they were concerned, mattered.

The guards, aware of the attitude of the engineers, of whom they were obviously afraid, harried their charges to the point of physical exhaustion. When anyone collapsed they were brutally assaulted back into a state of consciousness, then made to resume their task.

POW work party commanders, officers and NCOs did their utmost to counteract punishment. Often, because of their interference, they too, were severely bashed.

Jack Williams—Java Party—who had suffered extreme torture at Koenigplein gaol, Java, when he refused to answer questions relating to military installations in Australia, was one who was repeatedly attacked as he endeavoured to protect his men from the savagery of the inhuman guards. Despite what he had to suffer, he never let up. His troops worshipped him, and rightly so.

Day after day force commanders complained bitterly about the lack of food, medicines and drugs. In the main, the diet consisted of just plain rice. The first meal of the day was always a watery pap mixture, rice and water. One bladder evacuation and the benefit, if any, of that hunger appeasement vanished.

In this regard Ramsay felt impelled to make further submission to the uncooperative Nagatomo. His letter of 7 February, 1943, reads:

I wish to invite your attention to the serious shortage of animals and vegetables received.

(1) ANIMALS.
On the 30th January permission was given by the Nipponese camp commander to kill 4 animals and 3 animals on each alternate day, that is a total of 7 animals for each period of 2 days. On the 4th February, 1943, we received 13 animals (which, we were informed, should have been 14, but that one had escaped) and we were told these animals, together with those we had left at that date, would have to be sufficient to include all animals to be killed up to the 15th February, 1943, inclusive. This enabled 3 only to be killed on each of 4 February and 6 February and 2 only on each of the other 10 days for over 1800 men.

(2) VEGETABLES.

	Weight claimed to have been delivered by Nipponese soldiers	Actually received	Short
1st February 1943	1,086 kgs	770 kgs	316 kgs
2nd February 1943	1,093 kgs	795 kgs	298 kgs
3rd February 1943	1,093 kgs	786 kgs	307 kgs
4th February 1943	2,186 kgs	1,418 kgs	768 kgs
Total	5,458 kgs	3,769 kgs	1,689 kgs

These rations for some time past have been consistently short of the scale set down by Nipponese Authorities and is a very large shortage, especially as extra men are being asked to go on railroad work.

I would greatly appreciate it if something could be done to improve this serious position which is affecting the health and strength of my troops who are required to work.

Thanking you in anticipation.

(signed) G.E. Ramsay, Lt. Col. POW Camp, Kun Knit Way.

*

As was the usual case there was no written or, for that matter, verbal reply. Nagatomo never, at any time, committed himself on paper, other than issuing rules covering prisoner of war behaviour.

The animals referred to were yaks, small beasts and normally in very poor condition. Three, or even four, spread over 1,800 men provided so little nourishment, few POWs were aware of the fact meat was supposed to form part of their diet. Vegetable matter, too, seemed non-existent. So little amongst so many was hardly noticeable.

On many occasions the yaks were in such poor state they could not even walk. They were thrown into trucks, their legs tied, then delivered to POW camps. Their meat content was practically nil, but did serve to provide weak broth for the very ill. The entrails were hungrily snapped up by Dutch personnel; from that habit they inherited the nomenclature of 'The Offal Eaters', a name they hardly appreciated.

At all camps from the 4, 14, 18, 26 and 40 kilo, came the same news of hunger, illness and injury. The brutality of the guards was climaxed by the murder of Sergeant O'Donnell at the 18 kilo camp on 27 December, when he sought permission to go into the jungle to relieve himself. At the usual roll call he was found to be missing. A search of the area where he was last seen revealed his body. He had been shot in the head and chest, obviously at close range, by Dillinger.

At the subsequent investigation Dillinger claimed his victim had attempted to escape. To prevent that happening, and in accordance with Japanese military rules, he carried out his duty and shot him as he ran away. The fact the murdered man was shot in the front of his body gave lie to the allegation of attempted escape!

The shocking incident enraged every man in the camp and it was feared the prisoners of war might take retaliatory action, thereby creating the possibility of a massacre. Lieutenant Colonel Anderson's coolness prevented a serious event.

Tempers were at bursting point and Dillinger was spirited away to Than-byuzayat where, so it was stated, Nagatomo, the pompous egotistical 'Lord of all', would hold an Inquiry. If he did, it was in-camera and the callous murderer was, some months later, again a camp guard.

However, it was subsequently learned a group of Japanese engineers took it into their own hands to make Peanut, later known as Dillinger, pay a penalty. They bashed him near to death and his face was a pulpy mess.

(Near the end of the war, when the Koreans feared the worst, the same Dillinger endeavoured to ingratiate himself with the POWs, claiming it was his *twin* who had committed the cold-blooded murder.)

By March 1943 it was obvious to Ramsay that unless the ration supply was considerably increased, many of his troops would be physically incapable of performing much work at all, within the very near future. He submitted a report, in writing, to Nagatomo:

Under date of the 12th March, 1943.

Now that the section of the railroad upon which my troops have been working for the past few months is nearing completion, and a move to another camp is expected shortly, I feel the time is opportune to bring to your notice the fact that the health and the general physical condition of my soldiers are rapidly declining.

Upon arrival in this area there were a large number unable to do any heavy work on account of age, war wounds, and other inherent weaknesses which could not be overcome entirely even under the best conditions. Many of these men are now at Thanbyuzayat hospital

It is however, the disturbing position regarding the decline in the physical fitness of the men who were comparatively much stronger at the time of arrival here (and who have been working regularly on the railroad) that I wish particularly to place before you.

Even these men who are accustomed to hard manual work are finding that present conditions impose so great a physical strain that it is already having an adverse effect on their health and consequently on their ability to continue such work indefinitely. Signs of this strain, in ever-increasing numbers, have been observed by my Medical Officers. Many soldiers are now less able to work as hard as when they first arrived; a fact which has been recognised by some of the Nipponese Railway Engineers who have been supervising the work.

The general effect is becoming so noticeable that indications are that under present conditions, it must be increasingly difficult as time goes on even to maintain the average number of railroad workers which has been supplied up to date.

To confirm my own observations I have consulted Lt. Col. Black, my Medical Officers, and several other officers on many occasions, and the general opinion is that the two greatest contributing factors are (1) the lack of sufficient vitamin content and energy value in the diet and (2) the length of the present working period of nine consecutive days.

Further details and suggestions in regard to these matters will be found, if desired by you, in the accompanying letter.

The recent increase in canteen facilities is much appreciated and in an endeavour to maintain the health and strength of my troops, extra beans, peas, etc., to the value of Rs 970 have been issued to the kitchens since 27th December, 1942, for use in augmenting the rations received. This purchase was made from funds advanced to the Red Cross Society by Australian and American Officers.

It is asked that further consideration might please be given to the possibility of effecting some further improvements in the quality and quantity of rations, perhaps on the lines suggested in the accompanying letter; and also to the possible reduction of the working period from nine consecutive days to six consecutive days.

*

The accompanying letter, also dated 12 March, read:

Supply of Troops for
Railroad Construction Work

Further to my letter No. 1 of today's date in regard to the general health of my soldiers and to the difficulties of supplying the number of railroad workers required; I respectfully submit additional details in support of my statements, for your information and consideration, please.

I might mention that representations on these matters have been made to me by many of my best soldiers who have been doing railroad work regularly and I know also (in civilian life) to be men of good repute, intelligence and integrity whose opinions are valued by members of the Governmental, Professional and Commercial communities of Australia.

Firstly, I would like to place on record my thanks to you on behalf of my troops for your verbal assurance that men would not be sent to work against the advice of my Medical Officers, and that since the incident mentioned to you has been honoured to the fullest extent by your staff in this camp.

I would appreciate your patience if you will be so good as to give consideration to the following points set out below in suggested order of importance:

1. RATIONS. Meat, potatoes and bread together with a variety of green vegetables, form the staple diet of Australians, particularly those doing heavy manual work. Although there has been a slight increase in the meat ration received by us, I understand that the meat situation generally is somewhat difficult for you at present; but from our point of view this could be obtained and a larger proportion of sweet potatoes, pumpkin, white beans and green peas could be included.

By far the greatest portion of vegetables now received, consist of melons which are not very tasty and contain very little of nutritive value, and provide little chance of men being able to build up any reserve of bodily resistance to disease infection. They would be subject to much less of this infection if their present diet were more suitable in both quality and quantity. Regular supplies of flour and cooking oil would be of considerable advantage in providing variety as would also the addition of extra cooking containers (buckets, etc.).

The recent increase in canteen facilities is much appreciated, and if regular supplies of eggs, tomatoes and fruit could be maintained this should do much to assist the present difficult situation.

2. WORKING PERIOD. Nine days of consecutive work provides too great a physical strain, particularly under these conditions; and it is asked that further consideration might please be given to six days working week, resting every seventh day (Sunday).

3. WORKING CONDITIONS. It is admitted the tasks vary from day to day and that the men finish earlier on some days than others, but this variation due perhaps to a day on softer soil after a hard day on heavy shale is one reason why the men have been able to continue as well as they have done, but some portions of the work parties frequently do not arrive back in camp till after the evening meal has been served, and it is not always possible to keep hot their portion of the meal once it has left the kitchen. The heat during the day causes additional fatigue and when men have to work in the sun until a late hour, there is insufficient time for them to recover fully before starting the next day's work.

Although conditions vary, additional stress is frequently caused by large numbers of men having to work in a confined space, causing cramped conditions; but possibly the greatest handicap occurs where the excavated soil has to be carried for long distances, the shortage of wheelbarrows necessitating the use of baskets which has resulted in legs and feet of my men being affected in increasing numbers.

In addition, skin abrasions become infected by the dust and form into ulcers which take much longer to heal due to the vitamin deficiencies and to the general state of health of the men and also to shortage of medical supplies, bandages, etc.

4. INCIDENTS ON WORKING PARTIES. While the majority of the Nipponese guards show every consideration to my troops there are still occasional instances reported to me of officers and men having been struck by railway engineer soldiers. These are due in most cases to the language difficulty causing failure by my soldiers to immediately understand the instructions given, but I am sure that a little patience on the part of these Nipponese Engineers would have obviated any friction or any undue delay to the work.

5. DISTANCE TO ALLOTTED TASKS. The shortage of boots is a factor in this regard and I notice that while my troops are required to march a distance of up to two miles to and from their daily tasks, one section of the railroad passing through the grounds of this camp is being constructed by Burmese coolies.

*

Day after day, the slave-like work proceeded in an automatic way, accompanied by the screams of dissatisfied engineers and guards; the constant cry of 'speedo' and 'currah currah', the sounds of bamboo waddies striking the body of someone who may have collapsed from sheer exhaustion, became so prevalent as to be expected.

As the day progressed weariness caused many to lose track of time, relieved only if nature called. However, it was not a case of just dropping whatever tool was in hand; permission had to be sought from the guard. Quite often there was a brusque reply, 'No benjo, no benjo'. A further request often resulted in a slap across the face, a kick in the groin or a savage beating.

Working in the extreme heat of a tropical day forced perspiration to pour from bodies. Unless the loss of fluid was replaced at regular periods, many workers would faint and fall. Then the booted feet of guards or engineers crashed into the stricken worker. POW work party commanders, officers or NCOs who intervened, often ended up on a bitter receiving end.

Perhaps the worst to suffer in that regard was Lieutenant Colonel J.M. Williams, commander of the Java Party. He fought relentlessly with Japanese camp commanders, as well as their commander, Nagatomo. He and his troops, mostly veterans of the Middle East campaign, neither feared nor curried favour with the Nipponese; they despised them, and bitterly resented not having been given the opportunity to come to grips with their forces in battle.

In March 1943, the second party of Australians, Americans and Dutch arrived and gave news of a nerve-racking voyage on two old cargo ships that had been bombed by British planes near Moulmein. The raid, apparently a successful one, resulted in the sinking of a vessel which contained over 500 Japanese troops, railway engines and rolling stock. Very few Nipponese survived and fifty-two Australians died.

Several near misses off the second vessel did little damage but they did cause panic amongst the Japanese Ack Ack gunners. They forgot to take aim, and nearly blew the stern off their own transport.

One young Australian, a 2/40 Battalion lad, saw what he thought was one of his mates in danger of drowning. He swam to and supported him until a rescue boat arrived. To his immense surprise, after the oil was wiped from the unconscious man's face, he recognised 'Turtle Neck', the Nipponese interpreter.

Some of the Japanese, who had been saved by the Australians (by intent or not) praised and thanked them for pulling them out of the water. Not so 'Turtle Neck'. As his saviour was later to learn, he had no gratitude.

ESCAPE ATTEMPT

A thought in the mind of just about every POW was how to escape the horror of the life they were being subjected to. Many plans were made, but due to lack of knowledge of the jungle and terrain, and the inability to harbour supplies of food and medicine, they had to be abandoned.

However, three men from Green Force did make a break, hoping to reach Assam, India. They were Captain Mull, AIF, who had been on active service in India and who had a wide knowledge of jungles and their treachery, and two other Australians. They planned to travel by night and rest throughout the day.

One, Gunner Dickinson, went down with malaria three days out and, as had been agreed, was left to fend for himself. Mull and Bell made good progress and eventually arrived at a point Mull estimated was one day's march from the border.

Being so close to freedom, they cast doubts aside and decided they would complete their trek in daylight. They were both very excited and the smell of home was, as Bell later stated, in their nostrils.

At dawn they moved out of the heavy jungle into light growth. They had not gone far when challenged by Burmese police. Mull, who was armed with a pistol, decided to shoot it out. In the battle Captain Mull was killed and his companion, Bell, wounded in the right elbow. He was captured, returned to Thanbyuzayat and condemned to death. Before his execution he warned prisoners of war against emulating his and his mates' escapade. The jungle, he said was an implacable enemy and the Burmese treacherous to a degree.

The latter was borne out in the case of Dickinson, who had been left with— so the three of them believed—friendly Burmese. The lure of money overcame the friendliness of the locals. They collected the bounty; Dickinson fell to a firing squad.

A Japanese officer who officiated at Bell's execution, paid tribute to the escapee's bravery. 'It was sad,' he commented, 'such a valiant man should have to die in a foolish undertaking.'

If ever the Nipponese needed proof they required but few guards for prisoners of war, the failure of Mull, Bell and Dickinson presented it. The inhospitable, hostile jungle was a major guard, the bounty-hunting Burmese its back up.

Repercussions resulted from the abortive escape attempt when the Japanese secret police were brought in to interrogate Mull's brother officers. One, Captain West, a Victorian, was forcibly escorted into the jungle and tortured to death by the dreaded Kempei; he told them nothing.

Other senior officers from the same camp were also questioned at great length, in an endeavour to implicate them as accessories to the plan. The wall of silence held, despite the thuggery of the questioners.

The deaths of Mull, Bell and Dickinson, in addition to the three at Mergui and eight members of the 2/4 Anti-Tank Regiment at Tavoy, put an end to any further attempts to find sanctuary from the sadistic Nipponese. It was now a case of suffer, hope and pray for a speedy end to hostilities.

And suffering there was in the work camps and Thanbyuzayat hospital huts. The saddest sight in the Base hospital area was the darkened dysentery hut with its dark green mosquito nets. From the emaciated bodies came unbelievable odours as the inmates fouled themselves. The shortage of orderlies was, perhaps, the main reason the 'Hut of Death' earned its frightening name. The moment a patient was told he was a victim of amoebic dysentery, the main killer in the hut, any belief in possible survival immediately vanished.

It was not long before the pre-dug graves began to fill, and as bed-spaces emptied in the 'HOD', as it became known, new cases came in, stools were examined and diagnoses made known.

The haunting expressions of the new inmates left no doubt in anyone's mind as to what thoughts were tumbling through their tortured minds. All patients began to dread the medical officer's diagnosis. No-one wanted a prognosis. In the main, it was accepted that if the letter 'A' prefixed dysentery, the end was probably not too far away. From that moment on, few would want food of any kind.

When this fact dawned upon the older men, even though many of them had the same ailment, they literally forced rice down their reluctant mates' throats. That act, cruel as it may appear, saved lives. The Dutch personnel who staffed the hut were amazed at the determination of the not-so-young Australians. In their opinion, if someone wanted to give up, let him do so. Why interfere?

The reputation of the HOD spread up and down the railroad-building system, from the 26 kilo to the 75 kilo point. The moment a camp medical officer suggested transfer to Thanbyuzayat, in the case of dysentery patients, darkened features blanched (due to the tropical heat most POWs had browned bodies) and expressions of horror were quickly observed. But the MO's hands were tied—no drugs, no treatment. The latter applied at Thanbyuzayat, too.

The first Allied bombing raid occurred at the base area and the exultant prisoners of war were speedily herded into huts against their will. One patient, 'Sonny' Morris, 2/15 Field Regiment, went outside to see where the bombs were falling, only to get a bayonet wound in his backside. He was most annoyed, as he had hoped to see the Nipponese huts and ammunition dumps go up in flames.

Unfortunately the raid was more or less unsuccessful, but morale building for the prisoners of war. The incident was the first indication the Allies had freedom over the Burmese territory and was most heartening.

The first hint of something new happening came when the drone of the Pathfinder plane engines were heard. Quite a few RAAF boys let out a yell that so frightened some of the Japanese guards that bayonets were immediately fixed in the expectation of the arrival of parachute troops.

The flares the Pathfinders dropped lit up the whole camp like daylight and many feared the attacking crews would mistake the hospital huts for Japanese barracks. Luckily, they didn't.

As a result of the raid, requests were made to the Nipponese for the installation of huge Red Cross signs; requests that were refused even when later raids resulted in the deaths of a number of prisoners of war and the destruction of huts.

It must have been obvious from the air ('recce' planes came over quite frequently in broad daylight) that Thanbyuzayat was a base camp for prisoners of war and Japanese troops.

Unfortunately, as later sorties proved, the pilot would have great difficulty in determining which buildings housed which. The proximity of the Ack Ack guns—which the Japanese used from time to time, to no avail—did not make it any easier for prisoner patients; flack often fell through the roofs of huts after abortive firing.

For many days after the initial bombing raid there was talk of little else. Some feared that the next one may result in the death of prisoners of war. On the other hand, all felt there was some hope of freedom in the not too distant future. Allied planes roaming at will was a true indication that the Nipponese were now on the receiving end. The all-conquering Japanese momentum was finished, at last. Judging by the sullen expressions of the guards and engineers, they knew it!

NO. 1 MOBILE FORCE
January-March 1943

FURTHER EXTRACTS from the diary of Lieutenant Colonel J.M.Williams:

[Wednesday, 13.1.43] Lt. Col. Anderson, Captain Drower (Interpreter) and Lieut. Yamada, and staff, visited the line job today as well as inspecting the 30 kilo camp, No. 5 Group. (They had lost 150 of their Group at Rangoon on their way to join the Burma-Thai railway building project.) Their losses to date, in this camp, due to malnutrition and allied diseases, total eight. They have had a very hard time.

Camp commander change. Lieut. Yamada has been ordered to report to Rangoon. Five officers 'invited' to attend a picture show at Thanbyuzayat. It turned out to be a very cold evening.

[14.1.43] Two Jap Colonels from 30 kilo camp paid Tanyin a visit. They were interested in the camp layout; one, if not the best, on the line. No work for the troops today and a concert has been arranged for tonight.

However, the next day was to be a long one for the workers. They did not return to camp until 2035 hours. They barely had enough time to finish their ablutions and consume the evening meal before lights out. The parade ground is being prepared for a game of football, but the question is who is going to play whom; the men don't get any daylight hours to themselves.

Advised there was to be a camp inspection today *[16.1.43]*; all preparations made, but nothing happened. One of our officers, Lieut. Webster, was brutally assaulted by one of the Japanese railway engineers. There was no reason given for the attack which resulted in him suffering lacerations and many bruises. He was bashed with a rod.

Subsequently he was approached by one of the guards who requested him to refrain from reporting the incident. That was not possible as his injuries were so obvious and serious.

The guards are now cause of a lot of trouble at night. They are demanding the 'night watchmen' (one hourly stints) wear hats. They are not allowed to sit down, must not be under cover and are required to salute all approaching sentries.

Last night quite a few were slapped for failing in their duties one way or the other.

*

The guards refused to believe sheer exhaustion could cause 'watchmen' to seek rest during their hour of 'watching' by seating themselves at or near the entrances, particularly in wet weather.

*

The behaviour pattern of the guards has changed a great deal since the arrival of

Anderson Force. The atmosphere has altered quite considerably. The understanding on both sides had reached the point, within the camp compound, where everyone knew where they stood.

Not so now. The influx of the new (to us) guards has spoiled many things and the change is far from acceptable.

[18.1.43] The chilly nights are taking their toll of the troops; today 215 men affected. Just three days ago we had reached our lowest sickness point in two months, 25% as against 55% for the group from the 18 kilo camp.

Trading between the POWs and guards has resulted in the latter reaping huge profits; all prices up about 75%. No supplies have arrived for the canteen for the last six weeks. The men are hungry, have money to spend but nothing available, officially, except from the profit-making 'thugs', the Japanese guards.

Despite the warning orders from Ohama, Nipponese quartermaster, to the guards, not one article they have for sale passes through correct channel, the POW canteen. Unofficially, it was a two way market with the canteen being bypassed. A three star Jap (NCO) said it was up to the Force Commander to catch the culprits. He, or they (the Nipponese staff) were unable to do so.

A medical check revealed a slight drop in the numbers of sick men today *[19.1.43]*, down 15 as compared to the most recent figures. For some unexplained reason the Nipponese are confiscating all wire in the camp. They have not missed even the smallest bit, beds have been pulled to pieces, clothes lines dismantled, tables and anything bound or held together with wire of any sort, absolutely wrecked. The whole haul would not be worth a 'bob' in any market. Some of the 'valued' pieces would not have exceeded 2 to 3 inches in length at the most.

They were so determined to clear the camp of wire they instituted three separate searches. During the foray one of the guards copped a severe bashing. (Needless to say, not one POW intervened.)

*[20.1.43]*Visited the railway job today in company with Lt. Col. Anderson, only to see our men toiling 'coolie'-like as they moved backwards and forwards at the end of a rope. They were the 'horses' that hauled up the piledriver and let it go, accompanied by a mournful dirge from the engineers.

A second gang had to manhandle beams weighing over a ton in weight and to a height of 20 feet. One of the boys copped a bashing because he flatly refused to hand over his water bottle to a guard. In any case, the guard was not a worker and there was hardly enough liquid in the container for the lad's own needs.

[21.1.43] Today an unexpected but nonetheless welcomed increase in the meat ration. Allowed to slaughter four yaks and we have another three for the same treatment tomorrow. Counting bone and meat weight, we will have approximately 650 lbs for consumption by 1,700 men, a mere two cubes of meat per man. Hardly a banquet!

Cause for worry; our water supply now very low and little prospect of rain. Never comes when it is needed. Can only hope the soak does not fail us.

Situation greatly worsened by the arrival of the remainder of Anderson Force from Tavoy. They had to remain there due to illness. At the moment, they all appear to be in a reasonable state of health.

Trouble on the line again today *[23.1.43]* when an officer from Anderson Force was badly beaten up. The sadism of the Japanese and Korean guards has to be seen to be believed. The men on the receiving end really do!

Rumour has it our Batavia survivors are in the gaol at Moulmein. Their convoy was bombed and quite a few prisoners of war were killed in the raid. Have not been informed as to their destination. An additional 'latrine-o-gram', 10,000 blankets and a similar number of pairs of boots were alleged to have been part of the cargo on the ship that was sunk.

The railroad and camp guards are really turning on the heat at the present time. Hard to guess the real reason, except, perhaps, reverses on the fighting fronts.

[24.1.43] Yasumi today and an opportunity to sink the well another three feet. Good result, greater soak flow; water level increasing.

Many of the troops suffering sore mouths and we are experimenting on a berry growing prolifically in the jungle. The taste, as most say, 'is 'orrible' but if it cures the ailment, what matter the taste.

[25.1.43] A great deal of illness in Anderson force; 403 out of the complement of 525. In our ranks, the figure is 212 out of 778. Seven recently hospitalised at base returned to camp today. Unfortunately, they were not given the opportunity to bring canteen supplies back with them.

[26.1.43] Very bad news on the work front. Anderson and Williams Force Commanders, accompanied by Captain Bill Drower, ordered to report to the Japanese Railway Headquarters today. The reason was soon made known. The look on Bill Drower's (the interpreter) face indicated a problem.

There was. The edict—work tasks to be increased and many more men required out on the job. Despite a very spirited objection by both Commanders the Nipponese were adamant.

As far as one Jap was concerned there was no argument. He was heard to say, 'Why should we argue with them; they are only dirty white prisoners'. Conference closed!

At least, out of the gathering came two things; (1) a determination by the Nipponese to squeeze as much work out of the prisoners of war as was possible, and (2) the Australians no longer had any doubt as to what their captors considered them to be.

Confirmation of the loss by the Nipponese of one ship and a second one severely damaged. Seven Australians wounded and, regrettably, three killed.

Ration reduction on again, no yaks delivered and no one able to say when any can be expected. Usual Japanese bland reply, none available. However, some canteen supplies arrived for Williams Force; half a block of sugar, one egg and some cigars per man.

As from today *[27.1.43]* every rail worker has to work harder as all tasks increased. This requirement, on near empty stomachs, is harsh as rations considerably reduced and will be, unless cattle of some description is received.

Another day has passed and still no information as to when we can expect food on the hoof. Sufficient quinine tablets on hand to issue one per man.

As from this date *[28.1.43]* the Japanese intend to record the weight, height and chest measurement of every POW each month. Based on recent experiences at hospital camps, once the combined weight of prisoners decreases, so do rations accordingly.

[29.1.43] Another 24 hours gone and no sign of any increase in the ration supply despite the fact meat has been out of supply for some days. The cooks are managing to produce 'bull' (a POW expression) soup; a kind of watery stew with the rice meal. Improvisation in the kitchen has reached a high peak. The staff there work wonders with rice and whatever they can find to improve it. The workers pay tribute to their ability.

Some canteen supplies have arrived for the Anderson Force group, plus some flour as part of the ration scale. The boys are flat out constructing a 'baker's oven'.

The railroad workers are now working from daylight to dark, there is no let-up. The increased tasks are taxing the physical abilities of every man wielding tools on this mad rush to build a railway.

Today *[30.1.43]* we were issued with a few Dutch hats in addition to three buckets. Whilst they cannot be eaten, at least they are useful.

The great strain on the strength of the men out on the job is now only too apparent, they come back to camp just about washed out; their faces exhibit absolute fatigue. One of the lads was beaten up by two 'brave' guards today. *[31.1.43]* They hit him with everything; it was a cowardly attack.

The brutality of the guards yesterday on one man was bad enough but the mass bashing by an enraged Japanese today was unbelievable. He had found a pick—someone may have off-loaded it into the jungle—and he went completely berserk. One of the 27 suffered severe head injuries and was felled to the ground. Nearly all the men in the mass bash were struck around the head as they weaved and twisted to avoid the flailing dangerous weapon.

[2.2.43] There was an incident today that may have serious consequences for Sergeant Scanlon. He was apprehended outside the camp area whilst on a trading mission. The Nipponese guard accused him of attempting to escape, well knowing, should the charge be substantiated, the penalty was death.

There was no question of what Scanlon was attempting, it was the sale of some clothing to obtain foodstuff. But, his accuser, priding himself on the 'capture' of an escapee, was adamant and believed by the camp commander.

The acting camp commander, a three-star private, refused the intervention of the Force Commander (Williams) who submitted *he* would punish the lad for his indiscretion; fine him 60 days pay (yap) plus one month on extra duty.

It was an extraordinary accusation to level at Scanlon; he was totally unprepared for such a serious undertaking. He had neither food nor sufficient clothing, had nowhere to go, no maps or a guide nor was he an acquaintance of any of the natives. But, the bestiality of the two Japanese overrode clarity of thought, reasonableness or plea for clemency by his (Scanlon's) Commander. He was sent to base under guard.

So determined was the acting camp commander he petulantly ignored the communication prepared for transmission to Brigadier Varley. The letter never left the camp. The Nipponese attitude bode ill for Scanlon!

The following day [3.2.43] was unpleasant for the men of Tanyin camp, the Japanese presented the Force Commander with a bill amounting to 32.35 rupees, postage fee for the cards the POWs had been allowed to send to their families, some weeks back. The cards, all believed to be well on their way to the various countries concerned, were still at base.

Lieutenant Naito, gentleman type when sober, which was seldom, visited the camp duty and the Force Commander took the opportunity of presenting the facts of the Scanlon case to him. When correctly informed, he assured support for the lad when the hearing was listed.

After quite a long discussion he promised extra supplies for the canteen. One of the possible reasons for this was the fact of the high incidence of illness. Being a well-educated Japanese he viewed many matters in a different light to his not-so-lenient brother officers.

Rest days appear to be something thought and talked about but not agreed to by the Japanese railway engineers and sadistic guards. Twelve days since the last yasumi was granted. Despite strong representations by the Force Commander there was no relenting by the Japanese determination to keep the workforce constantly on the go. Seven ill men sent to base.

Perhaps the three star 'generalissimo' was implicitly obeying the demand of his supreme commander, Nagatomo, who said all prisoners must work 'diligently' and 'cheerfully' for the Imperial Nipponese

The oven is a success! The cooks outdid themselves today (5th) and produced a bun for every man in camp. The flour supply will probably last another five days. Now able to produce yeast; all sick personnel in receipt of 6 oz per day.

Captain Bill Drower struck twice today. His ability as an interpreter is undoubtedly a thorn in the side of the Nipponese.

*

It is probable that his knowledge of their language resulted in some sort of retaliation. Or, as some may put it, the guards concerned wanted to prove they was as good, if not better, than officers.

*

No matter how good our cooks are they cannot disguise the melon content in 'stews'. They are as tasteless as they are lacking in nutrition; they make a bit of bulk, that is all one can say about them, except, perhaps, they are better than nothing at all.

Decrease in the number of sick today [7.2.43], 70 less on the list. Decided yeast to be on issue to all personnel in the camp. A spot of water trouble, the pump is out of action. Work party now deepening well.

The rations now on a very low scale; mostly pie melons. One bright note, sugar and cigars arrived for the canteen. Supplies soon exhausted and shelves empty again.

[9.2.43] A surprise visit by Lt. Col. Y. Nagatomo and Nipponese medical officer. When the matter of the Scanlon case was raised little satisfaction resulted. Informed that kumichos and hanchos of the day, all witnesses and owners of clothing involved (which the accused claimed was for sale) are to be individually punished.

All verbal submissions concerning on-the-line and camp bashings by Japanese engineers and guards received scant consideration. Instead, Nagatomo responded with an order for a complete listing of all clothing in the camp. Also informed, the Nipponese 'doctor' would view all sick prisoners of war on 11th instant.

Brigadier Varley and Major W.E. Fisher, physician, called into the camp with unpleasant news. Scanlon was being held in the local goal and his future could not be viewed in a good light.

At last, a holiday today *[10.2.43]*. The reason, not just to rest the workers but to celebrate some religious function. At least the POWs benefited from the Japanese worship.

Opportunity to slightly better our diet. Able to purchase 100 blocks of sugar and some eggs. Very welcome change from the inevitable pie melons.

As demanded by Nagatomo, a complete inventory of the clothing possessions of all personnel in the camp now under preparation. A requirement, no doubt, resulting from the Scanlon incident.

Yesterday's yasumi had some repercussions today when one of the guards, a corporal, called into the orderly room and made threats against any prisoner submitting official reports concerning bashings.

One of our lads (Mason) was knocked about by a Jap down at the well for no reason, other than just plain desire to inflict hurt upon someone. When challenged for an explanation, the Jap had none to offer.

[Saturday, 13.2.43] The Japanese 'doctor' made an inspection of all sick cases. He ordered 465 men suffering from dysentery out to work. A few, very few, he considered so ill they should be transferred to the base hospital. He put Anderson Force through the mill. Just about every sick man was, in his opinion, fit to resume full duties.

Handed in the required returns at 1000 hours today *[14.2.43]*. Maybe as a result of that the Jap Economy Officer is to pay us a visit in two days time.

One of the boys was caught red-handed in a trading deal with a native but fortunately for him, no charge of attempted escape lodged. However, it was not an easy matter preventing him receiving severe punishment. The acting camp commander is not one too easy to get along with. Possibly, he was in one of his good moods; well, maybe.

*

Perhaps not intended as a reminder of the fateful 15 February 1942, but it was an ironic date as far as the prisoners of war taken in Singapore were concerned.

Many wondered if the rest day was a subtle gesture to Jap 'superiority' twelve months after the fall of the British Bastion of the Far East stunned the world.

*

For some unknown reason the men are all very quiet even though they have a free day. Their intention to gather firewood was thwarted when the guards wanted to play football. They refused to supply a guard for the party. However, at 1200 hours they relented and as preparations were being made to go out, the Economy Officer from Thanbyuzayat arrived. That ended the work party.

The exhibition of changing clothes was an eye opener; a general warning, 'if any man received any clothing and still had some in his possession, he would be punished'. How they expected men to work in any kind of weighty cloth in the tropical heat, is beyond anyone's imagination. But, the Nipponese did!

In daytime, and especially out on the line job, the temperature feels anywhere in the vicinity of 120 degrees Fahrenheit, as men haul the ropes to pull up the piledriver or swing a pick and/or shovel.

As the line of men moved along and they were seen to be wearing any kind of rag at all, no shirt or shorts were issued.

If what they were wearing was torn or worn out they were told to mend the article concerned. The fact no needles, cotton or material of any type was on issue, mattered not. As far as the (well named) Economy Officer cared, if they were wearing something, that was it. They were clothed, even if it was merely a G-string that only protected one's modesty, it was sufficient.

The fact that it was completely beyond the point of repair due to climatic conditions still did not matter.

*

It is possible that the Nipponese 'generosity' officer was influenced by the Australians' reputation for ingenuity and their ability to improvise the impossible.

*

As a clothing issue it was as disgraceful an exhibition as anyone could witness. One particular instance was a glaring example; a lad, wearing a pair of shorts that could only be accepted as a grass skirt, was refused a replacement. Not one man in the whole camp had received any clothing replacement for over twelve months. The shorts, or part thereof, they wore had been issued to them in the Far East, being their last issue of clothing (one pair of shorts each); no shirts since the Middle East. Every pair of shorts now worn had long since lost identity as such. What they wore was merely rotted material.

It is doubtful even Lieut. Yamada—who had returned from Rangoon that day—could have influenced the Economy Officer had he tried. No one approached him to intervene and he did not offer to do so. He looks a tired, worried man.

The following day the new Camp Commander arrived to take over from Lieut. Yamada. The men are sorry to see Yamada transferred. In his own way, and in accordance with his conscience, he had helped the POWs a lot. However, it is possible his replacement might be somewhat of a similar nature. Time will tell.

Prior to his departure at 1700 hours, he gave a short address; told of the heavy bombing raids on Rangoon, but gave no details of damage, etc., left that to our imagination.

Lieut. Hosoda, now the Camp Commander, wasted no time in calling a conference. Assured us, Lt. Colonels Anderson and Williams and the interpreter Captain Bill Drower, he would look into our troubles. It turned out to be a welcome gathering. The atmosphere was quiet; offered his 'guests' some brandy. Lt. Col. Anderson accepted a nip and the get-together ended at 2300 hours.

[17.2.43] Hosoda made an inspection of the camp at 1000 hours and said he would look into the matter of canteen supplies in the afternoon. He appointed Major Kerr as officer in control (canteen).

Water problem again; the pump is playing up. In a manner of speaking, it is a case of 'too many cooks'. We had a pump expert on it but he has been given the 'ancient order of the boot'.

The railway workers are still working very long hours and are returning to camp late every night. Lieut. Barker was struck today. The Japanese corporal in charge of the work party came to the camp commander and apologised for the hasty temper of his man.

[18.2.43] Another day gone and the pump still out of order. No one had a bath tonight; weather has turned very cold. As from tomorrow all clocks and watches (for those who have any) are to be put on 15 minutes.

Advised of new rates of pay to apply after today (19th). They are: Privates, 25 cents per day; NCOs, 30 cents; Warrant Officers, 40 cents; Night work, 5 cents extra.

A few head of cattle delivered today, plus four cases of tinned stew (mostly fly-blown) and some of the tasteless pie melons.

*

Those pie melons were enough to turn one off eating for life except for the fact every man was hungry to the extreme and ready to eat anything that looked like food, without taste or otherwise.

*

Surprise today *[20.2.43]*, canteen supplies arrived, comprising one block of sugar per man; 1300 (mostly rotten) eggs. To counter that, there is no water. The well is completely dry.

Camp Commander, Lt. Col. Anderson, informed all light duty men must be sent out to work tomorrow *[21.2.43]*. They are required to labour for half a day.

Lt. Col. Y. Nagatomo prevented the order being carried out, but the railway crowd (engineers) are insistent; half a day's work for half a day's pay.

Situation desperate today *[22.2.43]*—no water, no rations! Two men returned from base hospital wishing, under the circumstances, they had been retained at Thanbyuzayat. Only for canteen supplies we would be without food of any kind today *[23.2.43]*. As it is we are dependent upon vegetables; peas, beans, etc. Yesterday's ration arrived today. The bags of egg fruit are useless even for frying. Luckily, we still have a few bags of beans in the canteen. But we cannot afford to provision ourselves on 10 cents per day. Our earning rate provides us with two bags of beans daily, only if everyone, sick included, goes out to work.

Bashings out on the job are on again; two men assaulted, one from each Force. One struck a heavy blow on the head with an 8lb hammer, the other clouted with a shovel. The injuries so bad they had to be hospitalised. Complaints were lodged immediately but met with little satisfaction.

The guards are particularly vicious today *[24.2.43]* and one lad had his head split open when struck with a heavy piece of wood. When the Force Commander (Williams) protested vigorously he was told the cause of the attack was due to a smile at the guard by the man concerned. Prisoners are not allowed the privilege of smiling. The injured lad lost a lot of blood, at least one pint.

A general tightening up of discipline as all POWs *must* bow or salute any and all Japanese, no matter where. As far as Williams Force is concerned, it is Batavia all over again.

A rest day at last. After the incident of yesterday (the bashing) the men need it badly. Everyone's nerves are on edge as one never knows when the Japanese or Korean guards will attack.

*

If a smile is enough provocation, what would a nasty look be worth?

*

Lieut. Hosoda on his way to Thanbyuzayat today *[25.2.43]*. After his departure the guards went on a drunken spree and were in search of physical fun, bash type. They ordered everyone to remain silent, stand up and salute. Not satisfied with just that they demanded all men retire to bed at 9.45 p.m.

From that point on and until the early hours of the morning, they kept up a hell of a row, fighting and rowing amongst themselves. Fortunately, there was no further incident as concerned the prisoners of war.

Permission granted for the staging of another concert; the shows are important as the artists seem to improve every time they appear on the boards.

A wood-gathering party went out without a guard in attendance, a dangerous practice as it is against Nagatomo's orders. There is a distinct possibility someone will end up being shot one day as an escapee.

*

It did not need much of an excuse for a guard to make groundless accusations, as instanced in the Scanlon case.

*

Orders out today *[26.2.43]* for the move to Thanbyuzayat of—Lt. Col. Eadie, Lt. Col. Williams, the orderly officer and two sergeants who were concerned in the alleged attempt to escape of Sergeant Scanlon on 2nd instant. Matheson, Miller, Lincoln and two of the bamboo party are required to take part in the tribunal listed for the hearing of the alleged attempted escape.

It is a clear-cut case of selling goods and not escape but it is also a case of someone having to be the scapegoat!

Heard today we may be on our way very soon. In fact, it is so imminent it is only a matter of days. Our meat ration cut, again! But, the Japanese still get meat out of our kitchen in order to have fried steak for themselves. And, that is on top of their normal meat ration which is far greater than ours.

The tribunal party set off for base at 1400 hours, arrived at Thanbyuzayat at approximately 1700 hours. Very obvious improvement in the hospital huts; new buildings and better laid out and much cleaner. All the patients appear to be in better spirits. The party met up with some of the Unit (2/2 Pioneers) who had been aboard ship in a bombing raid. All are doing well.

The canteen and kitchen in good order and well patronised. Water supply so good baths were permitted. The group attended the weekly concert and were well entertained; it was a very good show. The instrumentalists were outstanding. After viewing the performance the Brigadier (Varley) held a conference which ended at 0100 hours.

The tribunal party assembled in the Conference Room at 1000 hours. Lt. Col. Y. Nagatomo took the Chair. Lieut. Naito, who was to be prosecuting officer, Lieut. Yamada, the Economy Officer and one other officer also present. Lt. Col. G.E. Ramsay appeared on behalf of Private Williams (Ramsay Force) who, like Sergeant Scanlon, was on a charge of attempted escape.

*

The other un-named Japanese officer is believed to have been exchanged whilst a POW in Australia.

*

In attendance, Lieut. Rossiter, Orderly Officer on duty the day Scanlon was alleged to have attempted escape, two orderly-room Sergeants, bamboo party Kumicho, Miller and Lincoln who were appearing as witnesses for Scanlon to prove that the accused (Scanlon) was only going out to sell clothes. They were seated with him throughout the trial.

The Trial

The proceedings opened by Lt. Col. Nagatomo asking questions in order to shake the statement already made by the accused (Scanlon). Lieut. Rossiter, the orderly room Sergeants, Miller, Lincoln and the Bamboo Party were all examined.

The whole of the examination of those concerned, was carried out in French and English.

As the case for the prosecution closed, Lieut. Naito gave out the sentences. They were—Death penalty for both Sergeant Scanlon and Private Williams, who up to that point had not been allowed to speak. Lincoln and Miller were each sentenced to two months imprisment. Lieut. Rossiter and the two Sergeants and witnesses were fined 20 and 10 days pay, respectively.

Lt. Col. Eadie, medical officer, was neither a witness or accused, but was fined 10 days pay.

Kumicho of the Bamboo Party was fined 10 days pay.

Lt. Col. Williams was severely reprimanded for writing lying letters about Scanlon.

Nagatomo then asked if anyone had anything to say. Brigadier Varley, who also attended the trial, then spoke on behalf of Lt. Col. Williams, saying his letter was a report on the incident and contained only the truth. Stated to the Tribunal that the Doctor could not stop Scanlon from going out of camp. The same applied for the Kumicho, the commander of the kumi (50 men) of which the accused (Scanlon) was a member, as he was sick the whole day and confined to his quarters.

Nagatomo closed the Court for one hour. At 1600 hours the hearing was reconvened. Whilst standing he declared *final* sentences: Sergeant Scanlon and Private Williams, two months imprisonment. Two months hard labour for Williams and one month hard labour for Scanlon.

Lieut. Rossiter, ten days pay fine.

Orderly Room Sergeants, five days pay fine each.

Miller and Lincoln, five days imprisonment.

All others concerned, a caution.

In the final address Nagatomo, after announcing sentences, said that he could not prove that the accused had attempted to escape and that the evidence did not prove anything either, yet he punished all hands.

Lieutenant Colonels Williams and Ramsay had to attend a conference the next day; the remainder of the party to return to camp the following morning.

*

If ever there was a farcical military trial, this was it. Nagatomo and Naito were bitter enemies, the former hating the latter. Naito, realising Nagatomo would go against him at the trial, told the Australian senior officers there was no question Nagatomo intended the two soldiers were to be shot; but he, Naito, would do his best for them. He did by trenchantly demanding the supreme penalty, well knowing his commanding officer, to whom he was 2 i/c, would not agree.

Nagatomo was most annoyed that he had lost face when he sentenced to death two witnesses who were not in any way involved in the actual charges of attempting to escape.

When this had been drawn to the attention of Nagatomo by the Australian officers he was, to say the least, nonplussed. At that point, Naito, taking advantage of Nagatomo's dilemma, again sought the death penalty of both accused.

Nagatomo refused, saying, in his opinion, mercy should be shown and condemned Scanlon and Williams to confinement in the guard house with hard labour. So came to an end an oriental personality clash.

*

During the night (it was the anniversary of the sinking of the HMAS *Perth* and the American cruiser, *Houston*) the base was bombed by Allied aircraft. One stick of bombs was dropped about one mile from the hospital. The bombing had been preceded by Pathfinder craft that dropped flares which lit up the whole camp like day. The Nipponese appeared to lose all control and refused to allow patients to occupy the slit trenches outside the huts.

★

It was during this incident that Bombardier 'Sonny' Morris was bayoneted in the buttocks by a fear-crazed guard. He was not seriously wounded.

★

The Nipponese all took cover in the trenches after warning patients anyone leaving the huts would be shot. On the 26th sounds of bombing could be heard coming from the direction of the sea. Today [28.2.43] two columns of naval (Nipponese) forces and one column of army were seen marching from the direction of Amhurst, carrying life jackets. Lorry loads of wounded were also noticed.

[Monday, 1.3.43] Visited patients in the hospital whilst waiting for the conference that did not come off. Apparently the bombing has shaken the Nipponese. One of the boys off the *Perth* passed away.

★

It was bitter irony for the survivors of the *Perth* and *Houston* that a lad off the Australian vessel should lose his life on the actual anniversary of the attack. They held a subdued commemoration service.

★

Warned today of a projected move from Tanyin to the 70 kilo camp.

One of the men who made an escape attempt (Green Force) was recaptured and shot at dawn this morning. He had been executed without trial. Brigadier Varley was not informed, neither was the Force Commander.

Arrived back at Tanyin at 1230 hours after a dusty trip. First bath in three days. Saluting blitz still on.

Request from base to select a team to play soccer at the weekend. A team will be sent. Had a slight increase in the meat ration today [3.3.43]. Eleven soccer and four tennis players, plus a manager, departed for base today [4.3.43].

All the rice bags we have been using as blankets have been confiscated by the Japanese. Few will be left with bedding and will suffer the cold at night. Hardly anyone in camp has clothing, what they have is just about worn out. Most of the boys have just a G-string to wear. That is why there are so many stricken with colds.

A well-earned rest day granted [5.3.43] but unfortunately we are experiencing water trouble again. What is in the well is muddy. But our overworked and underfed troops will enjoy the spell.

[Saturday, 6.3.43] The Japanese require full particulars of all Field Officers in camp. Date of birth, age, etc. The fires the boys keep going at night were put out by the guards (tonight). That is the last straw as the lads will not be able to obtain warmth from anything; no clothes, blankets or rice bags. By day, very hot. At night, cold.

Every night some members of the huts are required to act as watchmen for one hour each. If any POW attempts escape the next watchman is to be held responsible and will be shot as well. Japanese justice?

A service will be held tonight [7.3.43] by the lads who served on HMAS *Perth*. They will assemble at the Chapel. Padre Kellow will lead the commemoration.

Another bashing today [8.3.43]. The guard misunderstood an order and belted up one of our boys.

Ration shortage, no meat available; the camp commander makes plenty of promises but that does not seem to help the constitution. We found out it does not pay to ask for our meat entitlement. They give it to us alright, and when the cows run out (every 7 days) we go without meat until more cattle come along.

Twelve months as prisoners of war today [9.3.43] and what a twelve months! We all hope there will not be a second anniversary. If there is, we will all be 'cuckoo' or dead.

The Japanese killed a buffalo last night and, as usual, took most of the meat for themselves. They are 20 strong, we have 1,600 to feed. After tomorrow we will have 180 more, British and American POWs. Where we will house them no one knows. At the present time we have 285 men per hut built to house 200 at 2 per metre of hut. Perhaps worse still, water very low. One well has completely dried up. One well is used exclusively by the Nipponese; they must have their usual supply.

The natives do not spare water; they wash their bodies under the pump.

[10.3.43] Hosoda, the camp commander, is leaving Tanyin today. He has not helped in any way and made more promises than anyone; he is certainly no loss. Sergeant Tanaka, from the 18 kilo camp, is to take over. He promises nothing and does likewise. At least we know where we stand with him. Had to commence digging another well today, using green timber to line it. Sawn timber not available.

The English and Americans have settled in; we are squeezed up but still live. We are out of rations and the newcomers brought nothing with them. Result, no food for anyone.

A new interpreter, Mr. Hess, and Regimental Medical Officer arrived today [11.3.43] from the 26 kilo camp. They are to be attached to the latest additions (British-Americans). The Medical Officer had to be admitted to hospital and the interpreter was detailed to Williams Force.

Captain Bill Drower, interpreter, 18 kilo camp, was transported to base today suffering from a bad toothache.

Our water problem eased a little with good inflow, well No. 3. It will be used for the time being. Whilst we can use the well contents we have to put up with the mud-stained liquid. At least all troops can have a wash, mud or no mud. On hot days water of any colour is welcome.

A delivery was made to the canteen today, 3000 eggs; they will sell at the rate of eight per rupee.

[12.3.43] The new camp commander, Sergeant Tanaka, issued drastic orders.

'The Australian troops must conform as do the Americans and British and salute the Great Nipponese. The Australian attitude is to treat Nipponese like cows and pigs. This must cease; saluting must improve.'

As from this date, no lectures or concerts without permission, etc., etc. Lt. Col. Anderson paid his respects to Tanaka and came away somewhat disillusioned. Said he (Tanaka) was now a changed man since he last saw him at the 18 kilo camp.

*

Tanaka was never easy to get on with. The only change any one could expect from him was for the worse. Earlier experiences with him suggested he had uncanny ways. Now the mask was off!

*

Quite a few items arrived for the canteen today *[13.3.43]*; peas, coffee, cigars and dried fruit. Williams Force Quartermaster held in the guardhouse because of his refusal to give meat to the guard. His release was arranged but not before much argument was entered into.

The other kitchens were not so fortunate; they were compelled to give their meat ration to the Japanese in order that they would have fried steaks. The allowance for POWs (if they are lucky) is 1oz per man per day, if cattle are available.

There was a lot of trouble when one of the guards refused to return the salute given by Lt. Col. Williams. Much roaring and demonstrating before the salute was returned. The guard concerned, before moving away, threatened certain 'Chokos' (Colonels) would be done in.

Today *[14.3.43]* the heat is still on and the Japanese are out for blood. Major Meagher was forced to stand to attention at the guardhouse until the intervention of the Force Commander (Williams). He was then released. However, his detention was subject for fears as to his safety after the threat made by one of the guards yesterday.

*

It was a well known fact the guards considered Lt. Col. Williams as the 'No. 1 bad man' on the line. Subsequent events were to prove that.

*

The meat ration is still at a very low level and no advice given as to when next issue will be made. Some bananas came into the canteen from local suppliers. All village transactions are supposed to go through the camp 2 i/c but the deal is always ignored by the Japs who make certain they get their cut.

As a Japanese colonel is believed to be visiting the camp today *[15.3.43]* the rest day was cancelled. He failed to arrive. Half day workers ordered to move 1 cubic metre of earth (full day workers are required to move 1.7 cubic metres) for half day's pay.

[Tuesday, 16.3.43] Rest day granted and the workers need it badly as the ration supply is at a very low ebb. Luckily, the canteen had some vegetables, just enough as an additive to rice to make a meal.

*

The Japanese knew when they were on a good wicket, allowing supplies to come into the canteen and making a handsome profit for themselves by selling the food they should have supplied. Many of the Japanese must have accumulated a vast amount of money through ripping off the POW workers, in addition to their illicit trading gains, again at the expense of the men over whom they had control.

*

Tanaka came back from Base bringing with him cigars for sale via the canteen. He demanded 130% increase above normal prices. He was told, more or less, that he could keep them at that price. He retaliated by threatening to close down the canteen if the men refused to buy. Lt. Col. Anderson made a decision, probably to ensure the camp facility remained open. He ordered the purchase of the cigars, despite the inflated price.

Another (second-hand) blanket issue today [17.3.43], a grand total of 94; they were allocated to the most needy. Only a few of the men now without some kind of protection against the bitter cold night.

A water buffalo was sighted grazing near the camp and the Nipponese requested the meat on the hoof be made available. The marksman had a standing target, no more than 50 feet away. He let fly two shots; the good food turned and ambled away into a safer haven in the jungle. So much for the shooting ability of the Japanese soldiery.

[Friday, 19.3.43] The arrival of four yak cows heralded a change of diet today. It was not to be. The frail holding ropes soon gave way and the frightened animals took off and were out of sight before any attempt could be made to recapture them. All high hopes of different taste in the rice issue faded in a few moments.

Captain Griffin came up from Base today to select staff for the proposed new hospital to be opened at 30 kilo (Retpu) camp. The British and American group warned to make ready for a move to the 8 kilo camp tomorrow. They marched out at 1700 hours.

The combined Anderson and Williams Forces are living on the latter Force's rations. It is an almost impossible situation and the reason why so little food is available.

The projected opening of a hospital camp at the 30 kilo affected us today [21.3.43] when Captain Griffin, and most of our trained medical orderlies, moved out en route for the 75 kilo, 40 kilos away from their intended destination.

The troublesome 3-star Japanese left camp today [23.3.43] much to the great pleasure of all troops in the camp. He will be missed only for his brutal ways. Also to go was the last of the British and American boys.

As an outbreak of cholera is a likelihood the Nipponese supplied the vaccine for inoculation of all prisoners of war. They also presented us with 12 lbs of tinned Irish stew. Not enough to even alter the taste of rice when divided amongst 700 men.

Lt. Col. Eadie, and a number of medical orderlies, accompanied by 137 of the most seriously ill from Anderson and Williams Forces, moved to the new hospital at Retpu. We are now completely out of any medical supplies; what we had was needed for the now-to-be opened establishment.

Despite the transfer of many of our sick lads the camp hospital is still functioning and 20 of our men admitted there today *[26.3.43]*. Lt. Col. Hamilton suffered a severe bashing, administered by one of the crazed guards. The camp commander, Tanaka, refused even to take a look at the results of the attack. However, the matter will be reported to Nagatomo, via Brigadier Varley.

Tomorrow *[27.3.43]* we are to be transferred to the 26 kilo camp; one truck will be provided to carry the heaviest gear. The troops are to lumber all personal possessions on the 9 kilo hike. Actual time for the move is still indefinite; orders change as rapidly as Tanaka's moods.

It is now 2200 hours and the tired, hungry railroad workers are coming in off the job the Nipponese demanded had to be completed before a return to camp could be permitted. Huge fires provided illumination and the men kept at the task until the engineers were satisfied the project had been finally finished.

MEILOE (75 KILO) CAMP

ON 18 MARCH 1943 the working parties from the 26 kilo camp were transferred to a new area, Meiloe (as it was known), at the 75 kilo point from Thanbyuzayat. In some ways, the fears of a very unpleasant encampment were groundless. There was quite a decent stream, approximately eighteen yards wide, in which the POWs were allowed to swim, if they had the opportunity.

However, despite the availability of water and the chance to keep their bodies clean, the work demands increased alarmingly. From here on the 'speedo' was very evident. Two shifts worked day and night. All lighting came from vast bamboo fires and a hand-operated generator. There was no let-up and the worst possible guards thrashed men right and left.

The Boy Bastard and his mate, the Boy Bastard's Cobber were, perhaps, the worst of their lot. They had lost any veneer of humanity they once may have had and, as many believed, vied with each other in handing out the most sadistic of bashings.

In keeping with the guards' behaviour was that of their commander, the drunken Naito. In his alcoholic state he was a maddened bull. Proof of that was the occasion he jumped through the window of a guard hut and gave two Koreans a frightful doing over, much to the delight of the POWs who witnessed the event.

Rations, as usual, were well under the scale laid down by Japanese High Command. There was no doubt the Nipponese supply group was pilfering a large portion of rice and, as was suspected and later confirmed, trading with the Burmese.

As a direct result of food shortages and demanding physical labour, on occasions for up to eighteen hours, the illness rate soared. As far as the Japanese were concerned, sickness was no excuse and those suffering were ordered to carry out all camp chores. Force commanders fought the Nipponese at every opportunity and flatly refused to send out those diagnosed as medically unfit for work.

It was at this camp a cholera scare broke out and many men fell victim to the scourge. How the medical officers managed to contain the possible epidemic without drugs or medicines remains a mystery, but the feared death rate did not eventuate. Strict hygiene undoubtedly assisted in the control of a disease that ran unbridled in many camps, through no fault of the medical fraternity involved. Those highly dedicated men of medicine hardly rested, so determined were they to harness the dread disease that killed within hours.

For ten almost unbearable weeks the Japanese guards did their utmost to force the prisoners of war to work at a furious pace in an endeavour to finalise that section of the railroad. The labour was so arduous, the pressure continually on, the rations so low and lacking in quality as well as quantity, that illness increased at an alarming rate. Ulcers resulted from any break of the skin, mainly on the victims' legs.

Thanbyuzayat hospital camp became so crowded that, apparently on the orders of Japanese High Command in Bangkok, Nagatomo directed a new hospital to be erected at the 30 kilo, to be known as Reptu. It differed only in one respect, it had a boarded floor. Major Fisher, who was given a nickname he did not exactly appreciate but accepted in good humour, 'The Fuehrer', was to be the Senior Medical Officer; Lt. Col. C. Black, the camp commander.

Unfortunately for the patients who eventually tenanted Retpu, the Nipponese commander was none other than the perpetually drunk Lieutenant Naito. In the meantime, the huts at the 75 kilo camp, in tiered-type accommodation holding twice the normal crowded number of POWs, housed a high proportion of men incapable of performing any kind of work.

Typical of the Nipponese attitude to the sick were the remarks made by both Captain Mizdani, No. 5 Group, and Lieutenant Naito: 'Your sick shall starve until they die or go back to work. Any sick prisoner who can just make it to work and dies will not have died in vain, even if he has laid only one sleeper. No work, no food'.

Later, a senior Japanese field officer, name unknown, after listening to impassioned appeals for clemency towards the sick and injured in No. 3 and No. 5 Groups, quite indifferently answered: 'You do not understand us. We will build this railway. If necessary over the bones of the prisoners of war.'

And he meant it!

Throughout the month of April all camp commanders and medical officers were doing their utmost to have all unfit personnel transferred to Thanbyuzayat hospital; they feared the onset of monsoon rains would make all roads impassable. In that hospital, such as it was, there was more chance of them receiving some treatment than would otherwise apply in jungle camps.

At the beginning of May the Retpu hospital was filled to overflowing and Japanese pressure was being applied on Allied medical officers to discharge as many patients as possible for work on the line. As the result, the medical fraternity was forced to send back into the jungle men who were in a state that could hardly be classed as even approaching convalescence.

Many who were returned to work areas failed to make the grade and they now rest six feet below the surface in the foetid jungles of Burma. They had laid their quota of sleepers, and paid the price!

One of the Boy Bastard's favourite sayings was, 'You will never see your homes again. You will work for the Nipponese until you die. This is a one hundred years war.'

There is no doubt the Koreans did believe the hostilities would last a long, long time. In a way, they were echoing their treatment by the Japanese, who had warred with them for an extensive period; they had been vanquished by them, trampled underfoot to such an extent they accepted their status as 'Slaves of the Son of Heaven'. Slaves, no doubt, but Hirohito had no Heavenly affinity!

Now, their appointment by the Japanese as guards over thousands of white, brown and dark-skinned prisoners of war gave them power far beyond their wildest dreams, and they sadistically exerted it. The defenceless prisoners suffered undreamed-of physical punishments.

In his recollections of his POW experiences Tony Clive (8th Division Postal Unit) recorded his impressions of the 75 kilo camp:

One of the advantages the kitchen staff enjoyed at Meiloe was the access to a constant water supply. Their cookhouse was built on the river bank and a hand pump brought the precious liquid into large containers that, pre-war, were used to hold latex (liquid rubber).

The workers found their living quarters were much better than what they had occupied at the 26 kilometre encampment. Instead of lying on small bamboo poles, they split the larger type and spread them out in slat form. Much more comfortable than the round, 2 to 3 inch poles that made sleeping a hazard; the knots bit into the skin.

To accommodate the combined Forces (Ramsay-Green-Black), upper bunks had to be built otherwise men would have been packed shoulder to shoulder, as they had been in other camps.

One of the hardest tasks at the 75 was the construction of bridges, for which timber had to be cut and hauled from the jungle to the site. Before actual use, the logs had to be trimmed, shaped and made ready for pile-driving.

A rough bamboo frame would be erected, holes dug and the poles then placed in position. The pile-driver differed at various bridges, some were heavy iron or wood, but the actual work was similar. A team would raise the driver to about ten or more feet, let it go and crash down onto the head of the pole.

It was a monotonous job and very hard work; the pull and drop team chanted a variety of words in Aussie language instead of the Ichi-nie-san-sie Japanese counting invariably demanded. At (in explanation) 'one' the ropes would be pulled taut, 'two' and 'three' the weight (called a monkey) would be raised. On 'four' it would be let go.

On the average, 24 piles were driven on each shift and that was a physically draining task, which included the procurement of the ultimate pile from the jungle and the resultant trimming and shaping.

Had the workers been in reasonable health, fed well and not driven like work-horses, maybe the labour would not have taken so much out of them. But on starvation rations, long hours, belted and bashed, it was a heartbreaking job.

Due to the light bamboo platform they had to work on, many accidents occurred when weakened lads fell to the ground. The swaying and rocking of the rough scaffolding was almost akin to a ship at sea.

Natives engaged on the same type of work developed a rhythmic tune that ultimately appeared to 'fit in' and the Australians, always able and willing to mimic, adopted it, but in no way did the maddened Korean guards stop their yelling of 'currah currah' or 'speedo' tactics. Even a momentary break resulted in mass bashing.

Earthwork gangs were given no let-up as the Japanese steadily increased their daily metreage to 1.7 per day. With much more work to do, the hours out on the job became longer and longer, food less and less.

A visiting Japanese general, who was responsible for the line building, was visibly annoyed at the lack of progress and let it be known only four months remained of the time allowed for total completion of the line.

No matter the cost in human life, the line had to be operative at the end of September, 1943.

He promised that once the task had been completed within the scheduled time, all men would have a very long rest.

To meet that deadline the Nipponese increased the earthwork parties' tasks to 2 metres per man per day!

Despite strong representations by Force Commanders to the Japanese to increase rations and decrease labour requirements, there was no relenting. The POWs had to work until they dropped, as many did, some forever.

However, the Nipponese reckoned without Australian ingenuity, they found a way to confound the increased work tasks, long hours and lack of nutriments.

They realised the harder they worked the more they would be expected to do as the Japanese word was worthless; their many promises unfulfilled, their brutality a common factor with every one of them. So, the workers decided on implementing the 'Government Stroke' tactic, go-slow. The first instalment a sit-down strike; caring less for the result.

On the first day of the new plan and at the hour they would have finished, 7.00 p.m., only about half of the demanded work had been completed.

The Japanese were astounded; they questioned the officers who told them the men were too weakened by lack of food, hard work and long hours. It was a physical impossibility for any of them to carry on under the conditions imposed.

They requested the men be returned to camp.

The answer. 'Many mans will collect bamboo, light fires and work until they all finish their 2 metres of earth removal.'

What the guards failed to observe was quite a few of the workers had sought solace in the jungle and were sound asleep. Skeleton crews kept working. The latter, known as the 'scrub turkeys', gave the impression the whole party was struggling to complete the day's work task.

For the next two weeks this practice continued and the Nipponese were at a loss to understand why less work has been completed at 2 metres per shift, as against the former 1.7 metre task.

Bridge gangs were also working at night but were not dependent on bamboo for illumination. They had electric light supplied by a power plant and a hand-winding generator. The latter, one of the hardest jobs devised by man.

There was far too much light at bridge-building sites to put on 'scrub turkey' act, but the 'go-slow' was definitely on.

The Japanese required specialists in various capacities, truck drivers, mechanics, etc., and those with the qualifications volunteered well-knowing if they did not do so compulsion would result.

Additionally, and that was the main reason, they were aware the monsoon season was about to start and the conveyance of foodstuffs from the Base Camp, Thanbyuzayat, to the jungle camps would be in jeopardy if the Nipponese lacked the vehicles to transport beyond the limit of the railway line.

With the foundation of the line complete to near the 26 kilo camp No. 1 Mobile Force (combination of Anderson and Williams Forces) was formed to lay sleepers and steel rails and join them with fishplates and dog spikes. Ballasting was also to be part of their task.

The death rate at the 75 kilo camp began to escalate as the Medical Officers had nothing in the way of drugs or medicines of any kind. It was at this camp Lt. Col. Coates, AAMC, fell victim to scrub typhus and was completely immobilised. He was subsequently transferred to the 55 kilo hospital as Chief Medical Officer. (He was taken there on a stretcher and for the first couple of weeks did his rounds the same way, on a stretcher.)

Some three weeks prior to the move to the notorious 105 kilometre (Ankanan) camp, native labourers and their families arrived to work as labourers on the railroad construction. They, too, were in a bad way as they had no doctor with them, and they either recovered from the diseases they suffered, or died. The latter happened to many of them. Sometimes seven to eight bodies would be found in between huts. Their plight was sickening, and a further indictment on Nipponese behaviour.

During April occasional thunderstorms swept the area and did cause quite a bit of inconvenience, as prisoners of war were required to continue toiling irrespective of weather conditions. The parched ground soon absorbed the rainwater and prevented mud piles, luckily for the workers.

The advance party, fittest of personnel, moved from the 75 kilo camp on 13 May, 1943. They were force-marched 32 kilometres (actually over 40 due to the route taken by the Nipponese) to their last camp in Burma, Ankanan.

The month of May, 1943, heralded the approach of the rainy season, a period all POWs dreaded but knew they would have to endure. To have to work hard in dry weather is much easier than when tropical monsoon rains make life an absolute misery, but as far as the Japanese were concerned, the work as demanded by the Emperor—or so the Nipponese camp commanders claimed—had to be carried out, regardless of the weather. Cost in human life did not matter!

On the 22nd of that month the wind sighing through the trees gave way to an unbelievable deluge of rain. For the next 72 hours it teemed at an alarming rate. There was no let-up of either ravages, work or the relentless downpour.

Rather than the Japanese agreeing to a lessening of the work contract they increased their demands from 2 metres per man up to, within a few days, 2.8

metres; not just of earth, but shovels and bags of mud! Backs of the beleaguered workers gave under the enormous strain until, in sheer exhaustion, they fell forward, sideways or backwards as nature dictated they should.

When that happened, barbarism took over and the thuds of booted feet against gaunt bodies would be heard above the roar of the incessant downpour of water from the leadened skies. How it was possible one human being could so torture fragile bodies as did those fiendish guards, is beyond belief. But they did, and obviously relished it.

Many an unspoken thought of the workers was: 'If there is a God above, why are we made to carry the burden now being imposed upon us?'

In moments of great stress, be it from pain, fatigue, hunger or punishment, one is more likely to seek succour from someone 'up there' than at any other time.

But on that stretch of railroad, many felt the protection men of religion preached was theirs if they sought it, had filtered away as the rain came tumbling down, the guards' waddies, rifle butts or heavy footwear, bashed their skeleton bodies.

There is supposed to be a limit to human endurance but on that Japanese building project, it did not appear to apply. Strong, healthy men would have undoubtedly given up outside POW camp requirements, but not on the Burma-Thai railroad mammoth undertaking; the emaciated prisoners were driven far beyond believed human endurance to the point where Nipponese utterances proved to be only too correct—'We will build this railway over the bodies of prisoners of war.'

The rain, in its fury, converted tiny watercourses into raging torrents against which tired, weakened men fought nature as they dug into mountain slopes. The extended work contract demanded by the Nipponese meant the minimum of 2.8 metres of thick, black mud, actually became 3.2 metres per man!

The sting of rain upon bared bodies (very few had more than a bedraggled hat and a G-string) was like hundreds of needles being pressed into their skin. That feeling, in itself, was an irritant without having to achieve impossible tasks.

An example of the inhumanity of the Japanese was the sight of a body of Nipponese troops, loaded down with full equipment, forced to march under appalling conditions en route to the Burma Front. They had to pull carts filled to the plimsoll with food and ammunition. Additionally, mountain guns had to be manhandled out of very deep mud, miles of it.

To the prisoners of war, watching with grim satisfaction, it was proof positive, the Japanese were devoid of human feeling; they meted out treatment to their own as they did those who had the misfortune to be under their dominance. They actually witnessed distressed troops getting kicked in the face, and other parts of their bodies, when they fell in the mud as they slipped and scrambled to pull or push carts or guns.

As Officers and NCOs flailed their tiring troops, the first sight of the plight of the advancing front-line soldiers created a feeling of satisfaction but that then gave way as pity replaced pleasure at someone else's ill-treatment. The Japanese soldiery had two enemies; one from within and one from without.

May, 1943, was to be another terrific ordeal for the personnel of Ramsay, Black and Green Forces. A move to another camp was imminent, a thirty-kilometre march for the majority, after a long day of labour completing the last section of 75 kilo camp. No one actually knew the exact date, the Nipponese did, possibly, but as always, it was to come on sudden notice to the work-weary and weak prisoners of war.

As early as 4:30 p.m. on the 22nd, the guards ordered 'all mans back to their living area'. That was when the workers realised something unexpected was about to happen. And it did!

They hardly had time to cleanse their bodies, have a meal of plain boiled rice—or that is what it tasted like—and prepare for a tiring, winding hike to the new establishment; the ill-fated 105-kilo mark. They were told all gear had to be carried as only the most seriously ill men would be transported.

Thirty kilometres to walk in pitch black, almost impenetrable jungle was ahead of them. By direct route, it probably was only thirty ks, but by the twist and turning that was always the Nipponese way of finding their way, it was forty-two ks they had traversed when they eventually arrived.

The journey, for those who accomplished it, was an unforgettable one. Whilst the moon was out, the going over the rough surface which was bad enough, was not so bad, but as the rays disappeared a jet black void took over.

Few of the marchers had footwear of any kind and many slipped and slithered over the rock and slippery track. Dozens, drunk with weariness, loaded down with their own gear and sometimes that of two or more of their mates, finally collapsed and fell down embankments. Legs, feet and arms suffered cuts and bruise as fallen men scrambled up the banks, grabbing on to thorny bushes and knife-like rock outcroppings.

At the rear end of the group came the Boy Bastard, who delighted in scaring the wits out of the tailenders as he fired bullets above their heads. Some wondered if it was his aim in the darkness that saved their lives. There was no question that he would have shot them like he would a wild animal, if he could have actually got them in his sights. Perhaps a loss of the moonbeams acted as a saviour after all.

As the words, 'resting up ahead', filtered back to the stragglers, most drew sighs of infinite relief, then fell on the ground. Bone-weary, gaunt figures could be discerned in the eerie darkness sprawled grotesquely. To all appearances, they could be dead. In a way, they were, but fortunately in sleep. The 90-k stop was a heaven-sent blessing, but not for long.

Someone discovered dead bodies (Burmese natives) in a hut in a bit of a clearing. Almost immediately, the Japanese guards began screaming at everybody to get to their feet and move on. 'Cholera, cholera camp', was heard up and down the ranks.

Those dreaded words acted like magic on even the most wearied, and soon the struggle was on again. It seemed a never-ending drudge to put one foot in front of the other. Personal gear, now like a ton weight, was cast away. Anything to lighten the load. In that kilometre-long length of stumbling humanity, one was reminded of zombies that they had read about but could never visualise.

Just prior to the yelling and screaming after the decaying bodies had been found in a hut, one POW, wearied beyond measure, but denied rest, heard 'something' coming from the rear. He looked up just as a 'milky' moon struggled through the clouds to see a herd of wild elephants approaching the sleeping men.

For a few moments the blood in his veins turned to ice as he imagined the broken bodies that would be found after the huge animals had passed through. It seemed but seconds later the leading bull elephant curled his trunk high in the air, looked around, then, to his amazement, he saw the twenty-odd beasts step over the prostrate bodies like, in his words, mammoth ballet dancers.

It seemed as if time has stood still at that happening occurred and he wondered if it had been an optical illusion or, indeed, a fact. As he was not the only one to see the daintiness of those big, but marvellous jungle 'angels', he was convinced fate and nature go hand in hand. The combination was given proof time and time again as the railroad work went on.

When the going was tough and the logs hard to lift and place, the working elephants seemed to know when help was needed; they gave it!

*

The go-slow tactic described by Tony Clive was not the only form of resistance practiced by the POWs in their attempts to disrupt the progress of the rail and to allow the slave-labourers some respite. Lieutenant Johnny Kreckler describes the ploy of moving the pegs:

Prior to our arrival at a new work site, it was usual for the site to be surveyed and pegged out by engineers, commanded by a senior NCO or an officer. The subsequent work could then be supervised by an NCO and of course assisted by the guards.

With this knowledge I thought it reasonably safe to gamble on a lack of communication between the two groups: The engineers and the supervisors who followed to oversee the work. I put the proposition to the 30 to 40 POWs in the team. The plan was that I would change the pegs around, thereby reducing the overall workload. Each person would work as long as before but expend less effort to do so. The men agreed. The plan was to make it look as if each man was hard at it. If everyone acted out their parts we would all gain.

It worked well for six or seven weeks, until one morning we arrived to see a group of engineers commanded by a sergeant. We knew the 'Day of Judgment was nigh'. I realised it was 'nigh' when I picked myself up from the ground the second time! I was marched back to the camp; the men remained to continue the work. When I reported to Colonel Ramsay he was anything but the 'Gentleman George' he had been christened by the men. It was a very anxious wait in the guardhouse. It was dark and some time early in the morning when out of the darkness we heard singing, and then saw the men marching in formation with picks and shovels on the 'slope'. They were singing 'Oh Johnny! Oh Johnny!' The colonel put his hand on my shoulder and said, 'They don't blame you so why should I? Actually, you should be proud.' I was.

*

In *4000 Bowls of Rice* Linda Goetz Holmes noted that turning harassment into an act of absurdity was a more subtle form of defiance, and any opportunity was quickly seized. Cal Mitchell recalled one such an occasion, at Kanburi camp: 'One night in the pouring rain the Japs said there had to be another rollcall. We were all in our bunks, with clothes off. One man stood up and started to leave the hut naked. The others said, 'What are you doing going out like that?' He said, 'Why should I get my clothes wet, and have them soggy all night and into tomorrow?' We all decided that made a lot of sense, so 800 men went outside naked, and it was the Japs who got their clothes all wet.'

NO. 1 MOBILE FORCE
March–June, 1943

LIEUTENANT COLONEL J.M.Williams' diaries continued to record his and his troops' experiences after Williams and Anderson Forces had combined to form No. 1 Mobile Force.

Quite a few of the overworked lads were more than just furious at the Japanese insistence they be kept out so late (26th March), they threw their tools into fires, in utter disgust. They didn't arrive back into camp until after 2200 hours.

At 2300 hours Lt. Cols Anderson and Williams, and all other officers, were ordered to report to Camp Headquarters immediately. To ensure they did, a Japanese corporal, armed with a large stick, herded them along in no uncertain manner. He had no intention of carrying that waddy for his personal protection. It was to exhibit his expertise in wielding it against human bodies, irrespective of rank.

When they were all assembled they saw a Japanese Lieutenant, from the railroad building staff, standing on an elevated platform. He was raving and stamping his feet like some demented, caged animal.

As his rage increased he began to move backwards and forwards brandishing a loaded revolver. The two Australian Lieutenant Colonels stood a pace in front of the officers and the maniacal Nipponese appeared as if he was intent on shooting at least one of them. That thought was uppermost in their minds when it was explained to them that, if a Japanese soldier damaged a tool or tools, the penalty was he be shot, *immediately!*

The now-beside-himself Nipponese officer looked certain to carry out his implied threat, except for one thing. He had no idea what might happen were he to execute either of the two high-ranking Australian officers. It was possible he, too, would die if he committed a cold-blooded murder, just for the sake of a few burned tools.

The end came when he was calmed down and told it was not possible to know just exactly what did happen in the darkness. The explanation worked but he had a final say. If the same thing ever happened again, the actual culprit would not be singled out. All prisoners of war would be killed out of hand.

There was no question, he really meant it!

Any idea of a sleep that night went by the board; at 0300 hours Reveille, for the move to the 26 kilo camp, put rest out of the minds of all. Not only that, the late night events and the many possibilities arising therefrom had aroused everyone to the point there was an air of expectancy and uncertainty. It was a knife-edge situation.

The combined Forces were on parade and ready to move off at 0500 hours.

Forty minutes later they were on their way. For the first half of the march it was bad enough, but when it commenced to rain it became a virtual nightmare.

They were plodding along the newly formed railway track which soon became muddy. Crossing the timbered bridge was a terrific hazard. Just about everyone who ventured over the green, slippery timbers faced a fall of over 100 feet to the waters below. The pitch darkness was in no way a help. The moon was hidden behind rolling black clouds.

Dawn was breaking as the vanguard arrived at the 26 kilo camp. It was a bad one. The men had to be packed into the useable huts like sardines; there were no latrines and no tools available to dig any.

Every structure was in very bad disrepair, filthy and overrun with millions of flies. That night was one of the worst the troops had to put in. Bed bugs, hordes of them launching attacks on the numerous human bodies. They were ravenous, smelly and the overtired troops had hardly ever felt worse.

No sleep the previous night, now this torment. There was no way anyone could get rid of them. As fast as one was killed its relations retaliated. It was a night of misery!

Then came the rats. That was the last straw, so everyone thought. But then into the fray came more adversaries, fleas. The encampment was plagued with vermin beyond belief.

Hygiene being of the greatest importance, tools were 'acquired' and the digging of latrines began as fast as possible. The whole day was spent in an attempt to cleanse the area as soon as possible. A group of Dutchmen, about 150, moved out this morning (30th) and we learned they had been living on our rations— apparently delivered there in error—for the past three days. The locals had no food, until they, somehow, latched on to what should have been ours.

Luckily for us our canteen supplies had not been exhausted and we were able to provide the troops with meals, small but welcome just the same. Our larder carried us through for three days. How very fortunate we were, we learned when word came through that the POWs at the 75 kilo were completely out of rations of any kind.

Diarrhoea (100) cases reported today (31st) due, no doubt, to the presence of many flies. They are so bad one has to eat food as fast as possible to beat the maggot bearers to it. Making things worse—the open latrines. Until planking is available it is a problem we have to try and combat.

The food situation eased a little today when some nearby residents sold us quite a few eggs. The latter, and bananas, are like pieces of gold and many risks taken to acquire them. However, they, like everything else, are not always readily available. We have been ordered to make 100 men available for railway tasks.

The last of Ramsay Force, those who were too ill to travel with the main group to the 75 kilo camp, moved out today (1st April). In normal circumstances it would have been a fun day. Unfortunately, there is little revelry left in any of the POWs and even knowledge of the actual date would evade the majority. For them it is a case of day follows night, irrespective of the calendar specifics.

Every available man is flat out today on camp hygiene; more latrines have been dug, but lack covering. Some canteen goods arrived and will be on sale tomorrow. In the case of sugar there was enough to supply ½ lb per man. However, as the prices have doubled (inflation is high) our purchasing ability has been considerably reduced.

Saturday, 3.4.43: Only 50 men required on the railway job, the remainder are building grease traps, pits and latrines. The fly menace not so bad; the swatters are gaining control. Despite every precaution possible an outbreak of dysentery has occurred and more cases being reported daily. A few more canteen goods delivered.

A cattle party set off with 20 cows today for the 45 kilo camp. One was so poor it fell and was unable to get to its feet again. One of the party stayed with the animal (they wanted to save it if possible) at the 40 kilo peg.

When the droving group returned there was no sign of the man or beast. Lieut. Naito, camp commander, was very worried and questioned all officers concerned, as well as Williams Force Commander. At 1030 hours a lorry was made available and a search commenced to find both the missing man and the debilitated yak. Surprisingly, a wide sweep of the area revealed nothing; the animal and its keeper had completely vanished.

At 0200 hours word was received of the arrival at the 45 kilo camp of the lad, Lucas. He had coaxed the stricken cow along until he had, by an unfrequented track, been able to complete the delivery. On his return to camp Naito rewarded him with three rupees. By using his bushcraft knowledge he had worked out a short cut to his objective. And, was determined his mates at the 45 kilo camp would not be done out of meat on the hoof.

Today (4th) the new rail line reached this camp (26k) and Thanbyuzayat can now be served by an actual railway. The Burma-Thai railway is now fast becoming the real thing.

An unexpected influx of 520 American and British troops arrived today and are to take up occupation. When the Nipponese were told there was insufficient room, the bland reply was, 'Make room'. Many are now forced to sleep out in the open. If it rains it will not be difficult to imagine the crush there will be in the already overcrowded huts. To make things worse, the watercourse has dried up.

Our water supply ran out completely at 1600 hours. Our only possible salvation will be if the soaks can produce water. If they don't, our situation will be desperate.

All but sick men are required on the line job and it is tough going in the extreme heat. The workers are losing fluid as fast as they consume the allowed ration. A few more items arrived for the canteen, the demand will probably exceed the supply.

Wednesday, 7.4.43: The Japanese demand for all animal hides to be sent to base has ruined all our chances of repairing footwear. It is said the prisoners of war are to be paid all profits after sale. That was a 'pie in the sky' statement. We have lost both ways, the use of the hides and any monies received when they are sold.

In accordance with the Nipponese order the butcher stakes out the wet hides near the camp headquarters prior to their being transported to base.

The staked hides incurred hurt to the Nipponese feelings. To have them (the hides) in their immediate vicinity was, to them, an insult. Result, a punishment. We are to be denied any further supplies of animals. Naito has spoken! We are back to a meatless diet from now on.

The Nipponese are demanding more and more workers; they are questioning the veracity of the sick parades. Naito was told he must expect illness within the ranks of the troops whose only food is pie melon. He authorised the killing of three lean animals today (8th).

Tomorrow is to be a big day; the Japanese General, Commander of all prisoners of war in Burma and Thailand, is due to inspect the camp and inhabitants.

Prior to his arrival the troops were assembled, in proper formation, outside the Nipponese Headquarters. He came, had a quick look, made no comment and departed. Lt. Col. Y. Nagatomo and Brigadier A.L. Varley accompanied him. Our camp was reasonably, under the circumstances, clean.

The men he inspected stood tall and straight, ill clad they may have been, but true soldiers, and proud Australians, every one of them.

Very late evening meal due to the Nipponese determination to keep the workers out on the job as long as they possibly can; some came in at 2030 hours. the remainder about one hour later. Dysentery is rife in the camp. No medicines or drugs available. So we are back to the old fashioned medication—crushed charcoal, fast for two days.

The rain came today (11th) and there was no work demand by the Japanese. All those who had been slaving day after day took advantage of the unexpected yasumi and really spine-bashed. They deserved the respite. The downpour settled our immediate water problem.

Only showers today (12th) and it was work as usual; one of our officers badly beaten up due to a probable misunderstanding. A guard ordered him to move his men to a point 9 metres away. No sooner had he carried out the order when another 'slap happy' guard came, disbelieved what the officer said, and did him over.

Lieut. Barker corralled a water buffalo and our butcher boy carried out an immediate operation, which resulted in the troops having a taste of meat after a very long time. The yak issue (when we get it) is always so small, by the time what meat there is on the beast is added to the rice its identity is lost.

The unwarranted and cruel beating up of the officer out on the line job today (12th) reported to the camp commander by Lt. Col. Anderson, but it is highly unlikely that any action will be taken against the guard responsible; there seldom is.

The heavens opened up again today (13th) and our water supply is again assured. The Japanese issued everyone with another card which we must complete, in ink, within 24 hours. As we are not permitted writing materials of any type or quantity, how we can comply with the directive is going to prove difficult!

The particulars they require are: name, nationality, rank, staff duty, place of capture, parents' names, age, army number, unit, date of capture, occupation, address, next-of-kin and a short history of life!

Enough eggs delivered to the canteen to supply one to every man but as our pay has not arrived, credit must be extended to all purchasers. Men out on the line job are not returning to camp until after 2100 hours. The only possibility of a rest day depends on the weather; heavy rain, remain in camp. (A change in policy from the early stages of railway foundationing.)

A buffalo sighted today (15th) and a party was sent out to bring it into camp. No ropes issued, rifles and ammunition denied. Five animals found but catching them with bare hands proved impossible. It was very disheartening to see all that food on the hoof take off into the jungle. The only good thing for the day was the arrival of pay for the workers.

Friday, 16.4.43: Lieut. Naito checked over the sick men today and ordered approximately forty of them out to work. Simply contrariness of Naito's part. The Engineers had too many on the railway then and sent fifty back to camp.

Naito, the confirmed alcoholic, is drunk every night and the result is, everyone ordered out on parade at all hours for no apparent reason.

Heavy rain pouring today (17th) resulting in a rapid change in policy—'men must work'. Some very badly made boots, local manufacture, arrived and will be distributed despite their faults. At least some of the lads will have foot protection.

The propaganda Unit is putting on a cinema show for us, no doubt a repetition of the one shown at Thanbyuzayat; three shorts (one of general interest, one about Tokyo and the third depicted Japanese in song).

The main film was, as expected, the attack on Pearl Harbour and the sinking of the HMAS *Prince of Wales* and *Repulse*. The captive audience was somewhat polite; not the enthusiastic one the Nips may have hoped for. Anyhow, it broke the monotony, if nothing else.

A case of smallpox reported today; the patient isolated and all known contacts, ten, separated from the main body of troops. The Japanese Medical Officer ordered immediate vaccinations to prevent spread of the dread disease. As the vaccine was made available everyone in the camp willingly accepted the needle.

Unfortunately the day was to end in an unexpected way, 20 so-called fit men taken out for a full night shift. They returned to camp, had a meal and were ordered back on to the job, working until 2230 hours. Almost 24 hours with only a short meal break.

No change in the condition of the smallpox victim and the contacts are still in isolation. A very necessary precaution as an epidemic could wipe out everyone.

No question the troops are steadily losing weight; the lack of proper foodstuffs and the constancy of work is surely taking its toll. The ill-made footwear is so rough the wearers are becoming crippled by them. The only reason they are persevering with them is in the hope the wearing may eventually force the boots to assume the fitting of their feet; a rather forlorn hope, they were not craftsmen who made them.

Another late night (19th) for the line workers, came in at 2330 hours and the Japanese claim they are treating us well. We are forced to live in native huts full of bugs, fleas and rats. The men are crammed into a space of 10 x 12 feet, sleeping on bamboo poles; the atap roof leaks like a sieve, resulting in wet blankets (that is the one thin-as-tissue blanket per man), very few have clothing. The blanketed lads wrap themselves in the thin article hoping against hope for some measure of warmth, despite the dampness and the flimsy body cover. The daily working conditions are worsening as a 15 hours shift appears to be what the Nipponese consider as a normal day. Rest days seem to be but memories. Meals consist, in the main, of pie melon water sometimes flavoured with a little, very little, meat, no tea, and no means of providing the troops with boiled water so essential in these areas to prevent disease.

The vexed question of medical supplies is never far from one's mind; the lack of them is a direct threat to life. All that for a miserable pittance of 25 cents per day, just enough to purchase two eggs at a cost of 12 cents each. We have to suffer all this, like it or not.

Wednesday, 20.4.43: The Nipponese have relented a little. The workers have been allowed a four hours rest, 0830 to 1230 hours. They are so physically drained they have flopped onto their bed spaces and fallen asleep almost before they hit the bamboo slats. There is hardly a sound in the camp.

Right on 1230 hours, the overtired workers trudged back on to the job that saps their strength so severely. They came back in at 2330 hours. Seven and a half hours later they wended their way back to that never-ending back-breaking labour that is making zombies out of the once-healthy troops.

One of the worst aspects of long hours of work and little rest is the determined demand of the Nipponese to make each man do a one-hour tour of sentry duty every night. Tired and listless, they do it in the interest of their mates. If one fails to remain awake all hell breaks loose. How any of them, wearied as they are, can actually keep their blurred eyes open for that period is a wonder.

We were able to buy 200 rupees of beans and they went straight into the cookhouse. Our 20 cents donation per man from the Red Cross Funds has now ceased. Instead, the amount is now directed to the 30 kilo hospital. The inmates there are in dire need and what that money can purchase may save lives.

A guard who is to go to base today (21st) has offered bring back canteen supplies. Wary of what happened on an earlier occasion we agreed, providing sugar and cigars were available at a given price. If not, leave the goods behind.

When he returned he had 40 pineapples for which he demanded one rupee each. We subsequently learned he paid 60 cents for each piece of fruit. There was nothing we could do but pay up, even though it was outright robbery. The Japanese are out and out black marketeers. Ned Kelly was a gentleman compared to them.

Another very long day for our railway workers, out at dawn and worked throughout the day, and half the night, in pouring rain. They returned to camp at 2330 hours.

Came in contact with a mobile trader today (22nd) and he sold us a few blocks of sugar, which went into the canteen. Whilst the deal was going through every guard who was near demanded, and received, a rake-off.

A very dangerous situation developed today for Captain Drower, our interpreter. Lieut. Naito ordered he attend his (Naito's) office. But, due to tropical ulcers on his legs, he was unable to answer the summons. A clearly annoyed Naito called for the pay sheets, saw that Drower was marked as fit for duty and took immediate action.

The obviously near-crippled officer was forced to proceed to the smallpox compound where he was made to get in under the net covering a confirmed smallpox patient

Naito made no bones about his intentions as he stood over the bewildered interpreter with the added support of a guard, bayonet fixed and ready for action. Naito told Drower he was to stay there indefinitely. To make absolutely certain the Captain did as he was told Naito stationed the guard at the door of the hut, to ensure Drower did not attempt to crawl out from under the mosquito netting.

Still not satisfied, he decided that all Drower's belongings be put to the torch. He personally supervised the guard he had ordered to complete the destroying of every item Drower owned. The guard, to his credit, endeavoured, with the aid of one of the Medical Officers, to salvage some of the gear from the fire. Naito, quick as a flash, saw what was happening and bashed the Medical Officer, Captain Rowley Richards; the guard escaped punishment.

More bad news today, informed our workers would not be returning until 0300 hours and a meal has to be taken out to them. They were fed and it was back to the hazardous job of laying sleepers and rails. They worked under frightful conditions; showery and cold. Their clothing consisted, in the main, of just G-strings.

Friday, 23.4.43: The men had worked all night under similar conditions as applied last night, except neither food nor drinking water made available. They have been ordered to return to work at 1500 hours.

The workers who had returned to camp at 0730 hours today (24th) have been ordered to prepare for a move to the 45 kilo camp. At 0845 hours instructions came for the proposed movement to commence at 0930 hours, not less than 150 to be prepared to entrain at that hour. Kitchen equipment, 3 kwalis and two bags of rice, plus some buckets, were loaded but it was a very tight fit.

As was usual, the Japanese never commenced anything on time. The train did not leave until 1015 hours and it took some four hours to travel 5 kilometres. The group detrained at about 1230 hours and entered one of the filthiest huts they had ever encountered. The previous occupants had been natives. Night soil was everywhere, bugs came out in their millions.

The cooks lost no time preparing a meal of rice, nothing to go with it except boiled water. At 2100 hours Lt. Col. Anderson and Lieut. Naito arrived as the men were endeavouring to set up a decent camp; preparations had to be made for the housing of the remainder of the combined Forces due to arrive late that night; they came in the next day. Housing was the great problem and the troops were packed 200 to a hut, except in the case of two where they had to accommodate 300 each.

No-one had time to eradicate the swarms of bed bugs and they were in every piece of cloth or clothing. One lad, tiring of trying to brush them off, preferred like others, to lay out in the rain rather than suffer the bites of the disgusting vermin.

*

Captain Rowley Richards, who had replaced Lt. Col. Eadie (Williams Force Medical Officer) when No. 1 Mobile Force was formed, worked himself almost to a standstill in his determination to keep his charges not only alive, but as well as it was humanly possible without drugs or medicines.

He walked many miles up and down the line making certain any medical need could be administered within his capacity and province, despite the opposition he met with from the Japanese and Korean guards.

His name is legendary amongst all prisoners of war who served on and survived the Burma-Thailand railway project, particularly those who came under his immediate care.

*

Sunday, 25.4.43: One hour after the arrival of Major Meagher and the balance of No. 1 Mobile Group at the 45 kilo camp, the men had settled in, but were given no grace by the Japanese. At 1300 hours they were back on the line job, ballasting, laying sleepers and rails. They had spent the previous night out in the open parade ground. The advance party of line workers had been unloading sleepers practically all night.

The work party that had returned to camp at 2300 hours today (26th) were ordered out again at 0900 hours. Strong protests as to the long hours the men were being forced to put in met with little response, except that the number of workers had to be increased.

At 1700 hours, Yamanoto, a guard, inspected the sick lads, took the names of about 75 and ordered them out to work. Those obviously unfit men had to carry sleepers until 0500 hours next morning. They were not even allowed a few minutes break; they were driven like slaves on a task even the fittest men would have found daunting.

Two of the worst affected collapsed and the whole group finished up in the camp hospital. ·

Lt. Col. Anderson suffered for his inability to submit the number that would be available for work the next day. Due to the precarious state of health of all the men, it was almost an impossibility to forecast who would be capable of undertaking heavy work 24 hours ahead. As far as Lieut. Naito was concerned that was merely an excuse. The guards tied Anderson's hands behind his back and almost threw him into the guardhouse.

Williams Force Commander sought audience with Naito and explained how difficult it was to correctly prepare figures, as it could only be assumed what men would be capable of carrying out the heavy labour involved in sleeper and rail laying.

Naito, who could converse in English quite well, gave an assurance Anderson would be released the next day. 'However,' he said, 'he is a very bad man.'

The following morning (27th) 250 men marched out to work at 0900 hours and an additional 420 left camp for the work site at 1300 hours. No-one could hazard a guess as to what time either party would be back at their quarters.

Rations were delivered last night; they consisted of pie melons and some pumpkins. As usual, the Nipponese confiscated what they wanted irrespective of the fact they were the food issues for the Mobile Group. As expected, they took the pumpkins despite all objections lodged. Their contempt for the needs of the prisoners of war was exemplified in their attitude concerning the health and welfare of the troops they guarded, bashed, starved and treated like animals.

The workers streamed back into camp at 2100 hours, had a meal and quickly 'hit the sack'. They were completely worn out and, many, past caring. It was their first real rest in four days and nights.

The one compensation in this camp is the river, and the Japanese permitted—providing it did not interfere with work requirements—the men an occasional swim. Their very first since becoming prisoners of war. It was a luxury few believed would be allowed them.

All 'fit' men sent out to work at 0830 hours and they faced hard tasks before they would be returning to camp that night or next day; 28 April, 1943, was not going to be an easy day for the members of No. 1 Mobile Force.

Lt. Col. Anderson and Captain Fitzsimmons (USA) were ordered to report to the base camp, Thanbyuzayat, for a conference. They had no prior notice as to what it was all about and were quite puzzled as to the reason or urgency.

Every man who can do even the lightest of work is flat out at the present time endeavouring to cleanse this filthy camp. Everyone is aware of the tremendous importance of maximum hygiene. Their very lives, to a large extent, depends on it. Hence their determination. The line-laying workers did not get back until 2030 hours.

Today (29th) two of our lads were caught trading with a Burmese in the local village. Two more were apprehended because their breath smelled of brandy. The four of them were paraded to the camp commander, Sgt Shimojo. It was only too evident they were facing severe penalties, the bashing had already commenced when Lt. Col. Williams intervened.

The ill-treatment came to a sudden stop but the Nipponese had not finished by any means; they turned their attention to the Australian officer. He was commanded to stand to attention for two hours whilst the enraged Shimojo berated him.

At 1230 hours the line-laying party went out to work and returned at 2045 hours; one of the shortest shifts they had had for a very long time. Whilst they had to complete a heavy job in searing heat the reduced hours made it all worthwhile. The same hours will apply tomorrow.

The food situation is a bit grim today (30th) as our expected ration issue did not materialise. To worsen our position in the food line, the Japanese are taking our rations to supplement their own. Any attempt to prevent acquisition ends up in a bashing for someone, irrespective of rank or status.

One of our lads on the line party, A.S. Mills, was brutally beaten up today. His crime, accused of driving a dog spike into a sleeper on an angle. The alleged incident was supposed to have occurred at 1300 hours.

The eagle eyes of the Japanese ganger perceived the happening and refused to acknowledge it as an accident. (Obviously the hole had been bored incorrectly. It happened many times as the boys on the blunt augurs tried desperately to bore straight. They knew to fail to do so meant one of their mates would ultimately suffer, as Mills did.)

So as not to 'lose face' the ganger reported the incident to the Nipponese Officer, but lied when he said Mills had struck him. The Officer closed his fist and savagely hit Mills on the jaw, twice.

Lieut. Burgess, who was in charge of the kumi, and who was nearby when the ganger committed the act of assault, did, in an endeavour to defuse the issue, explain it all resulted from the language problem.

The Nipponese accepted the explanation admitting there was great deal of difficulty. However, should any such further incident occur, it was to be reported to him immediately.

Throughout the rest of the afternoon Mills was belted by every Japanese who went past him. When they returned to camp the two guards took Mills, Lieut. Burgess and Lieut. Staples into the jungle and repeatedly hit Mills about his face and chin with rifle butts in order to force him to say he had, in fact, struck the line ganger. When he refused they ordered the two Australian officers to get back to camp. The menace of the two loaded rifles was something they could not ignore.

They had only moved a few paces when they heard a rifle shot, turned and saw Mills was still on his feet and realised the shot had been fired over his head. They demanded Mills be allowed to accompany them back to camp.

The officers stood their ground and escorted Mills back into camp and when his injuries were examined by Captain Rowley Richards, he diagnosed a fractured jaw and abrasions. Mills was admitted to the camp hospital immediately.

*

When the facts were related to Lieutenant Colonel Williams he acquainted the camp commander of his intention to forward a submission to the base camp commander. Shimojo, the cur that he was, refused to listen to Williams, saying he had heard all about it, but he did agree Mills should be transferred to the 30 kilo hospital as soon as possible, but not immediately; the next day.

Mills was taken away at 1030 hours the following morning and Williams presented Shimojo with a written report. When he read about a shot being fired over Mills' head, he flatly refused to accept the report or send it to base.

Shimojo then passed judgment on the two men whose breath, it was alleged, smelt of brandy. Without actually seeing either, he pronounced sentence—thirty days each in detention, a similar punishment on one of the men caught trading.

*

Sunday, 2.5.43: The line party that went out to work at 0900 hours did not return to camp until 2100 hours. Major Meagher and Sergeant Black left for the base today and 180 sick troops sent to the 30 kilo hospital. Church service at 2100 hours.

Our ration problem is steadily worsening, no sign of the arrival of any cattle; vegetables now in very short supply. Our breakfast is a plain rice meal. And, not too much of that.

The American and British POWs marched out to the 14 kilo camp today and a warning issued of the impending movement of 300 Dutch. They, it is reported, will pass through here tomorrow and will have to be fed. Rice, the only food available.

Lt. Col. G. Ramsay and Lt. Col. Miller, both from 105 kilo camp, passed through here today after attending a propaganda film at Thanbyuzayat. They were disgusted at the hypocrisy of the Japanese making a film portraying a well equipped hospital; a dispensary filled with bottles of medicines and just about everything else needed to tend the sick and suffering prisoners of war. It was, to use Ramsay's word, a sickening affair.

They even had a lad sitting up in a bed allegedly reading a letter from home. That was pretty tough, rubbing it in like that, considering not one POW has received any news from home at all.

There is very grave doubt the cards filled in by the troops have left Thanbyuzayat yet. And, as regards to that film, so much footage was taken of faked scenes the eventual viewers will, no doubt, believe the prisoners of war are in a 'country club' atmosphere.

Lt. Col. Anderson returned from his wasted visit to the Base camp; the conference he was called to attend, was not held. He, too, was exasperated at what went on, propaganda-wise, at Base.

Five minutes' notices was given to prepare 100 men to pack and be ready to move back to the 30 kilo camp, where a railway siding was to be built, but they took longer and were fed a meal before boarding a train.

Some cattle arrived today (5th); two were killed and approximately 230 lbs of meat became available to feed to 1,100 men. It was the first taste of meat for over a week.

The native drovers claim they lost five animals on the trip and that means we have one cow left—it will be killed tomorrow—out of the eight we were supposed to receive. They, the natives, have a lot in common with the Nipponese, out and out racketeers.

This was exemplified when the Camp Commandant demanded 93 rupees commission on goods purchased for the canteen, and another payment of 20 rupees to the Nipponese quartermaster, for watching over our interests!

Australian bushrangers of old were innocents in the field of robbery by comparison. The Nips, and natives, of this jungle area are professionals in the art of theft by menace and intimidation.

The railway party went out at 1230 hours today and are not expected back before 2130 hours. A pleasant surprise, managed to catch a couple of tiny bream from the river. As some eggs arrived for the canteen (15 cents each, 10 at Base) the combination was indeed quite tasty.

Today (6th) is going to be a tough one on the line-laying team; they are expected, and will no doubt have to, make up for the time lost awaiting supplies, sleepers and rails. It proved to be just as tough as expected, they didn't return to camp until just on midnight (Tokyo time). They were completely dead-beat. The engineers had had their worth of those lads on the long shift of nearly 15 hours duration.

Been advised the 30 kilo (Retpu) hospital camp is closing down and 40 of the patients will have to be bedded down here, prior to moving on to the 75 kilo camp.

Heavy and consistent rain today (7th) but that means nothing to the Nipponese again. 'Men must work' irrespective of weather conditions. The despised line has to go through!

The Dutch group, 300, are to stay here overnight. That means the loss of one meal. We have one good meal per day, providing the ingredients are available, rice and stew. A second one is of vegetable water and rice; third one (if possible), rice only.

Whenever a party passed through here it means they have to be fed at the expense of our larder. At no time is there sufficient to have three meals a day if hundreds more men come into the camp. It is our lads who miss out.

The Camp Commandant has drastically cut our meat ration, one yak, thin as it may be, has to provide for 1,350 men. By the time it hits the dixies the taste of meat has degenerated to such an extent, it is odds-on few know there has been a meat additive. The Commandant, however, knows no limit for himself. His ration is 15 lbs, yet he seeks more.

The propaganda is on again! The workers have been ordered to don their non-existent shirts and shorts. They are to be photographed laying the line. Unless a miracle occurs, any audience who may view the finished film will only see G-stringed POWs, thin as a match with wood scraped off, slaving in zombie fashion. Shirts and shorts! Memories!

*

Saturday, 8 May 1943 marked the beginning of many hours of extreme torture for Lieutenant Colonel Williams. It all began when he was ordered to provide the film crew with a bugler. He told the Japanese quartermaster he would do so when the workers returned to camp, which would be somewhere in the vicinity of 2300 hours, as the bugler was out at work. As the Jap QM did not appear to understand, he repeated the information. In addition, and as a precaution, he informed the cameraman. Neither he nor the crew seemed to mind and the matter was left at that.

At 2200 hours they called for the bugler and he again explained that the soldier they wanted was out on the line. The sergeant put on a real act. He told Lieutenant Colonel Anderson he was to remember where every one of 600 men was twenty-four hours a day, and that the same applied to Williams, who had 887 under his command.

When Williams told the sergeant his office staff had been made aware of the absence of the man required, due to their work requirements, he was called a liar. In order to confirm the fact that he had provided the correct information, Williams told the Sergeant the cameraman had heard him tell the quartermaster.

This enraged the camp commandant who again accused Williams of lying and ordered him to *stand to attention in front of the guardhouse for three days!* Punishment to begin immediately.

He was then marched, under guard, to the standing point at 2359 hours and he remained there until 0200 hours when he was told if he was prepared to apologise to the sergeant (the camp commandant) he could retire to his bed. As he had done nothing wrong, he refused, telling them it was their own fault entirely.

During the ensuing twenty-four hours they made many similar attempts but all to no avail. By that time the stoical Australian officer began to feel the effects of his inability to even move. His feet were swollen, his body ached all over. He was refused food or drink, except for one mug of broth someone gave him during his ordeal. At 1900 hours heavy rain started to fall but he was refused the cover of a cape or permission to move under the verandah.

By that time his mind was in a whirl, he was wet through, his strength taxed to the limit. But, despite the pain in every muscle of his body, no-one could break his determination. He was the epitome of courage, far beyond any call of duty!

Finally, after twenty-six and a half hours of agony, he was released.

At 0820 hours on 9 May, five hours and fifty minutes after his release from his traumatic experience (one which few thought he would survive), the officer whose spirit and strength was never broken, led a party of 350 (advance group) men onto the train that was to take them to the 61 kilo camp.

En route the train collided with a motor lorry and a leg of one of the guards was broken. They arrived at their destination at 1100 hours.

As was usual, they entered an area of filth and vermin. It was the worst camp they had ever encountered, as Williams' diary recorded:

As they entered the huts millions of flies greeted them. The filth of the whole area was unbelievable. Every part of the encampment had been fouled. The latrines were in a disgraceful state.

An immediate clean-up was a necessity and the troops lost no time in entering into another phase of living areas to be made livable. Two dying natives were found; they both expired shortly afterwards. Six huts had to be completely cleaned out, one was taken over for the housing of the guards and the Japanese staff.

No-one minded the Nipponese occupying that particular building as it had been used by natives who had contracted smallpox. In fact, one dying from that dreaded disease was actually an occupant of the hut at the time the men set to, to turn it into the Japanese camp quarters.

There were other pock-marked natives, covered in human excreta, under the hut. Later that day the balance of No. 1 Mobile Force arrived, plus 30 kilo hospital patients and staff who were returning to camp. They had been discharged and considered fit to work. No rations were delivered.

The Japanese were totally devoid of feeling, either to the work rate or living conditions of the prisoners of war. Human decency should have dictated that the total cleansing of a disease-ridden encampment must have first priority. Not so; the troops were no sooner in their huts than a demand came for 110 workers, immediately. There was a rail washout in the vicinity of the area. Hygiene, as far as they were concerned, was of secondary importance. Request, as a health necessity, refused.

The next day (10th) was to be a hard one for the 600 workers who had to toil in pouring rain, ballasting, laying sleepers and rails. The Mobile Force faced one of the toughest jobs in the construction of the link, Thanbyuzayat to Thailand. The moment the material arrived the 'speedo' was on. There was no let-up; long hours, the hardest of hard labour, on a ration issue so low it was no wonder the death rate was accelerated. The brutality of the Korean guards was, in part, cause of fatalities.

The huts they now occupied had mud, in some places a foot deep, down the centre of each one. There was not one waterproof hut. The atap was rotted and the now continuous rain just poured down on the occupants, their bed-spaces and the floor. They were being forced to live in abject misery. This, their second wet season, heralded the outbreak of cholera which Captain Rowley Richards and his dedicated staff fought relentlessly to combat. They worked selflessly, without the help of drugs.

*

While at the malaria-ravaged 40 kilo camp (Beke Taung), no quinine had been issued for over a month. The health of the Force—they were then ballasting the line—deteriorated rapidly. Sixteen died at the camp and eighty of the remainder subsequently passed away.

*

After the 600 of the work party had departed, those remaining in camp, despite the incessant rain, did their utmost to prepare latrines, constructed the cookhouse and many were detailed to build housing for the Japanese. Some canteen supplies arrived; the Nipponese purloined 50% of what came in.

The whole of Anderson Force was inoculated against cholera and during the day the Japanese Medical Officer reported in, saw the condition of the camp and immediately cancelled visits to the area by Nipponese troops.

*

The fact that the Nipponese medico was of the opinion the camp conditions were too dangerous for the welfare of his troops, even if quite good enough for prisoners, showed just what a bad area it was. But as was generally known, prisoners of war were only two a penny.

*

The 600 workers who had been slogging hard all day returned to camp at 2100 hours, tired, listless and hungry. There was little to satisfy the latter. What rations came in today (10th) were not worth two bob, 40 pie melons and nothing else. What a menu to offer men who had been working almost to a standstill in teeming rain.

As it was, we ended up with only 32 melons, eight were taken away as rations for the men at the 40 kilo camp. Late in the night four bags of onions came in and it did appear as if the taste buds of the troops were to be exercised at last. False hopes; when the bags were opened the odour was unbearable. Every onion was rotten.

The blitz against non-saluting is on again, even the sick copped a bashing for failure to pay deference to the Japanese and Korean guards. It was so bad Lt. Col. Anderson gave the lads a 'pep' talk.

An innovation in the newly set up canteen; sweet rice coffee at two cents per mug. It is such a change the liquid was rushed by eager buyers who had just enough money left to enjoy at least one mug full. The idea has caught on well and looks like being a huge success.

Another native died today (12th) and many more will be joining him soon as they will not follow proper hygiene. In any case, many prefer death to the treatment handed out to them by those who professed to have released them from 'bondage'.

A division of work today, part of the Force sent out at 0900 hours, the remainder are to be held back until 1230 hours. They will not return until 2300 hours.

All men required for re-weighing, a nasty habit of the Japanese as they assess rations in accordance with gross bodyweight of all camp inmates. The procedure went on until 0300 hours (next day).

Quite a number of the troops were dead to the world in needed slumber and had to be awakened to do the winning jockey act, weigh-in. When it was all over, it was announced the average weight loss amounted to one kilogram per man. Far too much in their debilitated state.

Rations for the next two days arrived today, two bags of beans, two bags of rotten onions; the whole supposed to feed 1,270 troops. Some good did come of it, we caught and killed a small yak cow.

The bad news—our new Camp Commander arrived!

The saluting blitz is still on; before anyone can attend to their ablutions they have to make seven salutes.

Ordered to send 187 men back to the 45 kilo camp and to take with them enough rations to last ten days. At that suggestion the men laughed. The Japanese failed to see the funny side of the almost impossible, and put on a great act. When the lads moved out, one-fifth of the kitchen gear went with them.

The native huts were in such a deplorable way the Nipponese ordered the Australians to clean them up. A dead native child was found and the Japanese wanted the natives to throw it, and one of their dying members onto a fire. They refused even though they were unmercifully bashed tor their failure to cooperate with their 'colleagues'.

Some canteen supplies received today (13th) at a staggering price, one bag of onions—risky buy as they could be rotten—for which the Nipponese demanded, and got, 100 rupees, eggs at 15 cents each, oil 43 rupees per kerosene tin. Hungry men will pay a 'King's ransom' for food.

May 14, 1943, is a day a lot of No. 1 Mobile Force will long remember. Exceptionally heavy rain, everyone and everything sopping wet, and the midday meal had to be taken out to the workers who were all supposed to be on the one task, a kilometre away. When the orderlies arrived there they found 110 at that point, the remainder had been sent back to the 45 kilo.

The guards told them to await the arrival of a train scheduled to pull into there at 1500 hours. No train and the men then ordered to carry the food to where the men were working, by that time 20 kilometres away.

The mess orderlies, all sick men, were dumbfounded; it was a good four hours march for *fit* men.

A complaint to the Commander did, this time, produce results, he arranged transport and the men were fed at 1800 hours as they were returning to camp.

Coffee stall now set up in canteen, 5 cents per mug; even contained a taste of sugar. The men relished it and 52 gallons were sold in a short time. It was good enough for some of the boys to think momentarily, they were back in Changi.

*

No-one could stop them dreaming. The very name of their first POW home flooded their weakened frames with memories, envy and the hope they would soon see something much more valuable than that 'country club' . . . Australia!

*

They were soon brought back to earth when told the rations that had been delivered that day consisted of four baskets of onions, nothing else. Today (15th—anniversary of the departure of the first POWs leaving Changi for an overseas destination), the Japanese Quartermaster made a deal, some salt in exchange for one bag of onions. It was quickly closed. However, the pleasure was to be short-lived; the Nipponese promptly seized a second lot, leaving the POWs with just two baskets to feed 1,270 hungry men! A little rice with a wisp of onion to ease the gnawing pangs of extreme hunger.

The Mobile Force workers faced one of their hardest, grimmest days on this 16th day of May. Out to work at 0830 hours and slogged and slaved until, worn out and weary, they were allowed to return at 2320 hours.

How it is possible they can carry on is a mystery no human can solve. The gaunt faces, skin and bone bodies personifying film-covered skeletons. Yet they survive! They work long and hard; have little rest and food.

Dysentery is rampant and on the increase. No wonder, this camp was a pestilence when the men moved in; dying natives, corpses in huts and surrounding areas, disease-carrying vermin infesting even the bamboo slats the men had to lie on. And no time allowed by the Japanese to thoroughly cleanse the whole, in order to provide proper hygiene.

As dedicated as Captain Rowley Richards and his limited staff may be, they cannot defy the inevitable without the control necessities now lacking.

Like the workers on the line, there is no limit to the hours the medical staff have to keep going to ensure, as far as humanly possible, all efforts are made to salvage as many lives as they can in this frightening situation.

Despair and disillusionment is with them every minute of the day; they know what is needed, and also know they will never get it. But, despite the almost impossible conditions, they do succeed in snatching many dying lads back from the very edge of the grave.

Some rations came in today (16th) that will have but little impact, just a few egg fruit. Also, and this is surprising, some goods for the canteen. If the Japanese can find items to put into the canteen, the very same that would normally comprise our ration issue, why is it we have to find money to purchase what we are supposed to get as food to live on under normal circumstances!

Actually, the answer is a simple one, their rake-off is 130 rupees from a 700 rupee turnover. Just their normal black-marketeering!

The ballasting of the line is as back-breaking a job as smashing the hewn rock to provide it. The workers at the 45 kilo camp have the job of loading it onto railway trucks and the men in this camp have to unload and spread it. Lunch leaves the kitchen at 1115 hours but due to the distance the mess orderlies have to carry it, some get it at 1400 hours, others somewhere between that and 1800 hours. The last to receive the food are the worst oft; it is stone cold and unappetising but they eat it, well-knowing they must do so to maintain enough strength to carry on, if they want to survive.

The workers had a long wait for their evening meal today (17th); it arrived at their work-site just on 2300 hours. At that hour they should have been back in camp. Not so, said the Nips, 'Eat and get back to work'. What time they will finish only the sadistic Nipponese have any idea.

Working on Tokyo time can be very disconcerting as 0830 hours Australian time is well after dawn. Here, in this seemingly outlandish part of the world, dawn is just breaking and the workers are already preparing for a start, having breakfasted on watery 'pap', at 0830, Nipponese time.

More canteen supplies came in today (18th), Burmese cigars about the size of a fat cigarette, but priced almost as high as a 'Havana' in a peacetime market; 8 cents for a one cent 'fag'. Packets labelled 100, only contain 50. The men are caught both ways, price and quality.

The 20th is not a good day for us; three of our yaks died overnight due, it is suspected, to starvation. The Camp Commandant has granted permission for the slaughter of four of the remainder today. And, if the last three are still in the land of the living tomorrow, the 'generous' Commandant will permit their sacrifice for the camp inmates.

Some pineapples arrived for the canteen today but at a price that will be far beyond the 'pocket' of any of the workers. Luxurious as the fruit may be, and everyone longs for a taste of it, finance is the insurmountable problem and the Nipponese do not believe in extending credit. This is one time they can eat their own wares.

Throughout today (21st) rain has been falling almost all the time but there was no let-up in work tasks. Ballasting the line would be hard for fit workers, but for the men, in their condition, it is a heartbreaking solid grind. They went out at dawn this morning (0830 hours) and returned to camp just on midnight. If that was not bad enough, they had to line up for a blood test. It is believed the Nipponese are seeking malaria carriers.

Actually, all the tests they take appear to amount to nothing, there are never any results given. The time taken up in the needle-pricking only ends in all the tired-out men losing valuable rest.

It is now Saturday (22nd) and the rain is pelting down on the lads out on the line spreading ballast as fast as it can be unloaded. Miserable, weary beyond belief, they are driven like cattle as the guards keep up the blood-curdling 'currah currah' and 'speedo speedo' as they bash and wallop those they believe are not working hard, or fast, enough to satisfy their demands.

Another three of our ration animals passed away during the night; the carcasses cannot be used for human consumption as no one is actually sure of the cause of death. It could be malnutrition; on the other hand their demise may have been the result of some communicable disease. As much as the hunger-tortured, hard-working men are keen to take the risk, it cannot be permitted. Life is too precious.

The recent inoculation against the contraction of cholera may not have had the expected results. Today (24th) a Nipponese railroad ganger, inoculated at the same time as the workers, died. His death diagnosed as from the dreaded cholera. The Japanese have pressed the panic button in their own lines, particularly when they were informed of the passing of a Burmese woman worker within the precincts of the camp. Cause of her expiration, cholera.

As the natives use the same latrine as all our Force the risk of contagion is greatly enhanced. However, one of the greatest assets of our boys is the inborn determination to practise hygiene to the highest possible degree. By doing this, they lessen 95% of contamination.

The continuous rain is taking its toll of the workers who have to slave under the most unimaginable conditions. The sick parade is up by at least 100 per cent. Only 199 men available for line tasks today (25th) out of 600.

Despite the high frequency of increasing ill-health the Japanese demands for more and more workers may result in a blitz to force the hand of Captain Rowley Richards, who steadfastly refuses the accede to their fiendish intent to make unhealthy personnel work to the death on their railroad construction project.

The Jap propaganda machine knows no limits and they are now bent on using us for that very purpose. We were all handed a lettercard today (25th) to send to our families. The text reads:

'I am still at a POW camp near Moulmein, Burma. There are 20,000 prisoners being Australian, Dutch, English and American. There are several camps of 2/3,000 prisoners who work at settled labour daily. We are quartered in very plain huts. The climate is good. Our life is now easier with regards to food, medicine and clothes. The Japanese Commander sincerely endeavours to treat prisoners kindly. Officers' salary is based on Japanese officers of same rank and every prisoner who performs labour on duty is given a daily wage from 25 cents (min) to 45 cents according to rank and work. Canteens are established where we can buy extra food and smokes by courtesy of the Japanese Commander. We conduct concerts in the compound. A limited number go to the picture show about once per month.'

Two lines were left to write messages!

The reader would gain a very wrong impression as to living conditions, treatment, clothes and the very important fact, food. The Japanese wording was in direct contrast to the truth. However, perhaps the folks at home could gain some comfort from the card—if they ever receive it!

The real facts are—our plain huts are overcrowded, full of holes, bugs and fleas; food and clothing stores are at a bare minimum or non-existent (80% wear G-strings and no footwear); quinine, one tablet per day perhaps, no other drugs of any kind. As an example, 150 cases of malaria in this camp today.

Officers' salary, after deductions for board and lodgings, 20 rupees a month, 5 rupees to our local sick. Canteens; never sold anything good over the counter since we have been here. Everything received is rationed. When available, sugar is rationed to 5 lbs to 50 men. Cigars, if in stock, which is rare, one per man. All beans, etc. go to the kitchen. Pineapples, if and when available, one to 50 men.

The cost of a mug of coffee represents six days' work for the purchaser and that is too high a price for the average worker. Pictures, only two shows to a limited group. Never believe a Japanese, ever!

Demand for 100 out to work from the light sick; 50 came from Williams Force and the other, similar number, from Anderson Force. A request for consideration as to the type of work the ailing men could perform met with derisive laughter.

The Nips put them to the toughest jobs they could conjure up. The physical strain was so great they, subsequently, allowed ten to return to camp, but they drove the other 90 to the point of utter exhaustion.

That was the Japanese Commander's sincere endeavour to treat the prisoners kindly!

One hundred and nine of Williams Force, other than light sick, were kept working throughout the night in pouring rain (as it has been doing for the past 24 hours). They came back into their quarters at 0830 this morning (26th). They, too, were utterly worn out, physically and mentally. Much more of this and our ranks will be just about decimated. There is just so much the human body can take.

One of the ten who were allowed back to camp yesterday died today (27th), cause of death believed to be cholera. His body was interred at 1330 hours. Three more from that group are now very ill.

Two deaths today (29th), one from each Force. All ranks receive a 1cc anti-cholera injection. The Japanese blame the prisoners of war for the cholera outbreak and ordered everything in the camp to be disinfected. The only bother there is, WHAT WITH! We have no disinfectant whatever, and we have not been issued with any since capitulation.

We had a surprise visit from a Japanese Colonel, railway construction staff, who inspected the lines. He never uttered a word but from the look on his face it was apparent he had many thoughts about what condition the POWs were in.

Earlier in the day (31st) Lt. Col. Y. Nagatomo, accompanied by Brigadier A.L. Varley, Lt. Col. Hamilton, Doctor Larsen and others had also made an unannounced call which we all thought would result in a close inspection of the whole camp. We were wrong. Nagatomo refused to look at anything. He even turned away from the refreshments the Camp Commander had provided. Despite the fact it had been prepared from their kitchen.

Brigadier Varley did carry out a very thorough inspection and he was absolutely disgusted with what he saw; men packed in like sardines, many of them emaciated, diseased and on the very threshold of death.

We learned, too, of the impending demise of a lad at the 45 kilo camp where no Medical Officer is in residence. Two medical orderlies are endeavouring to care for 520 men, out of which only 96 are capable of any type of work. Those lads have been working continuously for two months without one rest day. The Japanese are treating them in a diabolical manner.

Tuesday, 1.6.43: Major Krantz and Captain Bill Drower, surgeon specialist and interpreter, respectively, returned from Base camp and were amazed at the state of health of the two Forces, Williams and Anderson They could hardly believe men could be so low, and yet be still alive.

To relieve the food situation at the 45 kilo camp, No. 1 Mobile Force sent 350 rupees to the lads in such desperate straits. That would allow, if supplies are available, them to buy enough to carry on.

The fear by the Japanese of a cholera epidemic prompted them to make provision for another test. Sergeant Westgarth, a probable suspect, is very ill.

Lt. Col. Anderson ordered to attend the Japanese Camp Commander's

Headquarters and was informed by the Commander that Lt. Col. Williams was not being fair to the Japanese as he was not sending enough of the sick men out on to the railway job.

They said he was 'a very bad man and did not play fair with them'.

To quote the officer concerned (the 'very bad man'): 'Well! Well! Don't give 'im a ruddy medal!'

BLACK-GREEN-RAMSAY COMBINED FORCES
105 Kilo Camp

THE 105 KILO CAMP, Ankanan, Burma was, undoubtedly, the worst the prisoners of war in these forces had encountered in their work on the railway. It had absolutely nothing to recommend it. Everything was short—water, food and rest days.

From the medical point of view conditions could not have been worse; no drugs or medicines, with just one exception, two injections per person against contracting cholera.

The medical officer for each force, Captains Anderson (Green Force), Cumming (Ramsay Force) and Higgin (Black Force) carried out their tasks in a manner that would seem impossible to anyone uninitiated in jungle conditions.

The miracle is, they saved hundreds of lives by their ingenuity, understanding and dedication. They had no statutory surgery hours, in fact they had no surgeries at all. Regimental aid posts, in the military sense, did not exist. Parades of the sick and injured were held more often in the open than in any kind of building.

They were driven to the point of exhaustion in their efforts to prevent the Japanese from exploiting the unfit, and ministered with care and devotion to the needs of the skin and bone apparitions who had once been men in the best physical condition.

No prisoner of war in any force lacked attention from his medical officer. Those men of medicine acted as a bulwark between the bestial Nipponese and the emaciated hulks the prisoners of war had now, in the main, become.

Day after day the work groups slaved on road-building, smashing rock for line metalling, corduroying roads that were feet deep in mud. Working in torrential rain, they were feverish from constant attacks of malaria, undernourished and suffering one of the worst scourges of all, tropical ulcers.

The adjacent hallowed cemetery gave daily proof that there was a limit to man's endurance.

The new camp was one of filth, mud and discomfort from the outset. Exhausted men just collapsed inside the supposed good huts; for many, the condition of their new home at that moment, meant nothing. They only wanted to lie down and sleep. Every muscle and tissue in their bodies ached as they had never done before; not even a stint of up to eighteen hours hard work on the railroad had tired them so much.

But for the worn-out cooks, there was to be no let up; all the marchers had to be fed. It was their job to provide a meal as quickly as possible.

The great majority of workers considered the kitchen fatigue as a 'snack'. There, they argued, you found the best fed POWs, no skin and bone merchants there. The falsity of that assumption was later demonstrated when

Ramsay Force company quartermaster, Sergeant Jim Mitchell, lost a leg due to an ulcer, contracted dysentery and passed away at the 55 kilo camp hospital on 20 December, 1943; the year that claimed so many lives.

Casualties of that frightful forced-march along forty-two kilometres of the indirect track from the 75 kilo camp, resulted from parched men drinking from many of the streams they passed en route. They became victims of cholera and failed to recover.

In all possible respects, the 105 kilo camp was a horrible nightmare for all who tenanted it; back-breaking work on the last section of the Burma side of the railway, very little to eat, and death waiting!

Additionally, the monsoon season was at its height, but despite the never-ending downpour, the work went on. There was a roadway near the camp that was rendered almost impassable by up to two feet of mud. The Nipponese, accepting the advice of the Australians, decided to corduroy it. That, too, was a slave-driving job. Trees had to be felled and carried to the mud-churned track.

As the work proceeded, the distances the timber had to be manhandled became greater. It was at this point the massive and wonderful elephants came to the aid of the prisoners of war. Even though they, too, were ill-fed, they seemed to sense the need of the prisoners ('light sick' who had been driven out by the bestial Japanese to build the roadway) and, without even a mahout, wrapped their trunks around heavy logs, found the balance point and carried them to the lay-down area. When the Nips woke up to what was happening they said that the heaviest timber should be carred by three Australians or one elephant!

That was an order, they meant it and observed it to the letter!

Every tropical disease that Burma presented was present in this camp; malaria, cholera, ulcers, dengue fever, scrub typhus, black water fever—the lot!

It was at this camp the forces of Black, Green and Kerr converged upon Ramsay Force, the last-named being the advance group.

One of the most dangerous of all diseases struck early at the 105 kilo camp (named Aunganaug by the POW 'host'), dreaded cholera. Victims died within four hours. However, the medical officers worked miracles in preventing the deaths of many who displayed the symptoms.

In the forefront of that dedicated group was Captain Gordon Cumming; he was tireless and worked very long hours as his compassion for the sick and injured overcame his own personal safety. How he survived the potentially dangerous ailments suffered by so many is one of those marvels of the Burma-Thailand railway.

Much has been written about the overworked medical officers who, in their own way, slaved as did those who toiled with pick, shovel and chunkel. The medical teams were compelled to improvise; how, only they know, but in their improvisation they could have rewritten all medical journals.

In every force the same story is told—'But for the medicos, few would have come through the horror life on that rail link from Thanbyuzayat, Burma to Bam Pong, Thailand'.

The water supply at the 105 kilo camp was very grim; it had to be carted from a creek nearly one mile away. To do so a human chain had to be organised; the labour—the 'light sick'.

By courtesy of Tony Clive, below are extracts from his memoirs relating to the 105 kilo (Ankanan) camp:

The Big Wet. Two weeks after our arrival at this infamous camp the monsoonal rains commenced. Fortunately for us the huts had been constructed on sloping ground and we had no drainage problems.

In our previous encampments the rain resulted in the creation of mud walkways, sometimes over 12 inches deep. In some instances, even deeper and waterlogged to a depth of two feet in the rainy season.

The buildings were not new and had earlier housed native labourers; they had moved out, apparently, some months prior to our taking over the site. So long ago, in fact, vegetation had crept into the huts. The grounds of the area were just about overgrown but not to a great height.

The hutments, as was usual, were of bamboo and roofed with dried-out atap. Gaping holes allowed the downpour to sodden just about everyone and their possessions.

Where and when possible repairs, of a sort, were effected and considerably reduced the discomfort. However, the lads in the upper bunks were not quite as comfortable as those beneath them, but they accepted the situation.

The work we were to be engaged on was, more or less, of a pioneering type. We were faced with virgin jungle out of which a road had to be built in addition to the railway line. It was a frightening future we faced.

Quarrying for ballast was one of the first tasks, a hard one at that, we were assigned to. The road being the first priority resulted in the haulage of ballasted rock to make the foundation. Long distances, heavy loads and not one real healthy man to perform such a backbreaking job. But, it had to be done, and the Japanese demanded the maximum of available men every day. Fit or otherwise did not concern them one iota.

For all its drawbacks the 105 kilo camp had one thing going for it, attractive surroundings; tall trees on a slope that, in normal circumstances, would be considered a place of beauty. But, for the prisoners of war, an area that engendered hate against sadistic guards, such as the notorious Boofhead who was one of the worst of the Korean group. His co-guards the BB (Boy Bastard) and his soulmate, the BBC (Boy Bastard's Cobber), Mickey Mouse, so named because of his size, who, at every opportunity, aired his knowledge of English; it evoked no admiration.

Then there was the Bull. A massive brute who obviously set out every day to smash and bash every POW he came in contact with. He took every advantage he could to wield his waddy against skin and bone bodies. He, like the BB and his mate, the BBC, was top of the reprisal list, for the moment the war ended.

Every guard, large or small, was a proven thug in every possible way. Their hatred of the White Race was exhibited daily. They were no respecter of persons, rank or state of health. No matter the nationality, so long as they were of light skin they considered it their right to flog, flail and brutalise the unfortunates. Few, if any, POWs missed out on a daily dose at the infamous 105!

In analysing the absolute worst of the bunch perhaps the Boy Bastard came near to that nomenclature. His favourite pastime was to force his victim to stand to attention whilst he worked himself up to a state of near dementia, mouthing obscenities of Australian and Korean origin. Once at his topmost pitch he was ruthless in administering a savagery of punishment of unbelievable proportions.

It was almost impossible to 'ride' the blows; the best one could do was to protect extremities, head to groin, the latter his very favourite area in which to land boot or rifle butt. Once he had his 'target' writhing in agony, his day was made.

Another of the guards' great pastimes was to thieve POW foodstuffs, palm oil particularly. From anything up to twenty tins supposedly to go to the workers' kitchen, at most the prisoners of war would get half of one tin. Sugar suffered the same fate; a little to the prisoners, a lot to the guards. They were shameless in their thieving.

As was usual, food was on short supply, so much so the men physically unable to work on the railway were forced back down the line to the 95 and 100 kilo dumps, to *carry* back bags of rice!

The long line of pitifully weakened men trudging through ankle deep—and sometimes even worse in places—mud in teeming rain, was enough to cause the strongest man to want to take to task the inhuman guards flaying them with rifle butts to keep up.

That was on the forward journey; the return trip, be it 10 or 15 kilos, was sheer agony. Those unfortunate lads were now distraught zombies bent almost double as they staggered along under not only the weight of the rice, but the added water the grains soaked up from the relentless rain.

Day after day the now named 'rice coolies' plodded along those sodden tracks. Some managed to walk a short distance, fall and then suffer a flogging from the well-fed, bestial-minded rifle-butt wielders whose chief delight appeared to be causing as much pain on those human hulks as was possible.

Of 60,000 prisoners of war the Nipponese had under their control building that notorious railway, there would not have been many who had but hate, real hate, in their hearts for their torturers. A hate that will, no doubt, linger in their minds to some degree forever.

On one well-remembered rice-carrying march under the worst possible weather conditions, slushing through mud, feet down in parts, and burdened beyond belief, one poor devil who had just undergone a real doing-over by a noted evil-bred Korean, let fly a string of Aussie oaths that staggered the guard. For one breathtaking moment it appeared the lad's worries were going to be over forever. But, for once the guard was speechless! He just slunk away and not one finger was raised against any of the carriers from that point on and into camp.

Day after day the Japanese demanded from all Force Commanders a higher than possible number of workers. Never once did the commanders submit to the unreal requirements. The ranks of the workers were daily becoming more and more depleted.

Lt. Col. Nagatomo, Commanding No. 3 Branch Thai Prisoners of War, Thanbyuzayat to the Three Pagoda Pass area, became so frustrated by the constant refusal of Force Commanders to comply with his work orders, he travelled to the 105 kilo camp to personally examine all diagnosed, or as he put it, believed unfit personnel.

He demanded everyone in the camp be paraded before him for his determination as to their fitness or otherwise. Despite his peculiar oriental outlook as to who could work or be permitted to remain in camp, he was visibly shocked when he saw the condition of the line after line of men incapable of even standing. His nose twitched and he almost retched as the odour of putrefied ulcers and dysentery-fouled bodies assailed him.

When Lt. Col. George Ramsay invited him to inspect the bedridden patients, that was the last straw. His horrified expression told its own tale. Nagatomo had seen enough!

Without doubt he accepted the obvious fact the POW Medical Officers had correctly diagnosed their patients' state of health. So much so he assured all concerned a hospital camp would be opened at the 55 kilo point. Very shortly after that, Nagatomo, for once, kept his word.

In company with Brigadier Varley he paid a surprise visit to the 75 kilo camp to discuss the new hospital camp possibilities with the then quite ill Lt. Col. Albert Coates, the officer Nagatomo considered as suitable to act as Chief Medical Officer. Ill as he was, the great Australian surgeon accepted the office, and subsequently arrived at the 55 kilo camp on a stretcher.

Whilst Nagatomo was at the 105 kilo camp Lt. Col. G. Ramsay sought to elicit a reply to the letters he had written to him under date of the 31st May and 1st June of that year, 1943. However, the wily Japanese commander dismissed them as mere correspondence, the responsibility of some other member of his staff. But Ramsay held his ground, and courteously requested the matters submitted be dealt with there and then. Nagatomo reluctantly agreed he would look into and study the contents of both submissions. As was usual, nothing eventuated.

With silence the only result of his personal approach, Ramsay decided the interests of his troops would be better served were he to submit copies of the earlier letters, which read:

ANKANAN (105 kilo camp)
31.4.'43

Lt. Col. Y. Nagatomo
Chief of No. 3 Branch, Thai War
Prisoners Camps, THANBYUZAYAT.

The number of men in this camp at present is 1,930. Unfortunately, owing to some statistics being left at Meiloe (75 kilo) camp it has not been possible to prepare a sickness graph for the month.

WORKING CONDITIONS AT 75 KILO CAMP

For several days prior to moving working conditions at the 75 kilo camp were appalling. Fit men were paraded at 0830 hours and were kept at work on the railway line until 0200 hours or later on the following morning. On several occasions men were taken from the sick parade and marched out to work immediately after lunch and kept at work until a late hour. The advice of medical officers was ignored and protests were unavailing. Naturally this procedure had an adverse effect upon the health of the men.

MOVEMENT

Upon the 13th May, 1943, at 2100 hours, approximately, 1300 men of this force commenced the march to the 105 kilo camp. Owing to the primitive conditions under which we had been living, the men were loath to leave any article behind and consequently many of the men carried excessively heavy loads. The conditions of the march were very trying. Much of the road consisted of sharp unbound metal which was very severe on the men marching in bare feet. Later, pitch darkness accentuated the difficulties.

Next morning the men rested for a few hours at the 96 kilo camp and then continued on to the 105 kilo camp. During the succeeding days, parties of sick men who had been left at Meiloe marched into this camp. Although most of the personal equipment of these sick men had been transported by MT, the march was very difficult for them owing to their weak condition. Some of the very weak were forced on at rifle point.

RESULTS OF MARCH

Many of the men suffered from exhaustion and there has since been a large number of recurrences of diarrhoea, dysentery and relapses of malaria. Many men suffered abrasions to the feet.

CONDITIONS AT 105 KILO CAMP

This camp is situated on gently sloping ground and consists of dirty old Burmese huts with fairly good roofs. Water supplies are very poor and it is necessary to carry water several hundred yards from soaks and a well to the cookhouse. Frequently rains have alleviated the position a little. Burmese were in or adjacent to the camp previously and flies are very numerous.

SICKNESS

Diarrhoea and dysentery have shown a marked increase in this camp. Several cases of amoebic dysentery have occurred and treatment is unsatisfactory owing to the lack of supplies.

MALARIA

Few new cases have occurred probably because practically every man has now had malaria but relapses have been very numerous. Many of these men who have had frequent relapses are becoming very anaemic. Each man is receiving 0.25 grams of quinine daily and this is obviously insufficient to prevent relapses.

RESPIRATORY LESIONS

Several cases of coryza and a few cases of influenza have occurred.

SKIN LESIONS

These are showing an increase and since the onset of the wet weather they are healing less rapidly and several cases of tropical ulcers have developed.

CHOLERA

An outbreak of cholera occurred in this camp on the 25th May. This patient had abdominal pain, copious vomiting of watery material and a passage of large 'rice water' stools. He had very severe muscular cramps and rapidly developed into a state of extreme collapse. His condition improved satisfactorily following intravenous saline infusions. Upon the night of 27th May was reasonably good although he developed some muttering delirium. He died suddenly next morning at 0300 hours on 30th May. Two other fulminating cases occurred on the 27th and 28th May respectively but each died within 24 hours.

At present there are two cases of cholera in the camp hospital. One of these is in a critical condition; the other has a less severe type and is making very satisfying progress.

The source of this cholera outbreak has not yet been definitely localised but is probably in the adjacent Burmese camp. At least three deaths have occurred among the Burmese and the majority of the other Burmese have left. The matter has been reported to the Nipponese authorities. All precautions possible under the present circumstances for preventing further spread of the disease have been adopted. The last case was admitted to the camp hospital 36 hours ago.

CHOLERA VACCINATIONS

All men received a cholera injection prior to leaving the 75 kilo camp and the majority have received another injection in this camp during the last few days.

(Signed) G.E. Ramsay, Lt. Col., Commanding Ankanan Camp

*

P.O.W. Camp, ANKANAN
1st June, 1943

Lt. Col. Y. Nagatomo,
Chief of No. 3 Branch, Thai War
Prisoners Camps, THANBYUZAYAT

In accordance with article 86 of House Rules I respectfully submit the following petition to you for your favourable consideration.

You may remember in my letters 1 and 2 to you dated 12th March, '43, I invited your attention to the failing health of my troops, particularly of those who have been working regularly on railroad work for the preceding months.

My fears expressed at that time that, with the continuance of such conditions the health of my troops would be still further adversely affected, has been confirmed, as my Medical Officers state that the troops here are in a worse state of health than at any time since we have been prisoners of war.

This is partly due to the long hours worked during the last days of our stay in Meiloe, where men had to work all day and the greater part of the night, followed by a particularly arduous march to the 105 kilo camp.

I recognise that the numbers required for daily working parties by the Nipponese Commander here would be most reasonable under normal circumstances but I respectfully submit that the present conditions are far from normal as the continuous work in the rain and on wet and slippery ground. Makes the work doubly arduous. This is further aggravated by the long continuous work periods as a rest day on every 10th day seems to have been discontinued. The very high sick rate is almost impossible of improvement and in fact must become worse so long as the Nipponese staff at this camp are permitted to send men out to work against the advice of my Medical Officers.

Lieut. Hoshi and his staff show us every consideration within the limits of their instructions received from higher authority, but the fact remains that some men are being sent out to work whose health is being seriously, perhaps permanently, affected. My Medical Officers advise that there are many cases of diarrhoea in camp at present and these need careful watching as, with some cases of cholera in our midst, they are more liable to contract this dread disease if their bodily resistance is further lowered by being sent out to work in wet, unhealthy conditions. Further that a reduction in rations, as threatened, would retard the restoration to health still more of many of these men, with a consequent reduction in the number available for work.

I enclose copy of a report from my Senior Medical Officer and he advises that experience has shown that men sent out to work before they have fully recovered from fevers have suffered relapses which makes those men unfit for three or four more days than otherwise would have been the case.

In the past week there have been three deaths from cholera and one from dysentery in this camp, and while this imposes a very heavy additional strain on my Medical Officers, every effort is being made by all ranks to take every precaution possible against disease.

A further disability which has made the present sick rate so abnormally high is caused by the great majority of skin abrasions, of which there are many, turning into ulcers which often make it impossible for men to work.

While assuring you that every effort is being made by myself and my staff to meet the constant demands of your officer and staff at this camp for large working parties, the object of this petition is to advise you of the alarming extent to which the state of health of my soldiers has fallen during the last few months and to ask that you would be so good as to give favourable consideration to:

(1) That no men be sent to work against the advice of my Medical Officers who undertake to mark as fit as many men as possible.

(2) That regular rest days be restored, at least one day in ten, and

(3) That rations be not reduced.

Thanking you in anticipation of these matters receiving your kindly consideration as I feel that the granting of these requests would be quite consistent with the terms of the letter card which we were kindly permitted to dispatch to our people in Australia recently.

I would like to mention that the personal interest taken and the efforts of Lieut. Hoshi towards obtaining water and rations are much appreciated.

(signed) G.E. Ramsay, Lt. Col. Commanding ANKANAN Camp

*

Even at camps like the 105 kilo, there were moments of grim satisfaction that at least bordered on the humorous. Johnny Kreckler recalls the tomato patch:

At the railway's 105 kilometre mark the Japanese wanted a tomato garden prepared. Who better than Rex Salier, a captain from Scotsdale in Tasmania. Rex, who had been in charge of an experimental government farm, selected me as his assistant. Thoughts of gaining a tomato or two made us very keen, although anxious farmers. Two gardens were prepared—one large and one small. We were hoping they would give us some plants for our own use. The plants arrived and we were told, 'Yes, you can have some ... but no water for Australian garden'. I immediately told them what they could do with their plants—in English, of course. Rex said don't worry; he though we could manage with cultivation and the morning dew. Rex's idea did work, and it worked well. Our plants, while smaller than those in the large plot, looked good and healthy.

One day, whilst cultivating around the 'Japanese garden', along came a sergeant who proceeded to give us a lecture, 'No dig, only water. Australians stupid.' He then gave a few slaps across the face for good measure. He wanted water so we gave them water and as we did we marched around each plant until the ground was like cement. Their tomatoes turned out to be very small, like marbles. Ours were quite a good, regular sized tomato. We never did get to taste the tomatoes, but we won our point knowing our captors did not like to lose face over any issue. Looking back I am sure we never expected them to let us harvest our garden; these men were not built that way.

No. 1 Mobile Force
June-August 1943

LIEUTENANT COLONEL Williams, like all other force commanders, was adamant sick men should not be compelled to work on any project. However, despite their uncompromising attitude on that subject, there were many times when they were forced, punished and eventually made to defer—to a point; that point being that such troops be given the lightest tasks.

The Japanese would ultimately agree to this, but never kept even the spirit of the agreement. Particularly on No. 1 Mobile Force, unfit personnel were forced to carry out the heaviest jobs Japanese could find for them. Williams' diaries supply many instances:

*

[Thursday, 3.6.43] Sergeant Westgarth's condition deteriorated so quickly Captain Rowley Richard decided his only chance of recovery was via a blood transfusion.

On a bamboo bed and in a stable wherein millions of flies hovered around, filth beyond description within the vicinity (no camp staff available to cleanse the area), the life-giving operation was carried out. He lived, but only by the grace of God and the competence of the dedicated Medical Officer and his staff.

*

The sacrifice of man, true mateship, irrespective of rank or creed, did wonders for the stricken lad. A cup of steaming chocolate (the chocolate Williams had long carried for an emergency) did much to cheer up the very ill 'Westy'. The choc-bar was gone, a soldier lived.

*

In an endeavour to rid the camp of some of the bugs and lice that made miserable lives more miserable, the bamboo slats were burned from a hut previously tenanted by Burmese. Many of those occupants had been suffering from smallpox and cholera. To have left the contaminated bamboo would have meant the Australians who had to take over and live in the hut, would run an awesome risk.

*

The destruction of the infected bamboo was a crime against the Emperor as far as the Japanese were concerned. The fact that it probably saved many lives, including their own, did not register. Had Williams not ordered the burning, an epidemic of uncontrollable proportions may have broken out. The results for Australians, and others, could have been catastrophic.

For his foresight, which was in the interest of everyone in the whole camp, he was given a verbal dressing down. That was the least of his worries. His only concern was to prevent a calamity and save lives. He achieved his objective; nothing else mattered.

The next day [4.6.43] he again proved his capacity for doing everything possible (and within his competence) to prevent death taking toll of the whole force.

The condition of Sergeant Westgarth was very worrying and Williams and the Medical Officer were determined to defeat the disease that was slowly but surely sapping life from his debilitated body.

The Japanese refused to supply drugs or medicines of any kind despite the imminence of an epidemic; cholera or smallpox. Westgarth, it appeared certain, had but a short time to live. The transfusion he had been given helped, but he needed more than that. His commander found it. Perhaps the very last in that part of Burma, a tin of milk!

From the very first sip, Westgarth seemed to benefit, and his wan smile oozed gratitude towards the donor, Williams.

That day Williams had to take over a role least expected. That of a doctor. He was near the isolation hut and observing another transfusion. As he watched, the orderly assisting Captain Rowley Richards passed out and fell to the ground. He heard the MO say, 'Leave him there, come and do what he was doing'. He did, and three minutes later the MO has also hit Mother Earth.

Apparently quite unperturbed, Williams stepped into the breach and called for a volunteer from one of the inmates to act as the orderly. Moments later he took over as the treating medical officer. Five minutes passed before the overtired medical officer, and his equally run-down orderly recovered.

When some of No. 1 Mobile Force members were stricken down with cholera, volunteers were called for to man the isolation hut. Two of the 2/2 Pioneer Battalion immediately stepped out. Williams warned them of the gravity of their decision, pointing out the possibility they, too, could become afflicted.

But they were adamant. Some of their mates needed help; they would get it! Those two lads, Lance Sergeant Johnstone and Corporal Kirby, fought hard to do the job that became their lot in that 'Hut of Death'. They were incredible; two doing the work of many, working long hours until they dropped from sheer exhaustion.

They now rest alongside each other in the Kanburi Cemetery, Thailand. 'Greater love hath no man than he who gives his life for a friend'.

It was not only on the field of battle that heroes were found; time and time again, in those disease-infested jungle camps, the same scene was enacted. Many paid the extreme sacrifice as they tended their mates.

In the almost intolerable conditions existing in POW camps in Burma and Thailand, the word mate held greater significance than in any other sphere of life. Selfishness was rare. Few ever gave it a thought; 99 per cent never knew the meaning of the word. Lieutenant Colonel Williams' diary continues:

*

Some canteen supplies arrived today [5.6.43] but not near enough to supplement the rice diet. Two more men sent to the isolation hut; they had been in the same building as one who had died after contracting cholera.

Orders given for the transfer of 460 men to the 40 kilo camp where it is expected they will be engaged in very hard work. The men of the Mobile Force now have the hardest and most exacting job on the near-final stages of the railroad construction.

Gloom has spread over the camp; the legendary Captain Rowley Richards, Medical Officer, has been admitted to the isolation hut. He and his orderlies deserve the highest possible praise for their unstinting efforts, not only for the cholera patients, but for everyone in the Force. What they have done to save lives with just about nothing but personal skill and dedication in salvaging men from the very brink of death, is incalculable.

Tomorrow Williams Force of 480 men move to the 40 kilo camp; they leave behind 44 who are too ill to be included. However, they will be in good hands.

The cholera patients are doing well at the moment and will be pleasantly surprised when served with chicken broth, eggs, custard and pineapple. There was no doubt about the surprise, and it certainly bucked them up 100%.

The chickens came from the local natives, pineapples from a contractor, milk (from an in-camp source) made the custard with eggs purchased from the canteen.

Everyone appears to be in good spirits tonight and there is an air of brightness. It is marvellous what a really good meal can do for morale. These days such luxuries are mostly dreams. To have one realised is almost unbelievable. Unfortunately, 170 men had to work.

A total of 483 of the Force moved out today [7.6.43] at 1300 hours; 474 Williams Force and 9 from Anderson Force. The whole morning was spent in preparing and shifting engineers' stores, tools and the personal and kitchen gear of the prisoners of war. It was quite a haul as the railway is situated some distance from the encampment. Throughout the whole exercise the rain never ceased.

By the time everything had been loaded three trains were packed and the men crammed into trucks with all kinds of equipment. The rain ceased when the trains had been unloaded and the men assigned to the huts. A problem. Not one decent, dry hut. The men are spread over an area usually housing 1,600.

Water is over 600 yards away and tubs have to be hand carried. That was overcome when an old cart, less oxen, was found. It held four tubs and made the transportation so much easier.

A work party of 150 required and supplied; the remainder are busily engaged in cleaning camp, digging latrines; some of the more enterprising managed to catch a fair quantity of rain water. That is far better than what is held in the well-soaks.

Another group managed to catch a grazing yak; very surprising how nice the rice tasted for that meal. In fact, it had a very real meaty taste! Seemed like Christmas had arrived early.

Quite a few of the boys are down with fever; probably brought on by exposure to the rain two days ago when the move was made to this location. Rations down to a bare minimum again. Rice only, once per day. Luckily, the cooks kept enough yak meat to make a weak stew. Just as well. One meal of rice, and a small issue at that, is not enough to sustain men engaged on very hard work. At least onions in the stew, watery as it was, did give some semblance of taste.

We received 240 pineapples, canteen stock, today [8.6.43], but not enough to meet the demand.

[Wednesday, 9.6.43] Just in time, rations delivered but one can hardly become ecstatic over four bags of mud beans and three sacks of rotten onions. Can consume the beans, onions will be returned to nature. At least we have some fresh water, rain filled our tubs.

The Japanese are now seeking tradesmen such as fitters, turners, motor mechanics and drivers. No men available in the categories required, except drivers. They appeared satisfied with those detailed.

Just after dawn today [10.6.43] we welcomed the warm sun; all sodden gear, blankets and the few cloth possessions men have, will soon be dried out.

There is a first time for everything. It has happened and everyone was astonished. An issue of hot tea! Our first in Burma. The 170 workers out on the line will be more than pleasantly surprised.

What an anti-climax. Yesterday a brew of tea, today [11.6.43] 15 Japanese on a brutal, 'bandit' spree went through our quarters like a wind storm. Stole everything they could lay their thieving hands on.

They disappeared as quickly as they had appeared but with a difference. They left loaded down with paltry belongings of poorly equipped and impoverished prisoners of war, who could ill afford to lose even one tiny item of their prized possessions.

The shock of the happening was felt very keenly, especially by the lads in the huts, too ill to do anything else than abandon their bed-spaces and await what turned out to be horrifying discoveries. Personal gear, in pitiful packs, thrown in disarray and looted.

No one would have believed even the Japanese would stoop so low as to rob men of personal items that, in some small way, still linked them with home. But it had happened; it was a case of grin and bear it.

Official stern complaints to the Camp Commander came to nothing; he could not have cared less. Nor did he give any undertaking to prevent similar attacks against POW property.

That was only too evident next day [12.6.43] when another roughhouse group arrived. The same tactics were applied; everyone, irrespective of their state of health, was driven out of their quarters and the marauders went to town again.

They were worse than a plague of grasshoppers; what they could find of what was left after the previous day, went out with them as they made their quick exit. For a wonder, the expected bashings did not take place. Maybe the grinning group considered plunder was plenty. There was so little left, the whole Force was almost destitute.

The rampages through the camp may have resulted from the Allied bombing raid on Thanbyuzayat yesterday when they plastered railway rolling stock.

Unfortunately, unconfirmed at the moment, the only fatalities were prisoners of war. A bomb landed near the hospital hut and ten patients died, nine were wounded.

Apparently the Nipponese opened fire on the six four-engined bombers with light machine guns and rifles and those unwise acts drew the attention of one plane; an 'egg' was dropped and the POW group at the well suffered a direct hit; from the air the crew would be unaware they were prisoners.

Despite the events at base our ration supply arrived today [14.6.43] and should last out for another ten days.

Thanbyuzayat appears to have had more attention from Allied bombers again today [15.6.43] but we have had no details. It is to be hoped the hospital area was not the subject of their action. However, with no marking to indicate the whole camp is anything else but a vast Japanese staging camp and railway depot, anything could happen.

Learned today of the payments made to the Burmese labourers on the railway construction project. They are paid at the rate of 125 cents per day as against the insignificant 25 cents POWs receive.

We were not given any information by the Japs of what occurred at base yesterday. But we were informed of an increase in the meat ration in the very near future. Heard that one before, so we will not be holding our breath whilst we await that day. A minimal amount of canteen stores delivered.

[18.6.43] At 0300 hours this morning Corporal Hambley passed away. His end was painless. Padre Kellow officiated at his burial in grave No. 3, at 1130 hours (40 kilo camp). Many of his 2/2 Pioneer Battalion mates attended the interment.

Been very quiet in the camp today as the passing of one casts an air of gloom over nearly everyone. The thought in all minds is, who will be next to go?

To make it worse we learned of the heavy casualty list resulting from the air raid yesterday. Sixty men killed or wounded, amongst them 13 Australians including Captain Ray Griffin, Camp Adjutant, who died instantly when a delayed action bomb exploded. Lt. Col. Black suffered a bullet wound in an arm and Brigadier A. L. Varley, who had a very narrow escape as he was near Griffin when the bomb went off, has a badly bruised face. Lt. Col. Black is now at the 18 kilo camp and the patients in the hospital huts at Base have been transferred to the 4 and 8 kilo camps.

Sickness is on the increase in this camp due to the apparent determination of the Nipponese to force ill men out to work. Those with fever have little chance of throwing the ailment off, no rest permitted as work requirements are heavy. Official protests mean nothing. The constant demand for more workers can have but one result, toll on the health of all.

Informed today [20.6.43] that the men of our Force currently at the 45 kilo camp are to join us soon. It is to be hoped they do. Preparations now in progress to provide room to accommodate them.[.6.43]

Only 170 men available for work today and they are labouring in constant rain.

Sergeant Shimojo, our conniving Camp Commandant, ordered 30 very sick men out to work. Whilst vigorously objecting did subsequently send out the fittest of the unfit. Before the party departed two collapsed on the parade ground. Seventeen of those who trudged to the work site were sent back to camp by the railway engineers. Eighteen of the original 30 did manage to see the day out. To make it the more hazardous, they toiled in the pouring rain, the majority clothed only in a G-string. No wonder illness overtakes them; they have no resistance left. Physically and mentally, they are exhausted.

*

Shimojo was at his worst on 22 June when he demanded that no less than 200 workers be made available. It was such an impossible figure that Lieutenant Colonel Williams stood up to him. He unhesitatingly refused to be a party to what amounted to murder, if such an order was complied with. He said he would rather risk death himself than agree to such an unreasonable requirement.

*

The demise of O/S Kitchen is expected at any moment; his condition is worsening by the hour and nothing, absolutely nothing, can be done to save his life. Malnutrition and generalised weakness have taken him beyond medical care; if medication was available!

As was expected, Kitchen died, at 0300 hours, today *[23.6.43]* and at 1110 hours he was interred in Grave No. 4, 40 Kilo camp, Burma. Heavy rain was falling as he was laid to rest. It poured all day.

All workers returned to camp at 1900 hours and everyone was placed on scales. In the final analysis it was established the average weight loss per man was 2 lbs in the last month.

It is pitiful to look at so many who were once so strong and healthy now reduced to walking skeletons. They have been driven that way by the callous disregard for their health by the Nipponese.

Shimojo and the railway gangers played another dirty trick on our 'light sick' men today. A total of 20 were sent out on what was supposed to be an easy task. Instead, as happened on two previous occasions, they were ordered to endure the heaviest tasks. The gangers considered it a great joke and they laughed as the men struggled, with little success, to do what men in the best of health may have baulked at.

Five of the men collapsed and had to be carried back into camp. A very strong protest to Shimojo ultimately resulted in his calling a parade of all the sick. He went along the ranks picking out those he considered were able to do whatever may be required of them on the line.

That many of the men were burning with fever, quite a few suffering from dysentery and ruptures, and quite obviously unfit, mattered little. He was the diagnostician and that was that! One, who had a broken wrist, suffered less than a month ago, was told to bathe it in water and report for work next day, even though unable to use a tool.

Shimojo's 'medical' inspection was pathetic inasmuch he had no medical knowledge whatsoever, nor did he want to admit to making errors, as he was the camp commander. And, as such, what he ordered, he meant to be law. He brushed aside any and all objections.

He gave three days notice to prepare for a move up to the 65 kilo camp. Everyone was aware of the necessity of another big clean up, and digging of latrines before the troops could be properly settled in.

[Friday, 25.6.43] Eight of the men ordered to work by Shimojo were kept in camp by Lt. Col. Eadie, Medical Officer. His determination to protect the health of the men caused a real riot. Shimojo's face went a deep red, then turned white. He was so furious he immediately wrote a letter to his superior officer demanding the committal to gaol of Eadie and Sergeant O'Brien. He ordered they pack and be ready to move to Thanbyuzayat prison.

*

Lt. Col.Williams intervened in this dispute and was ticked off in no uncertain terms. Shimojo finished by saying he was the Camp Commander; and, what he said in relation to men being fit for work, was an order to be obeyed, even if it meant they had to be carried out to the work site.

*

Told today *[26.6.43]* there was no need for a cattle party as there would not be any more meat issues. From now on the prisoners were to exist on cucumber, rice and the few beans the Nipponese 'graciously' supplied, a whole 6½ bags per day. Only one conclusion can be drawn from such a diet; the Nipponese are wholesale murderers!

When the men, in their weakened state, try to swallow the mushy cucumbers they immediately throw up. The taste is beyond imagination and many would prefer actual starvation to consuming it. The small ration of rice, and beans, weevilly and bitter, can sustain life, but only just.

A trader sold us 15 eggs at a cost of 20 cents each and they were sent to the hospital patients. With one day's pay being only 25 cents, there's not much purchasing power. A few boys from the Unit returned to the 60 kilo camp from Base. We expect to meet up with them at the 65 kilo camp. Line workers in a little earlier tonight, some at 1830 hours, the balance one hour later.

Constant rain falling as the 170 men went out to work this morning (26th); many were quite ill but sent out by Shimojo. It has continued to pour ever since. No wonder illness abounds in the camp; labouring under the worst possible conditions with very little food and practically no clothes.

*

Of all the forces on the Burma side of the death railway not one suffered more than the No. 1 Mobile Force. This force, which combined Anderson and Williams Force, had to ballast, sleeper and lay the rails of the line. It was the fastest, hardest task on the whole project.

Trains loaded with sleepers, leading bogie, and rails would be shunted up to the end of the last rail laid. From then on the men would work at a furious pace, overseen by waddy-wielding engineers and guards.

The men worked in pairs running ahead and laying sleepers. The empty bogie would be pulled off the rails to the side, then the rails had to be unloaded and laid, a pair at a time. Eighteen or twenty men, depending on availability, would grasp a rail and carry it to the drop point on the loose-laid sleepers. Each rail would be pulled into position, fish-plated and bolted; holes would be drilled into the sleeper, either side of the joint, a dog-spike driven in, one in the middle and other end of the laid rail. The bogie would be pulled off, then the next one shunted forward. That pattern continued until the whole train was unloaded.

Following the laying gang came the dog-spikers; they had to spike the rails to the sleepers, one to each side of the rail on the straight and two to each on curves. The team of four workers; one, armed with a steel bar that weighed about 25 pounds (to start with, it got heavier as the work proceeded at a pace), had to lever the sleeper hard against the rail as the augurman drilled the two holes. Then came the hammer-men, each with a 12 pound (hammer) tool. They had to drive the dogspikes home, straight.

Occasionally, one, due to weariness, would mis-hit a spike and bend it. The engineers or guards, always on the lookout for such an occurence, would whip into an immediate fury and thrash the hammer-wielder unmercifully.

As the hours wore on the four-man crew suffered hell; their hands became abnormally swollen and their arms ached and groaned as they tried to carry their burden, remembering all the while the Japanese claim that they would build the railway over the bones of the prisoners of war. That they meant it, was only too obvious. Thousands of prisoners were still available. If some died, what matter! They just forced more onto the work until their goal was achieved.

*

[Saturday, 26.6.43] Had an opportunity to clean up and fence the cemetery today. It now bears a well-kept appearance.

We are out of meat again and look like being so for a long time; no information as to when any can be expected. We did, however, get some canteen supplies; 2 eggs per man and about 200 sent to the hospital. One bag of sugar allowed for an issue of ¼ pint per man; the sick were given a full pint each. Pineapples, 30, also sent to the hospital patients. We were lucky to get the goods and they were well received.

Only 160 required to work on the line today [27.6.43] and their task is quite close to camp. A train smash resulted in 90 men being detailed to clean up the mess.

A pleasant sound in the air today as three flights of Allied planes flew over. The detonation of exploding bombs was clearly heard; came from the direction of the 30 kilo railway siding. The Japanese subsequently admitted three separate attacks on the Base camp, Thanbyuzayat, and two at Retpu, 30 kilo camp. Excitement among the local inhabitants is very encouraging. Perhaps they are well aware the pattern of the war has changed, undoubtedly in Allied favour.

For the very first time since we became prisoners of war we enjoyed a few cubes of real meat. We had it for our evening meal and the taste reminded us of old times.

Had a visit from Major Krantz, who is encamped at the 45 kilo, today *[28.6.43]*. Told us the men at 45 kilo are in much better health than the boys here appear to be.

We were unable to make the quota of 160 near-fit workers today and, ultimately, had to add seven light sick. As much as it went against the grain, and despite strong objections, they had to go out.

An audit of the canteen books set in motion today with the appointment of Major Daly and Lieutenant Mitchell as official auditors. Some rations delivered, 6 bags of onions, one of garlic, and two of cucumbers. Supposed to be five days rations; without rice that is going to be difficult.

One pleasant event occurred today *[29.6.43]*. Shimojo ordered to report to Moulmein. He has gone, no one has any regrets. Only 140 men fit for work and are out on the line job. Our meat ration disappeared this morning with the death of the only yak cow we had. Raining very heavily, no let-up all day.

A shortage of buckets is proving a bit of a headache. Permission granted to make some out of a piece of corrugated iron, conditionally upon one of the receptacles being provided for one of the Nips. One big problem, can make the buckets without much difficulty, but have no way of preventing them leaking. No such thing as solder or, if we had it, no soldering iron available. (Shylock was an amateur compared to this crowd.)

Four men whose illness was diagnosed as dangerous were admitted to the camp hospital.

The last day of June, 1943. Hopes are high we will not be in durance and under Nipponese control this time next year. If the bombing raids are any guide, there is a big possibility we will be back in our homes in Australia by then. Well, dreams sometimes come true.

Two more of our lads, Pte J. Watson, 2/2 Pioneer Battalion and Chief Petty Officer E.F. King, have died. Deaths resulted from malaria, malnutrition and, in the case of the CPO, a throat ailment. Lt. Col. Eadie (Ear, Nose and Throat specialist) performed an operation but the patient had so little resistance death intervened.

They were both interred at 1150 hours after a service given by Padre Kellow. Unfortunately we now have six graves in the hallowed area here.

Advised of a move to the 60 kilo camp in two days time; this is bad news as we are aware it is already overcrowded with British, American and Anderson Force troops.

The Japanese HQ have made a request; they want the names of all dead heroes who met their deaths fighting heroically for their country. A 'nil' return was submitted.

Had a visit from Brigadier A.L. Varley who was accompanied by Lt. Col. Nagatomo and staff. After five minutes they had departed but left us with a four-hour job that must be completed by 0800 hours tomorrow, 1st July.

The Brigadier told us conditions at the 105 kilo camp were 'pretty rotten'. The troops there are suffering the same conditions, healthwise as we are here, malaria, dysentery and fever. Also informed us a hospital had been opened at the 55 kilo camp, but it is expected it will take some time before it is fully operational. He confirmed the rumour of air raids on Thanbyuzayat.

Private A.N. Prior, 2/2 Pioneer Battalion, passed away at 0800 hours. His demise was caused by malnutrition, malaria and fever. His body was laid to rest in Grave No. 7. Padre Kellow conducted the burial service.

We are to prepare to move out tomorrow at an unstated time; usual Nipponese habit, could be early could be late. Depends on their mood. Some of our men are now working at the 62 kilo mark. At approximately 1420 hours we heard sounds of another big raid at Base. Judging by the explosions three attacks were made. We can be grateful of two things today; no rain and Base being plastered properly. Only hope the bombs fell well away from where the prisoners are quartered. Major Meagher was supposed to travel to Base today. The new Camp Commander, relieving Shimojo who is away, refused to allow him to leave.

Death playing a big part in this camp now, Private Payne passed away and was buried at 1100 hours, cause of death, malnutrition malaria and fever. At 1600 hours Private Goth departed this life and was interred shortly afterwards. He, too, had similar complaints.

A total of 232 men moved out at 1500 hours en route to the 60 kilo camp. Lt. Col. Eadie and Captain Nicholson remained at 40 kilo camp to care for the 190 men remaining there.

The troops of the 40 and 45 kilo camps combined and arrived at the 60 kilo camp at 1700 hours. As usual, no room. To find some sort of accommodation, 350 men were squeezed into a hut that is normally overcrowded with 200 bodies. The whole of the Force now packed like sardines in 1½ huts. We had no option, told to get into them, and not argue.

We argued but what was the use, we had nowhere to go unless the boys elected to doss down in the open, weather notwithstanding. They could not be allowed to do that as their lives could be in jeopardy

As it was, 50 of our Force were sent out to work, returned at 1900 hours. Our strength has been sadly depleted, now down to approximately one-quarter (499) of our original rollcall.

It is a filthy camp; got what we expected when told it had been used by Burmese labourers prior to us moving in. Everyone able to walk is involved in a complete clean-up. Have to, otherwise accept the legacy of disease suffered by the natives.

From the third day of the month (July) up to and including the 7th, the going has been tough. Work demands by the Nipponese are beyond all reason, yet they want more and more.

On the 4th, eight of our 150 workers were caught buying sugar from a trader. The Japanese confiscated the lot then sold it to us for 2.50 rupees, normal price 57 cents.

American Independence Day. It was not the Yanks who were to celebrate, it was the Nipponese. They did so by blitzing the sick ranks for workers.

Anderson Force was hit hard. It was a case of you, you and you. Out you go and no argument.

Fifty per cent of Anderson Force totally unfit were forced out despite all protests. Then came the turn of Williams Force Commander to confront the guard detailing the sick men. Heated argument developed and the Nip was told in no uncertain terms that he and his like were killing the obviously unfit men by demanding they do hard work out on the line.

After the confrontation the guard marched ten of the sick men out to join the workers, but before doing so named another ten who, in his opinion, could work. They remained in camp.

Another very tough job in front of the rail-laying gang today (5th) and the 160 will be absolutely done in when they return from the hardest work demanded by the Nipponese.

For the very first time since coming to Burma the Nipponese issued No. 1 Mobile Force with a 20-lb sack of potatoes. Shades of the good days, but unfortunately, 30% of them had rotted away.

*

July 7 started badly for Williams Force Commander when he was ordered to report to the camp commander's office. He guessed why he had been summoned and he was well aware it was not a goodwill 'invitation'.

He was told very forcefully he was uncooperative and he had to detail more men to work. This he refused to do, telling the Commander and his staff he had no intention of committing his unfit men to an uncertain fate. As far as he was concerned the workers he sent out were the healthiest available and the maximum number he would provide.

The annoyed Nipponese told him he argued too much; in the Japanese army everyone did as they were told. They expected prisoners of war, him in particular, to do exactly the same. He also said they were doing everything they could for the workers. They were dying, he stated, because they refused to work cheerfully.

*

A work party of 161 sent out today [7.7.43]; had to walk 9 kilometres there and back. A task on its own without having to undertake very heavy work at the end of the long hike. Tools had to be carried both ways.

We have been warned to have an early Reveille tomorrow; fifteen minutes earlier than normal. By doing this they think we will provide more men. That is impossible as too many are quite unfit for anything.

A heavy storm last night played havoc with the Japanese rations in store. The sugar they had was standing in muddy water, half melted, and, as far as the Nipponese were concerned, unfit for consumption by their troops, but quite all right for the POWs.

For once we agreed, sugar was sugar, muddy or not; enough was salvaged to help the sick. May the heavens open up again this night; who knows what will be revealed and acquired by men who have known few delicacies in a long, long time.

Out of the blue came an issue of shirts. As was usual, the Japanese took what they wanted, then handed the balance over for distribution amongst the men who laboured today.

Another blitz on the sick ranks by the Nips and despite strong objections, 12 of them were taken. It is galling having to stand and watch your unfit men being hunted along to perform tasks well beyond their capacity. But, what is the alternative!

*

Many a time the men in all forces thought about taking over camps. No bother in doing that. But what would happen afterwards? They were in a jungle camp, miles from any place where they could call for Allied forces. There was no source for a continuing food supply, and many were too ill to travel even a short distance.

A takeover was a hopeless proposition.

*

Memories of home cooking revived today [9.7.43] when everyone in camp was treated to four boiled potatoes for the evening meal. It was a real banquet, except for what went with them, rice and little else.

Word came through concerning more deaths at the 40 kilo camp where eleven of our Force now rest.

Due to the lack of rails and sleepers only 30 men required by the Nipponese today [11.7.43] and they were taken from Anderson Force. That small requirement was offset by the arrival of one of the nastiest creeps of a guard who ever came from Nippon. He was formerly batman to Lt. Col. Nagatomo and a pity he ever left Thanbyuzayat. He is without doubt the worst guard No. 1 Mobile Force has had yet. I've never struck more rottenness in one man.

Unlucky 13th, another move; this time to the 70 kilo camp and we expect the same old routine will apply—clean up a filthy area after the former residents have vacated.

If they were Burmese and diseased, we are headed for a lot of camp work and probable health problems.

No transport provided; it was a ten-kilo march and all gear had to be carried. Lucky for us, the Japanese used vehicles for their equipment.

The Nips did accede to one request as regards our sick personnel; 100 were taken to the 55 kilo hospital. En route four passed away.

Nagatomo's former batman waved the big stick today [14.7.43] and forced every sick man from his bedspace to clean up the camp in pouring rain. He ordered them to dig latrines and bury all rubbish. But he forgot one thing, no tools available to dig holes for anything.

He brushed aside all protests and literally forced the men to erect two poles outside the guardhouse, make tables, stands and ladders, etc. for the guard's hut.

In addition, they had to erect a kitchen for the Nipponese cooks on top of all their other tasks. Tools were soon made ready for work concerning them but none for the needs of the prisoners of war.

After working many hours in the constant downpour it was no surprise that another 100 men had to be added to the sick list.

The inhuman attitude of the new guard was never more demonstrated than it was today [15.7.43] when he forced 100 sick men out on to camp cleaning and any other job his imbecilic mind could conjure up. It is a wonder he did not demand the ten, who had arrived from Thanbyuzayat ex-hospital, to join the work force immediately. He is certainly on the warpath.

Another 20 men arrived from Base today [16.7.43] and they confirmed all the rumours we had been hearing concerning the bombing raids in that area. With them came an issue of 159 pairs of shorts and shirts, clothing so badly needed.

There is no abating in the rain and the camp is just about flooded out; mud and water at least one foot deep in the centre walk-way of the huts. There's no hope of dry feet or, for that matter, clothing (such as the men have) either. Mud and misery have combined to render life one of anguish and despair.

It is bad enough for those who are partially well but for the sick it is almost impossible to avoid high fevers or malaria. No-one knows what other illnesses this filthy hole may present.

Despite the inclement weather the line work does not stop and parties are demanded every day; 115 out yesterday and 120 today [19.7.43].

The huts are so badly overcrowded the Nipponese finally agreed something should be done and allocated another half hut to ease the situation.

Our strength increased by 50 men when a party from the 40 kilo camp arrived this morning at 0300 hours. Captain was Officer Commanding.

Some canteen stores arrived today [22.7.43] for the Nipponese but nothing for the prisoners of war.

Lt. Col. Eadie and the remainder of the Force at the 40 kilo camp were taken back to the 30 kilo hospital.

The guards are on a trading spree again and the POWs are being made the scapegoats in the blackmarket schemes. They purported to sell us 1200 eggs at three per rupee. On delivery only 900 were handed over, the missing 300 were supposed to have suffered breakages. Included in the transaction was, so they said, 50 blocks of sugar, only 45 handed over.

The 23rd and 24th were very long days for the workers. A total of 104 worked throughout the day and night in pouring rain. Meals were sent out to them at 1200, 1700 and 0300 hours.

Approximately half of them returned at 0200 hours and another gang was demanded to take their place. This was disputed and the guards informed only 'No Duty' men remained in the huts.

For once, it worked. No-one was sent out.

The Nipponese engineers realised only too well their error in building the line in dry weather over a watercourse. With the monsoonal rain the fill was quickly washed away as were several bridges. Unfortunately our men had to suffer the consequences and repair the damages.

The remainder of the all-night workers returned to camp at 1030 hours after a 26-hours stint. They were absolutely done in. They were too tired to even want to consume a meal. Most were out to it on their feet.

Another party went out at 1200 hours and a second one at 1800 hours; a total of 80 workers, 10 ration carriers.

The 25th and 26th turned out to be very tough days for the 97 and 94 respectively. The numbers failed to satisfy the Nipponese requirements and more were demanded. But ultimately the numbers were not increased.

The work is hard, the rations very low. Sergeant Shimojo eventually allowed the slaughter of one small cow and issued a paltry amount of white beans. However, he displayed his 'generosity' by allowing us to *purchase* our own rationed sugar *from him*.

The Nipponese have laid down a new work plan for the laying of the railway effective as from the 28th July, 1943. The workers will be required to lay a minimum of five kilometres of railway line per day.

In order to speed up the project sleepers will now be laid one every two metres.

This new demand holds frightening connotations and, if carried out, must further harm the health of every worker in the No. 1 Mobile Force. Today we lost two more. At least they will not suffer any further agony of body or mind in a fight to live.

In our sadness at the loss of valuable lives every man feels determined to thwart the Nipponese at every turn, even though in doing so physical hurt may result. They will suffer that, but overcoming rampant diseases is another matter.

To overcome the dangers of malnutrition and diseases of this tropical area two powerful essentials are necessary, nourishing food and drugs. The POWs lack both.

An indication of the determination of the Nipponese to force this railway through, no matter the cost in human life, was manifested today *[28.7.43]* when another order was issued—'All office staff must work out on the line from now on'.

*

Despite every approach made to Sergeant Shimojo by the No. 1 Mobile Force Commanders (Anderson and Williams) for better working conditions for their troops and for food and medicine, nothing changed. When Shimojo demanded the office staff do the work and abandon all clerical duties, it meant no further records of any kind could be kept, formulated or handed over to the Nipponese in accordance to usual requirements. It made no difference to him. He was adamant; they had to go out.

In that case, the commanders decided, one out, all out. Seven from Williams Force and five from Anderson Force, including the commanders, lined up for work.

When the Japanese realised what was happening there was quite an upheaval, but orders were orders, not necessarily always obeyed in full by the POWs, but in this case, to the letter.

It was obvious he meant the two commanders had to undertake all clerical work whilst the rest of their staff laboured on the line. Although clearly astonished at the turn of events he refused to retract, even when he was told the staff could not be in two places at once. Neither did the two commanders, and they marched out with the men. The bluff worked in that the attitude to the sick on the following day was less severe. Williams continues:

*

The following day *[29.7.43]* only 95 men were detailed as fit to work and the railway Japanese ordered a parade of all sick personnel. The intention was to take as many of the light sick as they considered fit enough to do some kind of work. The engineer took one look at the line-up and dismissed the lot.

Received orders today *[30.7.43]* to up stakes and move to the 80 kilo camp. It is like a dog chasing its tail; another shift, more cleaning up and probable hut repairs. As the sleepers and rails are laid and the line lengthens, it is either a long walk to and from the new site or head off to another camp.

At 0730 hours we were informed the sick would be carried and the remainder had to walk. The Japanese took all the fit men to carry their gear and left the sick to the care of others hardly even able to help themselves.

The latter party arrived at the new camp at 1510 hours to find their accommodation consisted of two huts formerly occupied by cattle. Filth and manure lay a foot deep on the floors. Mosquitoes and flies abounded in millions, they were everywhere. It was a sickening sight and yet another horrible experience in what has become the pattern of life for No. 1 Mobile Force.

It was a surprise to find a hospital hut occupied by members of No. 5 Branch. They were in a bad way, with the majority suffering from tropical ulcers. Their ration was just plain boiled rice, and not much of that.

One man, who had one of the largest ulcers ever seen, was examined by Major Krantz. In the Medical Officer's judgment immediate amputation was the only chance, slim as it may be, of saving his life. His leg was open from knee to ankle. It was in a frightful state, suppurating and emitting a foul smell.

It seemed the plight of the particular lad has been brought under the notice of the Japanese time and time again. They were not the slightest bit interested.

As far as they are concerned men who cannot work get no food. And might as well die. That dictum applies generally by the Japanese, hence the extra light rations these boys are on.

*

The plight of the 190 totally unfit troops shocked Williams and he conferred with kitchen staff. Rice and sugar were sent to them immediately. A barber paid them a visit to help clean them up; they were acutely embarrassed but unable to carry out normal ablutions, or trim or cut their hair.

The Mobile Force cooks lost no time in acquiring a buffalo they saw tethered in a Burmese cattle pen. The edible portions were soon cooked and then taken to the hospital hut. To offset any possibility of the Nipponese seeking the whereabouts of the 'obliging' animal, the No. 5 Group boys were told to consume the lot as soon as possible.

The men were advised to bury all bones and leave no trace whatsoever of the food. The starving men lost no time in consuming what they called the 'Gift from Heaven'. It was the best food they had been served in months, and their gratitude to their benefactors knew no bounds. But such was the comradeship so often displayed on the Burma-Thailand railway.

As was expected the loss of the buffalo did not go unnoticed by the Japanese and it was not long before a search of the kitchen and vicinity was on. They found nothing. Neither a piece of hide nor a bone was discovered despite a very thorough search. The lads in the kitchen denied all knowledge of the missing beast and showed the Nips it was only rice they were cooking.

To return to Williams' diary:

*

Another one of our boys passed away today *[31.7.43]*; he was one of the HMAS *Perth* boys. No matter how dedicated our Medical officers and staff are, they can't perform miracles or cure ill men without life-saving drugs and medicines. The death rate is more than alarming. Prisoners of war working on this railway project are at risk every moment of the day.

There is no question the Japanese are absolutely indifferent to the health state of all over whom they are in control. Lack of food and living essentials continues, but, they demand even sick men must work.

That was proven again today when another blitz was made on the ranks of the obviously seriously ill men. Not satisfied with the numbers considered by them as sufficient the Nips again ordered, if not all office staff, a portion thereof, be sent out to the line job to improve the figures of available 'fit' men.

Two more funerals from the No. 5 Group hospital. Everyone in that hut stares death in the face. They are gaunt, ghostlike; their bodies emaciated. They are a forgotten body of men suffering the pangs of hell; rotting tropical ulcers, beri-beri, malaria and many other associated diseases that could wipe them out, unless some humanity is shown from the Japanese ranks.

They have no such humanity and thousands of lives lost testify to that!

The lads whose ulcered leg was so bad Major Krantz decided on an immediate amputation, has now only a very slim chance of pulling through. Weakened to a point of near collapse, fighting malnutrition and possible gangrene, game as he is, the giant struggle may be just too much for him.

With the monsoonal season now at its height the work on the rail line has increased considerably; washaways at low level areas, bridges down and the maddened drive by the Nipponese to overcome these problems, which foolishly were unforeseen by them but expected by the POWs, have made the lives of the workers a nightmare. The workers risk life and limb on flimsy bridge structures, constructed of the poorest materials, as they labour to rebuild them.

August Bank holiday if we were at home; unfortunately we are far from such gracious living. On present standards, our lot compares very unfavourably with the poorest races in the whole world. Men are grasping at every straw in order to maintain life, undignified in some ways perhaps, but life is precious.

A boxed-meat ration arrived today from the Base camp. It had been delayed along the way. So much so it was just a stinking mass and alive with maggots. Its odour preceded its arrival. However, it *is* meat, unpalatable, but beggars cannot be choosers. It was at least seven days old.

The Japanese took what they considered as edible and gave the troops the horrible remains. In no way could it be wasted. The kitchen boys washed the squirming crawlies off and made a stew out of what would ordinarily be considered unfit for animal consumption.

The Japanese are still demanding more and more workers. In the ranks of the 150 sent out today (2nd August) were some of the office staff taking the places of some less fortunate.

Three days into August and our living conditions are worsening by the minute. The non-stop rain has made a mockery of the huts' roof structure and the centre walkway is almost knee-deep in mud. Water is pouring from top and sides. However, the men are so wearied and done in, they just flop down on their bamboo bed-spaces and seek solace in sleep.

Mud everywhere and inescapable!

Anniversary of the outbreak of the First World War, that 'war to end all wars'; and, bad news has hit us hard. Informed we have to reduce our rice intake from 350 grammes per man per day to 250. If it was starvation previously, what now!

A strong protest did procure something, permission to slaughter a yak cow. The Nipponese confiscated the greater portion of the beast and gave the prisoners the ribs (can't eat bones), one shoulder and half of one leg.

Impossible to feed hundreds of men on such a meagre issue; but at least the sick will appreciate what broth can be made from it.

Another day and more rain, huts flooded, kitchen fires hard to keep alight with green wet wood. Our miseries are compounding daily.

No matter that state of the weather, the difficulties in procuring firewood, then trying to burn it, the Japanese demand hot water be provided for their daily baths.

A few cigars arrived today [7.8.43] to be sold through the canteen, but not near enough to satisfy the demand. When one lacks food the inhalation of smoke, be it from tobacco or rolled leaves, does tend to allay hunger pains.

Rain is teeming down and bridges disappearing into the streams, that means more of the hazardous work of trying to replace them, accompanied by the screams of the Japanese engineers who flog them into the desperate attempts at reconstruction.

Timber has to come out of the jungle and that is no easy task with blunt axes biting into sodden green trees. But the railway has to be built, no matter how difficult the problems.

Shimojo is at it again, the sick must work and he selected 24 who could hardly stand, let alone be able to perform hard toil. When they arrived at the work site they were so tired and ill, all but two just sat around in the pouring rain. No matter the inducement, pick handles, boots or rifle butts, not one of the dead-beat boys moved.

The haulage of heavy timber for bridge repair work was normally carried out by elephants. The Japanese have discarded that idea. As far as they are concerned, a few Australians can do more than the lumbering giants of the jungle.

Is it any wonder so many men are fading away.

In the last few days twelve have died at the 30 kilo hospital. In Williams Force, 58 have perished since arriving in Burma in the latter part of 1942.

There is no accounting for the Japanese intellect or their unpredictability. Time and time again they have searched the meagre belongings of all the men. In every swoop they have taken just about everything they could find, even of minute value.

They went through the huts again today [9.8.43] and took away every scrap of paper they could lay their thieving hands on, also quite a few keepsakes and eating utensils; the latter handed back after protest.

They were, supposedly, searching for dangerous weapons!

As proof of their peculiar thinking and even after a very thorough search of the huts, they requested the prisoners lend or hand over to them their *parangs*. Even if any of the men had happened to possess one, the Nips would never have got the use of it.

Something is in the wind. The guards are undergoing parade-ground drill; a most unusual event considering the 'speedo' drive to get the railway through. Maybe it is only wishful thinking, but it is possible the fighting in upper Burma is not going in favour of the Japanese and the guards are being prepared for battle action.

One very pleasing aspect of the unexpected drill session was that the severity of it so tired the guards, they could not have cared two hoots what the prisoners of war were doing. Everyone hopes the training continues. But unfortunately our wishful thinking has let us down. It was soon back to work.

A total of 98 went out to work today [11.8.43] and we were given no indication as to when they will return to camp. All Anderson Force were sent back as soon as they arrived at the Railway HQ. It looks like night shift will be on again.

Anderson Force went to work at 2000 hours and Williams Force returned at 2300 hours. They call that day work; 15 hours each day, seven days a week—and on half rations. Who said the Nips know humanity!

Something brewing. The Japanese doctor is inspecting the sick men. And when that happens it is never in the interests of the unfit. Nothing came of it except orders to take further blood tests for malarial content. No matter what tests they might take from time to time, we never hear anything about the results. It is possible they go to No. 3 Group Headquarters in Bangkok, but that is purely conjecture.

All fit men of Anderson Force sent out to work on the line last night at 1900 hours and returned today *[13.8.43]* at 1000 hours. From Williams Force 100 detailed at 0900 hours and were forced to work 36 hours laying sleepers and rails.

No wonder lives are being lost when men are driven to such extreme exhaustion. We lost three more today.

Brigadier Varley called in today *[14.8.43]* on a tour of inspection of camp conditions. Whilst he had very little time to converse with us—he had guards with him—his face expressed his feelings. The rows of sick men clearly astonished him.

The horror of this railway building project is gathering in intensity day by day. Particularly hard work, poor rations and ill health brought about by malnutrition, and exposure to monsoonal rains that begets disease.

The workers are bashed and belted unmercifully by guards, railway engineers and gangers. Somehow after pitiless attacks on just about every part of their anatomy, they rise again, and in a mechanical sort of way carry on, guided by instinct only.

[15.8.43] At 0900 hours today 87 men trudged out on to another hazard-filled day. They know the long, demanding hours that lay ahead of them during which they *may* get a meal and maybe a short rest now and again.

As the days pass, the rail and sleeper laying proceeds at an even faster pace; and the ranks of the workers correspondingly diminish. More graves are dug and more crosses dot yet another plot in the Burmese jungle.

There has to be an end to this seemingly endless torture of body and soul. Only those gifted with a terrific willpower can survive this mad drive to bring together two ends of a railway that engineers, well-acclaimed world-wide, considered impossible.

But, the Japanese needed a rail link from Singapore to Moulmein, rivers, mountains and jungle notwithstanding. They had the labour and the reason. That was enough; and within the next few months the impossible will have been overcome. The cost in human lives did not concern them.

BOMBING OF THANBYUZAYAT HOSPITAL CAMP

A little after 2.00 p.m. on 12th June, 1943, patients in the base hospital camp, Thanbyuzayat, were thrilled to hear the drone of Allied planes heading, as they thought, towards Bangkok or somewhere in that direction, to blast the Nipponese into perdition.

Some weeks earlier that same welcome sound pervaded the huts and all inmates gave thanks to whoever was responsible for the consoling belief the Japanese were now being paid in their own coin. On that occasion, those who were able, ran out and waved like maddened beings at the pilots and their crews. They were thrilled to see the red, white and blue emblems on those avenging masters of the sky.

Again the mobile sick hurried out to wave encouragement to their own kind as they flew quite low over the area. But the cheers and cries of delight faded when they saw the formation break off into groups of three. Cold chills radiated up and down their spines as it dawned on them the camp could be the target.

The Nipponese guards literally fell into any depression they could find as they saw the planes wheel and level out in attack. Moments later the sound of explosions caused ear-drums to throb and blood in bodies to freeze as pieces of shrapnel, bits of wood and splintered bamboo flew everywhere.

Then, just as quickly, the raid was over. The planes closed into formation and went on their way, southwards.

A few moments of dead silence was broken when a lad came racing up to the medical officers, screaming, 'They got the well party. They got the well party'.

Nobody even considered the hospital huts would have been the actual target. The nearest crater was some distance away, near the old hospital area. But it was possible the pilot of one plane saw the group at the well, thought it might have been an Ack-Ack post and let his bomber have a shot at it. The water carriers had only just arrived at the spot as the bomb burst in their midst. Twelve died and only two survived.

Some patients in the old huts suffered wounds from bomb splinters. Approximately fifteen were injured, some severely, others only slightly.

Rumour had it many Japanese were blown to pieces but the commandant, Nagatomo, admitted to the loss of only one guard. Subsequent activities near their quarters suggested Nagatomo had misrepresented the facts.

The fear weighed on the minds of just about every patient in the fourteen long huts; (which in no way differed from the appearance of the Nipponese barracks and storehouses, but were thronged with about 3,000 prisoners of war in varying stages of ill-health) that the day would come when all of the buildings at Thanbyuzayat would be at risk. The knowledge that an ammunition dump was situated very close to the hospital huts intensified these fears.

From an air force point of view, unless some source of intelligence had informed them that most of the huts contained ill POWs, it was a perfect target. They were beside a large railway yard packed with rolling stock and supply areas of major military importance that literally invited heavy bombing.

Brigadier Varley and staff pleaded constantly for permission to erect Red Cross signs in the vicinity or, better still, on every hut where incapacitated prisoners were packed. The answer was always the same. No!

Nagatomo ultimately made one grand concession; he allowed a system of slit trenches to be built alongside each hut.

At sunset every man who could walk or crawl made his way to the cemetery to attend the service that paid tribute to those who had lost their lives that afternoon. Amongst the dead were Australians, Americans, Dutchmen and an

Englishman. The services were conducted by Padres Bashford, Corry and Vergeest. Few in attendance had dry eyes.

In subsequent discussions, many spoke of the lack of air support throughout the Malayan campaign when it was so vitally needed. Now, as prisoners of war, they were being attacked because they occupied enemy territory. Many reasoned that it was possible the Allies were aware of their proximity to major military targets, and any bombs falling on or near the packed POW huts did so accidentally.

Three days later the camp inmates had just completed a rehearsal of what precautions to take if and when the camp again came under fire. Every mobile patient was allotted a trench to occupy the moment an air raid warning was sounded. Arrangements were also made for the protection of the immobile, time permitting.

The drone of incoming planes caused little jubilation; everyone felt uneasy. And they had reason to be! As had happened three days earlier, the Nipponese opened up with rifle, machine guns and, in some cases with pistols, at planes approximately 2,000 feet overhead.

There was danger enough from the weird shooting of the frenzied guards. They appeared to shut their eyes and let fly into the air. Bullets whistled very close to men huddled in the not-too-deep trenches. Many actually went straight through the hut walls and roofs, but absolutely none in the vicinity of an attacking plane.

There was no doubt whatever as to the target; it was the huts.

In flights of three they bombed and strafed the whole area. The aircraft dived very low and one stick of bombs made a direct hit on the workers hut in the old section of the camp. A hut on the other side of the parade ground was demolished. Many bombs fell near the ammunition dump, the canteen and the cookhouse. Others fell between the old and the new huts, showering red hot splinters in every direction.

One large bomb crater was formed within a few yards of a long trench which held over one hundred patients. It was quite easy to see the bombs leave the belly of the planes but it was a impossible to observe the strafing cannons.

As far as the Nipponese small-arms fire was concerned, the plane crews treated it with contempt. To many of the observers it appeared (to use a battle saying) to 'only draw the crabs'.

To be bombed and strafed in battle is accepted as a war risk, but a POW camp is not ordinarily considered as a battleground.

The raid lasted well over an hour but seemed much longer and as the planes climbed up and away, sighs of relief were heard. But the hard and heartbreaking part came as the casualties were found and counted. Sixty were killed or wounded.

Colonel Hamilton, AAMC, had accompanied Brigadier Varley to the office of Nagatomo to seek permission for the former to be allowed to travel to Rangoon and broadcast the location of the camp hospital. After much discussion, the commandant refused the request.

When news of the refusal was made known to all inmates, morale dropped to a very low ebb. Admittedly, only a faint hope was expressed as regards the broadcast possibility, but at least it had been a hope. Denial was the last straw. Now hope for future immunity had been dispelled.

It was obvious from the depth and width of the craters that 500-pounders had fallen into the camp area. The crater near the canteen was of a most peculiar shape and many feared it concealed a time-bomb, but fortunately it didn't.

As night descended, long lines of disease-ravaged men stood to attention as the last body was laid to rest. Ill-clothed they may have been, but the skin and bone men never wavered as they paid tribute to their fallen comrades.

The following day just about everyone in the camp had the jitters, including the Nipponese. When Padre Vergeest, momentarily at a loss for a word, turned his eyes skywards so did the whole of his congregation. To them it meant only one thing, planes and another raid.

The aftermath of the devastation was an alarming deterioration in the health of the sick. In the words of one medical officer, the reason was the raids. They did more damage, he said, than many months of treatment without drugs.

On the morning of the 17th Nagatomo ordered the evacuation of the hospital patients. However, despite strong approaches for transport, rail or road, none was forthcoming. Except for approximately fifty bed-ridden personnel, all, irrespective of condition, were ordered to prepare immediately for a move to a jungle camp. Personal belongings and all necessary gear had to be carried.

In batches of fifty men, and one officer, the march of nearly 3,000 gaunt figures began a trek beyond belief. Many of the marchers had scarcely walked more than a hundred yards in months. Now derelict, barefooted, with ulcered legs, many of them fever-ridden and hardly able to put one foot in front of the other, they were being forced to cover miles that healthy men would baulk at.

They made a sad, heart-wringing sight as they moved yard by yard. To make it just so much more difficult they were held up near the railway siding for over an hour for a tenko. As always, the Japanese could not agree on numbers and the angry, ill and frustrated patients were subjected to unnecessary delays.

As 2.30 p.m. approached all eyes scanned the skies, as that was the time of the day the bombers normally paid their call. For the halt, the lame and the blind—yes, some were actually blind—it appeared as if the Japanese were deliberately exposing them to a massacre, should a bombing raid eventuate.

At long last the leading batch began what could truthfully be termed an eight-kilo grind beyond human imagination. Young men, now old in features and physical ability, had to carry their own meagre possessions plus, in some instances, those of their weaker mates.

Tired beyond measure and filled with pain, they were nonetheless determined to get to their journey's end. Some moved crazily, leaning against cobbers, who in turn leaned against them for some sort of support.

To the onlooker, and there were some Burmese observing, it must have appeared that the writhing, swaying bodies resembled a large reptile in its death throes.

No-one really knows what time the first patients, almost dead on their bare feet, fell into the huts at the 4 kilo mark—a camp long since abandoned by the first group on the line job.

As this was to be the administration point, all apart from those in the first batch had another six kilometre struggle towards the almost ruined buildings that were to be their hospital.

Those who had to continue, and they were the majority, staggered along as best they could. Many collapsed, fell, were assisted back on to their feet, only to hit the ground again in utter exhaustion.

Those who died on that frightful death march were murdered by Nagatomo and his staff, just as surely as if they had executed them.

When the advance party finally came to their hospital camp they were shocked, bewildered and maddened beyond measure. Only one hut even remotely deserved the name. The remainder had been ravaged by rain, winds and native scavengers; they were roofless, and only ten had atap sides. Nature, too, had played a part, and the jungle was beginning to reclaim its own. But over 1,000 men had to find some kind of shelter in the ruins. All were too tired to attempt anything but grab at a bush or some almost leafless atap to protect them from the incessant rain.

The one giant out of the next morning's chaos was Major Colin Cameron, 2/4 Machine-Gun Battalion, who called the officers together to discuss the immediate future. Everything appeared so hopeless. A camp had to be built and there was not one fit man there to even consider a start.

To make matters even worse, there was not one medical officer to attend to any of the patients, some of whom now hovered on the brink of death.

As the days progressed, Major Cameron's drive and ability inspired everyone. The cooks laboured tirelessly, working day and night in a tremendous effort to establish a kitchen. Not one man missed a meal. Like Cameron, those great and compassionate men who comprised the kitchen staff deserved the great tributes which every man able to speak paid them.

Due to the lack of facilities and materials, humpies of all description were everywhere. The monsoon season was at its height and, unless the sun appeared, and that was seldom, no-one was ever actually dry.

Rohan Rivett, war correspondent, and a group of volunteers began the arduous task of preparing latrines. This was a work of the utmost urgency; hundreds of patients were suffering from dysentery or allied diseases and perfect hygiene, or as near as possible, was high on the priority list.

The Nipponese guards were a bomb-happy lot and insisted on all mobile patients moving out into the jungle well before it was time for the now almost daily overhead flight of Allied bombers on their way to Thanbyuzayat, which had been attacked at least five times in as many days.

However, although the jungle offered sanctuary from overhead blitzes, it was no fun spending hours without cover in pouring rain.

There was one comical side to the Japanese desire for the camp inmates to hide in the jungle. They would head for the tall trees and beckon (not yell orders) for their charges to join them for safety's sake. The Nipponese showed themselves to be truly unpredictable.

In many instances this bush hideaway offered a chance to meet up with Burmese traders. Unknown to the guards, a veritable market sprung up right under their noses. Quite a few of the more able lads even made it to a Burmese village where they traded for fruit and other food. The roamers were always back in time for tenko.

As soon as the light sick were able to carry out tasks of any kind, parties of up to a hundred at a time were forced to return to Thanbyuzayat at night to repair bomb damage. In teeming rain they carried rubble to fill craters.

Two inmates of the camp hospital operated a secret radio, and one night Les Bullock was on his bed listening to the BBC broadcast when a Nip guard came near. Bob Skilton, Les' mate, knowingly held the guard's attention until Les had heard the whole bulletin.

Great relief was afforded many of the very ill men when Nagatomo agreed to transfer some of the worst cases to the 18 kilo camp. A few weeks later all the sick had been moved to Retpu, the 30 kilo mark. Some were provided with transport, many walked the whole distance but were permitted to load all their gear aboard a truck.

Thanbyuzayat was by now but a bad memory; the 'Hut of Death' had been demolished, as were most of the buildings the camp had once boasted. The railway yard was in shambles, rolling stock wrecked and all semblance of a massive POW camp gone.

Not one prisoner of war who had resided there was sorry to hear of the complete devastation the Allied bombers had created in that horror camp. Their only regret was the fact that hundreds of their mates now rested in the cemetery there. The cross at the head of each grave tells its own story: one of man's inhumanity to man; of how physical torture, starvation and ill-treatment had brought them to that small plot of ground in a country thousands of miles from home, loved ones and all that was dear to them. Those gallant men who rest there found the peace their beleaguered bodies craved.

TOM FAGAN POW DIARY
June-July 1943 at the 105 Kilo Camp

ANOTHER SEAMY side of POW life begins in this camp, the 105 kilo as it is commonly called. Without doubt, the worst we have encountered. The wet season has set in, huts leak as the atap roofing is a thing of the past and the Nips refuse to supply additional covering. Everything is sodden; the floors ankle deep in mud.

There is no let-up in the work schedule as the Nip engineers are determined to complete this section on time. We are again facing the task of gouging rock faces with picks. Chips fly off and penetrate the skin, particularly the shins. Painful sores are the result and quite a few have developed tropical ulcers. Hope I don't cop one; they must be painful.

Thought luck had come my way at last. Some of my mates, knowing I had discarded all my few possessions, have made certain I have a dixie, a mug and spoon. In addition, a pair of shorts, a bit ragged, but something to wear. To whoever supplied them go my thanks. Of course, no-one gave them to me; they just happened to land on my bed-space.

Another slice of good fortune, so I thought. Ten of us were detailed to go back to the 98 kilo camp on a water job. We had to fill 40-gallon drums with water from the river, load them onto trucks and transport them to the waterless 105 kilo camp. Sounded a sweet deal. What a let down! It is a staging camp for Nip troops. We are the only white personnel and don't the Japs take advantage of us. We are at their beck and call all hours of the day and night. Might have been better off where we were. Who knows?

The only real difference is, we miss out on the seven to eight miles hike to work as the lads at the 105 kilo have to do. But we have a lodger, our Korean guard. He has to bunk with us. The Nips hate the sight of him, won't even talk to him. We did gain something though. The same rations as the Nip troops are served. Much better than the plain boiled rice we have been used to. Good tucker makes one feel somewhat better.

With the roads just a mud heap the trucks are constantly bogged. We have to dig, push and do all that is possible to get them out. Whilst we are at it the lousy drivers are yelling abuse and threats. Maybe one day we'll even the score.

It takes a full day to get one load from the river to the 105 kilo, but the eight-mile trip is fraught with absolute drudgery as we are in and out of the bogs both ways.

When we do get back there is no rest. Usually get a feed, then it's wash the Nips' clothing, grease and do daily maintenance of the worn-out trucks. It is nearly always after ten before we have a chance to clean ourselves up and bed down for the night. At least we are dry at night; we are domiciled in a tent. No leaky atap roofing, but we do have a muddy floor.

1st June 1943

There has been no let-up in the downpour for the last three weeks; we live and work in a quagmire. Our once-dry tent was washed out and the Nips allowed us to build a hut. At least we were able to ensure the roof was as near watertight as possible with atap.

I am a bit puzzled. We are hardly ever dry, nearly always wet through to the skin, but no-one cops a cold. If these conditions applied at home—wish I was there—runny noses and head colds would be the order of the day.

Yesterday we were told to have a yasumi, plenty rest. Their idea was driven home to us when we were handed sledge hammers and ordered to break rocks into metal to spread on the road, After we had completed the job we had to wade into the river, waist high, and gather stones from the bottom.

In the fast-running waters it was all we could do to keep our balance. That was difficult enough and we soon became exhausted. The guards realised there was a possibility the lot of us could drown and allowed us out of the water

Something doing up north. A large number of front-line Nip troops passed through here yesterday. Puny little runts, all of them. They had no transport and were marching loaded down with gear.

Their officers were well catered for as far as their possessions were concerned. I saw up to eight men roped to decrepit hand-carts that were full of the officers' baggage.

A few groups were hauling what looked like old-type mountain guns. In a way, I felt a little compassion for them, hooked up as they were like bullocks. Their faces were drawn, their physiques that of a small boy. Their legs buckled under the tremendous strain as they pulled with all the strength they had. They looked completely done in.

One of them could take it no longer, he just collapsed to the ground. An officer came, as we all thought, to give him assistance. Not so, he put his foot onto the lad's head, trampled it into the mud, then put his boot into his ribs until instinct, it couldn't have been anything else, brought him to his feet.

We could hardly believe our eyes. An apparent front line soldier treated so brutally. Such inhumanity! That boy was one of their own, one of their fighting men. No wonder we, as prisoners of war, cop their wrath. They are not really human.

One of our guards told some of the boys that company had been force-marched all the way from Bangkok and were en route to Burma fighting zone. If I am any judge, the only fight that will be left in them, will be to survive the rigours of the journey.

5th June 1943

According to the Nips, we of the water party have recovered from our illnesses (the reason why we were selected in the first place was because we were too ill to work on the railway job) and therefore ready to go back to the work requirements at the 105 kilo camp. We are there now.

It is a case of out of the frying pan into the fire. Cholera is rampant here, four passed away last night and many others are in the isolation hut. Only medical staff, who are risking their own lives, are allowed near them. Our orderlies and Medical Officers are simply marvellous. They fear nothing and do everything in their power to render aid to the sick and injured.

When we marched back into this camp last night I was amazed. No, staggered is more like it, to see the change in the faces of my mates. They were, as I thought, just skin and bone before I left; we all were. But during my stint at the 98 kilo something terrible has happened here. All I can see is taut skin over bones, men lying contorted in agony from sickening tropical ulcers, knees to ankles. Others, bedridden due to malaria and associated diseases.

If an epidemic of cholera spreads, this camp could be wiped out in a few days. Hygiene is very strict, it has to be, as it is the only real preventive action the medicos can offer.

We are now at the height of the monsoon season and the road, if one can call it that, is a river of mud, but the only route vehicles travelling north can take.

In this particular area the Jap engineers demand the prisoners be used to fell trees, cut them into suitable lengths and corduroy the roadway. Only the unfit men required; the better in health are needed to 'speedo' the railway job.

It is a heartbreaking task; wasn't so bad when the trees were close to the road, but now long distances are involved. The antique axes we have to use make the work so much harder for the men who have never used one in their lives before becoming soldiers.

The ration issue is at its lowest level, supplies are not coming through due to the state of the road. Corduroying is a practical idea until the weight of the vehicles forces the saplings down into the mud.

It is a seemingly hopeless attempt to make the road fit for vehicular use, but it is the only way to get supplies through, except by manpower, which we have been warned may soon be employed.

Due to the scarcity of food, fatigue is taking its toll; we are all tired, haven't had a day off since Anzac Day. Yes, we remembered it, even though we were not allowed to really commemorate it. Maybe we will come next year. I hope to be home then with my beloved wife and family who can watch as I take my place in the march.

We all feel filthy even though we are seldom dry due to the constancy of the rain. What clothes we have stink. Most of us have only G-strings and a hat, but even they pong.

We are living a terrible life and suffer bouts of despondency and then a honeymoon with optimism. The latter born of rumours of Allied successes in the various theatres of war; we tend to believe them because we want to, badly. Mostly they prove to be just latrine-o-grams, thought up by some morale builder. We are but men grabbing at straws.

10th June 1943

Four things govern our life at the present time—rain, mud, rice and work. It breaks my heart to see so many starving, unhealthy men. Deaths are becoming quite common now; three more passed on yesterday and many more appear to be ready to join them any day.

Hundreds are just lying on their bed-spaces and unable to move or fend for themselves. Dysentery, malaria, beri-beri, pellagra and malnutrition are illnesses making inroads upon so many weakened and crippled; the legacy of POW life.

Many exist, I am sure, purely on the power of prayer and a determination to make it no matter what they may have to suffer to be alive when this war is over. I, for one, have my faith and my religion.

The rice-ration for the sick is half of the normal or, as one wit said, 'What is half of nothing?' Good question! For that is what the servings indicate. A few grains of rice in a dixie, not balls or lumps, just teases the hunger pains.

A lot of the sick boys turn away from what is offered them. 'Give it to Joe' is often heard. Joe, or whoever he may be, has a better chance; the one that lives because one of his mates had given up or preferred the relief of death, rather than try to carry on under frightful conditions.

Tomorrow 500 of us have been detailed to go back to the 96 kilo camp and each to carry back 38 lbs of rice. It will be a hike of 18 miles there and back via the route we must travel. Those who have already had to do it 'heartened' us. They said every yard of each mile on the return trip is likened to a pilgrimage to hell. Wet rice swells, gets heavier and heavier as the carriers trudge through knee deep mud and slush.

Hard as the detail will be it has to be accomplished if we are to save the lives of both sick and workers. Half of the total strength is hospitalised. Rice, food of any kind is a must, if any are to survive.

The Nips are at the screaming rage stage because, as there are so many sick prisoners of war, work quotas cannot be filled. Those who feel they can more or less cope, volunteer, to save the very ill from what, in many cases, is death out on the job.

Our medicos determine who is really fit enough to face the hazards of the railway work or timber parties. However, as far as the guards are concerned, there is never enough. They defy our doctor's diagnosis and go into the huts and grab men at random. Whether they are 'bioki' (ill) or not worries them little. As long as they have arms and legs, they can work.

The result is many collapse from sheer exhaustion and then, and only then, will the ill-tempered sadists allow two men to take them back to camp. In many instances the carriers deliver bodies to the mortuary hut. Such is the penalty many pay because our captors do not know the meaning of care for the sick, or have any understanding of human compassion.

When the hut blitz is over those left behind are not really safe, the Nips have a habit of returning and grabbing more, just because they saw a leg or an arm move. That 'mans', according to the 'Tojoman', is well enough to swing a pick, axe or some other tool. It is a sickening process that goes on day after day. The resultant deaths don't worry the Nips; less rations to be provided.

Those of us who survive will always remember the railroad of death and our barbaric tormentors, who put us through hell and have caused the death of so many of our mates.

As each day dawns I pray I will live the hours out. Hours that may, and possibly will, be filled with the utmost degradation and physical torture.

Very few of us have footwear; our legs are filthy masses of tropical ulcers that run from knee to ankle. I have one and know the real meaning of agony at its worst. Little can be done for those so afflicted; our medicos are helpless without drugs and medicines. The only treatment is boiling water packs. There again, many of us are beaten; no bandages or cloth of any kind to use as advised; not even rice bags. The greatest fear is gangrene.

I hate and despise these barbaric Japanese, and the just as sadistic Korean guards, for the suffering they mete out to humans, and also to animals and birds. There is no end to the lengths to which they'll go to inflict pain. I seethe with fury as I feel or see their bursts of cruelty.

In pre-war days, or more particularly before becoming a POW of the Japanese, no-one could ever have convinced me I would see grown, supposedly educated men, go to such lengths to cause hardship and horror, or to perpetrate, deliberately, demoniacal acts of unbelievable violence towards men, women, children or animal life.

20th June 1943

I couldn't have believed that such a frightful state of affairs could exist as they do in this camp. It is not only bad, it's a mess. How some boys are hanging on to life has me wondering. The hut is terribly overcrowded; crippled and sick men everywhere. Those who can, help the more helpless. Some cannot put a foot to the ground; they move either on their backsides or revert to their baby days, and crawl. Such a despairing sight!

Some who attempt the trip to the latrines, just don't make it. We call them the 'trail blazers'. No malice. They get so embarrassed. Their eyes tell how they feel.

The odour in the huts, even outside, tells the story of dysentery only too well. It's impossible to eradicate. The hygiene squad do a mammoth job! We can never repay them, the medical staff or the cooks.

The middle of our hut, suppose everyone is the same, is a stream. The continuous rain has everything sodden. May as well be without roofing for all the good the worn-out atap is. Add that discomfort to those deprived of their ability to walk, even sit up, and some idea may be gathered as to what conditions apply. And this is said to be a hospital hut.

Hell, I feel awful today. I've got the lot, malaria, the runs, and agonising pains in my lower right leg. The only treatment is still boiling water. We get that for every ailment. No wonder the medicos look so done in. They do their utmost, day and night, to relieve the pain and despair felt by so many. If only they had the drugs!

Not a day passes that they don't approach the camp commandant who blandly shows the palms of his hands. No supplies available even for his own men, or so he claims. Their health record does not substantiate the claim. They have good food, drugs, medicines and even call on the knowledge of our medical officers *if* any of the guards appear to be unwell. A damned pity they do miss out on what we have to put up with.

Our doctors have tried just about everything they can to alleviate the distress of those badly affected by dysentery. Charcoal is the only remedy of any sort; it helps quite a few. But, in the main, nature takes its course. Cascara, what little there was of it, was also used.

As the rations for the sick are so low quite a few of the boys have been seeking frogs, a snake now and then, boil grass and bamboo shoots; anything that will produce bulk if not nourishment. Desperate measures for desperate men.

I get a lump in my throat every time I hear the sound of the Last Post; it means another poor boy has gone to rest. When we originally came here, no-one envisaged the necessity for a cemetery. Today we have quite a large one. Every hour we feel the spectre of death is above us—just waiting. We wonder whose turn will it be tonight.

Last week a large group of 'F' and 'H' Forces, Thailand, came past our camp. They had been on the road for days. They had covered 150 miles by the time they got here. Now en route to a site 50 kilometres away. They were, so we were told, all very sick men heading for a hospital camp.

They comprised English and Australians; sixteen had died on the trip from the same diseases rampant in this hell-hole. Throughout the long journey the guards had refused them any type of vessel to boil water. The result, they drank from any stream they came to; many contracted cholera, hence the terrible death rate.

Suppose I got a bit excited when I heard there were some Aussies from the Thailand side passing our camp. I felt crook, but I struggled out and was able, by dodging the guard, to speak to one of the Australians. He told me, shudder when I think of it, 92 (all Aussies) passed away in two days at the 130 kilo camp. As applies here, no medicines or drugs supplied.

Not one was buried!

So many had gone it was beyond the ability of anyone to dig graves. Huge fires were built and the bodies cremated. At last count, as he told me, over 1,900 prisoners of war were incapable of working due to illnesses.

To me, the death toll represented plain murder on the part of the animalistic traits of the Japanese. With the railway building nearing completion, what matter to them if a few hundred more prisoners did die!

I hope the day of reckoning is not too far away.

We have had a bit of news about other camps. The same story each time, the majority are down with the same health problems as exist here. Their cemeteries, too, are getting larger by the day.

Slaughter! What else can it be called.

Last night the Burmese, who will not work in wet weather, shot through. Even let their bullocks run free and abandoned their carts. We don't mind one little bit. They were a dirty mob, unhygienic and lousy with disease.

Their campsite was an eyesore and too darned close to ours. It is possible the outbreak of cholera in this area came from their fly-infested, uncleaned buildings. Their huts, if it is possible, were in a worse state than ours. Is it any wonder they headed for the jungle or some far-away village? God only knows how many of their bodies are left in the huts or are in the nearby bushes.

In a way, their sudden move and panic has proved to be a bit of a boon to us. Late last night, when some of our lads woke up to what was happening, two yaks were caught, butchered and ended up in our kitchen. It was done so quietly not one guard saw or heard a thing.

Quite a few of our boys suffered nasty after-effects when they were fed with pieces of real meat. Their stomachs, mine too, probably, must have shrunk on the rice-only diet. However, not one complained. I, for one, thought it great!

I am not blaming the deceased yaks for my return of malaria and dysentery; it is something I have to contend with periodically, like it or not. I am not the only one, far from it. Mates all around me are in the same condition. We are so weak it is difficult to lift a spoonful of the hated, but life-sustaining rice.

Just heard the Base camp at Thanbyuzayat has had another going over by Allied bombers. The worst part of it was that a lot of POWs were killed. Their huts were in close proximity to the Nip anti-aircraft batteries. A nasty habit the Japanese have, putting their 'guests' at risk.

30th June 1943

To our surprise the last couple of days have been fine, not one drop of rain. However, didn't have much time to enjoy it; the wet, the big one this time, they tell us, is with us again. It is a repeat of last year except the majority of us have been endowed in the meantime with injuries and disease we never anticipated.

How I wish I was home. My loved ones are never out of my thoughts, bless all of them.

I'm dreading the period ahead; monsoonal rains are unbelievable. It isn't just rain, it pours and pours. And we have to work and work in it. Like it? Like hell we do. Everywhere is a quagmire. The hut centre is churned-up mud and at least six inches deep. Overhead the roof acts as a sieve, we are never dry.

Despite our ill health we are out in the hills from daylight until dark, smashing up rocks to make ballast for the rotten railway we are building. It is no longer a pick and shovel job. Sledge hammers, big beauties, have been handed to us.

When our basket is full it has to be lumped over half a mile to the line site. Don't know what they weigh, except they feel like a ton. A bag of rice seems a snack compared to these arm-dragging monstrosities. Wouldn't be so bad if we had good weather, and didn't have to slog through knee deep mud, both ways. Can't even take a five-minute spell. If you do the impact of a rifle butt is soon felt on some part of one's body.

The most cruel punishment, quite enjoyable as far as the Nips and Koreans are concerned, is to put their boot into an ulcered leg. They really take delight in the agony the unhappy recipient suffers. We do our best to control our emotions. But only yourself and your Maker knows what the hurt is really like. Not to yell is a supreme effort. If you do, it invites a repeat performance. I know, I have had it; the dirty mongrels.

There is hardly a man in the camp who doesn't have an ulcer; horrible, messy-looking things, many alive with maggots and yellow, smelly pus leaking away from them. Very few have any kind of bandage. Some gather leaves and pack them in. They don't help much but at least the ulcers are covered a bit. The pain is maddening, it rips the strength from one's body and you feel absolutely wrung out, at least I know I do.

The only time any ulcer case is out of misery is if one can sleep; and that is very hard to do. The agonising red-hot needle feeling overcomes one's ability to obtain solace from such a luxury. It is nearly always dawn before I get a chance to nod off. It seems but seconds later we have to get up and make ready for another long day, smashing up rocks.

The time has come when I feel it is impossible for me to even put my foot to the ground. Yet I must. If I don't, someone worse off than me will be called upon to do my task. God grant I will never play on another man's suffering. I won't deliberately.

The situation is now at a critical stage. Fewer and fewer are able to do anything at all. However, that doesn't mean a thing to the vulture-type engineer guards. They want workers, any kind. Ulcers, illness or any other obstacle to a prisoner's ability to be mobile is not accepted as an excuse. The line has to be finished and finish it they will, even if hundreds drop dead in the doing.

It had to come. Colonel Nagatomo, Japanese Commandant of all prisoners of war on the Burma side, is arriving today to carry out a personal inspection of the 'alleged' injured. He is 'not very concerned with the sick mans'—his words—they can all be used breaking up rocks. If they cannot walk to the job, they must be carried. One concession; light hammers, if they are available, are to be issued to them. If they want to eat, then work for it!

All tropical ulcer cases are to be lined up so that he may determine their fitness or otherwise for work. 'The railway', he said, 'is behind schedule. Every available man must go hurry hurry so that trains may run from Burma to Singapore.'

Troop and supply trains is what he really meant as we all feel certain the Nips are being pushed back well away from India, and reinforcements are badly needed. Our 'Nightingale' sings sweetly. Believed rumours are sometimes correct.

As Lt. Col. Nagatomo approached the long line of men suffering the tortures of the damned due to the frightening looking ulcers, leaking and with eaten-away flesh and bared, smelly bones, his features turned green, the colour that would do justice to a seasick mariner.

The stench was awful, almost overpowering and it proved far too much for his delicate innards. He looked at about two. That was enough; he couldn't get away quickly enough.

He gave in! Point made in favour of the unfit.

All ulcer and dysentery patients were to be transported to a 'new, well supplied hospital at the 55 kilo railhead point.'

He never used the word 'equipped'; he couldn't, might lose face. So, as far as he was concerned, 'supplied' fitted the bill. Except he did not say what with.

'Those mans,' he added, 'need plenty good food and medicines. That is what they will receive at the new home for the unfit mans.'

He finally agreed 800 would be taken away from the 105 kilo camp on condition enough 'fit' men would be made available to complete the railway on time.

Fit men. Only the Nips themselves came under that category!

The daily death rate in this camp is becoming more than alarming. Good rations and drugs are essential if any of us are to survive. Seems to me we are to be sacrificed as soon as the first train can complete the run from Singapore to Moulmein. It is possible we will be starved to death!

5th July 1943

A very real shock! Out of the blue, a day off. Most unusual following upon what Nagatomo said about the work being behind schedule. Wonder what happened. We fully expected to be flat to the boards until the joining ceremony had taken place. That is going to be around this area somewhere.

It is a bit of a relief to be in out of the pouring rain even if the darned roof on the hut is that in name only. At least it is not allowing the water to hit us on all sides. Terrible job, smashing rocks with the rain belting our bodies non-stop.

We have had no pay for nearly two months; no smokes makes for bad nerves. No dough means no 'boong' baccy and tempers fray. I'm nervy and jumpy, not entirely due to the lack of nicotine strength, but also to the horrible ulcer on my left shin. It's real pain and I cannot put my foot to the muddy floor.

Don't know how many but quite a few have been sent to the 55 kilo camp and feel I might end up there. Unless a miracle occurs, this stinking ulcer can only get worse. It is so wickedly sore I just don't know where to put my leg to get a bit of comfort.

I am so downcast today my thoughts about my loved ones are uppermost in my mind. Must have had a bit of delirium last night. Can distinctly remember reading my obituary in the local paper. Hope it is not a bad omen. Gives me the shivers a bit. I could be marked down to go, many of my mates already lie in the cemetery here.

Rations are on the down grade; servings are so light one almost needs a magnifying glass to find the grains. Is this the beginning of the end? I feel sure that is how the Nips intend to dispose of us once we are no longer of any use to them.

There are a few snakes around the jungle fringe and some of the boys are managing to bag one or two. Have had a taste—real beaut!

Bridge-building by POW slave labour
(Australian War Memorial Negative No. 118879)

NIPPON Pile Driving.
BURMA-SIAM Railway 1943.

Bridge pile-driving. Sketch drawn from memory by Major L.J. Robertson, June 1946.
(Australian War Memorial Negative No. 128456)

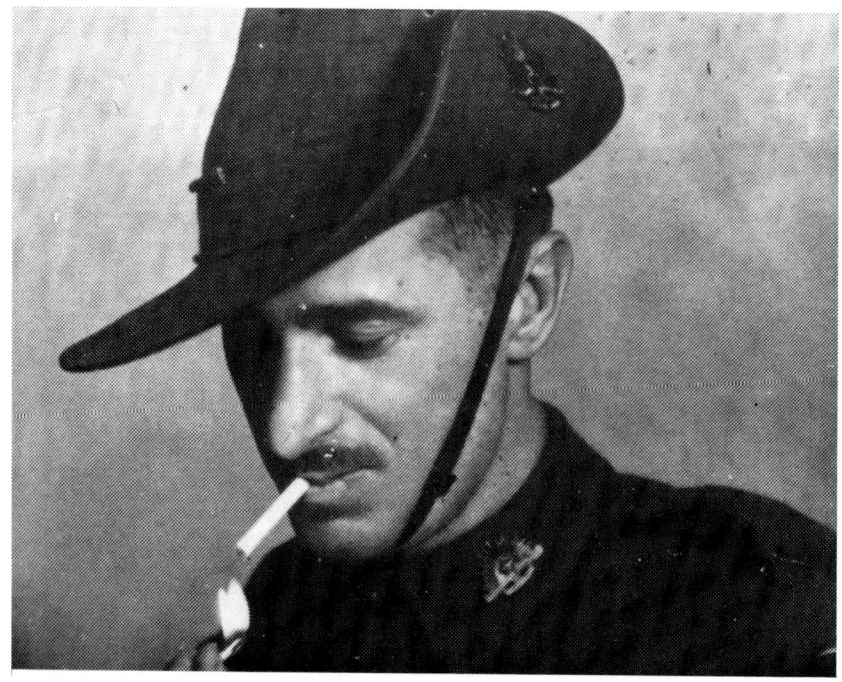

J.G. (Tom) Morris

Tony Clive, Postal Corps

Lieutenant Colonel J.M. Williams, CO 2/2 Pioneer Battalion and
Commander, Williams Force (Sketch by courtesy of Jim Collins)

POWs laying railway track
(Australian War Memorial Negative No. P0406/40/27)

Completed trestle bridge with members of a military party crossing over it
(Australian War Memorial Negative No. 122310)

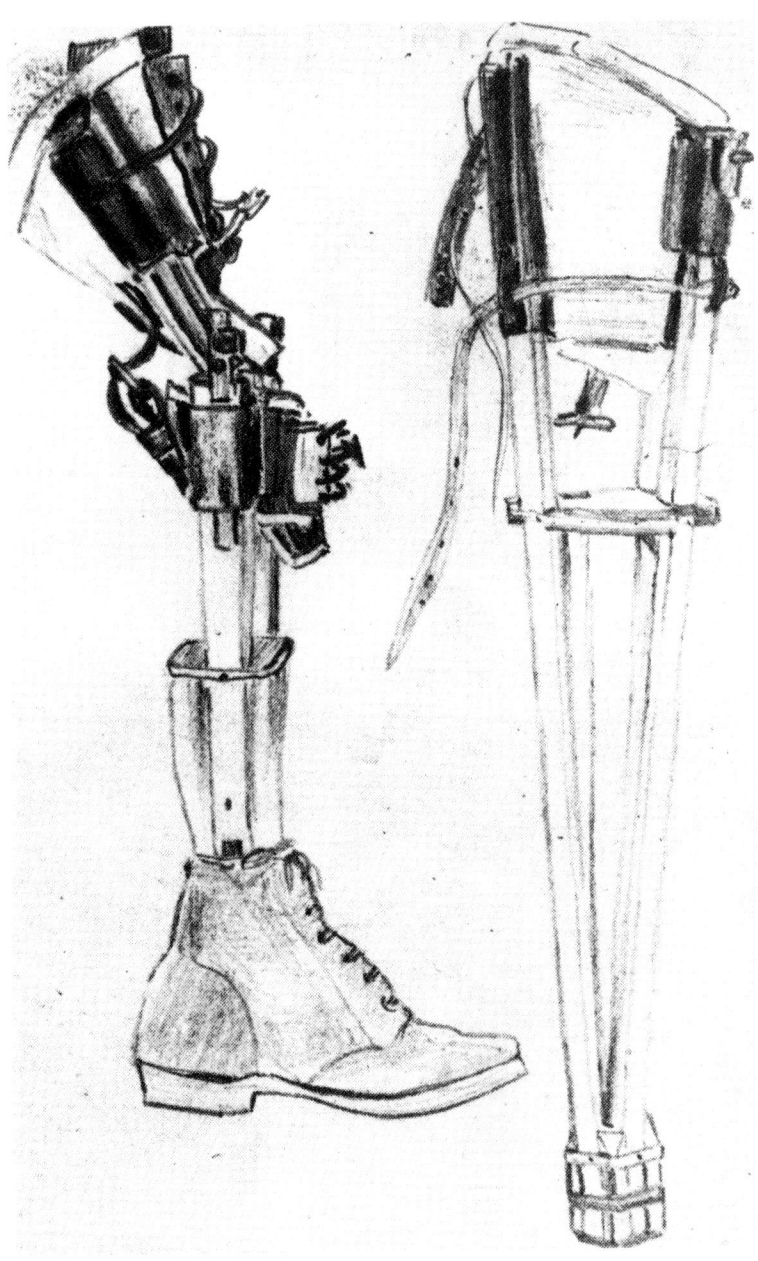

Artificial limbs manufactured from bamboo and miscellaneous
fittings scrounged by Sapper Teddy Dixon at 55 kilo camp.
(Australian War Memorial Negative No. 34475)

Captain Rowley Richards (2/15 Field Regiment), MO with Anderson and Williams Forces

Brigadier A.L. Varley, CO 'A' Force
(Photo by courtesy of Major Reg Newton. Australian War Memorial Negative No. 5515)

Major Syd Krantz, whose skills as a surgeon and ability to
improvise saved many lives

Survivors of the sinking of the *Rakuyo Maru* being taken aboard a US submarine
(Australian War Memorial Negative No. 305634)

Portion of Thanbyuzayat Cemetery
(Photo by courtesy of the Australian War Graves Commission)

AFTER THE ROADWORK came the formidable preparation for the laying of the rail line, clearing strips, building bridges and earth works. It was an awesome task made worse by the type of tools provided; primitive and unsuitable, but good enough in the eyes of the Nipponese.

Roadwork, 2nd Phase

The road gangs had cleared a carriageway to a width enabling two vehicles to pass, but for reasons best known to the Nipponese engineers, it had to be built of concave type. This had the natural result of forcing water to the centre of the road.

With usage it was not long before it became a quagmire and impossible for the passage of motor vehicles. Spinning wheels—even those fitted with chains—churned the mass of mud.

Native wagons, drawn by yaks, had the same problem as beset motorised transport. To overcome this difficulty the Japanese ordered the whole top, mud surface, be skimmed off and replaced by ballast.

Large parties of mostly unfit personnel had to quarry into rock faces to provide the ballast. Those engaged on that labour were the very first to suffer tropical ulcers at the 105 kilo camp. Splinters of rock would pierce the thin skin covering legs of the underfed, unhealthy workers.

Within a very short period the initial breaks would become holes, infect, lengthen and completely immobilise those afflicted. The only treatment the Medical Officers could prescribe was to cleanse the wounds, scrape away the suppuration and trust to nature to do the rest.

Despite the many approaches by Force Commanders and Medical Officers to the Camp Commander, Lieutenant Hoshi, for drugs and medicine, none were supplied.

*

Hoshi was a noted trader in iodoform powder, the use of which resulted in partial or complete healing of tropical ulcers. He was also engaged in trading in many other goods, particularly jewellery with those who managed to retain any.

*

Quarrying the rock was one thing, haulage to the road site was another. It had to be done coolie fashion—rice bags strung between two poles and loaded to the gunwales; weight, hard to assess but far beyond the capacity of the unfit men.

From the quarry face to the roadway was a kilometre-plus and the over one-cwt rock appeared to weigh considerably more by the time the carriers tipped at roadside. With the minimum set by the guards as 17 loads per man per day over a track covered in thorns and tree butts (stumps), slippery due to the soft, more or less muddy state of the walkway, it was a soul-tearing job and by the end of the day the workers had covered well over 20 kilometres.

After the first few loads many of the lads devised what they hoped was an easier way. For a few trips, yes, it appeared to be working, until the guard at the roadside became suspicious that only partial loads were arriving. He was spot on!

At the loading point the supervising guard would give each team a number which would be checked by the road guard. However, as the loads became smaller and smaller his oriental brain began to tick over. He became aware of the possibility the workers had a halfway point, dump some of the load there, return, pick up the balance and get credit for two loads. It was not long before that caper came to an end. Guards were posted along the track and they ensured every team carried the full load, start to stop, except for 'illegal' rests.

Despite the ballasting, corduroying and other road formative work, traffic (plenty of it) soon churned it into a seething mud mass. Many times it was absolutely unusable and the 105 kilo camp marooned, as far as motorised or any form of transport was concerned.

The result, all rations had to be manhandled, hence the rice carrying parties to squelch through mud back to the 97 kilo camp, to return with the life-saving food.

With the advent of the wet season came the normal outbreak of cholera and it did not miss the camp. Soon five cases were reported, four were fatal.

The trade-plying natives, so obvious up to this point, completely vanished overnight when wind that a cholera attack had struck the camp reached them. They just gathered their families, few possessions and did a bunk. Happily for the inmates they 'forgot' their yaks which began to roam the outskirts of the camp area.

The Australians could not let such a golden opportunity pass and soon a black market flourished on two fronts, meat, and wood from the dismantled carts.

The ranks of the workers were steadily decreasing as ulcered limbs and tropical ailments laid low so many. Fortunately, the Medical Officers, Captain Gordon Cumming in particular, managed by sheer dedication to thwart the source of cholera, but ulcers, malaria and dysentery took toll of the majority.

Japanese blitzes on the many sick resulted in the near-sacrifice of life as they forced ill men out onto rail and roadwork, heavy at that.

En masse 'medical' examinations were common; if a 'skeleton' exhibited no obvious injury or illness—out to work; and no explanation could dissuade them from their determined decision.

No matter what opposition Force Commanders or Medical Officers advanced, nothing influenced the Nipponese. No lacerated flesh; the man could stand, then he was fit enough to got out to whatever job he may be detailed for by them.

On completion of the exacting job on six kilometres of roadwork, the men were switched to the railroad preparation. Tough as the roadwork had been, this new assignment was considerably worse. The workers had a ten-kilometre march before they could even commence using a tool, shovel or chunkel, in the earth.

The inclement weather conditions made no problems as far as the Japs were concerned; pouring rain, mud feet deep—just slight inconveniences, not in any sense a cause for a lessening of the required metreage.

The initial earthwork at the 97 kilo point did not last long. Attention was then given to the grubbing out of jungle timber and bamboo clumps. For this job we were issued with crude tools labelled, by the Nips, as axes and crosscut saws. The only real resemblance was in name. Scrub hooks were also introduced and yielded better results than the so-called axes.

The torrential rain created an immense hardship for every worker. It was cut, slosh, slip due to the lack of footwear, be scratched by thorns (more often than not an ulcer would result from the cut) and bashed for failing to fell a tree or clear a stubborn bamboo clump speedily.

Yells of 'currah currah' and waddy wielding went on throughout the day as the sadistic guards vented their spite on the weary, worn-out POWs.

Meals, when they finally arrived, would be cold and the 'stew' watered down so greatly by the falling rain as to be of little value as regards nutrition.

On odd occasions the Japanese produced explosives to remove teak-like trees. By their manner of use all workers were apprehensive as the guards prepared, in an amateurish way, the shots. No question about it, they had little knowledge of the correct and safe method of handling the charges. More by good luck than good management, no-one suffered injury.

The 'speedo' was now on properly as the Japanese were determined come what may, the permanent way had to, and would be, ready for the rail laying come September, now weeks not months away. So, up went the daily task from *two* metres to *four* metres per man per day.

Bridge building was going on at a furious pace and long hours had to be worked to erect the flimsy gully crossings. It will be a miracle if some of the structures the prisoners built to carry trains ever stand up to the strain and stress. We all hope when our time comes to leave Burma it will not be by train!

With the work programme now progressing at a very demanding pace came the inevitable question of the right of the sick to rest. *No*, was the not unexpected answer, but every effort was made to prevail upon the humanity of the Nipponese to exempt the very ill from the death-promotional tasks.

Force Commanders and Medical Officers made daily representations to Lieutenant Hoshi, Camp Commandant, to relax his and the other Japanese's attitudes towards the prisoners who could barely stand, let alone perform hard manual labour. They may just as well have appealed to an oyster; they (oysters) do not speak, either.

*

Hoshi, a fat hulk, could not have cared less what his underlings did just as long as he waxed fat on profits from canteen goods he forced upon his charges at enormous prices. If any of the workers died at work, or in the camp for that' matter, why should he worry; less to feed.

*

With few men returning from hospital camps (presumably better in health and fit to work when they did) demands for more and more workers were straining the ranks of the very sick to the utmost limit.

The Japanese totally ignored the advice of the Medical Officers and Force Commanders and literally drove every sick man—the only exceptions being those actually bedded down in the hospital hut—to do at least a half day on some kind of a job, at full pay rates.

The latter was just another perk for Hoshi; the worker was paid for only half a day, the balance went into the pocket of the Camp Commandant. No wonder he demanded the maximum number of prisoners, who had been considered far too ill to work, based on appearance and Medical Officers' diagnosis, yet, in his un-medical opinion, and that of his minions, well enough to lift a tool, carry something and count as a worker earning pay.

*

Hoshi was considered a fat fool by many (probably even by his own men) and lazy by nature, but he had a ready-reckoner mind and amassed a lot of money in his nefarious dealings with all and sundry.

*

The sick men may have believed they were only signing the pay sheets for the amount of money they received when, in fact, their signature covered the payment for a full day's work.

On Hoshi's periodic journeys to Thanbyuzayat or Moulmein he would 'request' advance payment for potential purchases of POW canteen goods.

However, upon his return and delivery of items purchased, no invoices would be presented or any excess monies returned. He was too cunning to fall for an audit and entirely disregarded any questioning as to cash disbursements. Any suggestion he acted in any other way than honourably was to impugn his honour!

Not only did he make a profit on his actual dealings (purchase and sale) but he had the temerity to charge commission and cartage. That astute criminal would stoop to any lengths to satisfy his own ambitions as regards money.

Cigars normally priced at one cent at Base were ten of the same currency at the 105 kilo camp. Double that amount when the demand exceeded supply. The oriental black market thrived.

In actual fact, there was a similar market prevailing on odd occasions within the POW ranks. Ingredients that went into such edible goodies as rissoles, rice bread and coffee, were stolen from the Nipponese kitchen and retailed at very high prices to starving customers.

The Japanese suspected what was going on and were constantly on the alert to apprehend the culprits. When caught in the act, the subsequent punishment almost outweighed the risks run in order to increase one's financial status. Even so, as many were heard to say, it is a calculated risk and we help our sick cobbers. The prices charged enable us to acquire goods that, in the long run, benefit the needy.

As the end of August was fast approaching, that being the deadline to complete the railway earthworks, the hours worked were long, the work harder and harder. The sick suffered the pangs of hell as they battled against the rigours of disease and forced labour and the guards drove them unmercifully to handle work far beyond their physical capacity.

Although the combined Forces at the 105 kilo camp had completed their rail earthwork tasks, much maintenance was required as washaways were common; embankments 'gave' and repairs were essential.

No. 1 Mobile Force (Anderson and Williams) were steadily progressing with the rail and sleeper laying but at a frightful cost. Everything they had to do was at a pace; at times, they worked up to 24 hours and more. By necessity of their task, they moved camp constantly. As the actual line lengthened and they had to shift everything to be within reasonable distance of work location.

*

Extracts from Lieutenant Colonel J.M. Williams' diary appear throughout this history and describe, in graphic detail, the horror and suffering the men of No. 1 Mobile Force had to contend with. They, without any doubt, had the hardest task of any force on the Burma side of the Death Railway.

Tony Clive continues:

*

Ballasting of the line was another and not quite unexpected phase of the railway line. It was a case of back to the quarries and hew and bash rock that had to ballast the permanent way. Again came the back-breaking, ulcer-producing work that had been responsible for many deaths at both the 105 kilo and 55 kilo (hospital) camps.

It was at the quarry face the rock splinters pierced the thin-skinned legs of the workers. It would not be long before an ulcer set in, suppuration flow and then it was a fight against the onset of gangrene. Many of the patients were subsequently transported to the 55 kilo hospital. Some lost legs, and lives, as the direct result of quarrying rock.

*

On completion of the railway line in September, 1943, a memorial service was held in every camp. Lieutenant Colonel Nagatomo attended the 105 kilo camp and full details are recorded elsewhere in this volume.

Tony Clive was on the prison ship *Rakuyo Maru* when it was torpedoed and sunk by US submarines in September 1944. After four days and nights in the oily seas, with no food or water, he was one of the survivors picked up by the USS *Sealion*, which had been involved in attacking the convoy. He was repatriated to Australia later that year.

55 Kilo Hospital Camp (Kohn Kuhn)
July-December, 1943

IT WAS VERY seldom that the Japanese kept their word in any sphere of POW life. Nagatomo was notorious for prevarication and procrastination. His consistent refusal to reply to written, or even verbal communication, frustrated Brigadier Varley to such an extent he often told camp commanders that to make a complaint or request to Nagatomo was tantamount to bashing one's head against a brick wall.

The one big change came the day he agreed to open a hospital for the very sick at the 55 kilo camp. His visit and inspection of the unfit prisoners at the 105 kilo camp must have shocked him into a new way of thinking.

The sick must be cared for! A point of view he had not been known to express before!

Subsequently he invited Brigadier Varley to accompany him to the 75 kilo camp where Lieutenant Colonel Albert Coates, Chief Medical Officer, 'A' Force, was immobilised, due to an attack of scrub typhus. He was very ill.

When they arrived at his bamboo bed-space, he was, to use his own words, 'in my rags, but I received them with as much dignity as I could muster under the circumstances. I wondered what was the purpose of their visit. I was soon to learn.'

Nagatomo wanted to know if this great medical officer felt he was fit enough, physically and mentally, to take over the management of the new hospital at the 55 kilo camp. A real hospital, he was assured, where the very sick could be cared for.

Coates was incredulous. A proper hospital! That meant a fully equipped unit that had been promised by the Nipponese before 'A' Force departed Singapore for parts unknown. Was it another lie? Or, for once, was it possible Nagatomo was expressing the truth?

Those thoughts flashed through his mind as he envisioned what could be achieved if beds, drugs, medicines, surgical instruments and nutritious food were to be had in abundance.

The look on his face was as inscrutable as that of a piece of ebony, so much so Nagatomo questioned him, via the interpreter, as to the actual state of his health. Did the look of debilitation suggest he would not have the strength to undertake the gigantic task of caring for many hundreds of very sick men?

In the seconds before he answered Coates realised that Nagatomo had at last admitted many of the thousands of prisoners of war over whom he had supreme control were actually suffering to the degree all medical officers had been claiming throughout the building of the railway.

To the obvious relief of Brigadier Varley, Coates assured Nagatomo he would be well enough to take over control of the new hospital within a couple of weeks.

Just two weeks later he arrived at the old 55 kilo camp on a stretcher.

The moment he sighted the weather-worn bamboo and atap roofed buildings, his vision of a real hospital vanished as fast as clemency did amongst the Japanese and Koreans. This was no hospital in the real meaning of the word. It was just another camp the Nipponese had been using during their construction of a railroad link to Singapore.

Coates had an immediate consultation with Major Charles O'Brien and his adjutant, Lieutenant W.W. Tilney. It was agreed the strongest possible representations be made to Nagatomo for a complete group of working personnel to be supplied as soon as possible to build the necessary basic hygiene facilities. Kitchen staff, medical orderlies and, of greatest importance, drugs, medicines and bandages were also needed if the hospital was to have any semblance of a properly run health area.

The first sign of Nagatomo's lack of cooperation was the lack of food. He was apparently steadfast in the Japanese axiom; sick men do not eat! Major O'Brien made impassioned appeals via Brigadier Varley to have the situation rectified as starvation could only lead to a huge death rate.

Three days were to pass before the sound of the bugle gave the call everyone had been keenly awaiting—come to the cookhouse door!

When Lieutenant Colonel Coates was taken on his first rounds to see the patients at the 55 kilo hospital, he was staggered by the enormous number of patients, particularly those with tropical ulcers, many from just below the knee to ankle. The exposed bone had a greenish tint, indicating the possibility of dreaded gangrene.

Out of 2,400 patients at least 800 were ulcer cases, the remainder were sufferering from malaria, dysentery and other ailments of varying severity.

Day after day stretcher-bearers brought in dozens who were totally immobile, others limped in on roughly made bamboo crutches, while some just made it as walking wounded. In the main they came from the 75 and 105 kilo camps. For a great number, it was to be their last camp.

The following account is taken from the memoirs of J.G. 'Tom' Morris, volunteer medical orderly, and tells, in part, of the misery, mateship, medical miracles and other happenings in that Burmese camp of death:

*

As a result of Brig. Varley's earlier visit, it was decided to move Col. Coates and the remnants still at the 75k, back to the 55k, where a new 'base hospital' was to be maintained for the deluge of sick expected from the camps north of Meiloe. The camp had already been established, with Major Charles O'Brien (2/18 Bn) and Captain John Higgin (2/4 CCS) as camp commander and medical officer respectively. Col. Coates was to be the hospital's Senior Medical Officer.

Unfortunately, Coates was stricken with scrub typhus at this time, and for some days it appeared that he, too, would succumb to the ills of this relentless place. Dr Schrock, a Dutch medical officer, arrived at the 75k to take over whilst Coates was ill. Through careful medical care and nursing, together with his own tenacity, Col. Coates was able to move with us, on a stretcher, back to the 55k towards the middle of June. This journey was effected partly by motor truck and partly by 'our' railway, which by now had begun to function in an erratic sort of way, for part of its distance.

Kohn Kuhn—55k Hospital Camp: For me, my arrival at the 55k meant an end to my participation in the railway construction workforce. For the next twelve months I was to continue in my role as a medical orderly.

During the first two weeks Coates was carried on his stretcher from patient to patient, with Capt. Higgin as his only support in the very large ulcer ward. His badge was the inevitable large Burmese cheroot, which forever remained clenched between his teeth.

Being a camp of mostly non-workers, all sick were on a half ration scale. The Japanese had an inexplicable custom of weighing us all and then issuing rations in accordance with the combined weight of the camp inmates. The less we weighed, the less we received, with obvious compounded results.

The monsoon was now in full swing, and the torrential rain falling day after day for weeks on end was something I had not, nor have ever again, experienced. There was, however, no respite for the poor devils slaving away on the railway. Not only did they have to meet their daily quotas of work to keep the line construction on schedule, but they also had to repair the bridges and embankments washed away by the raging torrents which, only a couple of months previous, had been mere rivulets.

For the first few weeks I was placed, with Bruce, in charge of the hut which housed the milder dysentery cases, some of whom also had small tropical ulcers. I was then asked to work in the dysentery 'death house', where I stayed until the hospital was moved to Thailand the following December. There were few survivors from this depressing hut.

In the middle of this gloomy, isolated hut there was a 'thunder box' in the centre aisle, but few patients were capable of making their way to this offensive smelling container. For those bed-ridden patients on their bamboo slats, with nothing more than a rice bag or blanket beneath them, there was neither incentive nor required medicines to help them on the road to recovery. We had no bed pans, no facilities for bathing patients, no toilet paper and no special diets. Yet the Japanese had the gall to call it a hospital! For bed pans we substituted tin cans, old mess tins, half coconut shells and troughs or pots from large bamboo. Toilet paper, once again, was large leaves from nearby trees.

In addition to my work as a medical orderly, I was also called upon to prepare all the dead from the two dysentery wards for burial. I was also given the task of removing organs for post-mortem purposes—mainly brain or bowel— as requested by Colonel Coates. One of my most distressing experiences was to remove the bowel from Sgt Jim Anderson, a true gentleman, of whom I had grown particularly fond during the four months I had nursed him. He finally succumbed to the ravages of his amoebic dysentery, when his bowel perforated during the night. By morning it was too late to operate, not that this would have saved him, as past experiences had shown.

The sad thing was that a half dozen injections of emetine would have probably saved his life. Later a small amount of ipecacuanha was procured. However, taken orally it tended to act as an emetic on most patients. A Dutch chemist, Capt. Van Boxtel, extracted some emetine from it which, by injection, saved the lives of a few lucky ones amongst the amoebic dysentery patients. Too late, however, for Jim and so many like him.

The Japanese would not concede that amoebic dysentery was one of the diseases from which we were suffering. They continued to insist that it was only 'hill' diarrhoea. Higuchi, the 'horse doctor', the Japanese MO for all POWs in Burma, refused to allow the words 'amoebic dysentery' to be entered on the death certificates passed on to the Japanese. Eventually a microscope was procured, and Higuchi could no longer deny the presence of *Entamoeba histolytica*, of which Coates himself was also a victim. We still received no emetine.

Of the 2,000 patients at the 55k approximately 500 were ulcer cases. Tropical ulcers were usually sited on the leg but can, and did, occur on any part of the body. On 26 October 1943 Pte Dave Stuart, a medical orderly in the ulcer ward, had his arm amputated by Col. Coates, when a gangrenous ulcer formed on his forearm following an injury from a sliver of bamboo.

Tropical ulcers were essentially a local disease in Burma and Thailand. Where proper food can be provided the condition is easily cured without serious complications. Apart from diet deficiencies, the high rate of tropical ulcers could be attributed to the fact that most men had no footwear or protective clothing. Even minor abrasions became infected, and the ulcers spread with incredible rapidity. Once the infection reached muscle, its progress of infection and destruction was even more swift.

The only truly beneficial medication was iodoform, which was only obtainable in minute quantities. Although it could be purchased in Thailand it was extremely expensive.

Many substitutes were tried at the 55k—eusol, Condy's crystals, salt in solution, raw salt packed into the wound, lysol, hot rice poultices, ointments using axle grease as a base, and at one stage maggots were intentionally introduced into these great festering ulcers.

In the main ulcer ward the patients were packed three deep, with barely enough room for the orderlies and doctors to pass between their frail miserable bodies. Like the dysentery wards, there were no beds, and they had to lie on the hard bamboo platforms. For the desperately ill amputation cases, beds of rice sacks slung on poles of bamboo allowed a degree of comfort, as well as allowing easier access to them. There were no sleeping draughts or pain killers to help these poor unfortunates through their agonies.

The stench from this was indescribable. Bandages were made from rags, clothing and the bottom of mosquito nets. These putrid cloths were washed and used over and over again to cover ulcers, which often extended from knee to ankle with bone and tendon completely exposed.

(Col. Coates in his evidence at the Tokyo War Crimes Trials said, 'At the 55k camp I had the opportunity to visit a jungle hospital for Japanese troops and found it lavishly supplied with drugs and medicines of every kind'. Yet, Higuchi, the so-called Japanese doctor, once issued six two-inch bandages to a hospital containing 1,200 patients.)

Daily curettage, using a curette and a spoon substitute, was another heart-rending form of treatment, again without pain-killers. It was not unusual for eighty to a hundred patients to have their ulcers scraped and gouged in this manner. I well remember Bobby Bell, one of my unit, who had quite a large ulcer on his leg. Each day a friend and I held him down, while his ulcer was being curetted In spite of the abuse he hurled at us, in between his screams of agony, he would apologise profusely, begging us not to be offended, and ask if we would repeat the performance the next time. It was pathetic to hear the screams of those poor souls, whose shattered nerves could no longer even stand the strain of seeing the doctor approach with the curette in his hand.

When the first ulcers became fly-blown, they were viewed with revulsion by the poor unfortunate patients. Coates merely said, 'Don't worry lad, they never eat sound flesh'. Some patients with small ulcers visited a shallow stream close by and let the little fish nibble away at the rotten flesh. Although it was in itself quite painful, a number of men cured their ulcers in this way.

(At Tanbaya, 50k camp, in Burma a 'base hospital' was set up for POWs from upper Thailand, who were categorised as being unlikely to recover in two months. It was occupied on 3 August 1943, by 1,250 patients. Here 420 ulcer patients were treated. Of these, 250 died and 40 had limbs amputated, only four survived, patients from 'F' and 'H' Forces, Thailand.)

Between July and November at the 55k, Col. Coates carried out in excess of 110 major amputations, using scalpel, a saw borrowed from the cookhouse, sutures from the gut of oxen and a novocaine solution for spinal injections. This had been extracted from a small supply of cocaine held by Col. Coates. Again Capt. Van Boxtel was responsible for this feat. Minor amputations of fingers and toes were performed without anaesthetic—a snip of his surgical scissors and that was that!

A lean-to at the end of the bamboo-and-atap ulcer hut was the only operating theatre Coates had. Those with strong enough stomachs were able to stand back and watch the major amputations from beginning to end, with Coates giving a running commentary as he went along. At one stage he was performing four such amputations a day. Approximately 40 of Coates' amputees survived. The remainder died through gangrene and/or the added problems of dysentery and malaria, which gave them virtually no hope of recovery.

(Can you, therefore, understand the stark fear that overtook me at Tamarkan, Thailand, in 1944 when a piece of bamboo pierced my left leg just above the knee. Since 1943 I had a horror of such wounds. Below the knee, you at least had a second chance of survival, as slim as that might be, should a further amputation of the limb be necessary. Fortunately it was the dry season and I was in much better physical shape. The wound abscessed, was lanced and successfully drained. That small scar which I still bear is always a reminder of the 55k and those dreadful ulcers.)

The Japanese finally issued small quantities of iodoform and the improvement in the ulcers was remarkable. Sadly, it was in such minute proportion in relation to the demand, that few patients with the very large ulcers received any lasting benefit from it.

*

One of the greatest efforts to save life on the Burma-Thailand railway was enacted at the 55 kilo hospital camp. The medical team headed by Albert Coates was increased when the number of sick and injured grew beyond expectations, with additional medical officers arriving to take over the responsibility of various sections.

They were: Major Alan Hobbs, pre-war surgeon in Adelaide; Major Fisher, physician, Sydney; Colonel Norman Eadie, eye specialist, Melbourne; and, for short periods, Captain Don Cumming, Sydney and Captain Claude Anderson from Perth.

In the whole of 'A' Force there were thirteen officers whose care for the sick and injured is legendary. They performed miracles; they were selfless, dedicated, compassionate and brilliant. Hundreds of prisoners of war who survived the horror of the infamous railway project, owe their lives, in the main, to this group who never gave up the fight to preserve life.

In addition to those listed above, there were: Colonel Thomas Hamilton, Newcastle; Major Krantz, Adelaide; Major Chalmers, Hobart; and Captains Rowley Richards, White and Tom Brereton, from Sydney.

In the field of surgery, 'A' Force was fortunate to have three of the most eminent in Lieutenant Colonel Coates, Major Alan Hobbs and Major Syd Krantz.

Captain John Higgin was MO with Black Force, Captain Don Cumming, MO with Ramsay Force and Captain Claude Anderson (Perth) was with Green Force. Except for short absences, they remained with their forces throughout the Burma incarceration. Colonel Norman Eadie served with Williams Force until he was too ill to carry on and was then admitted to Retpu and later to the 55 kilo hospital.

Except for Thanbyuzayat, which was abandoned due to the many bombing attacks, the 55 kilo hospital held the greatest number of patients. It was a place of tragedy—tragedy that could have been averted had the Japanese been humane enough to provide necessary drugs, medicines and nourishing food.

The odour from just about every hut (the few exceptions being the camp workers' area) was nauseating to the extreme. Foulness predominated from the dysentery and ulcer wards. It was so powerful as to upset the strongest stomach.

If comparisons were to be made it could be truthfully stated the ulcer ward gave off the most offensive smell. Hundreds of afflicted men lay close to one another in pathetic rows. Some moaned in agony, others prayed, and prayed hard, for a quick release from the purgatory that was theirs. For many death came quickly; mercifully so!

Flies abounded in millions; the ulcer ward attracted them constantly. Affected legs became maggot infestated, much to the horror of those affected.

However, in a way, they had some advantages, and Coates quite often told 'his lads' the repulsive creatures were his little orderlies, 'they only eat the diseased flesh'.

It was soon quite evident to the Senior Medical Officer and his 2 i/c Major Alan Hobbs that the only way to preserve the lives of the men whose ulcered limbs verged on gangrene was to amputate. But what with?

The only instruments available were those Coates had brought with him, a scalpel and one pair of artery forceps. Needles for sewing up skin were made from darning needles sharpened by Sapper Dixon. To cut through legs or arms a carpenter's saw was borrowed from the kitchen.

As ordinary cotton, even if it had been available, was unfit for stitching, gut strands came from animal entrails and were used quite successfully.

Normal methods of amputation had to be abandoned in jungle camps and at the 55 kilo. Coates and Hobbs adopted the Listerian style. A circular incision, scrape out the flesh (if any) and bone. Loosely stitch and implant a piece of well-boiled cloth for drainage purposes (described by many as a wheat bag finish, a proven necessity under the conditions).

In *The Albert Coates Story* this renowned surgeon wrote:

*

The operations we performed were similar to those done in the days of Nelson and Wellington with, at least, the added advantage in some cases of pain-relieving anaesthetic. It was field surgery without any modern frills. I was grateful for the thorough grounding I had received from men like Hamilton Russell, that disciple of Lister, and others in my student days.

I believe that in this camp, probably, the best work I have ever done in my life was accomplished.

As the months wore on, I made a request that, as this was now a hospital camp, a commander above the rank of sergeant should be appointed. Nagatomo sent us Lieutenant Aounuma of the Japanese Medical Corps. He called on us, asked me to drink tea with him and regretted that more could not be provided by our captors for the comfort of the patients.

However, he helped us when, during the months of September and October, I officially gave my blessing to the boys who went out of camp at night and contacted Burmese traders. They brought back the meat which was so badly needed, and which was paid for with money collected from officers' pay and administered by Keith Bostock.

This meat saved the lives of many of our patients suffering from nutritional oedema.

Some of my medical colleagues, who by this time had joined me from Base, frowned upon this 'clandestine business'. My reply was, 'The men are dying anyhow. The Japanese have not played Red Cross and I don't believe they ever will. Therefore let's salvage what we can. Never mind about us being good Red Cross boys and them laughing at us. We'll play the game.'

A group of men, returning late one afternoon from an excursion to buy meat and carrying it in a bag, was accosted by Aounuma on his afternoon stroll. Said he, 'Meat?' 'No,' said the boys, 'bananas.' 'Ah, you lie. Give it all to the Dutch POWs in the camp.'

I quoted this story at the Tokyo War Trials, as an example of a doctor who was prepared to look the other way in such circumstances.

He was a decent Japanese who let us alone to do the best we could. In that camp we had our regular radio news, not only from an Australian who operated his churning wheel in the jungle each night, but also from one of our lame men, LAC Caswell, who had a bamboo walking stick containing dry cell batteries made by Van Boxtel. I encouraged these ventures, although some of my medical colleagues disapproved and persistently criticised this breach of the Geneva Convention.

My own attitude was that we were not in a hospital. It was a working camp with no Red Cross facilities provided. Why should I seek to deter the brave men who, at no small risk to themselves, wanted to defy Japanese orders.

*

The author and compiler of *The Blue Haze*, Les Hall worked at the 55 kilo camp hospital, and stayed with Albert Coates and the other doctors after they were transferred to Thailand, as the following recollections relate.

*

On the morning of the 4th August, 1943, a volunteer orderly was bathing his mate, 'Tankie' Phillips (2/30 Bn) when he heard him call out, 'Tommy, Tommy, where in hell did you come from?'

Coming towards them was a young, short, skin and bone lad helping himself with a primitive bamboo crutch. He had ulcered legs and an obvious 'rice belly'. (The latter subsequently diagnosed by Coates as beri-beri.)

The two, as was eventually disclosed after much shaking of hands, mad chatter and a joke or two as to each having the same problems, had been workmates and neighbours in Sydney. The excitement of two close friends joining each other in a foreign country awakened the interest of just about every patient in that stink-filled hut. They wanted to hear more.

Tommy Busine, the new man, was amazed at what he called his good fortune to meet up with someone he had known for years and to have the 'privilege' to bed down alongside one he had thought had passed away.

'I believe,' he said, 'there is a wonderful MO here. Who is he and is he saving many boys' lives?'

'Yes, he is. His name is Coates, rank of colonel. He is coming now and heading this way.'

Tommy liked the look of the cheroot-chewing medico and was pleased when he stopped to examine his badly ulcered right leg.

Coates said, 'New patient, eh laddie. Let's have a look at that leg of yours. I won't hurt you . . . just an examination at the moment. Sorry we have no medicines or antibiotics here. Hosts tell us they are fresh out of everything. Been bathing this well? Yes, an ulcer all right. We'll do what we can for you. We've probably caught you just in time. I'll see you later.

'Don't worry and eat up your rice. *Your ticket home is in the bottom of your dixie.*'

From that day on until the 15th August Tankie and Tommy both had to suffer the torture of the 'spoon'. Like many of the others in a similar state of ill health, they accepted it as stoically as was humanly possible, well-knowing that unless they did, there was but one result.

On that morning when the MO examined their legs, he straightened up, shifted the cheroot in his mouth, and said, 'I have to give it to you straight, lads. You are both on the verge of gas gangrene. Amputation is the only chance we have of pulling either or both of you through. If you agree I'll operate tomorrow afternoon.'

In that instant their countenance went deathly white as the fateful words hit home. Tankie was the first to speak, 'Whatever you say, Sir. What are our chances?'

'Amputation, I would say about 60/40. Without . . . none at all.'

'I'm a punter, Colonel . . . in whose favour is the 60 per cent?'

'Both of you, Tankie. Is it a bet?'

'You're on, Sir. We'll make it.'

As the MO walked away, Tankie turned towards Tommy, saying, 'Well, at least he gave us a sporting chance. It's pounds to pence no-one will ever believe that conversation.'

Tankie need not have worried. The nearby patients not only heard the exchange of words, they winced as they knew that they, too, may be told the same thing.

Les Hall told them the MO was a very humane and compassionate medico, one who talks to each patient in his own language, not one filled with funny-sounding medical terms.

The two T's looked at their orderly mate. (He and Tankie had been together since March 1940, in Wallgrove Camp, New South Wales, then in the Malayan Campaign. Now they were still together in the POW camp hospital. A great bond had grown between them that was to last unto death.) Then Tankie remembered he had observed the Colonel and his mate talking very confidentially the night before.

'You knew about this then, didn't you, mate?'

'Yes, Tankie, I did. Worse luck.'

'No wonder you talked long and late to both of us . . . what would happen if we lost our legs, the handicaps, struggles to be overcome. They were real, the words you used, but you couldn't tell us. We understand, don't we, Tommy?'

The next day the two T's proved their worth; despite the fact they had had a needle they believed would prevent all pain, they, to use their words, 'went through hell on earth. It was as if they were on fire as the scalpel made the first incision.'

Blood trickled out of clenched teeth, fingernails bit into flesh (what there was of it) in the arms of their mate who stood at their head . . . they never whimpered. But it was the *longest eight minutes of their lives*, a period they hoped they would never ever experience again.

They didn't have to. Fate, if that is the term to use, intervened.

In the early hours of 20 September 1943, the sound of singing awakened just about all in the hut. It was a song Hall had never heard before and the singer appeared to be close to where the two T's were bedded down. As he felt for pulse, wrist and throat, he heard a voice say, 'It's too late, he has gone.'

At that moment the orderly felt the splash of a drop of liquid on his arm. It was a tear from the eye of one of the most compassionate of men who ever held the title of doctor, Lieutenant Colonel Albert Coates, the medical marvel of that Burmese jungle hospital.

He was not just a military medico; he was more; he practised his calling with feeling and emotion.

It was not only the MO who was upset when Tommy Busine, the singer, had gone to rest. The loss of a patient in that infested, primitive encampment was almost a family tragedy and Tommy and Tankie had been popular. They had been the closest of friends, more so since their meeting in that out-of-the-way area in a foreign country. It was feared by many that Tankie would take the demise of so close a mate so badly that it would imperil his own well-being.

It did not actually happen like that. Tankie, who had been so bright the previous evening, had fallen into a semi-coma in the early hours of the morning and was unaware there was an empty bedspace beside him.

For three long days and nights the tiny lad, son of an Australian mother and Afghanistan father, lingered on the very edge of an abyss. He was in another world . . . one where happiness abounded, where pain and suffering were not known . . . he was again courting the girl he had subsequently wed . . . starvation and agony were no longer his . . . all that had gone!

Most of what he said was very private; no-one wanted to try and intrude upon his thoughts.

A little after 2.00 p.m. on 23rd September of that tragic year, he opened his eyes wide, gave a happy smile, sighed and passed away.

Les Hall found it was difficult to go on as if nothing had happened; he did miss the two T's. When people asked him how he felt now that his two 'star' patients had left him, he would answer, 'They are stars, now. Right up there in the "Southern Cross".' The ache he felt was with him all his waking hours. No matter how he slogged at work, the two faces were always there. Snatches of conversation would often remind him of how they once were. Of Tankie, his beautiful smile and thoughtfulness of others. No matter how bad that little bloke felt, he was the one who silently and gently helped others who, in many cases, were not half as bad as he was.

A mate of Tommy's told him they were a pigeon pair in more ways then one, both built along the same lines, both physically and mentally. In Black Force, ex-Java, the lad from Chippendale, Sydney, threw himself into the maelstrom of the injured and very ill, carrying and fetching even when every movement meant extreme pain for such a 'weed' of a man. 'No wonder he ended up as he did,' the mate said. 'Fate was most unkind to him. But there are many who will always remember the name of Tommy Busine.'

As the days filed on and more leggies filled bed-spaces, the medical orderlies, trained or volunteers, were flat out caring for each of them. Once a POW was an amputee he was automatically a bed-patient. However, Sapper Dixon, the 'miracle man', found ways and means to craft bamboo poles into crutches. How he did it no-one ever found out. He had no wire, nails or screws to assist him, yet he was never beaten for a practical idea, no matter what medical officers or anyone else asked him to supply.

Early in November 1943, another load of tropical-ulcered, beri-beri and dysentery-ravaged patients arrived from the 105 camp. Only God knew just how bad they really were. Colonel Coates just shook his head in despair as he examined those with dreadful tropical ulcers. One after another came the same diagnosis . . . amputation!

To Les Hall's surprise, one of the was a close 2/30 Battalion friend, Staff Sergeant Jim Mitchell, Ramsay Force, whose right leg, knee to ankle, was a green suppurating mess. No possible treatment other than amputation. 'Sorry, laddie . . . it has to come off. Book you in for the late afternoon session. Hall will take care of you in the meantime as he is out of the same unit and it's good to have someone you know to help you out. See you in the morning.'

With Jim came another Black Force member, who had known Tommy Busine at the Bicycle camp, Batavia. 'He was with me for quite a long time,' Fagan said. 'Not a bad kid, sorry to hear he has "cashed his chips". Hope I don't cop the beri-beri if that is what really cost him his life. This blasted ulcer is bad enough; certainly hate to land something worse.'

The fears of Tom Fagan were borne out, as he was laid low on many occasions with malaria. But, as he often said, 'It could be worse. At least I'm still alive.' Not so fortunate was Jim Mitchell. He lost the urge to eat, saying, 'Give it to Joe'. Despite every urging he just would not or could not eat; not even one spoonful; told the orderlies the sight of the rice gave him nausea. He passed away peacefully on 16 December 1943; Les Hall was beside him as he breathed his last.

Joe Noble (2/30 Battalion and Ramsay Force), an amputee, had been so close to death some weeks earlier, Colonel Coates had instructed Hall to have him transferred to the mortuary. On the way, Joe realised where he was being taken and pleaded with Hall to take him back. 'I'll eat elephant dung if you will take me back.' And, due to Jim Mitchell and his own determination, he survived the war.

In December 1943 Colonel Nagatomo advised Lieutenant Colonel Coates of the impending transfer of every patient to Tamarkan, in Thailand, where he said they would enjoy better medical supplies and food rations. But before they left he mounted another search for the hidden radio set. The search was unsuccessful, and at various times up until the end of the war the 'nightingale' continued to sing like the one in Berkeley Square.

In one respect Nagatomo was quite correct. Accommodation and food in Tamarkan were much improved. The POWs in Burma had only dreamed about vegetables like the green spinach-like leaves that were piled high near the cook-houses. The cooks themselves were out of this world in the way they varied each meal—except for breakfast: it was still water pap but even it was somehow different.

Even so, thoughts of food continued to consume every POW in Japanese hands. A lot more suffering, starvation and dying were to be endured in the period from Christmas 1943 until (and for many, beyond) 15 August 1945.

Les Hall was still with the leggies at Tamarkan and one tragic event he witnessed there was to linger in his mind for many years. It involved the loss of a twenty-two-year-old naval rating, Selwyn Jones, who had been a survivor of HMAS *Perth*. He had lost his lower right leg at the 55 kilo camp. Due to many subsequent haemorrhages, he had to endure further amputation above the knee.

Darkness had fallen on the evening of 29 December 1943 when Jonesy called Hall to his side. 'I'm losing blood,' he said. 'I can feel it trickling out of my stump. Please call the MO.'

As if fate had intervened, Major Alan Hobbs had just entered the hut on his night round. He heard what Jonesy had said and hastily applied pressure to slow the loss of blood. It proved useless, the artery, almost at hip height, was beyond repair. However, to dispel any concern on the patient's part Hobbs inserted a sterilise plug of material—a piece of old bed sheet—and with an assuring pat on the worried lad's head, walked away, stopped and called out to Hall to follow him.

'There is nothing anyone can do . . . the artery is finished . . . sit beside him, make conversation and contact me when he is gone!'

'You mean, Sir, he is bleeding to death?'

'Yes, more's the shame. I . . . we all feel so frustrated . . . not a thing can be done to stop the bleeding. His passing will be painless, take only a short time.'

A very worried Hall went back to Jonesy's bed-space to sit out a man's life! He felt awful and tongue-tied. 'It's all right, Les,' Jonesy said. 'I know I'm on the way out. When I have gone give this ring to my wife . . . that is, of course, if you make it! Brighton Street, Rockdale. Please memorise it. I don't want the Nips or anyone else knowing it. You'll know what to tell Yvonne and the kids. Don't tell them too much about how we've been treated.' With near-cold hands he grasped Les's. 'Thank you, mate.' His last word was slurred, a smile and he was gone.

The first leggie death at Tamarkan saddened the remaining twenty-four who feared, above all else, the cry of, 'So-and-so is haemorrhaging'. Unless it was below the knee, the medical officers had little or no chance of tying off the damaged artery.

A couple of days later a chap he had never seen before came to see Les Hall. He said he was a close friend and neighbour of Jonesy. 'As I know his wife and family, it would be better if I take the ring back to his widow,' he said.

'Not so sure about that,' Hall replied. 'I have made a promise and I don't like breaking it. Better I think it over. Who are you and what is your name?'

'Walker, Frank Walker. I was with 30th Battery, 2/15 Field Regiment. We were with your unit from Gemas to the island. I'm told you know Sonny Morris. He'll vouch for me. We only arrived here yesterday and he hopes to see you today, but he is not the best. He has a touch of malaria.'

TOM FAGAN POW DIARY
July-November 1943

THE NIPS ARE on the propaganda trail again. We have been given newspapers extolling the outstanding successes of their Army, Navy and Air Force. If we are to believe what we read, then the Allies have lost everything; have no troops, ships or planes.

If that is the case what the hell are we doing here in a POW camp? We should be on our way home. But then, of course, with Nippon rulers of the entire world, we will remain their slaves forever and a day. As one told me, 'No-one go home. All die here.'

One paragraph amused all readers. It read: 'The Nip Air Force were bombing over India. They bombed and machine-gunned. The cowardly British did nothing but run. After wiping out thousands, the planes returned over the Bay of Bengal.

'A very brave Nip pilot saw a British destroyer and flew to attack it. As he made his run he discovered he was right out of ammunition. He was not outdone; he turned his plane onto its back, swooped down, drew his sword and cut off the Admiral's head'.

Another beauty. 'As the pilot of a bomber prepared to land he found his undercarriage had been shot away. The brave pilot kicked his feet through the fuselage and landed the bomber by running along and carrying the plane'.

Dozens of others in more or less the same vein were in for our benefit and, they probably thought, to create dismay in our minds. The articles were so inane they must have thought we were but stupid school children, mere babies, or certainly, lacking in grey matter. Maybe the editor is a comedian.

In one part the Allies have lost their all, then comes the snippets and proof the British, if no other nation, had at least one ship still afloat; minus the Admiral, of course!

We were well aware of the progress of the war, our 'Nightingale' often sings lustily. The tunes serve to lull the bodily aches and pains; builds up our morale, too, to know the tide is on the turn!

15th July 1943

The ulcer on my shinbone has worsened and I am officially hospitalised as it is a sheer impossibility for me to put my foot to the ground. The throbbing prevents me getting more than a couple of hours' sleep at night; the ache and red hot jabs of pain are there all the time. The hut, hospital to give it its title, is crammed to the bamboo rafters with ulcer and dysentery patients. One disease seems to go with the other. Life is hardly worth trying to hang onto. I must, though. I have my loved ones home and awaiting my return.

A very popular officer died last night, Captain Watts, of the Engineers; he was a highly regarded officer who always stood up for his men. His passing is a great loss. He was only 25 years of age.

Despite the daily pilgrimages by our medical officers to the Japanese Camp Commander, not one particle of medicine, nor a drug, has been made available, even though promised time and time again. You can't believe one word the Nips say. They are liars, torturers and completely unpredictable. Sadism seems to have been born into them. They thrive on it.

Don't know where it came from, certainly not from the hated Japs, but we have a small quantity of lime to which is added portions of charcoal, then applied to ulcered areas. Whether it will help or not remains to be seen.

When we arrived at this disease-infested blot (105 kilo) in the jungles of Burma, we had a strength of 800 men, in varying states of health. That number has now dwindled to 200. Deaths, and evacuations to the 55 kilo camp have been responsible.

Something serious has gone wrong as far as the Nips are concerned; they appear to be in a spate of madness. Almost daily they blitz the hut and literally pull very sick men off the bamboo-slatted bed platforms. Bashings are on all the time. Some poor devils, for no reason at all, are singled out, made to stand to attention and then cop an unmerciful belting.

Not a day passes without one, sometimes more, prisoners seen standing, quite often on a round stone and holding a heavy one above their head. At every hourly guard change we can hear screams of rage and the thud of some heavy waddy whacking skin and bone bodies.

My blood runs cold and the procedure goes on and on. Intervention by anybody is added satisfaction to the murderous and brutal guards. Another one to tear into, boots, rifle butts or anything that can be used to inflict hurt.

24th July, 1943

I am still stuck here in this so-called hospital, have not moved; cannot get off the slats even for toiletry purposes. Very embarrassing; have to depend on my mates to help me in every way. Wonderful blokes. Some almost as helpless as myself, struggling to assist me no matter how much I implore them to look after themselves and forget my wants.

What a miserable life it is at the present time. I am in so much agony I do not know what to do to relieve it. Fact is, there is nothing I or anyone else can do except to apply hot packs, and that means calling on someone to go to the kitchen to get me a dixie of hot water. That I cannot do, it would be an imposition on a near-crippled mate.

I am so tired from the want of sleep I feel I could just close my eyes and doze off for a week. Trouble is, I can't. The intense pain in my leg is so terrific it overcomes all other bodily feelings. Dear God, if you can hear my prayer and plea, end it all for me, but in such a way I can go home to the family I love beyond all else. My loved ones, I know, are praying for my release. I am thankful they are not aware of what I am suffering.

The smell of my ulcer is worse than what comes from a dead, decaying body; the latter would be like incense as compared to the rotten odour my leg is emitting. Add mine to a couple of hundred more similarly affected. It is nauseating to the extreme. My shin bone is exposed; looks green as the flesh is rotting away. Now I can feel sores coming onto my back. Bamboo slat knots press hard against skin. Lots of the boys have them.

Just been told some more lads have passed on. Our Merciful Father has granted them peace. I wonder am I soon to follow. The rate this ulcer is degenerating it will be an absolute miracle if I come out of it. Maybe if I can get to the 55 kilo camp where the great surgeon, Colonel Coates, is operating, I might just have a chance.

I am finding it very hard to write; my ability to concentrate is dictated by physical pain, numbed brain and shaky hands. Hard to say if anyone will ever be able to read my writing, but I intend to keep on trying whilst I still have breath in my body.

I cannot remember what has happened during the last two or three days; it all seems so vague. Am sure someone had a go at my leg, appears to have been scraped out. But, oh, the burning, fearful pain sensation has increased and I don't know if I can hang on much longer. One of the lads told me I kept on repeating or saying a litany, usually the prelude to death.

That knowledge scared me a bit. I don't want to die; want to get home as soon as I can. I'm damned if I am going to give in. Me speaking a litany; must have been out of my mind. Have heard some of those no longer here mumbling in a strange way. Now I understand; they must have been seeking to make peace with God. Maybe I *was* on the way out, but Our Saviour has given me a reprieve!

We have been told the first party to go to the 55 kilo camp had a very bad trip down and were given no food whatever for two days. Wouldn't have had any them but for the boys in Williams Force. They voluntarily gave up their rations in order that the near-dead at the 55 should at least have something to eat. Colonel Jack Williams was the instigator of that. He paid a visit to the camp, saw there was a kitchen without rice. His boys knew what to do. What spirit misery engenders!

What was believed to be hospital huts turned out to be huts that had housed Burmese labourer-prisoners who left them in the usual frightful, half-wrecked state. The sick and injured had to almost rebuild every one to gain protection from the elements. How they managed it is a mystery, but some of them did. At least they had dry quarters after repairing the rotted atap roofing.

Within three days of arriving sixteen prisoners paid the extreme penalty and now rest eternally. Their bodily ills are no longer, they remain in the memories of those who live. They gave their all to help others. They will not be forgotten!

The medical officers, headed by Colonel Coates, a Melbourne surgeon, Majors Fisher, Hobbs and Krantz, were completely frustrated in their efforts to gain the medical supplies promised by Colonel Nagatomo when he outlined his plan after his inspection of the 105 kilo camp.

Their task? To perform the impossible. No matter how dedicated they may be, it surely won't be enough, without drugs and medicines. Only the Almighty can direct them. It is a repeat of the old story, the myth of medical supplies.

The rumour-mongers are at it again. We finish the work on the line here in August and will then return to Changi to recuperate. Boy, I hope that is one latrine-o-gram that comes true.

Really can't believe it, but am like someone clutching at straws and am full of hope. We were told the same thing in May, but we are still here on the Railroad of Death! Aptly named and unfortunately true.

20th September 1943

Must be two months since I have been able to put pencil to paper. It has been a terrible time for me—pain, pain, delirium, fantasies whilst hovering on the very brink of the end of my life. Today I have managed to sit up and am determined to record as much as I can of the happenings and the unbelievable horrors have suffered. Others, too, have had the same experiences. As I write of myself so, in a way, I do for others.

There is not a man in this hut who isn't just skin and bone. Features of my mates have become distorted due to the agonies they have had to endure. We are a mob of skeletons who have, miraculously, defied death. How? I just don't know.

The medical officers can only gouge out ulcers in a despairing effort to rid the affected limb of the encroaching gangrenous, killing disease. The gouging is so cruel men scream in expectation of what is to come, even before the doctor gets near them. My innards turn turtle the moment the instrument sets fire to my ulcer.

If only this war would end; all this would then be but a horrible memory, one I'd rather forget. But for now, I'm part of it and it is, I am sure, far from over yet. Despite the morale builders, the jokes, the tender care mates give one to the other, we have much to go through as weeks, possibly months, pass by.

I feel very low down at the moment; the poison, the medicos tell me, has got into my system and is the cause of my inability to get my issue of rice down. Once there, it isn't long before it is on its return journey. At the most, it is only minutes before I lose the food I need so badly.

Worse still, my leg has contracted under me. No matter how hard I try despite the pain due to the effort, I cannot straighten it. I have just been told there is only one possible treatment. Must have it.

I swallowed more than twice when I was told, but come what may I'm all for it. I have been through so much it will be impossible any treatment can hurt me more. Here they come! If I come through it, my diary will know.

Thank God it's over!

Three men held me down as the medical officer went to town with a pair of scissors. He cut through what little flesh I had at the ulcer centre site beneath my shin bone. It is now exposed from knee to instep. My leg looks like a tin one, green and nasty.

When the scissors bit into the flesh all the fury of hell hit me and I was afire. Although the operation took but a few minutes, it was a lifetime for me— of indescribable agony. But it may have saved my life and I am grateful for that. My body revolted at the measures and every inch of me throbbed and trembled. I hope I didn't yell. If I did, no-one said a word about it.

At last, a cessation of pain and I can hold my food down. Best of all, I have had a sleep. So sound I heard nothing for many, many hours. What a blessed relief!

To the MO and his helpers, my gratitude knows no bounds.

Almost daily now we hear the plaintive notes of the sounding of the Last Post. It means one or possibly more have gone to rest. Some envy them; others, like me, grind their teeth in anger at those perpetrators of death, the hated Japanese.

In a way I suppose I am a bit lucky. I am bedded down and cannot move but I can see many of my mates hobbling around, forced to work even though they can just put one leg before the other. They are just like ghosts.

I cannot possibly describe the scene, it is like something out of a horror movie. But, this is no Hollywood make-believe, it's for real! Men, many destined to die prematurely, because they are riddled with malnutrition, malaria, beri-beri and, of course, the cursed tropical ulcers. Their movements are mechanical; zombies, hundreds of them!

Food is at an all time low.

As I watch the boys get around their eyes are on the ground all the time; hunger is in their expressions. They seek anything that moves, cats, dogs (although they went long ago), snakes, lizards, frogs, bamboo shoots and any grass one can boil with the measly bit of rice we get. All I can think of, when pain allows, is the luxury food I used to have, and sometimes grumble about, at home.

My eyes fill with moisture as in my mind's eye I see my beloved wife load plates of steaming, delectable foodstuffs. Hell, now I can only dribble and crave. If fate decrees I will one day get home, and my Faith tells me I will, I'll never ever criticise any meal put before me.

Bad news from the 55 kilo camp. Already over 150 have died and thirty legs have been amputated in an effort to stem the death toll. A cold shiver ran down my spine as I was given the dreadful news. What a gruesome prospect faces all who may one day be a patient in that make-shift hospital. I wonder what I will be thinking if ever I am told I must lose my leg.

Just heard, and it is official news, thousands, yes, thousands of all nationalities are dying the length of the line in Burma and Thailand. Is it possible our captors have planned mass elimination of prisoners of war now that the line is almost completed!

I am not alone in that line of thought. The mere mention of it has caused many to plan something to beat the Nips at their own game. But, what can any of us really do?

26th September 1943

At last, a break in the constant, wet, miserable weather. Now and again we get a glimpse of the sun. Not much of it yet, but I feel sure the rainy season has run its course. I can feel the dampness going; well, at least I think I can. Maybe it is only wishful thinking. Hope not, the mud and never ending water through the worn out atap roofing, has made our lot so much worse.

THE LINE IS FINISHED. The link up was made on the Thailand side. Maybe, from now on, the Nips will treat all POWs a bit better. Or, will they?

What now? The 'speedo speedo' gone. To what use can the unwanted manpower be put. I don't have the answer, but am sure the bestial inhuman Japanese and Koreans will find one.

The Jap camp commandant has stated there will be plenty of rest for all workers as from now on. All there is to do is fettle and maintain the new link, which brings Burma and Thailand together in defiance of the age-old determination of Siam, as it was once known, never to have a railway line within miles of the Burmese border.

The Nips changed that, and much, much more.

Rumour has it *all* the sick, suppose that includes the injured as well, will be transported to a very large, and fully equipped hospital in Bangkok. I like that last bit, *fully equipped*. Nagatomo has always evaded that word. But he won't be in Thailand. We don't care where he and his cruel crew go to. Won't be hell, that is too good an end for that lot. Anyhow, the 'Fiery bloke' wouldn't have a bar of them.

The Allied bombers have been at the Nips again. Believe they plastered Thanbyuzayat and many other dumps in various places. Can't find out if they hit Singapore or not. If they have or do, hope they know Changi is packed with prisoners of war. Be terrible thing if they unwittingly massacred thousands of their own. The loss already of many prisoners due to the accuracy of our own bombers has been heartbreaking. God grant they never do that again. It wouldn't happen if the blasted Japs would allow Red Cross signs to be displayed near all POW camps.

A few motor trains have been seen near here pulling heavily laden bogey trucks. They are solid proof trains can now run from Singapore to Burma; an engineering feat never believed possible. And we did it; more's the pity!

Apparently the link up of the line was considered a very important event by the grinning, gruesome Japs. A couple of days ago a film team was here taking pictures and making recordings. In one instance, they literally forced our boys to put on a mock funeral to show Christian burials are conducted.

To show how 'happy' the prisoners are they filmed a group marching out loaded with picks, shovels, chunkels and other tools. The picture must be intended to show the Japanese nationals how wonderfully the prisoners are treated and how happy they are in the Imperial Japanese detention camps.

As the 'work' party moved out they were ordered by the Nips to sing 'Pack up Your Troubles'. The lads enthusiastically agreed and as they passed the record unit, the song they sang, *heartily* was the Army version of 'Bless 'em All'.

The elderly Japanese recordists were all smiles. They may not be doing that when the recording is correctly interpreted. The boys nearly burst their lungs out so that the message would be loud and clear.

Last night I had one of my best sleeps for many a day—bless that medico and his scissors—and I really feel much better. I'm still hungry though, and swallowing every grain of my rice ration.

Another outbreak of cholera in several camps. Men are dying like flies and the inhumanity of our captors prevents supplies of any kind that may allay, or wipe out the disease. Callous coots! What I really think cannot be committed to paper, as it's not the asbestos type.

2nd October 1943

So much for the Nagatomo promises. The huts are jammed with sick and injured. Thought all the unfit—which means just about all in camp—would now be at the 55 kilo jungle hospital. The death rate here is so bad, never a night or day passes without the mournful tones of the Last Post. If it keeps up we will not be needing places like the 55 kilo camp.

Yesterday Major Hobbs amputated the leg of an ulcer patient who appears to be holding his own at the moment. At least, as he said, no more ulcer worries for him. We are all praying he gets better as each day goes by. We are making certain, too, he gets a little extra rice to help build up his strength. He is going to need the nourishment.

Very peculiar feeling in my leg. No real pain or the agony I suffered before, just a numbness and it's darned heavy. A dead weight and moving it is a real hard job. The whole of one side is open to the world; the main or big bone is as black as the ace of spades. The noxious smell even sickens me.

With the end of the rainy season the boys who are working appear to be a bit better in health, despite their languid looks. The zombie aspect seems to be disappearing; Not one man is really well. Too much malaria, beri-beri and the now almost universal tropical ulcers. The stink is so great, I'd bet this camp is so smelly that even the vultures won't come near it. Haven't sighted one for days; that's unusual.

The main job on the working parties is breaking stone to be spread on the roadway. Maybe the Nips think they will still be in front this time next year. Hope not! No news around lately as the 'nightingale' is in temporary recess. Needs batteries. That situation will soon be corrected. The lad concerned will make a changeover with a truck; a used one for a fully charged one.

Steam trains are expected at any time and work parties have been formed to fell trees and cut wood. Been told there are many stacks adjacent to the track.

The guards have eased up on their constant cries of 'speedo, speedo'. Bashings have been reduced and the boys are deliberately easing down on whatever job they are on. They take risks and get away with it. Has to be a reason. These swaggerers are too pitiless to remain somewhat human for long with the workers.

Rice rations have been cut once again and what we are being served is dirty and has a horrible taste.

Maybe the fear of a change in circumstances has induced a lessening of brutality by the guards. There is the occasional whacking going on, but it is not as frequent as it was.

I'm homesick, down in the dumps and have a feeling all is not going too well with this bunged-up leg of mine. Actually, at the moment, I am not suffering a great deal of pain with it. In fact, my leg is numb. Can see a bit of flesh; don't know where the sinews or veins are. If I haven't got circulation, how come I'm still alive. Has me beat!

Last night was a great lift for all of us; the Nips allowed the boys to put on a concert. Hard to believe how sick men can change so rapidly. A bit of a sing-song, some laughter, a joke or two and one's anguish is, for a few minutes, gone. We enjoyed the show even though those who rendered items did so only with a great deal of willpower. They, too, suffered from various ailments and a few propped themselves up on crude bamboo crutches. What a fantastic lot!

After it was over and we were carried back to out lice-infested bamboo slat bed-spaces, the yearning for my loved ones almost overcame me. I was saying my prayers, and must have been doing it aloud. In the middle of them, I heard a voice say, 'You all right, Tom?'

I hadn't the faintest idea anyone could hear me and I was so surprised I just mumbled, 'Yes.'

'Sorry, mate, I shouldn't have said anything, but I did think you were in a lot of pain. I know what was up. This terrible existence is tearing us all to pieces. Never been religious in my life. But I'm calling for help from the Almighty now. Maybe he will forgive me for waiting so long. I think religion has hit us all. Hope I'm not too late.'

'It's never too late,' I murmured, 'Most of us, I feel sure, just take Our Heavenly Father for granted, until we really need his assistance. How many of us ever think to say 'thank you' for all the blessings showered upon us in everyday life? Very few, I guess.'

Cannot say how long that conversation would have continued for we were told to forget the sermon and go to sleep. A few of the boys laughed a little, one said: 'A pity some of you blokes are unbelievers. The day will come when you of that ilk will go down on your knees and plead for help you may feel you need. Now sleep, if you have a clear conscience.'

A clear conscience! Did I have one? Did I ever do as I told Lennie? Or was I telling someone to do something I neglected to do myself? I began to wonder.

I was deep in nostalgia when a burning, piercing pain shot up from my near-dead toes into my brain. Brilliant lights cascaded before my eyes as my body struggled against the frightening feeling. Every nerve in my frame was jumping and I felt as if I could stand the agony no more. I felt hands holding me down as I struggled for breath; perspiration poured from me as the fight to hold on consumed me. It was then I mercifully passed out.

THE BLUE HAZE

For three days and nights, I was told later, I lay in a comatose state; the MO told an orderly I didn't have long to go. There was nothing, absolutely nothing, he or anyone could do to save me.

It must have been in that period I saw a very realistic vision, one I will never forget as long as I live. I am going to chronicle it here and hope, if I fail to make it, someone will give the diary to my beloved wife who, I know, will understand.

Don't know whether it was day or night but I clearly recall seeing a wisp of blue smoke up near the roof of the hut. It claimed my attention as it sort of shone. Hard to say smoke can shine, but this tiny bit did. As I gazed intently I saw a face emerge, then two smaller ones. The eyes of the three appeared misty as they peered down at my skin and bone body.

The smoke began to fade as I saw their lips frame the words 'come back, come back'. At the moment I knew the girl I loved so very dearly and our two children had been with me. They knew I was on the brink of death and they came to help me. And, help me they did! Even though I was unconscious I fought to live, because they wanted me to.

It was God's way of telling me to hang on. I did and will.

As I think back now I can recall voices near me in that lost period; must have been the MO and an orderly. The words I heard were, 'When he has gone, come and tell me'.

Flagging morale is almost an every day occurrence here and in that sphere I must pay homage to our respective Padres. It is not only what they say and how they say it, but what they do. They give as much physical help as they do spiritual. They are universally appreciated.

They hold services in the various huts and it matters little whether one is a Church of England, a Catholic or Methodist, or whatever. The denomination is of little concern. We all join in and pray not only for ourselves, mainly for our loved ones waiting back home.

Home, the word lumps in my throat. That is where I want and long to be and I need all the assistance I can get to achieve my great ambition. My eyes are filling as my trembling hand jots down my thoughts. Maybe no-one will ever read my writings. To put down on the bits of paper I have, what I am thinking from time to time, does something for me. In a way, it is security. I've got it down and, somehow, feel the better for it.

10th October 1943

I have been in this hell house for fourteen weeks and I am heartily sick of it. My luckless 'pin' seems to be at a standstill at the present time; neither better or worse. I find, too, there are times I can sit up without too much discomfort. It is a great relief to get my back off the knotty bamboo slats. What would I give for a real spring mattress, sheets and blankets. Oh, well, nothing to stop me from dreaming. At least that is one privilege we enjoy, Nips or no Nips!

Received one heck of a shock yesterday; I was weighed and came in at six stones nine pounds! Some jockeys would appreciate getting down that low. They'd then have no worries about wasting to get down to correct weight.

Quite a few ulcer cases are now improving even though the medical staff still lack the essentials to treat them. What they are doing, under the most trying circumstances, is nothing short of marvellous.

Whether it is due to the change of season or the knowledge the medicos are coming good in more than just a few instances, I cannot say, but it's a fact, a happier note pervades the atmosphere. As soon as someone breaks out in song community singing takes over. It's amazing; I find myself forgetting my woes for the time being and joining in the well known melodies ringing out through the hut.

Then, just as suddenly, all is quiet! It is as if somebody has suddenly realised this is not a military camp where freedom gives one a feeling of gaiety, but a mangy, lousy Nip-run prison area. The joy of the moment is replaced with despair. A few moments ago I heard a voice plaintively call out, 'I want to go home, home, someone please take me home'.

I don't know who it was; what I do know is, we all want to do what he in his wandering mind pleaded for. It was the cry of a human being no longer in full possession of his mind. One who probably believes he is in some place back in Australia, from which he can be taken to where he wants to be. If only that were true!

The organised quiz sessions do take our minds off the frightfulness of our way of living. To have to concentrate and rake our minds for answers is a great thing. Mental therapy they call it; good name, it sure works.

Great to see a bit of sunshine now that the wet season has gone for another twelve months. Much to our surprise and pleasure the Japanese decided to provide extra rations. They found a few tired old yaks and we are to benefit from the find. The tongues, liver, brain and kidneys, plus the blood have been delivered to the kitchens and we have been served jungle stew; weak but tasty just the same.

Our cooks, always on the lookout for something for the sick even boiled up the hooves, called the result soup and we enjoyed it. Some who expected the real thing made some jokes about the ability and vivid imagination of our 'babbling brooks', but just the same, expressed a kind of hero worship for those who cared for their welfare.

No purchases can be made from the canteen. Like Mother Hubbard's cupboard, it is bare. And, with the goodies gone, it is back to the plain fare of just rice.

Some of the Padres came good again. Don't know how or from where they obtained them, but they came around handing out Burmese cheroots to the sick lads. One chap was heard to say, 'they might be "Bible bangers", but their hearts are in the right places.

24th October 1943

It is twelve months to the day since we arrived in this stink-hole of disease-infested collection of horrible huts. One year, the longest and most miserable I have ever spent in my life. We have had to try and beat off vile vermin of every description, to counter grave illnesses; many just couldn't and now rest in the Hallowed ground, many have been laid low with life-depriving tropical ulcers, beri-beri, malaria and extreme malnutrition.

How any of us have survived the tortures of the hard labour, the bashings, starvation and everything that goes with it, is something to marvel at. That we lived, any of us, I am sure is due only to Divine intervention. What will happen if we remain prisoners of war for another long period will be determined by fate. It is certain many more will die for we lack the very things needed to prolong life in these conditions.

Something must be causing the Nips alarm up north. Troops and ammunition pass through here daily. They appear to have an inexhaustible supply of both. Maybe the Allied Forces are driving the Japanese front liners back and reinforcements are badly needed.

One of my walking mates just told me another troop train has gone through with soldiers hanging onto anything they can grasp. They packed closer than sardines and look just as unhappy.

We can hear but cannot see planes flying over here on almost a daily basis but we are certain they do not belong to the Nip Air Force. The drone of the engines tell us they are *ours*. And that makes us feel real good. They appear to flit at will, no opposition even in daylight! That can mean only one thing, the Allies have the freedom of the skies above!

As proof of our belief the Nip guards now wear tin hats and are armed to the teeth. They are as touchy as they can be and have issued orders, should a raid take place, we, the sick injured or even the dying, are to move to a corral-type enclosure not far from the camp.

If that happens, this fellow, Tommy, will be No. 1 man for the jungle even if I do have to hop like a wounded wallaby.

Big day for one of the English lads yesterday, a letter from his mother; the first one to hit this camp. It had been written fifteen months ago but that mattered little. It was mail from his home. All who could, clustered around him to hear news of the outside world. He didn't mind, was only too pleased his mates could share in his good fortune.

Maybe it is a false hope, but we are optimistic enough to believe if one missive can get through, there must be more to follow, and this time more than one boy could receive mail.

It is twenty months since I had word from loved ones and yearn every waking moment for even just one word. Dearest Kit, how I miss you and the kids. I live in a dream-world of my own these days, dreaming of you and the children and the good life we led until I responded to the call to arms.

Should I have may prayers answered, we *will* have that life and better when I return. From the minute I meet up with you, I will never leave your side.

Perhaps I am a bit maudlin today; it is that letter that brought so much happiness to the boy concerned, and to all those he read it to. I wasn't lucky enough to be near him, but I reckon he will be around to let us enjoy some of his excitement.

Big clean-up campaign on today as some high-ranking Nips are expected, a General, Colonel Nagatomo and his immediate staff. I was told this camp is to become a vast supply depot. The many raids on Thanbyuzayat have completely destroyed everything the Nips had there—oil, ammunition and workshops, plus many, if not all, living quarters. The bombers have done a great job and driven the Japanese out. May they do the same everywhere.

I had a crack at getting out and about on a pair of bamboo type crutches but the pain in my bunged-up leg beat me. I gritted my teeth, was determined but even my willpower wasn't enough. Might do better next time. I was so tired when I got back I realised the extent of my weakness.

5th November 1943

When the rainy season was on we moaned about the constancy of it. We were wet all the time. Now the position is reversed, no rain, water scarce and we are scanning the skies for a cloud that may cause a downpour. Vain hopes, I'm afraid.

Just looked around me. All I can see is skeleton-like figures whose features project the misery of pain and disease. Suppose I am the same. Don't know. Don't want to. My jockey-like weight suggests I am.

If it wasn't for the few books being handed around I'm afraid we would all go mad. Some are too far gone, of course, to read. But those who can, read and re-read the volumes available. They won't last too long if someone is able to get tobacco. Even a lot of Bibles have gone up in smoke.

So many sick boys are crammed into this hut it is almost impossible to avoid shoulder to shoulder bed-spacing. The only time we get a bit more room is when deaths occur. Some days a few go almost at the same time, but it isn't long before more are brought in. We are all getting a bit blasé about the death rate. Oft times I feel it will soon be my turn, then an overpowering desire to get home pulls me back into reality and I am glad I had the willpower to overcome the temptation to give in.

The infestation of vermin is now at its height and there is little anyone can do to eradicate the plague. Rats, fleas—millions of them bugs and chats swarm everywhere. There is but one cure, burn the lot to the ground. The boys would, too, if there was a chance the Nips would supply bamboo and atap to rebuild. They won't; said so, and that is that.

A big search was bunged on yesterday and many treasures the lads had hidden were found and confiscated. I was lucky. Well, in a way. Immediately below my bedspace some orderlies had buried two pistols, some maps, a compass and four diaries. Had they been found I would have been tied to a post and now be a statistic.

Luckily, one of the orderlies indicated to the Jap that I was tuxan-bioki (very sick) with cholera. I've never seen a Nip move as fast as that bloke the moment the name of the dreaded disease was mentioned. I breathed a great sigh of relief; so did many others.

If they were after the wireless set they missed out. I don't know where it was secreted, only the operator was aware of that, and he, wisely, kept his own counsel. Last night we heard that Italy had tossed it in. Germany and Japan are still battling it out. But for how long is just a guess. We all hoped it would not be too long before the Axis Powers were a spent force. Had the 'nightingale' been found we would have been unaware of that very important happening.

Apparently the senior Nips had not passed the information on to their subordinates otherwise another rash of bashings would have broken out. To our surprise, nothing out the ordinary happened. In my opinion, they kept it quiet so that the lying propaganda newspaper would not be doubted by their lower ranks.

I MOVE TO THE 55 KILO

At last the horror and fear of the 105 kilo camp is behind me and ten of my mates. We were adjudged the worst ulcer cases in the camp and transferred, by train, to the 55 kilo jungle hospital. Here, please God, we have a 50/50 chance of staying alive.

To me it is one chance in a million as I never believed I would get away from the dehumanising atmosphere of that frightful site and the Nip guards. Perhaps I am a bit selfish, feeling as I do. Hope not, I didn't want to deprive someone worse off than myself of the opportunity to get to this one haven. I am more than sorry and fear for those who still sojourn in that disease infested hole, a hell on earth.

We were made ready for the move two days before the train arrived; we began to wonder if our believed transfer had fallen through or by some miracle the wood burner would actually turn up. Eventually it did!

The moment the whistle heralded its actual arrival the panic button was pressed and we were more or less raced to where it stood waiting. The stretcher-bearers made absolutely certain we were going to get aboard the iron monster, and literally ran with us.

Amid 'currahs' and 'speedo, speedo' we were placed into the filthiest steel truck I had ever travelled. It contained stinking, maggoty fish and the odour was, believe it or not even worse than a hut packed with patients rotten with dysentery and vile tropical ulcers.

The orderlies did everything they could to rid the 'carriage' (Nip's term) of its crawling passengers, but there was so little time and their efforts, in the main, came to nought. The Nips only allowed three stretchers in.

It seemed but moments before we, too, were covered in the smelly, evil things. They crawled all over us seeking the ulcers on our legs. They had gorged themselves on the rotted fish, now turned to a change of fare.

Three of our near-dead boys were left on the stretchers and the other eight of us had to sit on and amongst the stomach turning, putrid prior residents of the River Kwai. The stench filled our nostrils, breath was hard to get and violent illness imminent.

My first trip on the Railway of Death was an unforgettable experience, one that will never be erased from my memory as long as I live. We had fifty kilometres to travel and thought it would be a journey of but a few hours.

We reckoned without the Japs!

Speedo, we were to find out, was meant for prisoners only, not Japs themselves, when it came to transportation. For eighteen long hours we sat in that pitch black steel 'cell' providing the loathsome maggots with an opportunity to worry the very daylights out of us. Before darkness fell we tried to make certain the stretcher cases were kept as clean as possible, scraping the crawlies off them. Only moans told us in the darkness what was happening.

At each camp along the line shunting operations gave us many unpleasant moments. At one, in particular, the engine, about the oldest one the Nips could find, crashed into our truck, threw us in a tangled heap from side to side. Gave the seriously ill boys hell.

We endeavoured to sort ourselves out the best way we could; hard when we couldn't see a hand in front of us. The impact was so great I was certain my bunged-up leg had broken. Luckily it was still in one piece. Not so our tempers, though. We let fly, properly.

The driver, if he heard us, had the most abuse hurled at him, his ancestors, family and the whole Nipponese nation. In very appropriate language our tormentors copped the lot. We expected harsh repercussions but couldn't care less. At least, for once, the Nip guards held their tempers and waddies.

At each incline the old locomotive would wheeze to a stop, the crew would let the train run back, the steam would be allowed to build up and away we would go. One rather steep gradient the old 'puffing billy' made six attempts to get over the top. We felt like cheering when at last it succeeded. We knew then, we were getting close to our destination.

The boys with dysentery had a hard time; no-one, at any time, was allowed out of the vehicle. The only way, other than fouling themselves, was for whoever could, to hold them over the edge and let nature do the rest.

It was 11.00 a.m. when we finally arrived at the 55 kilo hospital camp. We were physically and mentally exhausted. Every bone in our bodies ached and our ulcers were giving off an odour that could put a sewerage plant to shame.

Our misery was made worse when told we had about one mile to walk to the amp; a feat absolutely beyond our capabilities. The orderlies left us at the side of the railway and went for assistance. They returned with a work party of 44 men to carry us and the other groups to the hospital.

As soon as we were bedded down, bamboo slats again, we were examined by Colonel Coates who told me, and two others, we had but one chance of surviving—amputation of our ulcered limbs.

In a way I suppose his diagnosis was a shock, yet I had felt for quite some time I would eventually become one of the 'leggies'.

Met up with a lot of old mates I had thought I would never see again. A few of them not quite as I had last seen them; they were amongst the sixty amputees. Whether or not it was for the benefit of the three of us booked for amputation, they all appeared cheerful and gave us plenty of advice, plus a bit of badinage to build our peckers up. A bunch of good blokes.

From what we could see of our surroundings it was just another POW camp, looked anything but a hospital. But, as one chap told me, it had improved 100% on what it was when the first parties moved in. All I can say is, it must have been terrible in the beginning; it is very primitive now.

However, as I gazed around and across to the other huts I felt so nauseated I nearly lost my innards. The impression still clouds my mind as I try to put into words the horrifying sights.

Many once able-bodied men, and some mere boys, were now emaciated hulks. Their bone structure was clearly outlined by skin tightly drawn over every part of their frames. Gaunt and haggard is the common expression, but those words fail to aptly describe the frightfulness I was now part of.

What I was to learn later, was that many I was observing felt about me as I did about them. Thank God I couldn't see myself.

The camp is packed with thousands of the worst cases of ill health amongst prisoners of war. The most rampant being dysentery, beri-beri (many amputees were afflicted with that), malaria, scrub typhus, tropical ulcers and many other ailments too numerous to mention. The daily death rate is appalling; the cemetery is a very large one.

Because it is allegedly a hospital camp the rice ration is at a very reduced level. The Japanese stay with their claim that sick men don't need food. And, that is exactly what would have happened only for the determination of Colonel Coates, Major Hobbs and staff, to demand sufficient rice to keep as many of the patients as possible alive.

Surgery is not performed just now and again. It is a daily event here with the medical staff flat the to boards coping with requirements. Operations are a necessity in order to salvage as many lives as possible.

The instruments, call them that for want of a better name, were made by budding technicians and what they have turned out is quite remarkable. Exactly what they are I haven't the faintest idea. But without them the surgeons would have no means to assist anyone.

Heard about a chap named Dixon, a sergeant, whose ability to make something out of nearly nothing is beyond belief. It takes situations like that applying here, to bring the best out of men. He has produced instruments, crutches and a type of artificial limb that enable a few of the leggies to get off their backs and get around.

Dixon is a genius, a wizard who deserves the highest accolade.

Hope, when my turn comes, he can help me.

30th November 1943

If there is one very outstanding day in one's life; a day that is burnt into the brain, I have had it. Eight days ago at 8.00 a.m. a couple of cool customers came to prepare me for a loss. My left leg was due to part company with me within a very short time.

For a moment or two my spirits took a tumble. I knew that when I came back from where they were to take me I would be slightly unbalanced, a little lighter but rid of the foul mess that was still my left lower leg. I wasn't exactly scared—not too brave, either. All I could think of as they carried me to the lean-to bamboo 'theatre' was, 'Fago, from now on you will be a cripple'.

I cracked a joke or two, that was putting on a nonchalant front, but if the two bearers really knew what was going through my mind at that moment, I feel sure they would have turned around and taken me back to my hard old bunk. Not being mind readers, they just carried on. Then, the shock!

Waiting for me was Major Hobbs, comes from South Australia I believe, a great man of medicine, one who would inspire confidence in anyone.

'Hello,' he said, 'won't take long. Going to give you spinal injection of novocaine and brandy. You won't feel any pain, but you will know what I am doing.' Fine, I thought. The amputation will be a snack!

The contents of the injection resulted from a Dutch chemist who was able to extract juices from various plants and trees. Prior knowledge of his ability and the fact I *was* to be injected, took all my fears away.

The Major handed me a cigar, told me to chew on it and forget what was happening. Happily, I thrust the unlighted, funny-tasting cheroot into my mouth and just waited to be told when the operation was over. Easier, I thought, than what I imagined.

As the scalpel cut into the flesh left on my leg I lost interest in the 'baccy' chewing, grabbed a piece of blanket, shoved it between my teeth to prevent me from screaming.

All I could feel was the raging fires of hell racing through my body; I felt as if red hot pitchforks were being jabbed into every part of me. My vaunted courage went in a flash! The believed deadening effect of the injection was a myth; just something to calm pre-operation nerves.

Whether or not it worked for anyone else, it sure didn't for me.

However, I felt a great surge of relief when my stinking ulcered leg fell away. At that second, Major Hobbs was God to me. Wonderful man.

When I was returned to the hut I was given a big surprise, a rice-bag bunk. 'Gee,' I thought, 'VIP treatment for the new leggie.' Just after I was bedded down I was warned not to move about as I would suffer torment as the result of the spinal injection.

'How come?' I asked one of them. 'The biggest hangover you have ever had. Worse than the morning after the night before'.

From all sides of me came good advice from those who had lost legs long before me. One thing they did forget to tell me was the darned rice bag bed had other residents—lice, bugs and goodness knows what else. Their presence may have been a godsend, in one sense. They took my mind off the pain I was beginning to suffer.

The following morning I felt as if hot water had been poured into the bottom of my bed. I was wrong, what was there was my blood spilling out; I had developed a haemorrhage. In addition, I was in the throes of a bad malarial attack, one of the worst I could recall. Later the same day my stump became fly-blown and maggots were nearly driving me silly.

I really didn't know I had the dirty, crawling, smelling things plaguing me; thought the cut nerves were going to town. Next morning Major Hobbs came to see me, saw the mess I was in, removed the stitches and flushed out the stump with salt—a mystery where that came from, the Nips refused to issue any—and water. After cleansing he restitched the flesh.

The orderlies try their utmost to look after us; some are fully trained, many of them are volunteers whose greatest ambition is to help save the lives of their mates. All of them work flat-out, rendering assistance when called. No task is too much trouble for me, and they appear tireless.

Patients afflicted with dysentery make it hard for them; bedpans are small-M and-V tins, or old dixies. Urine bottles are made from bamboo butts.

The going here is tough, really tough. There have been over 250 deaths since July, 95% British, includes Aussies, of course, and the rest Dutch. Out of a total of 160 amputations less than 50% are still alive. The odds are not good and makes me do a lot of thinking. However, no matter what lies in front of me I'll fight as hard as my system will allow.

One thing about my operation I now recall was the scare I got when I saw the Major pick up a sterilised meat saw. Am told it was borrowed from the Nip kitchen. Am game to bet, had they known to what use it was being put, it would never have left their possession.

They wouldn't have been so compassionate.

Yesterday was an 'all man's rest day' to be respected as a Thanksgiving Day, in commemoration of those who gave their lives in the construction of the railway.

The hypocrites! The blame for every death lay at their feet and they had the hide to call for a thanksgiving. In what sense, I wonder.

After that, 'Feast Day'.

It was sure some luxury the rations they provided; watery meat broth, rice and a 'pork' pie made from ground rice.

What a let-down! We imagined they, in their peculiar way, may have really given us a proper meal; not our basic food disguised as something else. But such is the mentality of the Japanese, one never knows what is in their hard-to-understand reasoning.

10th December 1943

Only one word to describe the feeling I experienced today, fantastic! I was allowed to turn onto lay on my side. It felt heavenly to get off my back, for two reasons. Firstly, I feared massive bedsores—a lot of the leggies have them—and, secondly, the relief one feels after lying in one position hour after hour, day after day, and then being able to move.

What a marvellous gift is comfort, even if it is won on a rice-bag shakedown, vermin-infested and all.

I am in more trouble, my stump is not responding as it was believed it would. To make matters worse, I have been hit with another attack of dysentery, a bad one at that. During the last fourteen days I have lost a lot of weight, too much and it worries me.

Sleeping is another vexed problem as the night hours are continually broken by the pleadings of sick men for help. 'Pan, pan', is the prevailing cry. Others scream due to the agony caused by maggoty ulcers, the effects of acute hunger, pain from beri-beri and the ravings of many afflicted with severe malaria.

In a way, I feel the chill of possible approaching death; my bones are just covered by skin, drawn tight at that. Deterioration in the amputation area is the first sign that gangrene could set in. If I suffer a haemorrhage it could well be I am treading the path of others who are no longer with us.

Yesterday morning I heard someone call out, 'Blood, blood, please help me'.

I saw an orderly, a volunteer one, run and almost fall at the side of a young sailor boy who had bled a couple of times previously. Someone brought Colonel Coates and a few minutes later the lad was on his way to the 'theatre'. Later, I heard the Colonel had to tie off the aorta valve, but it was only a temporary measure. He had but a short time left.

A terrible shame, such a youngster who loved the Navy and had planned a career. I was told he had studied hard and had been in line for promotion to the upper deck. All that is gone now; soon, he will be, too!

Almost every day now we hear the sounds of the Last Post signalling more of our mates are forever resting. Hardly ever less than three or more pass on. Is it any wonder I am conscious of the possibility my life span is slowly drawing in? But I won't give in easily. Don't care what hits me, I'll fight like hell to beat it.

Looking at the pitiful sights around me I am reminded of the fact only a couple of years ago many of the men now almost skeletons, were very robust and weighed from twelve to fourteen stones. Today, very few would make six stones.

Some of my close mates I find hard to recognise, so changed are their features; sunken eyes, gaunt and fearful, they represent the last hold that separates living and dying.

Got to hand it to many of the boys here who are prepared to take their lives in their hands to go out on parties, meet up with the Burmese traders and barter for meat and fruit. They dare to do it in broad daylight. They do it, not for themselves, but their mates who are just hanging on to life by a thread.

They run two risks. If the Nips whack on a sudden body count and they are found to be missing, death, should they return, is what they will have to face.

On the other hand, the known treachery of those they chance to meet, most of them bounty-hunters, could have exactly the same result. Death by bullet or bayonet; they would be deemed to have been attempting to escape.

I have nothing but admiration for these game chaps. One Dutchman I was talking to said neither he or any of his countrymen would even dream of placing their heads on a block, even though such sorties might result in the obtaining of much needed food for the very ill. 'You Australians beat me', he said. 'Only wants one of the guards to change his pattern of patrol, and your friends will die'.

So far no-one has been caught, but the chances are they may go out just once too often. Those who do it are supposed to be the camp maintenance group and are known to the Nips. Some of them are so brazen they come out of the jungle almost on the heels of the patrolling guards. Only wants a Nip to turn around, catch one, and shoot on sight.

We who benefit from the activities of those courageous traders give only a mumbled 'thank you', when a piece of meat or a banana or two is given us. With all our possessions gone, what can we offer but gratitude? When I hear them say, 'she's apples, cobber; eat and enjoy it', I feel so very, very humble. A life risked for me and my mates.

Most of the amputees still living are looking a lot better, thanks to the game-as-guts traders. Without them, few of us would now be here. I am certain they have pulled me back from the grave on more than one occasion.

BLACK-GREEN-RAMSAY COMBINED FORCES
105 Kilo Camp

FROM JULY UNTIL December, 1943—the tragic year—many of the unfit personnel were transferred to the 55 kilo hospital camp where the medical staff, under the guidance of Lieutenant Colonel Albert Coates, fought against almost insurmountable odds to rescue life.

In November 1943 the Japanese granted all workers at the 105 kilo camp two days rest. It was quite unexpected, but more than welcomed by the very tired men.

The real purpose, however, was not to give the hard workers a holiday, but to celebrate (Nagatomo's word) the formation of No. 3 Thailand POW Group Organisation. A schedule was prepared, setting out the form the celebrations would take. It included a promise of additional foodstuffs.

The first day was to include a service at the cemetery for the dedication of a cross supplied by the Nipponese. The second day, after a parade at which an address was to be given, a concert and a sport programme were arranged.

The Chief of No. 3 Branch, Lieutenant Colonel Y. Nagatomo, issued his addresses which were to be read to the assembled troops by the Japanese camp commander at each camp.

On the first morning the whole camp at Aungganuang (105 kilo), numbering at that time about 2,000 prisoners of war, was assembled at the cemetery. The Japanese camp commander, Lieutenant Hoshi, informed Lieutenant Colonel Ramsay that as it was a memorial service, he would take no active part except to be present on the parade with his staff.

A small platform was erected from which Ramsay was to make his opening remarks, and then call on Hoshi to read a letter of condolence from Nagatomo. It was addressed—'To the souls of those who have died in war even though they may be enemies'. Ramsay was then to read a translation. In actual fact, the ceremony was impressive and everything went according to schedule.

On the second day the troops were again paraded and an anniversary address from Nagatomo was read by the Japanese commander, after which Ramsay read the translation followed by a reply which he had been ordered to prepare in writing forty-eight hours beforehand, so that the Japanese might know what he proposed to say. This was done and no amendments made. The addresses given on those two occasions were:

20th November, 1943

Lt. Col. G.E. Ramsay:
To Taicho Donna and Staff, officers and other ranks
In this assembly this morning there are representatives of the Navies, Armies

and Air Forces of Great Britain, Australia and the United States of America. If it should so happen that some of you are fortunate enough not to have any comrades from your respective services in this cemetery, I would like it to be understood that this morning's memorial service is all-embracing, and includes those comrades who have fallen in action in the various theatres of operations, both on land and sea; and also those unfortunates who have been unable to make the grade under the adverse conditions of a prisoner of war in other parts or other countries, since capitulation.

I do not propose to dwell on the responsibility for the tragedy of these latter deaths, which no doubt must be the subject for investigation in the future; and whatever misgivings some of us may have in our minds as to the sincerity of the instructing authority that ordered this parade, we are nonetheless grateful for the opportunity to honour, in a collective way, our glorious dead; nor need it detract in any way from the sincerity of our own tribute.

I must commend the team spirit and the spirit of unselfishness which has been apparent amongst you as evidenced by the readiness of so many of you to assist in every way possible those who in the matter of health have been less fortunate than yourselves.

Our hearts go out this morning to the relatives of those comrades who are no longer with us, especially when it is realised that their kith and kin are not yet aware of the sad losses which they have sustained.

I can only give you a message of courage and express the fervent hope that changes for the better must soon be a reality.

I can add no more, in speaking to the memory of our fallen comrades than by quoting those immortal lines

'They shall not grow old,
as we that are left grow old,
Age shall not weary them nor
the years condemn,
At the going down of the sun
and in the morning
We will remember them.'

*

LETTER OF CONDOLENCE ON THE OCCASION OF
THE MEMORIAL SERVICE FOR DECEASED POWs

As the first stage of the railway construction has now been completed, I have, on this day of commemoration, the honour of taking the opportunity of consoling the souls of the POWs of the 3rd Branch, numbering 655 [actually closer to 1,300], who have died in this district during the last year.

In my opinion it is a virtue, since ancient times, to pay homage to the souls of those who have died in war, even though they may be enemies. Moreover you were under my command and have endeavoured to work diligently in obedience to my orders, while always longing for the final repatriation to your own country once the war is over and when peace is restored.

I have always done my utmost to discharge my duties conscientiously, taking responsibility for you all as your commander.

Now you have passed on to the other world, owing to the unavoidable prevailing diseases and epidemics, and to the indiscriminate enemy bombings, I cannot see you in this world any more.

Visualising your situation, and especially that of your relatives and families, I cannot help shedding tears, sympathising with your unfortunate circumstances.

This tragedy is the result of war, however, it is owing to fate that you are in this condition, and I consider that God has called you here.

However, today I will try to console your souls and pray for you in my capacity of your commander, together with the other members of my staff, by dedicating a Cross and placing a wreath in your cemetery.

In the very near future your comrades will be leaving this district, consequently it may be impossible to offer prayers or place a wreath in your cemetery for some time to come. But undoubtedly some of your comrades will come here again after the war to pay homage to your memory.

Please accept my deepest sympathy and sincere regards and may you sleep peacefully and eternally.

Given on the 20th day of November in the 18th Year of Showa (1943).

YOSHITADA NAGATOMO, Lieutenant Col.
Chief of No. 3 Branch of Thai War
Prisoners Camp, Thanbyuzayat.

LIEUTENANT COLONEL ALBERT COATES
55 Kilo Hospital

'IN THE MIDST OF LIFE THERE IS DEATH.' This truth was evidenced in all jungle camps on the Burma-Thailand railway. At the 55 kilo hospital over 350 died, as did another 700 at the 50 kilo hospital—the latter patients from 'F' and 'H' Forces, Thailand side of the railway.

The death rate was so great in the two camps that, each morning, patients did not ask who had gone during the night, but *how many*.

Below are extracts from *The Albert Coates Story*:

Just before Christmas, 1943, I was ordered to move with the sick to Thailand. I walked on my stick to the cemetery and bade farewell to the many gallant boys who had been my patients and who were taking their last rest. I could not help shedding a tear or two for those who had given their best and yet died so miserable a death in the most ignominious conditions.

Varley visited the camp and informed me that, in Thailand, I was to take charge of a large hospital camp intended for all the POWs of the railway. This was confirmed by Aounuma and the sergeant of the guard. The latter invited me to dinner in the guard hut as a sort of send-off. He told me I was to go to Nakompaton and he wished to honour me with a rice and stew and sake meal. I was to bring some of my 'outstanding' medical orderlies with me.

The evening came and we repaired to the guard hut. A Korean interpreter, who had obviously read some books of the Regency period, asked me if I was a two-bottles or three-bottles a day man at home. I had not tasted alcohol for over twenty-one months. As the Japanese dinner got going with each man sitting cross-legged on the bamboo platform, the sergeant asked me to sing. I replied I only sang in a choir.

'How many?' he wanted to know.

'Thirty or more,' I told him.

'Then bring in thirty.' he roared.

So in came thirty of our prisoners of war and partook of the repast in the best Japanese NCO fashion.

As the sake went around, he asked me to lead the chorus. I chose the song—'Sons of the Sea'.

Soon, all the guards, as well as ourselves, were raising their voices in praise of the British Navy.

No. 1 Mobile Force
August-October, 1943

AS THE BURMA-THAILAND railway neared completion conditions did not ease for its POW slave-labourers. Lieutenant Colonel Williams continued recording the circumstances under which his troops had to labour:

With malaria now rampant, more tests by the Japanese. Just an inconvenience and a disturbance of what little rest the men can grasp.

Ill health is on the increase and the Medical Officers, and their staff, are fighting harder and harder to maintain a standard that is thwarted by lack of lifesaving essentials. The Japanese refuse to supply even basic medicines, let alone drugs.

Another batch (18) of the too ill to treat in this camp sent to the 55 kilo hospital today. They had a nightmare trip in torrential rain; many hours were to pass before they even boarded a train to take them 18 kilometres. Those who survive will not forget August 16, 1943.

It was also another more than just tough day for the workers who had to rebuild the washed-away bridge at the 87 kilo mark. It was a nightmare job as they slaved against the raging torrent that tore at every piece of timber placed into position.

Another 21 seriously ill patients sent away today [17.8.43] to Thanbyuzayat hospital. They included Lieutenants Richards and Campbell. Leading Seaman Garret (HMAS *Perth*) passed away. He had battled against terrific odds to remain alive and all had hoped he would make it. Fate decreed otherwise.

*

Garret had battled valiantly to beat the disease that had overtaken him. Almost to the last breath he believed he had won. He had the willpower; his body lacked the strength. In the absence of the Padre, who was too ill to attend, Lieutenant Colonel Williams officiated at the graveside.

*

A workforce of 101 sent out onto the railway job today but no-one has any idea when they will return to camp.

Rations were delivered but gave little reason for joy; boxed meat, days old at that, a few beans and some maize that had been wet, set solid, and filled with weevils. Hungry as the men are, the sight of the alleged foodstuffs was enough to ruin any appetite.

Another group (62) of our sick are on their way to the 55 kilo hospital. They had to wait many hours at the 62 kilo mark for the train. They sat in the pouring rain and looked for all the world like a collection of zombies. If any of them survive, it will be a miracle. Once aboard the transport they face an uncomfortable twelve hours, if not more, before they arrive at their destination.

The Japanese are obviously panicky now as the deadline set for the joining up of the railway in Thailand draws nearer. Today *[20.8.43]* we detailed 85 for the railway job. They demanded more and blitzed the sick ranks. Strong protests eventually convinced the guards the sick were really sick. None were taken. Four of the men (ex 30 kilo hospital) on parade had very high fever and were sent back to their quarters.

A group of 40 from the 30 kilo hospital had walked 20 kilometres before they arrived at this camp (80 kilo). Five of them were crippled and unable to move another step. One, they told us, was left lying on the ground three kilometres back. He was carried into camp.

Every one of those poor men had been diagnosed by a Nipponese doctor as fully fit for railway work and ordered to foot-slog it to the 100 kilo camp. They have another 20 kilometres to walk before they arrive at their destination. How they will make it, no-one knows.

Bad day for us *[21.8.43]* even though there was no blitz on the unfit men. A total of 80 sent out to work, four of them returned suffering high fevers, but Ori, whose main mission in life appears to be to bash up the sick troops, disbelieved three of them and had them stand to attention at the guardhouse.

An immediate protest was made to the Camp Commander and he very promptly had them released.

Only 73 fit to work today *[22.8.43]* as 72% of the force is down with malaria. That is the quoted figure; looking at the rows of sick men it is a very conservative number. To the observer, 92% would be nearer the mark.

The frequency of death in this camp is causing a great deal of alarm. And, as we interred four more of our men today, we can only view a bleak future, unless the inhumane Japanese change their attitude.

The Japanese Camp Commander is furious today and the two Force Commanders were called to his office. They wondered why, but hoping against hope it could mean a relaxing of work number demands, or perhaps better rations.

It was neither. Apparently rumours had reached him in respect of POWs trading with the Burmese. He said unless it was brought to a stop, rations would cease to be supplied! Some ultimatum!

There was no way the Commanders were going to admit their troops were engaged in illicit wheeling and dealing with the locals. But if it meant starvation, and cessation of rations would mean that, then a possible solution had to be found.

Hungry men will take all kinds of risk but no-one, irrespective of conditions, would deliberately imperil the welfare of their mates by ignoring what Shimojo threatened. He was capable of doing anything, as well the men knew.

The Commanders could suggest to their men that every care must be taken to ensure the Nipponese were unaware of any dealings, in the interests and welfare of all in the camp, particularly the sick to whom most of the food purchased or bartered for was given. Officially, orders would be issued and the Japanese made to believe all trading had ceased.

Only 88 detailed for line work today as rails and sleepers were, as happens quite frequently, unavailable. However, there would be no let-up as far as work was concerned. The Nips would see to that.

Some canteen stores arrived today *[24.8.43]* and included cigars, one tin of coffee and some rice cake at 10 cents per slice. Paid for, but did not receive, 1,500 eggs. Ned Kelly was a gentleman compared to the Japanese from whom we are compelled to buy. The difference between what they pay for goods sold to us and our debit, is anything up to 100%.

Ori, one of the most vile of all the guards, portrayed his true colours today when he went berserk and savagely attacked ten of the workers and one officer. His reason, contents of the medical bag were inadequate. It held the bulk of the stores issued to the Force by the Japanese. As far as the ferocious Ori was concerned, even though there may have been cause to use some of what was in it originally, nothing should be missing. An example of oriental thinking.

Well aware he had overstepped himself he threatened further ill-treatment to anyone who dared to report the despicable incidents to Shimojo. He obviously enjoyed venting his fury on prisoners but had no desire to undergo any himself. His threats were useless, a very strong protest was lodged. Whether or not he received his just desserts no-one knew. If he did, it was more probably verbal than physical.

Another boy buried today *[25.8.43]* and it is feared many more will soon leave us. Tragedy stalks our ranks as the ravages of disease take over.

One of the railway engineers caught and killed a yak out on the line and graciously presented the workers with some of the bones. Seems as if their rice bowls are on the light side as well. Maybe the flesh of the luckless beast will ease his hunger pangs, and the gift of the bones his conscience

Ordered today *[26.8.43]* to detail sick men for light duty; all protests waved aside and 15 of the unfit personnel forced to build huts and cut wood. There is nothing that hurts more than having to submit to Japanese inhuman demands for the too-ill to work. It is galling; we voice the strongest protests against such cruel treatment and are disregarded.

Later in the day Shimojo demanded more workers and the railway engineers put on an extra shift to enable the laying of the sleepers and rails. Five kilometres per day is a rate far beyond the ability of the workers available, but that does not worry the Nipponese. If the materials are there, then they must be laid.

The true example of complete indifference to the lives of the sick men was never more evident than it was today *[27.8.43]* when two medical orderlies were sent to help out the unfortunates in the No. 5 Group hospital.

Shimojo told the Force Commanders there was nothing he could do for them as they had been *sent there to die!* Few of the 194 survived the churlish Japanese treatment.

The day and night requirements of the sick ranks have been taking toll on the physical reserves of both Major Krantz and Captain Rowley Richards. They have denied themselves in every way in order to administer to the needs of the many sick men.

The arrival of Majors Chalmers and Hobbs today [28.8.43] enabled the transfer of Krantz and Richards to the 30 kilo hospital camp for a complete rest, Nipponese permitting.

An issue of meat for the first time in a month; two yak cows were slaughtered and every edible portion will be an additive to the rice diet and for broth for the sick.

A surprise arrival, 650 pairs of Nipponese clogs to be distributed to the bootless majority in the Combined Forces. Certainly unsuitable for railway work, but better, perhaps, than nothing.

Our lives invaded by a horde of Japanese at 1850 hours today [29.8.43] and everyone had to quit their quarters. For the next 90 minutes they played havoc with everyone's gear. There was no orderliness in their process of searching. Everything they did not take ended up in one heap. They played merry hell, no beg pardons. Hard to say what they were looking for (usually concentrate on one thing and ignore all else), as they favoured nothing. What they took included torches, table knives, blade razors (those safely hidden prior to the raids) kitbag locks, a camera (a wonder the owner was not savagely beaten, may have been had they found film), gift pens, pencils, scissors, pliers, screwdrivers and anything else that took their fancy.

Whilst the scavengers were wreaking havoc inside the huts, Japanese railway workers encircled the prisoners. Maybe they expected some kind of action and were somewhat apprehensive. Little did they know it, but many quiet threats indicated the hostility of the men. But a few cool heads kept all calm.

As Japanese time is followed religiously by the Nipponese all clocks were put on 40 minutes. Local time, 3.30 a.m. when we are aroused.

The speedo tactics are going to be very rough on our lads as from today ([30.8.43]. Sleepers and rails, plus dog-spikes and ballast have been delivered. The whips will be out, with the Japanese screaming their heads off and gangers wielding pick handles on everyone they may think is slowing up. And that does happen within a very short period of commencement.

The sequel to the hut raid of the previous evening was an impassioned approach to the Camp Commander for a return of all possessions taken from the troops. He assured the Force Commanders he would give some consideration to returning articles; did not say which ones, but as the prisoners are forbidden to have torches, they would remain confiscated. He reserved his decision.

The 1st day of September, 1943, was another one that did not promise any concessions from the Japanese. Not enough men out on the line; to augment the dwindling numbers Shimojo decreed officers must take their places in the ranks of the workers. He bluntly refused to listen to any argument against his ruling on that or any other matter the Force Commanders felt impelled to present.

The following day four officers went out as part of the work group and their rank was not considered a reason for preferred tasks. It is dark when reveille is sounded, same when breakfast—watery pap—is served, and tools handed out. It is still before first light when the men arrive at the work site. So much for Tokyo time.

[3.9.43] Another move tomorrow, this time to the 95 kilo camp where the same routine will undoubtedly have to be followed. A big clean-up, dig latrines and repair falling down huts.

Despite all protests 23 light duty men were forced out on to the railway job today.

Our last day in this camp and another lad laid to rest in the now enlarged cemetery. Grim faces are an indication of the feelings of the men who dig the graves, attend the burial services and gaze into an uncertain future.

Just as well we are scheduled to move out from here, cholera has broken out in the Burmese lines. Their lack of hygiene renders neighbours a grave risk of contagion of many kinds of tropical diseases.

Reveille was at 0730 hours but we were informed we would have to await orders as to the disposition of the sick as well as the remainder of the troops before any move could commence.

The orders came at 1000 hours and it was then the mad speedo was applied. It was an exhibition of stupidity so normal from the Japanese command when troop movements are in process. For a wonder, the sick personnel are to be transported whilst the workers have to do it the hard way, march and carry their gear.

It poured with rain the whole way and everyone was thoroughly wet when they arrived, and as expected, found filthy, weather-worn huts. Mud, at least nine inches deep lay in the walk-ways, the roofs leaked, bamboo decks (bed-spaces) broken.

The accommodation was absolutely inadequate and 18 men had to squeeze into a bay which would normally hold six. All that was bad enough but an immediate demand for 40 men to go straight out to work (1800 hours) was just a little too much.

This time the Camp Commander acknowledged the strong complaints and set the work time at 0200 hours next day and have the following day off; they returned to camp at 0600 hours but were told they had to be ready to report for work again at 1400 hours the same day.

The word of a Japanese was again shown to be worthless.

Perhaps the letter handed to the two Force Commanders was meant to be somewhat of a sop, an easing of the farcical charge of their accommodation. The charge was reduced from 70 rupees a month to 20. A grandiose gesture that influenced no-one.

Despite the fact this was supposed to be a staging camp for front-line Japanese troops, there was no provision for latrines. It was another case of dig and do so quickly to ensure proper hygiene.

The Japanese found their housing was somewhat in accord with what the prisoners had to occupy: To increase their comfort they called for 100 men to clean the place up for them. Their request was not fruitful and they ended up doing most of it themselves. The boys found ways and means of dodging the hardest part. For once the Nips did it real tough, whether they liked it or not.

The cholera infestation throughout the jungle camps did elicit some concern from the Japanese. Not that they cared whether the prisoners of war contracted it or not. Their only thought was their own welfare and the possibility that affected men could transmit the dreaded disease to them. The Japanese doctor decided on a glass rod test, via the anus. The only difference was the 'tool' he used; he used wire similar to fencing material which felt like very sharp barbed wire, at that.

On the 7th, reveille was at 0500 hours and workers had had only four hours sleep. What they did not know, but the Japs did, was a 19½ hour back-breaking task lay in front of them. How those exhausted men actually performed the arduous work of sleeper and rail laying is quite beyond imagination.

Those long stints are not just a few isolated instances; they come far too regularly. The astounding ability of the undernourished troops confounds even the medical fraternity. How can they continue?

However, whatever the job, its toughness and required speed, there is always a wag or two who can turn a sour experience into some sort of anti-climax with jokes, and this bewilders the guards and gangers.

One party returned to camp at 0100 hours, wet and frozen to the marrow, hungry and desiring undisturbed rest. The remaining 33 came in at 0500 hours slightly worse for wear than their mates who returned earlier. They were so physically beaten, it was a struggle for them to put one foot in front of the other. Like the others, they were fed and sent off for a well-deserved rest.

Line-laying materials appear to be arriving fairly regularly now and work demands are becoming greater and greater. The rails and sleepers seem to get heavier, the body-bashing more often and the yells and screams of the Nipponese and Koreans a continuous crescendo.

Williams Force had to detail 99 of their fittest men for the line job today [8.9.43]. A group of 66 commenced their march to the work site at first light. They were followed at 1200 hours by a second party of 33. In addition, the Nips ordered all sick men be employed on sledge-hammer work.

The return of the working parties was awaited with apprehension; hard work, a foot slog of seven miles each way, little food and torrential rain was enough to cause a tremendous amount of illness for the men concerned. A group of 33 came in at 2200 hours and the remainder at 2350 hours. All were completely exhausted.

At 0845 hours next morning, 100 men trudged off to another harrowing and long day. A few came in at 0010 hours and the remaining 60 at 0500 hours, next morning. Reveille was sounded at 0800 hours which meant the overtired men had but two hours sleep.

*

Williams Force Commander was so incensed at the treatment of the men he made no bones about seeking changes. He was fed up with the fact the men were forced to walk, carrying tools, 14 miles per day and expected to work like slaves on rations that hardly amounted to one meal if all meals in a day were put together.

His approach to the camp commander was a determined one and Shimojo knew it. He pointed out quite forcefully the lack of essential foods which were required if the Japanese were to expect workers to proceed at such a pace on such exceptionally heavy work. For men, who were anything but healthy, to be kept out working for those long hours could have but one result. And the camp commander must be aware of the lurking dangers, unless changes of work procedure were immediately implemented.

Rations too, would have to be increased to the point of adequate nutrition. It is thought he quoted to Shimojo the type of foodstuffs available that very day (10th September)—half a sweet potato and rotten meat for the whole day. Hardly a menu for a working man.

For once Shimojo did not react violently, but merely said the meals were, in his opinion, quite satisfactory. And, that was that.

Williams continues:

*

As the direct result of poor rations and hard labour, dysentery was again a very great problem. It was increasing to epidemic proportions despite the fight the Medical Officers were continuing to keep the outbreak in check.

For two successive days *[11th and 12th]* reveille was at 0700 hours and the Japanese demanded the men of the work parties that had returned to camp at that hour, be sent back to work just sixty minutes later.

The Force Commanders ridiculed the idea and instructed the men to remain in their huts. They did! And, we got away with it.

These men were sent out at 1200 hours, sat in the pouring rain for five hours then sent back to camp!

Been advised we move camp tomorrow and all men are to have plenty of sleep.

At first light the Nipponese demanded all gear be on the railway siding within thirty minutes, including their personal gear.

As was usual with the Japanese, tenko was a very lengthy one, 1½ hours to account for 600 men. The matter of transport was again cause for much discontent. Finally, the Japanese agreed all the very sick men and the cooks could travel by train, the remainder of the troops were to walk and carry their personal possessions, such as they are.

They set off on the hike to the 108 kilo camp; rain was teeming down and made the road a complete bog. So much so it took three hours to travel the first three kilometres. When they eventually arrived at the 105 kilo camp they were greeted by Lt. Col. G.E. Ramsay, Commander of Ramsay Force, and were provided with a meal which will be remembered by Williams Force for many years to come.

Tired out and drenched they filed into their new camp at 1300 hours. The first meal was served at 2100 hours; they were joined later by the work party that had gone out the previous day from the 95 kilo camp. They had been made to work practically non-stop for 26 hours, then foot-slog it to the 108 kilo camp. Their personal belongings had been packed and carried by their mates on the 13 kilometre march.

The Japanese are never satisfied. After the long trudge, through mud and loaded down, a work party of 60 was demanded to go out on line work at 2200 hours. Few of the men had slept the previous night and no-one will get much tonight.

For the first time in their many camp shifts they had come into a moderately clean area. However, one unpleasant aspect is the necessity to share one hut with Burmese labourers, as well as occupying a common kitchen.

We soon discovered four of the native coolies were victims of cholera. Isolation of the afflicted was effected without delay. A shock, not to be denied, 'request' for all the light sick to be out on the railway job by 0900 hours. Based on recent experiences we cannot expect their return to camp until tomorrow.

The men who went out on the night shift were supposed to return to camp for their breakfast. They did not come in until 1100 hours.

No matter the strength of protests launched by the Force Commanders the Japanese detailed 30 very obviously ill men to do chores in their lines. That meant the moving of a lot of heavy materials, then they were ordered to assist the Jap cook erect a kitchen.

That nasty character ensured the project was carried out with speed. As they worked he flailed the sick lads on their heads and backs with a heavy, long piece of bamboo. Quite one of the most vicious!

How these lads actually managed to work is something of a wonder. They could hardly stand up as their balance was affected. Feverish and badly weakened, their movements were impaired, bamboo poles fell from their hands, the atap was difficult to handle and hard to tie. On top of these problems, they had to suffer the cruel bashings.

*

On the morning of the 14th, Williams Force Commander again fell foul of the Japanese. One of the men detailed for the line job came down with an attack of malaria, just as he was due to parade. To keep the actual number correct, Williams replaced him by directing an officer to join the group.

As far as the Japanese were concerned, it was a last minute change in which they lost a worker even though the total number was no different; perhaps they believed it was intentional. The figures given the evening before were in order, but by replacing the sick man by an officer, who would not be a worker, they were, in effect, one worker down.

Williams was ordered to parade to the Nipponese camp commander, who upbraided him and made him stand to attention, in pouring rain, for just over an hour. He was then quite bluntly told he must not forget that he was a prisoner of war and as such must do as he was told, and that the same also applied to his men.

Under the circumstances Shimojo could have saved his breath. How could any of the men forget for one moment the horrible facts of their situation. The Japanese gave no recognition to the Geneva Convention, to the Red Cross and humane treatment.

*

The Japanese must be desperate in their attempts to lay the line. They are demanding that Force Commanders send out to work even the heavy sick. But that's impossible; many are in a semi-comatose condition, cannot walk, let alone work.

The men who were sent out did not return to camp until 2330 hours; they had laboured for 26½ hours in continuous heavy rain. Because of their state of health (they were the light sick) the guards, gangers and engineers were expected to allocate them to light tasks. But no concessions despite emphatic protests on their behalf.

If anything, they had to handle, and with speed, the hardest jobs the Nipponese could find. It was a miracle quite a few did not die; only sheer willpower kept them going, together with, or in spite of, the usual cruel inducements with waddies and boots.

The workers who were sent out yesterday [14.9.43] returned to camp at 0200 hours this morning. They would not have been back then only for the fact they ran out of sleepers.

Reveille was at 0700 hours, the usual 'pap' was served and the workers were away in pitch dark and heavy rain at 0800 hours (Tokyo time). If rails and sleepers have been delivered, it will probably be sometime tomorrow before we see them again.

Our ration issue is more or less on the starvation basis and there is no certainty we can expect any improvement in the foreseeable future. Major Hobbs, our surgeon, returned to the 105 kilo camp today [15.9.43].

Great to-do by the Japanese; five yaks arrived at the slaughter yard today [16.9.43]. Judging by the scrawny look of them the whole group would not make a decent beef sandwich. Even so, pennies to peanuts the Nipponese will take the lion's share before the POWs get even a hoof.

Some eggs were delivered for the canteen but, as usual, a lot less than what we had paid for. We were supposed to receive 600, counted 445, the Nips took the rest.

Advised we are on the move again tomorrow [18.9.43] to the 116 kilo camp.

The work party came in at 0430 hours, reveille was one hour later; breakfasted (sounds good but it was only watery pap) and the march out commenced. After covering four kilometres the Force met up with a train that had followed them.

It had to be unloaded and all the gear was to be manhandled the rest of the way, another four kilometres.

Strict orders were issued that all Japanese gear, work and personal, had to be taken to the camp before any POW possessions. The Force Commanders were furious and protested vehemently. All to no avail. The men had to make two trips, and then another one with their own belongings. It was tough going!

The camp is absolutely the worst the Force has experienced. It was necessary to squeeze 32 men to each bay, 10' x 8' with an upper deck necessary.

The previous tenants had been a group of unhygienic natives who could not have cared less about the placement of their nightsoil, scraps of stinking rice that attracted vermin, and other rubbish. The smell was abominable!

A Japanese officer took one look, said it was bad, but then just strolled off and went to his bed! He had no care that the POWs had been domiciled in a cesspool; his comfort was all he thought or cared about.

Not another Nipponese put in an appearance; maybe the vile odour emitted was just too much for their sensitivity. In addition to the lack of space, the troops had to contend with mud twelve inches deep, inside and outside.

Wearied beyond measure, after the march, and three trips back and forth to the railway siding to collect tools, other heavy materials and personal gear, all the men wanted to do was flop down on their bed-spaces. Many were even too tired to partake of the light ration of plain rice that had been prepared for them.

But not all were able to take a rest. The Nips demanded, and would not take no for an answer, 80 men for immediate line work. They would not listen to arguments that the men had been on the go for many hours and were too tired to undertake work tasks. There was little sleep that night, even for the men left in camp. Nature rebelled against the physical demands made on their bodies and they were so done-in that the luxury of sleep was beyond them.

Incessant rain is creating misery for everyone except, perhaps, for the Japanese who protect themselves from the inclement weather. Rain or not, the men must work and another 100 are battling it out on the rail job. They were despatched at first light.

The remainder of gear left at the siding yesterday has to be brought in today. The Camp Commander promised a lorry would be made available to transport the huge amount of material lying where it was unloaded. But, as so often is the case, the motorised transport failed to arrive and the Camp Commander ordered every man, sick or otherwise, to go back the four kilometres and manhandle the lot to the worksite or camp, wherever it was required. They left at 1330 hours.

The conditions of the camp where the prisoners of war are housed are so bad not one Jap will come near it. Their total absence does have its compensations.

The existing latrines, such as they are, are overflowing on the ground between the so-called huts. And as all the men are barefooted they are at risk. All kinds of tropical diseases can be transferred to the bodies through the feet.

Time and again Force Commanders have made appeals to the Japanese authorities for an issue of suitable footwear to all POWs. On rare occasions clogs and rubberised slipper type of footwear have been made available, but never in a quantity. In any case what was issued were not suitable for the work being done and were so fragile they soon wore out.

Major Meagher was aware boots were stored at the Base camp and were to remain there until the rainy season was over. So much for the vaunted kindness of the Nipponese!

Now the 19th September and still a lot of material to be brought from the siding four kilometres back. Sick men are still being forced by the Japs to carry heavy loads. Even though they may buckle under the weight, no concessions are granted. If anything, punishment is the penalty if one, for a minute or two, lingers in the sight of a guard.

*

The hope and wish of every POW at that time was to see the day come when those inhuman brutes would be brought to justice and dealt with in a proper manner for their sadism.

No pen can aptly describe the horror of incarceration under Japanese control. Young men, who had been in the bloom of health prematurely aged as they suffered slow starvation, potentially terminal diseases due to lack of drugs, medicines and nutritious food, plus unbelievable daily physical abuses.

Their cruelty was not confined to humans alone; they nailed birds to bamboo, played football with kittens and grown cats, set fire to dogs that might wander into a camp. They laughed in sheer enjoyment at prisoners forced to stand on oval stones and holding a heavy weight over their heads. That was one of the minor punishments employed at various camps.

There would be few prisoners who did not harbour resentment against their tormentors, or who, during their suffering, did not plan retribution at war's end. However, when Japan laid down arms the overriding emotions were relief and the joy of freedom.

*

A work party of 100 detailed for the line work today [20.9.43] as the rain intensified. It was coming down in torrents, but in no way was that an excuse to delay work. The five kilometres of line had to be laid, even if all the POWs on the job passed away in the effort.

The guards demanded a ration party of ten men, a sure indication of a day-night shift for the bedevilled 100 toiling their hearts out on the railroad.

A group of light sick were sent; the Nipponese sent them back with a message. They required *strong* men. The same group were told to report back. No men of the physique demanded by the guards were left in camp. In fact, there were no strong men in the whole Force. All near-strong were at that very moment labouring on the line and trying to cope with tasks and a pace beyond their capacity.

The reason the guards sent the ten unfit boys back was they feared they could be cholera carriers. If so, the Nips could contract it and return to their homeland in ashes. Very few suffered such an end, but they feared it.

On the move again! Advised at 0300 hours to prepare and have all gear ready for transportation at 0830 hours. Reveille was scheduled for 0600 hours. A working party of 25 required to report to the guardhouse to carry their gear to the railway or whatever point they might indicate the believed transport would be waiting to shift all materials, plus the troops.

No marching or carrying our possessions, kitchen gear, etc; a lorry or lorries would transport the two Forces. That intimation was accepted with a grain of salt. It would be out of character if, for once, they told the truth. Every POW is fed up with Jap lies, misinformation and promises never kept.

We walked *and* carried our possessions for six kilometres to another filthy, vermin-infested camp that had previously been tenanted by Burmese labourers. The conglomerate of supposed huts had a frightening appearance.

With heavy hearts the usual clean-up commenced; our two Forces were weary of the same happenings in every camp we took over. The work had no sooner commenced when orders came to down tools and wend our way back to the 116 kilo encampment to carry up more gear, arriving back at the 122 kilo at 1900 hours. We had our last meal at 0700 hours and it was 2200 hours before we could have our evening meal.

It was midnight before any of the bedraggled troops lay down to rest. This time they slept, despite the exhaustion and discomfort.

Next morning the Japanese told the Force Commanders they had to relocate their troops and provide one eighth of a hut for Nipponese accommodation. They brooked no argument, just barged in.

It is quite obvious the Japanese are on edge and fear the worst should cholera break out in the camp. To ensure the POWs are free they implemented another test. Whatever the results, as usual, we were not told. As they didn't vacate the portion of the hut they had taken over, it could be accepted the test proved negative.

The arrival of 70 men ex-hospital created a necessity for more housing; representation to that effect resulted in the overflow moving into a hut in the Dutch lines 300 yards away.

As anticipated the line parties worked, without a break, for many hours— shifts exceeding 26 hours. They come back in dribs and drabs, weary beyond measure and almost too done-in to concern themselves with anything except a meal and much needed sleep. They get both.

Although it was thought there could be no work harder than what the troops faced at the 116 kilo camp, it was relatively light to what they have to endure now. It is similar to working in a clay pit; up to their knees in soggy clay that prevents free movement. It is almost as if they are fettered with chains; instead, it is a clinging mass.

The embankments are freshly made from wet material that creates a quagmire. As the men battle to lay sleepers and rails, both just sink into the muddy surface; they just disappear. However, the yelling engineers and the guards force the issue no matter the conditions. A railroad has to be laid. Materials and human automatons are available and five kilometres must be put down each day. It will be interesting to see what happens the first time a train endeavours to pass over that area. The line is now to the 130 kilo mark from Thanbyuzayat.

It is a pitiful sight to see the lines of barefoot men heading out to the physical endurance tests and that is exactly what the work parties are engaged in now, under the worst possible conditions. Their feet just look like horrible blobs of skin and bone.

It was a sheer impossibility to field 100 men fit enough to go out on the line today [24.9.43] but the Japanese just commandeered men shivering with malaria or from any other cause to, as they said, make up the numbers required.

Protests of the Force Commanders are of little avail; it's just like talking to a concrete block. They want bodies out on the line job. To hell with the objectors; sick or not, out they go.

To make life more miserable there had been another outbreak of diarrhoea. Must be expected under the circumstances as rations are at their lowest point. A rice-only diet—and not much of that. The camp is plagued with millions of flies, despite the monsoonal rain. Many men have more than one complaint and suffer in silence, fearing their more unhealthy mates may pay a penalty if they report as sick. Not one man in the two Forces will play on another. They all have a mate, or mates, and do their utmost to protect each other.

The Medical Officers carry out a herculean task in caring for so many whose lives are imperilled through lack of medication. But they are limited in what they can do. They, too, put in long hours as they stimulate the minds of the hopeless with drive and influence that is evident as patient after patient responds.

The willpower they assert over the sick men has to be seen to be believed. How they do it is a mystery, which even their medical minds probably can't answer. But the smiles from the tight-skinned features is evident testimony they do succeed where success appears an impossibility.

It was after midnight before the line workers came in from the bitter hours of purgatory they had put in on the railway job. Whilst they hope for a long uninterrupted rest, they are aware it will not be too long before they are again on the way back to the worksite.

At 0900 hours (Tokyo time) 160 headed off for another long stint and they were followed at noon by another 100 men. There were many problems in getting them away today.

The Japanese belted one of the officers over the head with a piece of bamboo and took one basket of eggfruit and a bag of potatoes from our kitchen. He handed back one basket of *rotten* eggfruit. Complaints were lodged but to no avail.

At 1000 hours 50 of our men returned to camp, but it was another 24 hours before any more came in; then only a group of 50.

The *[26.9.43]* September heralded the first ray of sunlight for a long time. Its arrival seemed to give everyone a 'lift'. At least the men will be working in dry weather, and the sun might dispel some of the prevalent diseases and dry up the mud in the walkways in time. The remainder of the camp given the cholera test today.

One of the Anderson Force members so ill today he was placed in isolation. Only a precautionary measure against his possible contraction of cholera.

The ration issue is almost at zero point and we are endeavouring to improve the rice by the addition of a vegetable that looks very much like seaweed. It looks awful, smells terrible but it does alter the taste of the low grade rice.

At 0400 hours (28th) we were informed of another move and that we were to have all gear out on the road ready by 0730 hours. Told the Camp Commandant that was too short a period. He agreed on 1000 hours. Three trains were supposed to be made available to transport all heavy gear and our sick personnel. They were scheduled for 1030, 1200 and 1330 hours.

For about the first time on record one part of the timetable was kept. Some gear and 100 workers departed at 1030 hours. The marching group moved off at 1300 hours. By the time they had left six kilometres behind them they had caught up with and passed the train that had preceded their departure by 2½ hours. At 1700 hours the foot party arrived at the 130 kilo camp.

They were astounded when they saw two new huts they were to inhabit but suffered severe shock to find out neither had a roof. A total of 900 men to be squeezed into an area that may have provided elbow space for about 600. The eventual allocation was 23 to a space of 9' x 12'. A few hours later it rained! There was no let-up, teemed throughout the night.

Not one POW slept. How could they! It was a frightful night. To make things even worse, there was no kitchen available, therefore no meal could be prepared.

Daylight brought no reprieve; rain and plenty of it. Another problem, no latrines. What a camp. Roofless, small huts, unhygienic, vermin-infested blot on the landscape. Despite the inclement weather, digging of latrines and completion of the huts, material permitting, was of the utmost importance, after the erection of the kitchen.

A train arrived at 2100 hours with only a few of the expected sick men. The second one arrived at 0100 hours and the third, and last, at 0830 hours, 29th September. Aboard the latter was the camp staff.

Whilst the unloading of the train was in progress a guard took exception to the method employed by Williams Force Commander.

★

It was another ploy by the Japanese to savagely beat up Lieutenant Colonel Williams. They hated him as he had no respect for any one of them, from their Emperor down, and in no way hid the fact. The guard, using his rifle as a rod, struck the Australian officer several times. To avoid being hit on the face he used his hands to shield the blows. That enraged the guard and for the next five minutes Williams went through hell as the flashing bayonet and rifle butt crashed onto his frame.

Not to be outdone, the other guards joined in. Rifles, boots, fists and waddies gave the beleaguered officer one of the worst bashings witnessed throughout the building of the railway. It was a wonder he came out of the punishment alive.

When the frenzied group finally tired, the bloodied figure of the Australian officer, still on his feet but obviously in a bad way, glared at his tormentors and turned to the work in hand.

When the Japanese Camp Commander was called in, all he did was to say he would make an official report of the incident. There were no repercussions for the fiendish guards. Meanwhile, Williams was more concerned with the welfare of his men.

*

The inhumanity of the Japanese was demonstrated yet again when they detailed 60 men to work on the line, despite the fact they had had no sleep at all for the past 36 hours. There was no doubt they were in for a long shift, and would still be out there well into the night.

The POWs were further inconvenienced and handicapped when the guards took away all the tools to erect a hut and kitchen for themselves. As far as they were concerned, their 'slaves' just had to put up with it; like it or lump it.

Another night of living under the stars and hoping the rain keeps off. It passed, but the following day brought no improvement as regards hut completion or kitchen erection. Same thing applied to providing latrines. The guards still had the tools. No wood could but cut, no fires, no cooking.

It was an impossible situation and the Force Commanders voiced their complaints to the Camp Commander. This time with some result. Forty tents were supplied, six were used as a hospital. As many men as possible took refuge in the remainder. Some atap roofing was made available; only enough to roof one third of one hut. And that, said the Camp Commander, is all you are going to get.

The well-orchestrated bashing of all and sundry is on again, and the brutish Nipponese cook took a heavy piece of bamboo to flail the fatigue party working on the Japanese kitchen. One lad was so injured it will be at least three weeks before he is fit to work again. A deep laceration of one of his legs is open and bleeding profusely.

The cooks have managed to prepare meals under the most trying conditions. They are an ingenious lot and perform miracles with their ability to overcome the impossible. Just takes a little longer.

One small thin yak cow provided but the Nips commandeered half of the carcass. The amount of meat left was in no way anywhere near enough to even add taste to the rice, let alone cause mouths to water on succulent cuts.

[Friday, 1.10.43]: September was one of our worst months of the year and everyone is hoping the future, with the line close to the link-up stage, will be much brighter, healthier and more bearable.

A work party of 75 out to work but some of them sent back to camp under instruction to return to the worksite at 1200 hours. Some of the tools recovered from the guards—shovels and an axe. At last latrines can be dug and hygiene improved. Framework for a kitchen, too.

Rain is pouring down again and the lads endeavouring to dig the latrines are doing it tough, but what they are doing is of the utmost importance to every man in the camp.

No railway work today [2.10.43] so the Japs have ordered every available man be employed in collecting bamboo for the guards. They are going to build a bath-house for themselves. They said there was no more atap, but they have found plenty to roof and cover the sides of a hut for them to bathe in! Just another act that proves they lie in their teeth.

Rations low again, none delivered today [3.10.43] and no assurances there will be any in the near future. No wonder there is such widespread malnutrition.

Our first death in this camp (130 kilo) occurred today but judging by medical reports, unless Shimojo (Camp Commandant) can or will provide drugs and medicines, more are likely. But Shimojo promises nothing, gives nothing and does nothing. No wonder our medical officers are so completely frustrated. They know what is needed and if they could only get a portion, lives can be saved.

Lacking rail line supplies (sleepers, rails, etc.) bamboo parties have been called for despite the fact the workers are badly in need of rest after the long shifts they have been forced to work in recent months.

The engineers played havoc with our housing arrangements today when they confiscated 30 of our 34 tents. Shimojo did nothing to stop the acquisition. The occupants of the canvas homes are now out in the open. The comfort of the POWs, whether it be food or housing, is of no consequence to the Nips.

It was said more atap roofing is to be provided but when is what matters. Still only one third of a hut roofed and with only four tents left hundreds of men are victims of the elements. This is a terrible camp.

The torrential rain is falling and the lads out in the open are a pitiful lot. Their meagre possessions are sopping wet and sleep on a muddy surface is impossible. How much longer these conditions are to apply is purely a matter of conjecture. Shinojo and his minions are not the least disturbed and are doing nought to provide any kind of shelter.

Force Commanders' constant representations earn no response. They, too, are utterly frustrated and deeply concerned for the welfare of the troops.

The low rice ration, protected as far as possible by the kitchen staff, is fast becoming a soggy mess. Additionally, keeping fires alight in pouring rain, using only wet wood, is a tremendous difficulty. Without a roof above the fires (still no kitchen) the task of the determined cooks is a stupendous one.

A very small quantity of rice delivered today but no atap for roofing the huts and/or, when one can be constructed, the kitchen. But, although there is no atap available for the POWs, there is quite enough to allow the building of a Jap guardhouse in the centre of the camp.

Normally, such a building would be erected at the entrance to the camp. This is quite a departure from normal practice but for a very good Japanese reason.

Any POW who goes past or is near to the guardhouse has to salute the guard, or guards, on duty. Failure by prisoners of war to do so is sufficient reason for a guard to unmercifully bash the 'culprit'.

There was a crash during the night when one of the huts, by force of occupancy, failed to sustain the weight and collapsed. The frail building housed 500 men; it would have been overcrowded with 200. Just one more problem to try and surmount.

Another day of misery and depression as 100 men head out for the hated line-laying job. On top of what lay before them in the hours to come, was the knowledge a new cemetery was to be a permanent reminder that death stalks them. The death of a Dutchman, who will now rest alongside the Australian who predeceased him two days ago, foreshadows more white crosses in another hallowed spot.

The downturn in the health of the men can be attributed to a great extent to the conditions in the camp, lack of rations and work stints of up to 36 hours.

Weight of bodies caused a second overcrowded hut to come to grief; another rebuilding job IF materials are supplied. If not, more out in the open.

At 1100 hours today [4.10.43] one more lad found eternal peace. He was buried at 1400 hours. Additionally, all were saddened to hear of the death of a lad left at the 108 kilo camp. He had fought hard, but it was a losing battle.

Advised by our Medical Officers of the disturbing fact that at least 80% of the troops are suffering from beri-beri. Unless a complete change of diet is soon available, many of those so afflicted will also rest eternally in this vermin-infested jungle.

Rations at last, but not what we had been hoping for; some 'on the nose' fish and some white beans. In an endeavour to add bulk to the very light ration, leaves are being collected and added to the rice, together with whatever else the cooks can lay their hands on.

No work today [5.10.43] and no ration delivery either.

Captain Drower, interpreter, and Major Kerr were heard by a guard discussing the possibility of our next move—such as where, when and what it might be like. Shimojo was told and it was not long before the 'criminals' were sojourning in the guardhouse. They remained there for the next two hours.

The crime being none of the prisoners of war are allowed to think of or discuss such matters! Shimojo has spoken!

The heavy work is continuing and 150 detailed today [6.10.43]. They will have a long shift before they return, weary, hungry but defiant, as one man demonstrates when he brazenly whistles a tune entering the camp. He is a real morale builder.

Our ration increased slightly when we were allowed half of the carcass of a very small yak cow. The Nips took the other half. At least the sick will benefit and perhaps the rice may have a slightly different taste, for one meal.

Our cemetery is expanding rapidly; one of Anderson Force passed away today. His interment cast a gloom over the camp.

A workforce of 150 sent out today *[7.10.43]* and a similar number allowed to erect a hospital hut—roofing materials are now available; also to build a fence around the compound and improve the building housing the Nipponese headquarter staff.

The bestiality of the despised Ori, one of the most vicious guards on the line, is emphasised daily. He just belts up anyone and everyone he comes in sight of; apparently it is his way of overcoming the boredom of his job. He is a born sadist. It is hard to say how many feel the whack of his rifle butt or boot in the course of a shift.

A pleasant surprise today *[8.10.43]* some canteen supplies arrived and seven cigars and half a block of sugar sold to each man. Even the weather took a turn for the better, much warmer now.

The Nipponese still very wary as regards cholera; another test taken of the workers today and the aftermath of rough methods used was obvious when so many had to stand up to eat.

Another nine deaths reveal the precarious state of health of our men. To date, Williams Force has lost 107 since the inception of 'A' Force. The figures are devastating.

[Sunday, 10.10.43]: No rest on the Sabbath for the prisoners of war of the Japanese. It is just another day of hell for the 300 who are out on the line and who will have to lay five kilometres of sleepers, rails and accessories. They are well aware they have at least 24 hours of exceptionally hard work in front of them before they return to camp. They will be very lucky if they receive two meals in that period.

However, something went wrong with the programme; lunch was sent out to them at 1100 hours but they returned to quarters at 1230 hours—no explanation.

To get our ration issue 100 men had to walk five kilometres to get it and manhandle it back to camp. It comprised some dahl, small peas, beans and rice. Apparently three days supply.

Lost another tent last night when two guards came in and Shimojo had no accommodation for them. It did not matter to him where the occupants of the canvas cover were going to be housed. The Japanese have no accommodation problems in any of the camps they happen to be in. Three men to a bay as against 21 prisoners of war in the same given area.

Due to the loss of the tent, we now have 14 lads out in the open whilst just two guards have a whole tent to themselves. Just how long the situation exists depends on Shimojo. On that basis, irrespective of weather conditions, there is no way possible to house the unfortunates who are out in the cold. In the meantime, where it is share and share alike, there is no question their mates will take it in turns in and out of cover. No need to ask or issue an order.

Rations, for want of a better name, arrived today *[11.10.43]* in the form of dehydrated potatoes. Even if the whole lot goes into the rice no-one will ever notice any difference to the taste of the basic food.

Rain is pouring down and we are all in the same state, all and everything wet. The huts partially roofed, afford very little protection against the downpour. Everyone has to huddle in groups in the vain hope body heat may result in keeping them warm and their belongings a little dry.

Shimojo demanded 480 workers to be ready to move out to the line site at 0900 hours [13.10.43], but only 83 men were fit enough, and then not 100% by any means, to parade. He was so enraged he decided on diagnosing the troops himself.

As far as he was concerned, the fact everyone left in camp was ill was no excuse for missing work. He made sure, no matter their condition, they were going out.

Many of them could hardly stand as they were suffering from malaria and dysentery, with a few suspected cholera cases. Even those with exposed tropical ulcers had to shoulder tools and head out to undertake heavy work.

Shimojo finally detailed 100 of the sick, 60 from Williams Force and 40 from Anderson Force. He would, without doubt, have driven more out except for the fact they were too ill to move from their bed-spaces.

Another death today.

The day workers returned to camp at 2230 hours, tired, listless and mourning the passing of yet another friend.

At the rate the men are working (30½ hours, 2 meal breaks for the night shift gang, and the sick boys, who worked 18 hours, were not allowed to eat the meal taken out to them—they returned to camp at 0300 hours) how long can any survive the treatment?

The local guards had a field day [15.10.43] when they lashed out at all and sundry. Two men had teeth knocked out, one suffered spinal injuries when brutally booted.

Tiring of taking it out on the prisoners of war they turned their attention to the Burmese labourers. Every one of them was subject to a body search, then beaten up.

That behaviour was not quite enough for them and they demanded the services of our barber boys when they returned to camp after working 30 hours straight on the line. Hardly able to hold scissors they had to stand and cut the hair of all the guards. How they managed to carry out the task is beyond belief, but they did. Had they refused they knew that not only they would suffer physical torment but many others would as well.

The night shift (15th–16th) returned to camp at 1330 hours after completing 31½ hours straight. The day workers are still out and no-one has any idea when they will be back. No instructions to send a meal, or meals, out to them. We can just wait.

The bash artists are in their element today [16.10.43] and Captain Handasyde was badly beaten up. The reason, the guard didn't like the look on his face.

The day and night gangs returned to camp and ordered to get some sleep. They may be required to go out again tonight.

There is a very strong possibility the two ends of the Burma-Thailand 'Death Railway' may meet tonight, a momentous occasion for the fanatical Japanese. All work parties are still out on the last of the line construction.

Two more of the critically ill patients succumbed to the ravages of the diseases which plagued them and their bodies were laid to rest in the one peaceful area of this encampment.

THE END OF THE LINE

At 2330 hours last night, 17th October 1943, the historic moment came. The railway from Singapore to Moulmein, Burma, became a fact. But what a price! The lives of many thousands of prisoners of war and Burmese civilians!

*

On the 17th October, 1943, the Burma-Thailand railway was officially joined at the 131 kilo camp, Nieke, Thailand. It was a moment of propaganda at its oriental best.

To the accompaniment of a full brass band, Japanese dignitaries and others stood proudly as cameras filmed the world-shattering event as cheerful Japanese 'labourers', perspiration pouring from their well-fed bodies, drove home the golden dog spikes.

In the best film-making tradition it was pseudo-perspiration that poured from these bodies, produced by throwing buckets of water over the Japanese to create the effect they were hard-working hammermen. The gold on the dog spikes was in fact paint.

The bone-weary, empty-stomached prisoners of war who had carried out the work to almost the last second, had been ordered well out of sight. The Japanese audiences who may have viewed the film would believe, as they were supposed to, their nationals had been the real builders of this railway that linked Singapore Island to Moulmein, Burma.

But as thousands of others know only too well, they were not.

From Thanbyuzayat to the 130 kilo camp, the last camp to be occupied by 'A' Force personnel, cemeteries tell the story.

The number of wonderful lads resting in those hallowed areas testify to the barbarism suffered at the hands of fanatical fiends, whose sadism was beyond belief. No-one could imagine that one human could inflict such cruelty upon another. Not only did they do it, but they so obviously enjoyed the spectacle of battered, blood-stained living skeletons—their victims.

The prisoners of war who survived the building of the railway, and the 22 months that followed, only hoped that any punishment their tormentors might ultimately receive would be fitting for the crimes they committed.

NO. 1 MOBILE FORCE
October 1943-March 1944

THE BURMA-THAILAND railway was completed and officially opened in October 1943, at which time 'A' Force effectively ceased its 'unit' functions. However it was not disbanded—and the dispersed—until March 1944. Lieutenant Colonel Williams' diary records 'A' Force activity and privations up until that point.

*

The actual moment of the joining of the two stretches of the railroad was pre-empted yesterday morning by the Nipponese when they held a ceremony at the 153 kilo peg to commemorate the achievement. A lot of pomp and ceremony that meant nothing to the prisoners of war, except the high cost in lives; to the assembled Japanese it was a moment of glory.

The Japanese were so jubilant they dynamited the river and some of our lads gathered fresh fish which was cooked and fed to the sick lads in hospital.

This morning [19.10.43] a member of Anderson Force was interred with the usual dignity and now sleeps painlessly with many of his former mates in the secluded, sacred spot nearby.

Major Krantz returned today and told us of the ever-growing death rate at the depressing 55 kilo hospital, another eight patients had passed on before he left the area.

The savagery and despicable behaviour of the crazed guards is quite beyond belief, and quite without reason. They are on an orgy of bashing all and sundry. Even in the seclusion of the huts there is no escaping them. Frequent raids on the immobile men, many critically ill, result in deliberate bashing for no apparent reason whatever.

As issue of clothing was made tonight and all ranks had to parade to accept what was doled out; many missed out.

The morning of the 20th was not a good one for any of the Force as the belligerent Ori put on a terrible show last night. He bashed and belted everyone he came across. He roared and rampaged like a bull.

It is useless complaining to Shimojo as all he will say is 'Do not make any reports to Nagatomo'. Even if we did, the silence would be deafening.

As all prisoners of war had been promised a rest once the railway project had been completed every member actually expected that promise would be kept. Not so! Well, not for the No. 1 Mobile Force, anyhow.

Instead of being able to indulge in some spine-bashing, came orders to clear the jungle from the camp compound and prepare a parade ground. This will be a mammoth task, as bad as those forced upon the men at the beginning of their time in Burma.

Major Chalmers moved out today *[21.10.43]*en route to the 30 kilo hospital camp.

[Friday, 22.10.43]: We had a short concert last night, the singers were accompanied by a mouth organist. Actually, no-one felt in a festive mood, except the guards who put on a party and forgot all about us. One time we were left completely alone.

At least 100 workers are required each day to serve the 30 guards on fatigue parties including the parade ground job. The river is now very low and we are taking precautions against a shortage of water and sinking wells.

Rations are very low and no indication as to when supplies will be replenished. Our only food is the few sweet potatoes the cooks have been holding against an emergency. Just as well, or we would be on a starvation basis, with wishful thinking in place of a meal.

[23.10.43] Unusually quiet day and we are able to continue on the well project. The second one is down nine feet but no sign of water as yet. Some atap became available today and we were able to completely roof the isolation ward. Three bags of sweet potatoes—our rations—have been delivered, no rice. It is to be a reduced diet for all concerned.

Rumour of more deaths at the 55 kilo hospital was confirmed when we learned of the passing of two more.

*

The death rate at the 55 kilo hospital was appalling, despite the desperate fight by Lieutenant Colonel Coates and his entire staff to arrest the trend. They did manage to salvage many by sheer devotion and skill. Had Nagatomo supplied the drugs and medicines he implied he would, a large proportion of those who now rest in the Thanbyuzayat cemetery would have been saved.

*

A work party of 50 detailed to deliver rations today *[24.10.43]*. Included in the issue was some rice and sweet potatoes. What we were not keen to have were the melons, but the Nips took them anyway along with spaghetti, oil and sugar, which we did want. They live in luxury (melons excluded) on rations denied the POWs.

The guards have devised a new type of torture; they walk past us at regular intervals to obtain salutes. Heaven help anyone failing to respect the order. Two of Williams Force were badly kicked and punched by a guard today because they didn't salute him when he came up behind them. The guards have taken to sneaking up behind working parties and doing them over.

From then on it was a game to the guards; wherever working parties were labouring the guards would approach from the rear. The boys would be unaware of their proximity until they were bashed for failing to do honour by saluting.

Four baskets of fish were delivered today and were destined for our kitchen. The Nips confiscated two and out of the three bags of potatoes, we ended up with only one!

As ration carriers have to pass the Nip kitchen to get to ours the fat Nipponese cook snatches what he wants from our containers. Hence, low rations for the prisoners.

[26.10.43] We lost another lad today, Private H.Wadell. He could no longer fight the ravages of malaria and succumbed to the disease.

Great excitement amongst the Japanese today *[27.10.43]* when the GOC of all prisoners of war in Burma-Thailand visited and made an inspection of the camp. However, the only prisoners he saw, by Shimojo's arrangement, were those who had some semblance of wearing apparel. The near naked, which comprised the majority, were kept out of sight of the august officer.

After the visitation the guards decided to put on a party; the sake flowed and they behaved like hooligans. They went mad, but, luckily the prisoners were untouched.

The following morning some boots arrived to be distributed to the prisoners. They were badly made and branded sizes 8.4 and 8.5, but even those who normally wore size 6, had trouble with them. They were ill-fitting, but despite the discomfort, some of the lads managed to get them on. There are still over 100 lads without footwear of any kind.

A black-faced guard, apparently bored, decided on fun and games today *[29.10.43]* with every POW he came in contact with. He went to work with a zest and actually surpassed his previous attacks. He smacked and booted so many that, by 0830 hours, he was so tired out he was forced to discontinue.

We are again in trouble with rations, due in the main to the thieving tactics of the guards. When rations arrive 50% are allotted to the Japanese. But they fail to adhere to that arrangement and steal from our issue. They took at least 100 men's potato entitlement from the last delivery.

LOOKING BACK

The day 'A' Force was formed, 26 October 1942, almost 53 weeks ago, Williams Force strength totalled 884, all ranks. Today, October 30, 1943, only 296 are left in this camp. Out of that number 100 are moderately fit; the remainder are in hospital suffering from the acute stages of malaria, beri-beri, malnutrition and associated diseases, dysentery being one of the most prolific.

Along the 130 kilometres we have laboured, suffered the horrors of hell on earth, and lived on rations so low in vitamins and nutrients that it is only a miracle any of the Force have survived.

Today as we reflect, and contemplate the future, we mourn the 122 once healthy members of our Force now lying at rest in the many cemeteries from Thanbyuzayat to the 130 kilometre camp, our present location.

The *Death Railway* has been built, as the Nipponese vowed it would be, even if in doing so it was over the bones of the prisoners of war. And that it was! There was a death for every sleeper laid over the forbidding terrain of jungle and mountains.

Some day this war and purgatory will end but how many of us will live to see that day. At this moment, no-one knows.

Reality

Four more of our lads passed away today *[30.10.43]* and we fear more will follow.

A ration of boxed meat arrived unexpectedly; we were supposed to get two, only received one as the Nipponese stole the other. A Dutchman acquired some sugar and the Japanese noted the loss. The whole of the ration party (100) was lined up in front of the guardhouse. Lieutenant Templeman, Officer in Charge, was ordered to smack each man.

He refused and was badly beaten up by the guards using their iron-like fists and bamboo waddies. The second rank of men were then told they had to give the man in front of them three hits. They complied in such a way the guards believed just punishment had been handed out. In actual fact, the blows were so tempered the recipients were hardly aware they had been struck.

*

The guards then demanded the presence of Lt. Col. Williams. He was accused of failing to train his officers in the correct way. They gave him their advice in their normal way.

The Dutch lad was forced to stand holding a 50lb block of wood above his head. Each time he faltered or fell, he was subject to more severe punishment. Two hours later he fell in an unconscious state. Then the Japs allowed his removal to quarters.

*

From now on, so Shimojo ordered, all prisoners of war will goose-step when passing the guardhouse. Additionally all commands are to be expressed in the Japanese language.

No-one at the 130 kilo camp will forget the morning of the 1st of November, 1943. At 0600 hours (Tokyo time) Ori, the monster, entered a hut at piquet changing time. There was only one there; he gave him four very hefty punches.

Not satisfied, he called for Lt. Col. Anderson and the Interpreter, all the while belting into the bewildered lad who wondered why he had been singled out for the malicious treatment.

Minutes later the three hut piquets and the two officers were taken to the guardhouse. It was not long before the five of them lay on the ground. Bamboo waddies had done the job; they had been knocked out.

Very small ration received today *[2.11.43]* and some ill-made boots, marked sizes 7 and 8. As happened on the earlier distribution the footwear bore no relation to actual size markings.

For the second time in a very short period a 7 foot snake was captured in one of the huts. The taste of them is somewhat akin to chicken.

The fat Japanese cook was relieved of his position today *[4.11.43]* and we feel, from now on, our rations may be much nearer the mark, unless of course his replacement assumes the same habits as the 'Bull' (as he was known) and pilfers portion of our entitlement. No-one regretted the Bull's departure, even though he appeared anything but well.

Another death in the camp today [5.11.43]; one of Anderson Force members became the fifteenth to be interred in the ever-spreading cemetery at this point.

A mentally disturbed Dutchman disappeared last night and the whole of the camp occupants were turned out to search for him. He was found about 25 yards from the camp area. He was suffering from fever and exposure. He was taken to the guardhouse and questioned but he was unable to reply; totally incapable of giving any answers.

Finally, he was told to return to his hut. The two Force Commanders, and heads of departments, were ordered to parade to the guardhouse and given a lecture on how to treat fever-ridden patients. They were also informed *no man was allowed to acquire any kind of fever!* Nor must they be allowed to run away when they become mentally deranged.

The guards are still engaged on their bashing spree; quite a few copped beatings, mainly, it is presumed, for failing to salute when they are approached from behind. We were allowed to remove the atap roofing from an empty hut and complete the roofing on one of our partially roofed huts.

With the railway work completed (except for future fettling) every available man is engaged today [7.11.43] in shifting huts, erecting a fence around the cemetery and building a new Japanese kitchen to appease the new cook.

As there is no payment for camp duties our financial standing is about to take a tumble. Should canteen supplies arrive no-one will be in a position to purchase foodstuffs to supplement the present very meagre diet.

*

The Japanese thinking was hard to understand, and never more so than when it related to rations. They had always stated that sick men do not eat and put that belief into practice by reducing the camp foodstuff requirements accordingly whenever anyone reported ill.

During the railway construction there were periods when the ration issue was near to the scale laid down, but even then the guards pilfered for trade purposes. And there were the occasions, as happened with the Bull, when it was just outright theft from the workers' ration containers, considerably reducing the issue.

No. 1 Mobile Force, in line with other forces, suffered reduced rations with the end of the railroad construction. The Japanese belief then was no railway work, men eat less.

*

The Dutch complement moved out today [8.11.43] for an unknown destination. We took over their hut for a hospital. During the morning a Japanese officer, who was passing through this area, came into and inspected our living quarters. He wanted to know how many were housed in the one hut. When informed 450 men were crammed into it, he replied, 'Too many, not healthy.' A Nipponese Officer stated the obvious!

A recall for railway work today *[9.11.43]* and 100 men were detailed and have gone out. A group of 30 sick men were sent to the rail point to carry in our rations. However, the belief we were to receive the lot was soon dispelled. To the Japanese kitchen went the soya bean oil, peanuts, flour and cases of tinned food. The troops ended up with one bag of sweet potatoes.

The Nipponese still fear an outbreak of cholera and the whole Force was inoculated.

The huts are not so crowded now and where the officers were packed in 21 to a bay, now only seven occupy the same space.

We were pleasantly surprised when we received five bags of potatoes and a similar number containing rice today *[10.11.43]*. But our pleasure was to be short-lived. Our cooks were ordered to prepare all the potatoes for Japanese consumption.

There was no call for working parties today *[11.11.43]*. We commemorated Armistice Day in the normal way—two minutes silence at 1100 hours.

Rations have, unquestionably, been reduced and we are completely out of foodstuffs. No meals can be served today.

Cannot understand why, but 15 more guards arrived today *[12.11.43]* and that means the Japanese will undoubtedly reduce our ration to feed the extra mouths.

We are out of salt, and rice, when it comes, will not have a very appetising taste. We are certainly back to the bad days as regards food. Saltless rice is not so hot.

When we saw a herd of yaks today *[13.11.43]* our taste buds worked overtime in anticipation of meat on the menu. We need not have concerned ourselves, the whole lot was for the Nipponese, not one cut for the prisoners. Seven beasts meant a banquet for the guards.

Protests to Shimojo did have some result; informed we could have some every second day. Within two days we were apportioned a whole 40 lb for the hundreds of hungry men. That largesse meant very little when we were told that the issue of meat meant a corresponding reduction of vegetables, if and when any comes in.

We were allowed to purchase a small quantity of canteen goods from a local village. What there was went to the Regimental Aid Post for the sick lads.

With no railway work, the guards are demanding men be employed in their compound. A very distasteful job and hated by every man in the Force.

As expected, our rations are now on the lowest possible scale and there is no question, unless the unexpected happens, we are going to be on one meal per day. Some prospect!

Two more funerals today *[14.11.43]* and it was a depressed group who paid homage to their departed mates. Far too many of our lads are leaving us in a way we had hoped would never occur.

The despised railway is finished and they have paid the penalty exacted by a fanatical enemy.

The one meal per day is a reality now, rice only at that. Hunger is again haunting everyone. It is slow starvation and it can only lead to malnutrition and subsequent inability to ward off diseases.

One of the Japanese guards visited the Regimental Aid Post today *[15.11.43]* and booted one of the patients many times. For what reason only the crazed Nipponese can know.

Rations came in but we benefited very little, half a bag of coffee beans to make a 'stew'. As usual, the bulk of the rations ended up in the Japanese kitchen.

A demand for workers on the line job today *[17.11.43]* but not as fettlers, as line layers. When they arrived at the site they saw two rail engines derailed. The POW teams had to manhandle them back onto the rails. Not an easy job by any means but it was eventually accomplished.

Two of our lads were seen by a guard to accept a banana each from a passing native. For that crime they had to stand at attention for seven hours. Only then by virtue of strong protests made to Shimojo were they released.

A party of 30 detailed to carry in rations for the Nipponese. We missed out.

Permission granted to stage a concert and 20 men are engaged in the building of a stage and another 20 are cleaning up the area for audience comfort.

As hunters we came off second best today *[19.11.43]* when a 30 foot long snake eluded would-be captors. It was large enough to afford a real meal for those desperately in need of good food. The wily slithery reptile was too fast for the many who spotted the visitor near one of the huts. Succulent steaks just wriggled into the jungle.

We had an opportunity to do some buying in the local village but the traders refused to accept Burmese money, our only currency. To become their customers, Thailand cash only.

From wildflowers we prepared wreaths to be laid tomorrow for a ceremony to be held conjointly, prisoners of war and Japanese, but as far as we are concerned, for two very different reasons.

A dedication, Nipponese style, honouring the construction of the rail link and a memorial to those who lost their lives in its building.

For us it will be a memorial service for our many departed friends.

We were informed a cross would be provided for us to erect in the hallowed ground of the cemetery. It failed to materialise.

THE CEREMONY
0930 hours—20 November 1943

Lt. Col. Anderson gave the opening address and Padre Kellow took the service. The prisoners of war stood tall and straight and, despite the lack of uniforms, looked the soldiers they are; still servicemen and proud of it.

Sergeant Shimojo, Camp Commandant, read Lt. Col. Nagatomo's speech and Lt. Col. Anderson read the interpretation, whilst eighteen men placed wreaths on the graves.

ADDRESS OF THE COMMANDER OF NO. 3 BRANCH ON THE OCCASION OF THE FIRST ANNIVERSARY OF THE INAUGURATION

The first anniversary of the establishment of NO. 3 Branch occurred on the 15th August of this year. But at that time, the pending railway construction was at its peak and we had no leisure for anything else, therefore it was postponed until later. It gives me great pleasure to celebrate today the anniversary of the establishment of this Branch simultaneously at every camp, during the fine autumnal weather.

It may be recalled that this Branch was established in August last year. Since that time it has accommodated a great number of POWs totalling 9,545, from the nearer vicinity of Tavoy as well as the further Island of Java. Up to the present it has endeavoured with desperate efforts to accomplish the construction of the Thai–Burma railway.

Under difficult conditions, such as lack of transport facilities, imperfect and insufficient accommodation, provisions, rations and medical supplies, we have exploited untrodden jungles. Under the burning heat of the tropical sun and the daily torrential downpours of rain, we have achieved this epochal and brilliant feat in this period of time with the inflexible and indefatigable energies of those who have wielded the pick and shovel

The achievement reflects great credit upon us and must be attributed to the fact that each of you has been zealous in doing your own respective work, grasping my mind and aims, on serving my instructions of various times and many rules since the establishment of No. 3 Branch.

I extend to you many thanks for your labour with the deepest regards.

Now the organisation of this Branch is confronted with new dispositions which have developed in accordance with the change of the construction work, all POWs then ought to readjust their minds to the aims of the Commander and be absolutely obedient.

The members of the Japanese staffs should realise the POWs' actual conditions and should not miss any opportunity of contributing to their betterment. Both sides should try to understand each other In this way we are working together for the prosperity of this Branch. On this occasion I strongly emphasise the above-mentioned items.

Happily let us celebrate this memorable day by having a very pleasant and cheerful time to everyone's heart's content. Let this occasion be chiefly one of looking to the future and reflecting the memories of the past year. This is my address on the occasion of the official celebration of the Anniversary of No. 3 Branch, 21st November in the 18th year of Showa.

After Lt. Col. Anderson had read the interpretation of Lt. Col. Nagatomo's speech and a reply to the Camp Commander, we broke off and then had our official concert, which lasted until 1145 hours (Tokyo time).

Actually, the entertainment was an artistic surprise; an excellent performance rendered by a conjurer, a comedian, two piano accordianists, two guitarists and three singers.

It was a professional, refreshing show that proved beyond doubt, no matter the suffering, there is always a group who can minimise miserable moments and build up morale. The Dutch Force from Nieke (133 kilo) camp, were our guests for lunch. They left for their camp at 1400 hours.

One very sad happening was the interment at 12 hours of one of Anderson Force. His demise, although expected, was mourned by every POW in the camp.

At 1300 hours Major Meagher arrived with the Cross for the ceremony, pay for the workers and some canteen stores, comprising one third of a bag of flour, two thirds of a bag of beans, 85 blocks of sugar, 304 eggs and a few onions, plus some pomeloes, as well as cigars, 8 per man.

At 1600 hours four pigs were delivered, two each for Williams and Anderson Forces. They cost 150 rupees each.

Our evening meal of the 21st consisted of two pigs fried in rice and a flour bun. It was the best meal we had had for many months and eased the hunger pains that had plagued us all day and every day for some time. For one meal, at least, we enjoyed real food.

The guards put on a celebration dinner tonight and ended up fighting drunk by 11 o'clock. However, it was a relief that in their alcoholic state, they forgot the POWs, even though they played up a bit.

In anticipation of possible problems we had all decided on an early night. We need not have worried, they left us alone.

We benefited from the Japanese celebration supplies. We were given 10 tins of milk which went to the Regimental Aid Post.

Monday, 22 November 1943, was a sick and sorry day for the Japanese guards; they had imbibed too well and too much the night before. As a result, we had a very quiet day.

However, two funerals dampened the spirits of the whole of No. 1 Mobile Force. We now have twenty lads lying at rest in this cemetery.

A detail of 50 men required for rail work today (23rd) and 30 went out to pick up rations. We received 5 bags of peas, beans and dahl and some rice.

Unfortunately, another of our boys passed away, the third to go in 26 hours.

1944

For the next month or two the daily routine was the same. Short rations, work parties to the railway or for rations. The death rate continued on an average of one or two per day.

We have had our first mail from home. It arrived on the 23rd December and had already been censored, but that was not good enough for our Japs, they had to have a go at censoring too. A few Red Cross parcels came at the same time as the letters, and the guards demanded we hand them over to them.

We refused, stood firm and were severely beaten up; to even the score their way our normal ration issue was cut back to just plain rice.

A sign of the times. Allied aircraft flew over the camp several times on December 26th, but no raid was attempted. It is possible they were aware the huts below them housed prisoners of war. Is that wishful thinking?

The first group of stretcher cases have been sent into Thailand, destination unknown. Believed to be going to a hospital camp, but that may be just conjecture.

Ten of the worst guards we were ever associated with left for Kanburi Camp, Thailand, on Christmas Eve. They had made our lives a living hell subsequent to the joining of the line at Nieke.

They stole our rations, confiscated blankets and shirts which were supposed to be issue for prisoners of war. Eventually we were given their discards, old and very worn but in their opinion, good enough for mere prisoners of war. Their behaviour towards the sick men had to be seen to be believed.

Almost every night the drunken sots roamed the compound looking for or making trouble. Men visiting the latrines were at their mercy, and felt the impact of boot or rifle butt.

On the 25th January we were moved back to the 114 kilo camp, remaining until transferred back to the 105 on the 7th February. The food there could not have been worse, melons mixed with rice, nothing else.

The first group to be sent to Japan, from the 105 kilo camp, was selected by the Japanese and sent off to Thailand by rail, over the line few POWs wished to travel on; they knew its problems.

The Allied Intelligence must have been misinformed as to what the camp at the 105 kilometre area contained. It was machine-gunned on the 24th March by Liberator planes.

The following day, No. 1 Mobile Force entrained for the journey into another period in POW life, Thailand.

Anderson Force was posted to Tamarkan and Williams Force to Kanburi.

The troops of both Forces were integrated with others and ceased to function as actual units.

'A' Force, as it had been known, was no longer an entity. It had ceased to exist.

*

'A' FORCE DISBANDS—TROOPS RELOCATED

The completion of the building of the Burma-Thailand railway and its official opening and use in October, 1943, marked the actual end of 'A' Force.

However, it did not mean the promised long rest was to be theirs. Nor did it signal the end of the barbarities the Japanese and Korean guards had practised for such a long period.

Steam engines had to be fuelled; trees had to be felled, cut to size and stacked at strategic points throughout the length of the infamous line. Fettling, too, was necessary and was to take a very long time.

In December there were rumours of a move into Thailand and, for once, they came true. The main body of Black, Green and Ramsay Forces was transported to Tamarkan and Kanburi camps, Thailand, and eventually relocated from there to Chungkai and Tamuan. Other small groups were moved to various points along the line. The largest group was sent to Japan. En route their vessel was sunk by American submarines with a terrific loss of life.

Williams and Anderson Forces remained at the 105 kilo camp until March 1944 when they, too, entrained for Thai destinations, the former to Kanburi and the latter to Tamarkan.

Those two forces, combined as No. 1 Mobile Force, had been the first to commence work on the construction of the Burma–Thailand railway and the last to leave Burma.

Williams Force had the distinction of having served, as Corps Troops, with the 6th, 7th and 9th Divisions and shared and suffered the privations of prisoner of war life with the 8th Division.

The cemetery at Thanbyuzayat, Burma, is a lasting memorial to the frightfulness of what occurred in the building of the aptly named 'Death Railway' on the Burma side. The graves of 3,770 servicemen, and one Dutch civilian, testify to the horrors of atrocity and disease.

To the many patients in the camp hospital huts and the 55 kilo camp, main area for the sick and injured, the completion of the railway meant absolutely nothing.

It did not mean a miraculous cure for their many ailments, or any improvement in the ration supply. Neither did it seem possible the hated Japanese would relent and at last produce the many drugs and medicines the medical officers and force commanders had been fighting for throughout their imprisonment.

They were not even aware of the visit by Lieutenant Colonel Y. Nagatomo, commander of No. 3 Thai Prisoner of War Branch ('A' Force), to the 55 kilo hospital for the purpose of delivering a memorial address for the 1,300 who were lying in graves from Thanbyuzayat to the 105 kilo camp.

An extract from the memoirs of J.G. (Tom) Morris, Green Force, reads:

*

At last the monsoons dried up, the railway was completed and the influx of patients from the work camps fell to a trickle. Towards the end of November, 1943, Nagatomo visited the 55 kilo hospital to read a condolence on the occasion of a memorial service for those POWs who had died during the construction of the railway.

Nagatomo's hypocritical message was responded to by the senior Dutch Officer who, in good English and without fear, berated him and asked for the Red Cross parcels and mail to which we were entitled.

The Japanese got more than they had bargained for and, for those of us who attended that service, it was a great boost to our morale. Sadly, this fine man was buried in that cemetery before we left in December, along with 437 of his fellow countrymen.

Nagatomo, your penalty of death by hanging was far too swift and merciful for your heinous crimes against defenceless human beings.

The period I spent at the 55 kilo camp was, for me, probably the most emotionally scarring of all my POW years. As we pulled away from there I had time to reflect on those six months. It had been, in its own special way, a time of blood, sweat and tears.

The blood and sweat were real, as were the tears of rage, frustration and anguish I occasionally shed in the privacy of my own night-time quarters.

Something of me stayed at the 55 kilo.

*

The words of that dedicated volunteer medical orderly reflect the thoughts of the 61,000 prisoners of war who slaved and suffered in an aura of death and destruction as they were bashed, bullied and, at times, tortured as the orders of the Emperor of Japan were carried out in the building of that infamous railway.

'A' Force was born in the Bicycle camp in Batavia and in Changi. When brought together at Thanbyuzayat in December 1942, it numbered 4,000. However, the ultimate strength increased by a further 6,000 to 10,000. In January 1943 No. 5 Group was attached and Brigadier Varley commanded a combined Force of 12,000 troops.

Of that number 3,070 sleep eternally in Thanbyuzayat Cemetery as the direct result of Japanese ill-treatment in those many months of railroad construction. (Seven hundred members of 'F' Force are also interred there.)

Twelve alleged escapees were executed and thirty died in Allied bombing raids over various camps.

But for the absolute dedication of all medical officers and force commanders, the losses, staggering as they were, would have been immeasurably higher.

Post-war information also provides startling statistics as to the number of servicemen and civilians employed on the Burma–Thailand railway construction.

The civilians, most of them conscripted, came from Burma, Thailand, Malaya and other Asian countries, their casualties numbered in the vicinity of 270,000. There is no exact number. Their death rate was appalling and far greater than that of the prisoners of war.

Figures supplied by the Allied War Graves Registration (1946) state 330,000 workers, including 61,000 prisoners of war, were employed in the gigantic construction task. The total deaths of POWs were:

Australians	2,815
British	6,318
Dutch	2,490
American	356

During the ten months taken to build the Burma–Thailand railway, 4,000,000 cubic metres of earth was moved, 3,000,000 cubic metres of rock hewn and 14 kilometres of bridgework erected. [5]

Most of that work was carried out with picks, shovels, chunkels and a few pounds of dynamite. The explosives were used only when picks failed to even dent the solid rock.

It is said, but cannot be substantiated, that for every sleeper laid on that railroad, one human being died. Many grave sites were overrun by jungle growth, despite the post-war searches to find them. The names of all who died are engraved on plaques in various War Graves Commission-controlled cemeteries.

They rest in peace.

GROUP 5

Like Williams and Black Forces, which had preceded them from Java, Group 5 spent some time in Changi Prison Camp before embarking aboard the *Moji Maru* for the voyage to Moulmein, Burma, and ultimately, became part of the construction force on the Burma-Thailand railway.

The Group consisted of 450 American, 385 Australian and 965 Dutch troops under the command of Lieutenant Colonel Tharp of the 131st United States Artillery Regiment. The senior Australian officer was Major Robertson of the 2/6 Field Company Engineers.

They sailed from Singapore on 9 January 1943, in a convoy of two transports with a naval escort. En route the vessels were bombed and strafed by Allied aircraft which inflicted severe damage. One ship was sunk and approximately 400 Japanese troops were killed or drowned. Forty Dutch prisoners were also lost.

The report of the incident contained in Lionel Wigmore's *The Japanese Thrust* (Official War History) states:

*

Moji Maru twice near missed by bombs. Last stick holing starboard side severely, killing 7 PW's, wounding many others. Many Nips were killed or wounded. After-gun blew up killing its crew; forward gun, trained aft, narrowly missed blowing the navigating bridge to fragments. Behaviour of the PW's excellent. As ship circled round picking up survivors from the other vessel, sick bay organised on after-deck by Captain Lumpkin, USA and Commander Epstein, USN together with Australian, American and Dutch orderlies. Captain Kennedy is to be especially commended for his work in organising cookhouse to get tea and hot water ready and generally in controlling the troops. RAN personnel . . . also Corporal Imlach (2/40 Bn). Privates French and Coe. both of the 2/2 Pioneer Battalion, were generally outstanding in work of organisation and rescue of Dutch PW's.

*

In the rescue attempts one Australian lad, a member of the 2/40 Battalion, was responsible for the saving of many lives including, as he subsequently found out, 'Turtle Neck', a Japanese interpreter.

Whilst in Moulmein gaol Group 5 members were organised nationally and formed into kumis, as had been declared by Lieutenant Colonel Nagatomo and in line with 'A' Force, later known as No. 3 Thai POW Branch. They arrived at Thanbyuzayat on 26 January 1943, and immediately set out on a march to

Alepauk, 18 kilo camp. The group commanders spent a few days with Brigadier A.L. Varley and were briefed on the type of work and conditions the troops would face on the railroad.

For the first few days the workers were required to move 1.5 metres of earth per day. And like No. 3 Group personnel, they fell victim to Japanese duplicity. The 1.5 metres per shift was soon abolished and the constant cry of 'speedo' and 'currah currah' began to take its toll.

Very hard work and light rations soon resulted in illnesses, disease and a lessening of the number available for line work. Captain Hugh Lumpkin, MO, worked long hours as he battled against the almost impossible, without drugs or any kind of medication.

Major Robertson, the Australian commander, became the focus of Japanese fury when he intervened on behalf of his troops. He suffered many bashings, but they did not deter him. He never let-up in his protestations against the severity of the labour requirements, or the lack of nutritious food and rest days.

For some unknown reason the Japanese and Korean guards believed the Australians were capable of more work and could stand longer hours on the job than other nationalities.

In fact, every worker on the line suffered the utmost torment, cruelty and starvation, and became so debilitated that hospital huts became overcrowded. The spectre of death was ever-present.

When cholera struck in July, two Americans and one Australian died and an isolation area was rapidly prepared. Work quotas had to be reduced as very few even near-fit men were available.

The increasing numbers of very ill men for whom little or nothing could be done caused a terrific strain on Captain Lumpkin, and at the end of July he collapsed. For the next few days he fought hard to defeat his ailment but on 2 August the gallant, overworked and dedicated man of medicine succumbed.

Lumpkin's untimely passing cast gloom over the whole camp; but for him the camp cemetery would have held many more bamboo crosses. His interment was impressive and many a tear was shed by men whom he had worked so hard to keep alive. In doing so, he gave his life.

Group 5 thought the 18 kilo camp was a bad one, and it was, but it had nothing on what they were to encounter in subsequent moves. At the 85 kilo the huts were new and waterproof; the best they were to see throughout their railway work. However, even at that camp the Australians were given the toughest jobs, worked long hours on rations of mainly pie melons which, when cooked, were tasteless and just like water.

April saw them on the move again, this time back to the 80 kilo camp. It was an awful area in a hollow surrounded by thick clumps of bamboo which blocked off any breeze that may have brought relief from the extreme heat. The area was dusty and sickness soon struck just about everyone. By now they were all in such debilitated condition they were prone to the many diseases the jungle abounded in.

Work quotas could not possibly be filled and failure in that regard infuriated the Japanese. Blitzes on the sick became a daily event. As happened in other camps (No. 3 Branch), little, if any, compassion was shown to men totally unfit for manual labour of any kind.

Those considered fit enough to undertake the mammoth tasks set them had to labour until well after dark. The long, hard days soon began to tell on the weaker of the workers. By early May, out of the 322 Australians in the camp, only 220 could struggle out on to the line. It was a tough month for those forced out onto assignments far beyond their physical abilities. From early morning until just on midnight they were brutalised and driven at the utmost speed to complete that section of the railroad track.

At the end of the month they were ordered to prepare for a transfer to the 100 kilo camp. It was an agonising march. Every man had to carry his own gear (some also carried that of others as many could just struggle along, but were physically unable to carry anything). Kitchen gear also had to be carried. Over the last ten kilometres they ploughed through ankle-deep mud. It was a hellish struggle. Quite a few who collapsed in the mud had to be lifted and carried, piggy-back style.

At the 100 kilo camp the 322 Australians were almost completely done in. Even so, 170 were forced out to work despite their obviously unfit state. The Nipponese were not worried about that; the POWs were there to work and work they would. They were bashed, bullied and flogged, in a way you wouldn't treat an animal.

As in other camps the ration rate was low as the Japanese temporarily suspended transport due to the state of the roadway. They said a bridge was down at the 75 kilo and all transport was at a halt. Meals were cut to a very low level, with camp duty personnel being on less than the line workers.

The low death rate amongst the Australian troops firmly convinced the Japanese they were the healthiest of all the nationalities on the line project, and could therefore perform harder tasks and work longer hours.

In the seventy two days to 20 August, sixty-two died at the camp. Out of that number only four Australians passed on. The heavy loss of life at the 100 kilo camp was attributable to uncontrollable diseases, starvation, loss of appetite when food *was* available, and the resultant inability to combat prevailing illnesses.

At that time the total strength of POWs in the camp was 301 Australians, 363 Americans and 834 Dutch. A survey found the eating habits of the various nationalities differed quite noticeably. For example, the Australians ate everything available and sought more. The American troops despised the rice and consumed less than their issue. The Dutch, although avid rice eaters normally, ate less than anyone.

The result was the Australians were, in fact, in a better physical state despite pernicious diseases they, like the others, contracted. The Japanese, recognising that obvious fact, forced the near-fit and sick to undertake the hardest tasks on the railway.

Australians, in the main, worked hard, not by desire or from experience of pre-war occupations, but to ease the demands on their sick mates.

When blitzes were made on the unfit ranks and some had to go out to work, there were countless displays of selflessness and mateship. When many collapsed due to sheer exhaustion (and some actually died on the job), their mates, although not fit themselves, tried to do more to save cobbers from punishment or death.

The death rate in Group 5 was appalling. By late September 168 had passed away; 154 Americans and Dutch, plus fourteen of the Australian complement. Deaths were occurring at the rate of four per day. By 1 October the total had risen to 183. No Australian had died in the period 23 September to the beginning of October.

The workers of Group 5 suffered unbelievable treatment and were subject to the never-ceasing 'speedo', 'currah currah' and daily bashings. It was tough going 'knapping' solid rock into ballast and carrying it to the line from the 100 to the 105 kilo point. Burmese labourers carried out the actual spreading.

On 12 October the very first steam train, Burma end, went past the 100 kilo camp. On that same day three more Dutchmen died, bringing the total deaths in the group to 208.

If it could be said something amusing happened whilst construction of the line was at its height, it was the general instruction issued by the Nips to all prisoners of war (Australian and British, particularly) to cease using words which, although normal in all army circles, that were, in the Nipponese opinion, profane.

The reason? The guards were being contaminated!

October saw a slight change in the weather pattern with an easing of the monsoon rains. A change, too, in work requirement. The almost unheard-of rest days were reintroduced (much to everyone's relief), rations were on the improve and snakes, easy to catch, added to the taste of the rice diet.

Of greater importance was the fact two days passed without a funeral service.

Early in November, Group 5 received its first batch of mail from home. A whole six letter cards dated January 1943. All were addressed to Java.

The arrival of something from Australia created terrific interest and men crowded around the jubilant recipients, who did not hesitate to read them out. That again showed the degree of mateship so manifest in POW camps; share and share alike. The news, however old and touchingly personal, was of greater value than all the gold in the world.

That night they were re-read time and time again until at last the owners, cards clutched in skin and bone hands, settled down to rest. Dreaming, no doubt, of the loved ones at home who were waiting patiently for their return.

Everyone hoped and prayed a miracle would occur and that happy day would come soon. But even that hope was dimmed a little by the knowledge there would be great sorrow for many families who would never see their menfolk again. Some survivors would have the sorrowful task of telling how their mates had to be left in Burmese jungle camps. The grim details may never be told as that could be too hurtful.

November 20, 1943, was to be a day of mourning for those who had lost their lives in the building of the Death Railway. It was so ordered by the Japanese authorities in every camp. Memorial services were to be held in the various cemeteries from Thanbyuzayat to the 131 kilo camp.

For the troops in Group 5 the service was held at the 80 kilo, in association with that of the 100 kilo (hospital) camp. At its conclusion 'a day of feasting' was declared; unfortunately the daily menu remained the same.

The health of the personnel of the group was so bad that only 50 per cent were able to perform any tasks at all. With the railway now complete (it was joined at Nieke, Thailand, on 17 October) only maintenance work was involved. Even so, the work was hard and the guards just as sadistic as they had been all the way through.

There was some slight reduction in the call for a workforce to a one day on and one off basis. That meant a great deal to the tired out workers and they relished the rest.

In December Group 5 lost its identity and was absorbed into and under the administration of Group 3 ('A' Force).

On the 27th of that month the evacuation of the sick commenced and they were transported by rail to hospital camps in Thailand. Colonel Tharp, 131st United states Artillery Regiment, accompanied the first party out of Burma. Major Robertson, 2/6 Field Company RAE, assumed command of the remainder of the Java group.

In January 1944 they moved to the 105 kilo camp—127 Australians, and the remainder of the American and Dutch Forces. Transfer of all nationalities to base camps in Thailand continued until 23 March. As from that date, Group 5 was completely wound up.

Statistically the Australians fared better than the Americans and Dutch. Their losses amounted to 54 out of 385, compared with 98 out of 456 Americans and 322 out of 1,160 Dutch.

However, the total strengths and losses in Groups 3 and 5 in the period 15 September 1942 to 20 July 1944, from figures supplied by the Australian War Memorial, (Report on 'A' Force Combined 3 and 5 Branch Statistics) show:

	Total strength	Deaths	Percentage
Australians	4,851	771	15.8
British	482	133	27.5
Americans	650	128	19.6
Dutch	5,554	697	12.5

In addition 33 Australians, 17 British and 237 Dutch prisoners died in Burma before work began on the railway. Up to January 1944 the death rate in 'A' Force was 13.06 per cent; in Group 3, 13.43 per cent—far lower rates than those suffered by any of the forces with which Australians were employed in Thailand.

'During the whole of this tragic period of misery and suffering,' wrote

Lieutenant Colonel Anderson, 'Brigadier Varley's strong personality, his vigorous and fearless championship of the troops, careless of the rebuffs and determined to leave no stone unturned for the better treatment of the men, won for him the grudging respect of the Japanese, and I have no hesitation in saying he was probably instrumental in preventing a far greater tragedy than that which took place.'

MOVE TO THAILAND AND SINGAPORE

IN DECEMBER 1943 Colonel Nagamoto informed Lieutenant Colonel Coates, Chief Medical Officer, 'A' Force, that the 55 Kilo camp was to close pending a permanent move to Tamarkan, Thailand. Arrangements were to be made for a transfer—by train—of all patients and nursing staff to a 'prepared' hospital. Food and medical supplies were to be better provided, presumably as promised before the POWs left Changi on 15 May 1942. The CMO accepted that assurance, and there was no question in his mind that the proposed move meant a hospital would be found, irrespective of any destination, but it would be of bamboo and atap.

Chaos reigned as the Japanese and Korean guards screamed their heads off when they realised too few stretchers had been made available for the amputees and the seriously ill. Many of the stricken POW patients suffered intense agony as they staggered to the pick-up point. In the long hours of waiting, the train eventually arrived and, as usual, packing the trucks meant great suffering for many. Stretchers were loaded into the wagons, three in line, plus as many sit/ stand patients as could be crammed into very little space.

The guards, as usual, took up premier space near the open doors. Many dysentery cases, with little or no control of their bowels, created an odour impossible to dispel. Additionally, the rotting flesh of tropical ulcer patients emitted a stink so bad even the guards felt they could no longer suffer it. But accommodation was stacked to the absolute maximum and they had to remain, whether they liked it or not.

The alleged hospital at 55 Kilo had been bad enough, but this train was worse than any hell could possibly be. Profanity raged as the suffering lads railed at the train crew, Japs and Koreans in general, but all to no avail.

Cries for water, space and relief from pain stirred many to do all they could to help their desperate comrades. A sympathetic engine driver was approached for water but he could not provide for over 1,000 men, as he needed as much as he could to produce steam to haul the frightfully over-packed train.

The 'speedo'-built railway line was not conducive to comfort. The POWs had helped make certain of that, it was a form of passive resistance. Now they would have to ride on the risky rock and roll over a non-bedded line that rose and fell almost at will. Furthermore, they had to do so in oven-like steel monstrosities normally used for freight transportation. That trip remains fresh in the memory of Johnny Kreckler:

*

Having completed our work on the line, we were moved to Thailand. We travelled by rail along a track built with the blood and sweat of our fellow prisoners of war. Our train was a series of steel box trucks, with a sliding door on each side. Our ration for the trip was one bucket of raw turnips and one bucket of water. Two such buckets were supplied to each truck.

There were approximately twenty men per truck, space was at a premium and, after much buffeting as the train shunted back and forth, our precious water supply was greatly diminished. The doors were only opened at various 'comfort' stops and always at a camp site, usually nearby the camp cemetery— some small, some larger.

There was one cemetery, quite a small one, that caught my eye. It had a bamboo fence around it and above the entrance a small piece of flat wood. Someone had written on the piece of wood, using a burning poker. The message was not the usual 'Lest We Forget'. This was a little more direct: 'We Won't Forget'.

*

The agonising trip to Tamarkan came to an end in the early hours if the morning. The relief to the many sufferers was obvious as they were bundled out. The stretcher cases were handled with kid-glove care by willing hands. While few words were spoken, the look on the faces of the unfortunates was thanks in itself. At last the misery and horror of the run from the stinking and unhygienic jungle camp was over. What lay ahead?

To many, at first glance, heaven, for there piled high at the kitchen were mounds of what they called 'Popeye'. The starving POWs wanted to grab and eat the spinach-like vegetable even in its raw state. It was 'manna' from above. Following the interminable 'tenko', the housing plans were put into place, water was provided for ablution purposes and then the splendid meal the dedicated 'babbling brooks' had prepared was served. The meal was luscious and all wanted to be in the leggie line for any leftovers. Sadly, there were none. At least those who were able to partake of the food bonanza licked their lips in deep gratitude. Those too ill to consume anything were so far gone they were totally unaware of what was happening and were passively awaiting a merciful passing.

In Tamarkan there was sanctuary. However, although the new and seemingly wonderful camp was better staffed medically, there was still an ever-present shortage of badly-needed drugs, medicines, bandages, clothing and footwear. The medical officers continued to perform miracles with their make-do equipment and were able to nurse the seriously ill to such an extent that they 'brought back to the living' many of those who would most likely have died in the jungle hospitals.

The GOC of all allied POWs in Thailand, Brigadier Varley, was now quartered with his staff in Tamarkan and persisted in his mammoth attempts to better the lot of the men for whom he was responsible. Daily he jousted with the Nip commandant who was similar to the tyrant he had fought so defiantly at Thanbyuzayat, Colonel Nagamoto. The 'brick wall' of Burma was somewhat more pliable in Thailand, and the forcefulness of the Varley way did obtain minor results and benefits for the ailing POWs. The Japanese still adhered to their 'sick mans do not eat' policy, but Varley's pleas for medicinal requirements bore some little fruit.

When 'A' Force was disbanded at the 105 POW camp on 23 March 1944, all remaining POWs were also moved to Tamarkan. It was a large base camp and the supply of food far exceeded any provided throughout the frightful period of line-building in Burma. At first glance it appeared a God-given oasis, the likes of which they had only dreamed of as hunger and privation had caused some of them to contemplate suicide rather than attempt to live with that continuous craving for anything edible. If this is not a dream, they now thought, life might be preferable.

The very sight of the encampment immediately whetted the taste buds of the distraught, starving, stick-like frames of humanity. But protruding ribs told their own tale, and many who had been in that camp for several weeks were shocked at the appearance of walking death-like lines of emaciated bodies. Was it possible, quite a few wondered, that they too had looked like these pitiful feet-dragging men who laboured for breath? Willing hands were extended to the forlorn group, who could only gasp a 'thank-you' when laid on the bamboo slats which were to form their living quarters for the near and distant future— Japanese permitting.

Many of the starving men could not wait for a meal to be served and attempted to grab some of the long green spinach-like stalks in the kitchen area. Mouths watered at the sight of so much food awaiting the attention of the sympathetic cooks. When it was taken from them (for their own protection) they growled like hungry animals, resenting their missed opportunity to get even just a bite. Tears dropped from staring eyes. The craving for something to eat, no matter what, overcame their sanity and they lunged out for it like maddened beasts.

Few could understand why anyone would want to keep them from food when it was so tantalisingly close. Epithets flowed freely and all kinds of names were hurled at the interfering well-fed men guarding the piles of food—so close, yet so far away. All hated the Jap and Korean guards for their unbridled cruelty. Now it seemed their own kind were hurting the most deserving.

Still, they did not have too long to wait before their dixies were laden with the best the kitchens had to give.

Tamarkan, like Kanchanaburi and Tamuan, was a dispersal point for many of the POWs considered by the Japanese as fit to travel and work in Japan and other areas. It caused the breaking up of friendships and the separation of close relatives who had been together in unit order throughout their term on the building of the Railway of Death. The Japanese allowed no interference. They selected whom they considered 'fit mans'. The only exceptions were the older and the crippled. If POWs had two legs and arms and could stand, they were candidates for faraway Nippon. Les Hall was not among those chosen for the Japan party.

Following medical inspections, kitting out of multi-coloured garments (which many believed were women's pyjamas) and underwear, came the formation of kumis. It was at this point many groups of friends, brothers and other relatives were broken up. It was a case of you, you and you, irrespective of who or what they were. There was no negotiation as to manning. So long as there were 150 men in a kumi, that was that.

Officers were appointed to each kumi and were to remain with that group from there on. Some medical attendants were also attached and finally the Japan party was transported to Singapore, but it was not allowed near Changi. Some met up with working parties and messages were given for mates and/or relatives in Changi camp.

Brigadier Varley was desperate to get nominal rolls and a great amount of information to 'Black Jack', Lieutenant Colonel F.G. Galleghan, OIC of all POWs in Changi. Although his approaches to get out to Changi met with a blunt refusal, he found a way of getting all documents away safely. He trusted them to Gunner John Wade who, acting as a medical orderly, was escorted to a group of very ill men at the Changi encampment. John was aware of the risk he was running but was determined to carry out his task. He arranged for the walking 'wounded' to surround him on arrival at Changi and so avoid any suspicion the guards may have as to what he or the others may be carrying.

Luck was on the side of the party as all Japanese and Korean guards feared contact with POW personnel who may have been in a camp on the line where cholera had killed so many. No search was made and freedom of entry was allowed. When John informed 'Black Jack' of Brigadier Varley's endeavour to visit him and failure to obtain permission, 'BJ' told him to tell the brigadier to request dental treatment—the only practicable way of gaining the desired meeting. The advice was followed up and the two eventually met.

The Japan party selected at Tamuan was perhaps one of the most disappointed of any group. They were to leave a real camp haven (or so it appeared to them in POW terms)—good hutments, banana trees, vegetable gardens, swimming facilities, and the best kitchens they had encountered as POWs. To leave was a real blow and in the months ahead their thoughts were often to wander back to Tamuan.

The dress of the Japan party was cause for much amusement to the men of Changi. Catcalls of 'women's army' and 'pretty girls' and many other names provided much merriment to all but those wearing of the multi-coloured clothing, straw hats and Nipponese rubber boots—ill-fitting, but footwear at least. Still, the grinning 'A's gave the 'wharfies' as good as they got. Things could have been worse. Food was fairly good, a great deal better than that provided on the 'speedo' railway job. But after suffering hell as coolie labourers they now faced the very real prospect of being sunk by Allied submarines on the voyage ahead. Very few were happy at having been 'selected'.

Quite a few of the Changi wharfie guards poked fun at the men also, and made signs indicating that they would end up as 'fish feed' and never reach their destination. These predictions were, unfortunately, to prove only too true, although the frightfulness of a submarine attack was to be only one of the many disasters that lay ahead.

Singapore Island was not to be 'rest' camp for the Japan-bound POWs. They too were put to work on the wharves well away from the Changi boys, but the groups soon found means of meeting and exchanging experiences, renewing old acquaintances and meeting up with unit cobbers. They were shocked at the unbelievable state of Singapore. Gone were the teeming crowds, crowded docks, etc. The downtrodden looks on the faces of the residents indicated the savagery of Nipponese control of the once-busy city. The glamour of the past was but something to recall. It was no longer Singapore—it was a dismal, lifeless place where misery held top-billing.

The accommodation for the Japan party in Singapore consisted of time-ravaged, open-sided huts with leaky roofs. On one occasion a hut collapsed and about fifteen POWs, mostly British, were hurt and transferred to Changi. Luckily for them, they missed the boat to Poppy-land.

One of the unsung heroes of the Japan party was the fresh-faced doctor, Rowley Richards (known to the Jap guards as the 'baby' doctor). Like all other medicos, he had only a stethoscope and little else with which to monitor the health of his many patients, yet he worked miracles in his treatment of tropical ailments that beset his growing list of patients each and every day, and in his struggles against the screaming guards who demanded more and more 'fit mans'. He had a complete nominal roll of the 2/15 Field regiment, plus every detail relevant to their health prior to and during the Malayan Campaign. Quite remarkably, he had maintained and updated these records throughout their period in captivity even on the Burma-Thailand railway. In build, Rowley Richards was not a big man; his enormous strength was demonstrated in his determination to stand up to the might of the Nipponese and Korean guards. One instance stands out as an example.

After conning his way into Changi and arranging for safe custody of his valuable records, he returned to River Valley Road camp to be informed they were to move to a small island, Paulau Damarlaut, in the south-west of Keppel Harbour. It has no facilities, no water, little food and was commanded by an obnoxious, sadistic commandant who the Aussies quickly named the Jeep, because of his squat, pudgy build. To 'enhance' his status, the POWs renamed Paulau Damarlaut Jeep Island. In his ignorance of wry Australian humour, the Jeep believed that to be a compliment.

The Japs were constructing a huge drydock, one large enough to accept a battleship. As on all jobs, the pudgy one demanded more and more workers. Ignoring Richards' claims that the men were far too ill or injured to turn out for hard work, the Nip 2i/c, Greenpants, decided he would be the judge and began to 'medically' examine the sick. He picked on Gunner Maurice Barkley, who was recovering from a severe bout of malaria with associated dysentery and was obviously totally unfit for any kind of duty. Richards was just as determined and told Greenpants: 'If you send this man to work, he will die! After the war I will speak to my government, which will speak to your government and you will be tried for murder.'

Screaming with rage, Greenpants lunged at Richards. He bashed him over the head with a piece of wood and beat him with his fists, chipping the doctor's teeth. Richards was determined not to fall down, knowing that he would get the boot if he did so.

Finally Greenpants walked off huffing and red in the face and muttering imprecations. A few minutes later the Jeep approached Richards, carrying a bowl of tea and three small rice balls, saying, 'So sorry. Now OK?' Richards replied 'No', pointed to Barkley and reminded the Jeep that the issue was as yet unresolved. The Jeep yielded and as he left Richards smiled grimly through swollen lips. 'We won,' he said. 'You won,' Maurice Barkley corrected him.

On 3 September 1944 the Australians were told 'all mans to Nippon' and that they would be returning to River Valley Road, there to join the rest of the party and board ship the next day. Many POWs believed this was not going to happen. None of them wanted it to.

SINKING OF THE *RAKUYO MARU*

ON 5 SEPTEMBER 1944, remnants of 'A' Force, under the command of Brigadier Varley, boarded the *Rakuyo Maru*. It was to convoy 1,310 ORs and eight officers to Japan, along with a number of other POWs not from 'A' Force. Not one of the large group imagined this was going to be a Manly ferry voyage, even though the size of the vessel appeared somewhat similar. Nor was it to be. Aboard the ship, the members of 'A' Force were faced with the horrible realisation that the *Rakuyo Maru* was twice as bad as they had feared, or even allowed themselves to imagine.

As each man boarded he was told to take with him a lump of rubber weighing twenty to twenty five pounds. It was to be their lifesaver should it be necessary to undertake a saltwater and oil bath. Seeing this as another way of exporting more rubber to Japan, one lad 'accidentally' dropped his into the water and it sank like a stone. So much for its lifesaving qualities!

The accommodation presented was frightful—way below decks, dark and forbidding—and no-one wanted to descend the ladder that lead down to the unknown. The leaders stopped dead and would not move any further despite the yelling and screaming guards who prodded the unwilling passengers with sharpened bamboo sticks that drew blood but failed to move the POWs. Of the three cargo hatches, only one was open. Looking down was bad enough. How could anyone expect so many men to fit into such a confined space? Only the Japanese. It was impossible to see much in the dim light of just one low-powered light bulb, but it was obviously an airless area and, if filled to capacity, bodies would be crammed together as closely as sardines in a tin.

Despite the urging of the Korean and Japanese guards, men spilled all over the deck—they were everywhere. At least they could breathe top-deck. Down below it would be near impossible. So, not one man went and stayed below. As the hours passed and water-bottles emptied the impasse remained unresolved. The Nips believed they held the trump cards. Go below as ordered or lose the privilege of food and water until all had descended. Still, not one man moved.

Finally a British officer urged the men to accept the situation as, no matter what the representations made by Brigadier Varley and the American Air Force Colonel Melton and others, the Japanese were adamant . . . 'Go below or be driven'. Still no move. Sullen guards were growing desperate and it was soon evident that blood was going to flow, and it did. Instead of the traditional sharpened bamboo sticks, out came the rifles fixed with bayonets and the guards flayed everyone within reach. Slowly but surely the battered and bleeding POWs were forced down the hellhole. Many braced themselves against bulkheads. It made no difference, the frenzied Japs and Koreans meant what they said. Death was a probability and the stench of jam-packed bodies struggling to find room where little was to be found rose up to greet them. It was war, but the unarmed could not withstand the sustained attack, as many injured bodies testified. One of the POWs, Colin Latham, was the son of a former Australian ambassador to Japan.

Despite the determination on both sides, there was no question who would ultimately win out. If the stand-off had not been broken, lives would have been lost. Had all-out fighting occurred (as many wanted) the deck would have run with POWs' and guards' blood. Varley, Melton, Rowley Richards and others battled hard with the oppressive Nipponese, but to no avail. It was not the weight of numbers that won, but bayonets and the threat of bullets.

The scene below decks is impossible to imagine. Over 1,000 bodies were crammed together in one of the holds, some standing, some crouching down, chin on knees, with insufficient headroom to sit up straight. To the 'A' Force boys it was worse even than the *Celebes Maru*, and that was considered the hell-ship beyond anyone's imagination. Not only that, but hanging over them all was the unspoken question: even if they managed to survive the deplorable conditions, what if the ship were attacked by Allied submarines? In fact many stated that they preferred the prospect of trying to survive on a life raft to remaining cooped up in this fetid, filthy area, drenched in their own sweat, urine and—if the dysentery sufferers could not make it up the ladder—faeces. But if the ship were attacked, the rush for that solitary ladder would allow few any real chance of survival. To the guards, of course, none of this was of any consequence. There were POWs aplenty.

The rations, water or rice, were strictly limited, with distribution haphazard. Quite a few of the POWs had mealtimes with no food.

Availability of toilets was of constant concern to the sick POWs, whose sufferings included not only dysentery, malaria and allied illnesses, by near suffocation and complete exhaustion from the never-ending battles for space. The heat from closely-packed bodies was almost unbearable and the concerned medical orderlies were done-in—calls for assistance were coming from just about every inch of the dimly-lit two-tiered 'bunk housing'. There was no hope of lying down and sleep was out of the question, because when one man moved, or tried to move, it created a domino effect ... an effect in the semi-darkness like a wave at sea, a swaying movement which only served to increase the frightful discomfort.

All this, and the vessel was still at anchor. What was it going to be like once the convoy was under way? Only deaths could provide more space, unless the combined approaches of the officers could convince the ship's captain to allow 200 or more men to bed down on the upper deck. Brigadier Varley and Captain Rowley Richards, on behalf of the Australian and British officers, continued to seek succour for their troops, but it seemed nothing was to be changed.

The officers themselves were in no discomfort. They wandered at will in the clean air and had the full deck wherein movement was unrestricted. But to their credit, and realising their men were expected to live in conditions beyond human belief, they risked being bashed and continued to demand better conditions. If any of the below-deck POWs died due to the inhumane treatment now being meted out to them, they threatened, representations would be made at governmental level to charge all Japanese and Koreans concerned with murder.

As a result, rules were eventually changed as regard night movements. POWs would be allowed on deck to use the 'slung-over' toilets, but queues would not be permitted. Any violation would result in a reimposition of earlier conditions. It was a small concession, but at least a chink in the wall of indifference so evident since the ship was boarded.

With the ship still at anchor, the hours passed slowly and the atmosphere grew worse with every passing second. The hatch cover was open but there was no wind to give relief to the herded mass below. It was a frightful experience for every man, so cooped up he felt as if there could be only one way out— death. As they struggled for breath and fought to get the next lungful, the chain reaction was disastrous. Many near choked on their own sweat as it ran into their mouths. There were no handkerchiefs, not even a tiny bit of cloth to use as one. The men were caught like rats in a trap with no way out. The smell of urine and excrement filled every part of the overpopulated area. There is no word that could even begin to express what it was like in the hole of hellish deprivation that the Nipponese considered adequate quarters for prisoners of war.

The convoy was beginning to form but it took thirty-six hours before any ships got under way. It was the morning of 6 September 1944 before any relief was accorded the suffering throng down in the bowels of the *Rakuyo Maru*. Then and only then did air percolate down into the seething mass of human beings. But from the moment the convoy slipped out of Singapore Harbour came the new fear—the threat of a torpedo slamming into the hull.

Some wags bet it would not be very long before the Yanks had a picnic with so many ships out to sea. Fear spread through the masses. If the vessel was attacked, how would it be possible for the men to evacuate the hold via one ladder? They were soon to find out.

An aid station was set up and each morning a parade was permitted top deck. Due to the misery of the POWs confinement, tropical illnesses including dysentery, malaria, beri-beri and other painful ailments began to make their presence felt. Captain Richards held grave doubts that the men would actually be able to withstand the conditions that prevailed, day and night, in the hold. He had good reason to be so concerned. A man of wondrous compassion, for whom the loss of just one man was a very real tragedy, he just kept going along in his caring, hoping way.

After the passing of days, the POWs were so filthy they could hardly stand the odour of their own skin and bones. Each and every man stank, as Colin Latham put it, like the famed American skunks, as dirt, grime and sometimes human waste ran down their skeleton-like frames.

The continued pressure by Brigadier Varley and other officers finally opened the heart of the Japanese a fraction. About one-third of the 'mans' were to be allowed top deck at nightfall, and the rule was not strictly enforced. Some of the guards even began to exhibit a friendlier attitude towards the POWs. The limit of one-third at a time soon fell by the wayside—who could be bothered to count? It was not too long after this that the rule was relaxed during daylight hours as well, but many found the piercing sun too much to handle and preferred to seek solace down below, now that the area was not crammed body-to-body.

On the fifth afternoon, 10 September, fresh water came in abundance when torrential rain fell on the convoy. Topside of the vessels, men danced in their birthday suits in sheer joy, mouths agape letting the stinging, pure water assault their faces and bodies. They filled canteens, anything that would hold water, and drank greedily. For the first time since leaving Singapore, thirst was not a problem.

After sunset, the rain slowed to a steady drizzle, sweeping the decks and blotting out the stars. It became suddenly cold—in fact so cold that the men topside even considered returning to the hold.

As the convoy neared the middle of the South China Sea there appeared to be more vessels, and one of the crew intimated some came from Manila. The resetting of shipping ended up with the *Rakuyo Maru* as the last ship, starboard side, in the convoy.

Judging by the attitude of the ship's crew, it seemed that fear of submarines was uppermost in their minds. The unhappy prisoners had more to fear than anyone else. At most times through the day hundreds of them would be below decks, with little chance of escape should Uncle Sam's boys let their presence be felt. Just about all had a feeling of restlessness and their thoughts were filled with foreboding. The air was thick with consternation. Some even welcomed the prospect of an attack by the US as a possible means of escaping the tyranny of their captors.

The Wade brothers began to plan what they would do if the old tub justified submarine attention. Of course they were not the only ones pondering the possibility of being killed, wounded or tossed into a sea probably flowing with burning oil. It was not a pleasant prospect, but one that could become a reality at any moment. Fred Brown and Colin Latham had also developed a plan: they were ready should the worst happen. To a great number, the pleasure of sleep eluded them as the waiting game occupied their every thought. A heavy atmosphere of tension hung over everyone, and when the gun crews began to stack sandbags alongside their weapons, the time for waiting was surely nearly over.

Some POWs formed syndicates to take bets for and against attack, and each day the odds for one shortened. Quite a few of the non-swimmers had the jitters and feared what might happen to them should a 'dip' be necessary. Despite assurances of help, it still concerned them that they might end up in burning oil and unable to swim away from it.

Most of the military personnel aboard the *Rakuyo Maru* had only ever received rudimentary training (en route to Singapore) in 'abandon ship' procedure. Only the POWs who had crewed HMAS *Perth* or the USS *Houston* had any real working knowledge of what to do in a sinking ship, and they endeavoured to transmit their knowledge to all khaki boys who cared to listen. Those who did were to put their newly acquired knowledge to good use when the acid test finally came.

Life preservers were distributed, but it was soon evident that an insufficient number had been provided. It was agreed that non-swimmers had to take priority and that all others would have to take their chances if the ship was hit and had to be abandoned. In spite of their hate for the Japanese and Koreans, the majority of men hoped to make land without experiencing a submarine attack.

Captain Rowley Richards stressed to all that, if the ship was attacked and in danger of sinking, all excess clothing and footwear should be abandoned. Hit the water as lightly clad as possible, he said. Those with life-preservers were instructed to make sure that their arms prevented the water forcing the preserver up around their necks, as necks could be broken. Above all, the instruction was DO NOT PANIC!

The evacuation of the seriously ill was of great concern should the emergency arise. Richards' compassion was unceasing and he hoped that all assistance would be given. Swimmers were to aid the sick, and to swim away from the hull ASAP, to avoid being sucked under should the vessel sink swiftly.

Many of the boys eyed everything on the deck, searching for anything that could be turned into floats. They knew the Japanese would want the wooden, lashed-down rafts for themselves, unless they got to them first. In a battle for survival, the fastest would be those on top deck. It was quietly arranged that there would always be a number waiting near the rafts if and when a torpedo struck.

It was obvious that the POWs below decks would be in the most danger and eyes looked everywhere for anything that might offer a life-saving opportunity. They overlooked nothing because each POW knew it would be every man for himself and that interfering guards would be hurled overboard. Those who had water bottles vowed to keep them topped up. Others even prepared head coverings to protect themselves from the hot sun should they be in the water for days. Brigadier Varley warned the men that they were not to go overboard too quickly—that they were to stay on board as long as possible to avoid being covered in oil. Care was to be taken when tossing life rafts, etc overboard in order to avoid injuring those already in the water.

John and Ernest Wade, Colin Latham and Fred Brown were all asleep when they were rudely awakened by some thuds on the hull of the *Rakuyo*. It was 0525 hours and they knew immediately that what all had been fearing had occurred. Torpedoes had hit fore and aft. It was 12 September 1944.

Luckily they were amidships, even though below deck. Colin estimated that approximately 1,500 POWs were in that area and about 500 lying top deck.

Despite the fact that water commenced to pour in, some initially doubted that they had been hit. Soon, however they were fully aware of the situation.

The most immediate thing to do was to get up on top deck. Peculiarly, there was no panic. A very orderly evacuation began and soon ropes were thrown down by the top-deck POWs to assist those below.

John and Ernest Wade made their way up along a long plank of wood. Others pulled themselves up via the suspended ropes. On deck, they saw the very real fireworks. A tanker was on fire, burning oil on the water, and guns on the escort ships (frigates and destroyer) were blazing away. No-one knew what was going on except that it was like Guy Fawkes' Day gone mad. The flame from the burning tanker lit up the area like daylight. One advantage for those going over as 'abandon ship' was ordered was that they could see floating debris, including pieces of wood about four feet square with ropes hanging from each side.

The Wade brothers—Ernest a good swimmer and John just a 'dog-paddler'—both reached a float where they were joined by four others. One who was injured was placed on top; the rest just hung on.

As daylight dawned an awesome sight was revealed. Heads were bobbing up and down in all direction and voices calling for help. Some were assisted to any bit of floating wreckage available. No matter what it was, so long as it floated, someone was hanging on to it. It was a case of every man for himself, but help if you can.

To the wonderment of many, the *Rakuyo Maru*, whilst listing, gave no indication that they were about to sink. Brigadier Varley, Rowley Richards and other officers were doing their utmost to maintain calm and went about distributing life-belts. Canteens were filled with water, but many had no corks or screw tops and attempts to lower them resulted in complete loss of their contents. Many who had dived overboard climbed back up again, searching for food and water. Sergeant Frank Tome, 2/30 Battalion, and another Aussie were busily occupied building a raft large enough to hold twenty or more survivors.

All the Japs had gone off in lifeboats, with no attempt to save any POWs. At last, however the tyranny of the sadistic guards was forgotten. Some had been 'assisted' overboard, but at that time retribution was not something many thought about. The two things uppermost in most minds were self-preservation and the need to help other POWs where possible.

Following depth-charging for subs, Japanese frigates began to take aboard only Japanese and Korean personnel. The Wade brothers and their float companions were witness to a submarine blowing a Nip destroyer out of the water, a most miraculous act of attacking bow-on as the destroyer tried to ram the sub.

John Wade painted a graphic picture of the whole scene. 'Ships—must have been well over twenty in the convoy—were zigzagging in an attempt to evade torpedoes, a heck of a lot of shooting. Maddened Japs running everywhere aboard the confused, turning and twisting vessels no doubt afraid. The Yank submarines were having a great time. So many targets, goodness knows how many large and small ships were eventually sunk. It was like watching a huge bonfire, really amazing.

Within a few hours no ships of any size were visible, but some boatloads of Japs had been picked up and the swimming POWs salvaged the lifeboats. The Wade brothers and others aboard the float grabbed one. Some hours later a Jap ship came alongside and machine guns were trained upon them. No doubt they would have all been shot except for the fact that a Japanese officer had sought and found sanctuary in the boat. He ordered no shooting.

For the next three days the boats of hopeful survivors drifted to the will of the water. Hardest to bear was the constant thirst—no rain fell, besides which there were no containers to catch any nature might have provided. Tongues were swollen and sore bodies covered in salt which the sun caused to harden. Many survivors were also coated in oil. It had been hell aboard the *Rakuyo Maru*, but they felt they would have few misgivings were they still aboard that crammed craft.

The descriptions of the sinking of the *Rakuyo Maru* are many and varied. The best, perhaps, were those given by POWs who were topside and actually saw the two torpedoes heading for the starboard hull. They yelled a warning and many, so it was said, headed or slithered to the port side, away from the immediate danger zone. In fact, in the initial attack on the ship, not one POW was killed— only those who came from the Land of the Rising Sun. Was that appropriate retribution? It certainly seemed to redress the balance, at least in part.

From the moment of impact, the Japs went mad. Some were screaming orders, others were running around completely immersed in panic. Gone was even residual care for the POWs as self-preservation took over completely. Not surprisingly, no POW was allowed near a lifeboat—a Jap holding a machine gun saw to that. Who cared amongst the POWs? Even if other crises and dangers beckoned, the yoke of the inhuman Japs and Koreans had been magically lifted.

After the explosion, a great wall of water flooded the deck and many thought it would be minutes at the most before Davey Jones would lay claim to the now-wallowing vessel. However, the *Rakuyo Maru* appeared only to gasp and groan, the list to starboard as water flowed into the aft hold. Some survivors later suggested that the cargo of rubber helped keep the wounded ship afloat.

While the ship still floated, Captain Rowley Richards, Brigadier Varley and other helpers were lashing together anything and everything that would float. A small lone lifeboat was discovered, lowered overboard and very smartly manned. Some of those in lifeboats the Japs had abandoned decided to row to China, though none of them knew their exact location or the distance to be covered. They were never seen again. Brigadier Varley was one of their number.

Amongst the other POWs on the *Rakuyo Maru*, tribute must also be paid to Vic Duncan, who had been Chief Petty Officer on the *Perth*. Not only did he direct the movement of those below decks when the ship was attacked, and plan its orderly evacuation, but he also took command of a number of tied-together rafts and was subsequently responsible for saving many further lives. He was eventually recaptured by the Japanese and taken to their homeland, where he and a number of others—including the Wade brothers—endured almost a year of brutal cruelty, hunger and cold.

All the POWs on rafts or hanging on to them suffered horrific experiences. Of the Japanese attempts to attack US submarines John Langley 2/30 Battalion and a survivor of 'A' Force, later said: 'It was one of the worst times of my life. I had a funny feeling down my back, then I felt the concussion, the vomiting and bowel evacuations at the same time. If the depth-charges did that to us, no wonder subs do get blown out of the water.'

The *Rakuyo Maru* eventually sank, bow-first, twelve hours after the torpedoes hit. For those destined to stay afloat, the ongoing problems related to exposure, to their being encrusted with oil, and to the lack of food and water.

Three days after the attack, 15 September, a lookout on the submarine *Pampanito* sighted and a large quantity of debris floating on a calm sea. An account of the unique rescue operation which followed is given in Joan and Clay Blair's *Return from the River Kwai*:

The Officer of the Deck McMillan H. Johnson notified the Captain [Peter Summers] and began to prepare to lower the lifeboat. He noted the position as 18° 42' north longitude 114° 00' east. He logged that this spot was a little to the north of the spot where *Growler* and *Sealion* [submarines] had first attacked the convoy. It was about forty miles north-west of the position where *Sealion* had sunk *Rakuyo Maru*.

Summers approached the lifeboat warily. There was a belief in the US Submarine Force that the Japanese used Lifeboats and debris as lures for American submarines. When the submarine stopped to inspect the lure, the Japanese submarine would torpedo it. There was no proof of this, no officially reported lure attacks. However, all submarines viewed lifeboats and debris with scepticism and respect.

The inspection was carried out without stopping. *Pampanito* passed close at fast speed. The lifeboat was abandoned, Summers logged. He noted no markings. It might have been one of the four lifeboats abandoned by the Vic Duncan group, or it could have been one from the *Nankia Maru*, sunk by *Sealion* along with the *Rakuyo Maru*, or from the unidentified tanker sunk at the same time.

A few minutes later, at 1610, quartermaster John Greene reported an even more startling discovery on the horizon—'two rafts with men on them'. All hands on the bridge swung binoculars to the bearing. The men were waving 'frantically'.

Peter Summers logically assumed the men on the rafts to be Japanese, survivors of *Growler* and *Sealion* torpedoed ships. If he took one of them prisoner, he might gain some valuable intelligence on the ships that had been sunk.

The rest could be disposed of by the boarding party, a special commando type of team trained to board smaller vessels for intelligence purposes or to sink

them by lighting fires. Disposing of Japanese survivors was not officially condoned.
Nor was it officially disapproved. There was simply no policy. It was left up to
the skipper.

Summers headed for the rafts and called away the boarding party. The torpedo
and gunning officer, Ted Swain, was its leader. The artist-gunner, Tony
Hauptman, was the chief enlisted man. The big torpedoman, Jim Behney was
his main assistant. Swain, Hauptman, Behney and half a dozen other members
of the group rushed topside. Among them was another amateur artist, Motor
Machinist Clarence G. 'Mike' Carmody, twenty. They went out on the forward
deck. Hauptman carried a 12-gauge double-barrelled shotgun. He gave Behney
a .45 calibre Thompson machine-gun.

There was no doubt that the boarding party was preparing to kill the men
on the rafts. A reserve officer, John N. Red, Jnr—'We all thought they were
Japs'. Peter Summers passed the word to break out the small arms—'we'll have
some target practice'. Dick Sherlock—'Pete passed the word below to open the
gun locker. Anyone who wanted to shoot a Jap got a Tommy gun. A whole lot
of guys came up with guns, all set to have a "ball".' Tony Hauptman—'We
thought they were Japs. We were not going to pick them up. The captain told
me to do away with them. I was going to shoot them.'

Again *Pampanito* closed the debris warily. It could be a Japanese trick, a
human lure. Hauptman and Behney held the gun ready. As *Pampanito* swept by
the debris for an inspection, they noted the scantily clad men on the rafts were
black. Some wore Japanese hats and caps.

The fire controlman, Bill Yagemann, had been on the bridge adjusting the
TBT when the rafts were sighted. Now his attention was focused on the drama
unfolding. As *Pampanito* turned and re-approached the debris, he saw that there
were about fifteen men on, or clinging to the rafts, makeshift structures of hatch
boards and timbers. He did not doubt they were Japs. Now he could hear a
jumble of unintelligible shouts. Then suddenly—and startlingly—one clear
obviously Western voice. 'First you bloody Yanks sink us, now you're bloody
well going to shoot us.'

Down on the forward deck, Tony Hauptman was stunned. 'Who are you?'
he called.

'Prisoners of war,' came the reply. 'Australian, British prisoners of war. Pick
us up please.'

Summers, Swain, Hauptman, Yagemann and others topside stared in disbelief
and amazement, and suspicion. Hauptman tossed a rope to one of the rafts, held
up one finger and said, 'One man and one man only'. One grabbed the rope
and they pulled him towards the boat. Other survivors jumped from the raft
and started swimming towards the boat. Hauptman shouted menacingly, 'Stay
on the raft'. Behney raised the machine-gun.

Frank Farmer, the Australian schoolteacher, had joined a large raft supporting
many men. One was Harold D. 'Curly' Martin, who had been in his outfit but
with whom Farmer had had little contact on the railway or on the *Rakuyo*

Maru. The submarine was first sighted by a raftmate who earlier had been delirious. His claim of seeing two masts on the horizon at first went unheeded by his companions. However, he proved to be right. The submarines had two periscopes which at a distance did appear to be the masts of a small fishing vessel. 'I stood on the raft and waved my hat. The size of our group and the height above water caught the attention of the watch. As the submarine swept past, those on the deck appeared puzzled, somewhat, both by our appearance and actions. But the factor which undoubtedly brought her back was a report to the captain that "Curly" Martin had fair and curly hair, suggesting that we were in fact European.

'It is difficult to describe our feelings as we saw that the sub was returning. But as it approached, they signalled for one man only to take the curling rope thrown from the fore deck. I grasped the rope and was hauled across the intervening water to the sub's side, where I was assisted by two crewmen. When I thanked them in English, they were incredulous. I heard one call out to the bridge, 'They're English, Sir'. I was escorted to the foot of the conning tower, where I met the submarine's second in command, Lieutenant Commander Davis. He was both distressed and dismayed that over 2,000 POWs were in the sunken convoy.'

Frank Farmer thus became the first survivor of *Rakuyo Maru*—and of the Railway of Death—to return to Allied control.

Pete Summers' next order was decisive: 'Take them aboard'.

The officers and men on *Pampanito* had never drilled a contingency like this, or even dreamed of it. They responded to the challenge immediately and magnificently. When the incredible word spread through the boat, dozens rushed on deck and volunteered to help. Under Ted Swain's direction, they formed teams. Some swam out to the rafts with lines. Others crawled down on the bulging saddle tanks to pull the survivors aboard. Another team stripped the survivors of clothing and gave them a quick rub-down with diesel oil in an attempt to wash of the encrusted oil. Still others lowered the men down through the after battery compartment the small crew's mess where motor machinist C. Boyd Markham and others gave the men another washing down. Markham— 'We started out using alcohol, but they screamed in pain, so we put that away'.

The swimmers, of course, had the most dangerous job. They left the ship to enter what is known to be shark-infested waters and if an aircraft forced the boat to crash-dive, they would have been left behind. The chief swimmers were Torpedoman, Second Class, Robert Benneth, Fireman Andrew L. Curries, Seaman Gordon L. Hopper, Jim Behney, Bill Yagemann and Tony Hauptman.

They were assisted on the saddle tank by Mike Carmody, Edmund Stockslader, Electrician's Mate Third Class John G. Madaras, Fireman Richard E. Elliot and others.

At first, some of those below failed to get the correct word. One of these was the ship's ebullient yeoman Charles G. 'Red' McGuire Jnr, twenty-four. The word he got was 'stand by to take on prisoners'. He thought that meant Japanese prisoners. When the first survivor was lowered into the crew's mess, McGuire was there waiting. McGuire—'I grabbed his head and smashed it into the ladder with all my strength. This guy says, "Blimey!" I said "Who the hell are you?" He said, "Prisoner of war of the Japanese". I nearly died.'

Topside, the men worked quickly and efficiently as *Pampanito* moved from raft to raft. All were shocked at the sight of these oil-encrusted, emaciated and foul-smelling survivors. For most of the crew—who lived and fought in an isolated, clean, bloodless environment—it was the first contact with the grim realities of war. Some were so revolted they could not carry on. Frank Fives— 'I started to get involved, but my stomach could not take it. It was terrible. It was the first time most of us had seen the bloody side of war. I didn't want to see that. That was why I chose submarines. I went back up to the bridge and took over as officer of the deck.'

The survivors continued to be stunned, disbelieving or overwhelmed with gratitude. Harry Pickett recalls—'I'd been on my own for quite a while. It was darkish. I could feel the regular pulse of a mate through the water. Then I saw a sort of shape. Someone with a good old American accent shouted, "Can you catch a rope, buddy?" My spirits went straight up. So I go the rope and they pulled me, the exhaust of the sub blew spray in my face. The man pulling the rope was Jim Behney from Florida, a big torpedoman, whose name I will never forget. He carried me below.'

Summers' log starkly recorded the progress of the rescue:

> 1614 Took fifteen men off the raft. The survivors came tumbling aboard and then collapsed with strength almost gone. A picture none of us will ever forget.
> 1712 Picked up a second raft with nine on board. This group was in a little better shape. They were cleaner and could tell a more intelligent story.
> 1721 Picked up another six men.
> 1730 Picked up another six men.
> 1753 Picked up about eleven men.

All hands on *Pampanito* began to feel a sense of history. Nothing like this had ever happened in the submarine force. It was unique.

Electrician's Mate First Class Paul Pappas, Jnr, twenty-three, rushed below to get his camera to record the moment for posterity. Private cameras were strictly forbidden on American submarines, but Summers was happy Pappas had broken the rule. He not only encouraged Pappas to shoot all the film he had (three rolls), he gave him the ship's official 16mm movie camera.

By this time, there were probably fifty men topside on *Pampanito's* deck, including both crewmen and survivors. At 1753, what Summers feared most happened. The signalman, Herm Bixler, cried out, 'Three planes in formation astern'. Summers, in turn, shouted, 'Clear the deck! Clear the deck!' It was a moment of sheer panic. Survivors and crewmen alike jumped or tumbled down the hatches in a mad evacuation. But the crisis passed immediately. The three planes turned out to be birds. Later, Summers logged the discovery with strained humour—'Fortunately, one of the planes was seen to flap its wings, proving the formation to be large birds gliding in perfect order'. Summers cancelled the dive.

There seemed no end of survivors in sight. Summers broke radio silence, requesting immediate assistance from *Sealion*. Then *Pampanito* moved on to the next raft, while high periscope plotted the bearings on more distant ones. They saw many grisly sights in the water. Summers logged: 'While heading for the next group, a small raft was passed close aboard. Its single occupant dead, with part of the head gone—probably by a shark.' This did not build confidence among the swimmers.

At 1840 a second panic swept the topside. High periscope reported what was believed to be the mast of a patrol boat. Again Summers ordered the decks cleared and prepared to dive. The next report from high periscope was worse. The patrol boat turned out to be a submarine. It appeared to have a gun on the aft deck. That could not be *Sealion*. Some of the POWs had incorrectly cautioned that there was a German U-boat in the vicinity. The submarine could be German or Japanese. Summers keyed to SJ radar—a method of communicating between American submarines and exchanging recognition signals or call signs, but got no response. At 1905, now 'very suspicious', Summers dived and ordered his men to get *Pampanito* back in fighting trim.

Warily—very warily—Summers closed the submarine, submerged and called the tracking party to their stations. It was then noted that the other submarine 'was practically dead in the water'. That seemed odd. After a most careful periscope inspection at close range Summers decided it was *Sealion* after all. She was probably stopping to pick up survivors. The 'gun' on the aft deck proved to be a knot of rescuers. At 1940, Summers surfaced to resume the rescue mission. The light was fading rapidly.

Pampanito searched until dark. A lookout again startled the bridge with a report of a 'light' on the horizon. On closer inspection John Red thought it was not a light but someone waving a white flag or hat. Another raft. Summers closed the 'hat' to find a single man on a raft. The 'hat' turned out to have been his hand, bleached white from the immersion. He was brought aboard at 1957. Eight minutes later another raft was found in the pitch darkness. Twelve more men were brought aboard.

For the next ten minutes, Summers cruised back and forth over the area. No other rafts could be found. At 2015—after four hours of rescue operation—Summers ordered the search terminated. When an exact count could be obtained it was learned *Pampanito* had recovered seventy-three survivors, forty-seven Australians and twenty-six British. Among these were the Australians, Alf Winter and Wally Winter. Alf Winter grinned wryly as he recalled—'I always thought it remarkable that *Pampanito* picked up two Winters and the captain's name was Summers'...

Summers set a course for Saipan—the nearest Allied territory—at four-engine speed. He again broke radio silence and made his first transmission to Pearl Harbor. He reported his attack on the convoy, the sinking of the three ships and damage to one and the discovery of the POWs. He suggested that *Sealion* might not be able to accommodate all those remaining and that Pearl Harbour consider sending other submarines to the area.

Pampanito, like other limited US submarines, had only a single man trained in medical care. He was Maurice L. Demers, twenty-six, a Pharmacist's Mate first Class. Born in Manchester, New Hampshire, where he graduated from high school, Demers had worked as a bell-captain on a Miami-based cruise ship before his military service. In 1940 he enlisted in the army and became a dental assistant.

Realising he had made a 'horrible' mistake, Demers was discharged from the army, joined the navy in 1941 and ended up on the *Pampanito* doing a doctor's job. He had sparse medical supplies, but he worked like a beaver, cleaning out gobs of oil from mouths—patients could not swallow or spit out the oil as they were far too weak. He managed, with crew assistance, to rid eyes and ears of oil. They were wonderful, the whole crew—all wanted to help and did.

Charles Armstrong, rescued by *Sealion*, had dreamed three nights in a row he would be rescued at sea. His dream came true.

*

Other remnants of 'A' Force were aboard the POW ship *Rachidoki*, which was also torpedoed and sunk on the night of 12 September. The survivors suffered the same horror as those who had been on the *Rakuyo Maru*.

Vic Duncan, in his group of lashed-together rafts, rationed their meagre supplies of food and water. Some time later—so John Wade related in an interview—they were rescued by a Japanese frigate. When the skipper, who hated Americans, realised they were Australians he decided to show them mercy. Jack Langley (2/30 Battalion) told of the luck they had to end up with a tender-hearted Nip captain. He saw they were fed hot tea water with some kind of sweetener, which tasted good. At hourly intervals they repeated the feeding. Captain Rowley Richards was in this group and noted that the ration was biscuits wiped in some sort of soup, with brandy in it, plus two-thirds of a pint of water.

The ship sailed through the area of the earlier attack, where they saw the destroyer *Zuibo Maru* still burning days afterward. The rescued POWs were deeply affected by the sight. But after their hours in the oil-covered water, when they were free men, now they were back as POWs. It hurt.

On the morning of 15 September they were transferred to an empty tanker in which they were to voyage to Japan. The prospect awed them—anything but an oil tanker. The 136 men were feeble, and still more or less covered in oil. The heat on the vessel was enough to fry an egg. Hundreds of English POWs were already aboard and in a frightful state. They were still covered in oil, some moaning and delirious, others blind from the oil caked in their eyes, some with broken arms and legs. Someone was endeavouring to set a POW's limbs and the injured man was moaning in great pain—there was nothing to relieve the agony he was suffering.

Rowley Richards was near heart-broken. Men were just lying anywhere, with all sorts of frightful injuries compounded by a thick covering of oil. He was helpless. There was nothing he could do for them. He tried to help but, even though he was a medical man who had worked on the Burma-Thailand railway, the sights he saw on that vessel caused him to throw up. It was beyond his ability to stomach the sight of those grotesque and blackened figures. They were brutally hurt and no-one was able to do a thing to help them out. How was it all going to end?

Richards went from man to man doing what he could. Others from the *Rakuyo Maru* followed his example but they could only offer so much. The Japs were not concerned with treatment. They did not even want to have the men on board and regarded them as little more than a nuisance.

Wally Williams, 2/19 Battalion, a Burma-Thailand railway veteran, was a recaptured POW on a whaleboat when he and others heard a terrific explosion. The immediate thought was—another torpedo; we are in for another oil bath! All the windows on the bridge of the ship were blow out. Apparently an escort, a small one, intercepted a torpedo meant for the whaler. It was gone in a flash. All they saw was a cloud of smoke, flames, and then nothing.

On 28 September the whaler berthed at Moji and when the ill-clad POWs marched off the vessel they trod earth for the first time in twenty-two days (almost six months since they had left Tamarkan). John Wade and his brother Ernest felt humiliated as they walked into the township wearing any bit of covering they could lay their hands on. Many were absolutely naked and some dysentery patients were fouling themselves as they plodded along like zombies. They were objects of curiosity to the locals. The Wade brothers, with about thirty others, were then taken by train to a camp at Sakata. Of the men who had sailed aboard the *Rakuyo Maru*, only eighty landed at Moji. Eighteen of them now rest up near the Russian border.

Meanwhile the submarines *Pampanito* and *Sealion* arrived at Saipan, just five days after they had taken on board the ex-POWs. Most of them were tortured, frail and anything but well, but they were permitted on deck to see the 'Seventh Heaven' they had dreamed of since Singapore fell on 15 February, 1942.

From the shore the now-clothed ex-POWs looked just like crew members, but with a crucial difference. They were skinny and still somewhat bewildered, trembling with suppressed excitement as they gazed at the naval base and reflected on their escape from the waters. Unbelievably enough, they were alive. And they were free! But for those compassionate Yank submariners, not one of those who had known the hell of life (in every possible sense) would now be gazing in heartfelt thanks at Allied-controlled land.

The seventy-two ex-POWs shipped ashore from the *Pampanito* were so excited and happy they could not find the right words to convey their appreciation for what Peter Summers and his boys had done for them. They may have been speechless, but in their hearts they worshipped their saviours. As for Pharmacist's Mate Maurice Demers, he was so exhausted when the last POW was taken ashore, he turned in and slept for thirty-six hours.

The figure (given by official report) as to the total number of POWs rescued by the US submarines were: *Pampanito* 73 (one died), *Sealion* 54 (four died), *Queenfish* 18 (two died), and *Barb* 14. In sum, the four boats had rescued 159, of whom seven died en route to Saipan. Of the 152 survivors, 92 were Australians and 60 British.

Colin Latham, of Granville, and Fred Brown, Parramatta, were two of the men who astonished their families by their early return. It is impossible to adequately describe the excitement and tears that accompanied their homecoming, they were so overcome with emotion.

Les Hall's wife Gladys, his mother and his daughters Marjorie and Betty had all heard of the POWs picked up in the South China Sea and hoped Les was one of them. In fact he was still in Thailand, but within days of their return to Australia Latham and then Brown visited the Hall family at Parramatta and told them that they had last seen Les in January. He had not been especially well—few of the POWs were, of course—but he was alive. Fred Brown was somewhat circumspect in his account of conditions on the Burma-Thailand railway, but Colin Latham gave a more graphic and accurate description of the horrors suffered by those who laboured on its construction. Colin told them of deaths and of amputations, and that the Halls' old friend Tankie was dead. While the news of Les was welcome, it was not encouraging enough to dispel all worry.

Meanwhile, there was so much happening at home that Gladys Hall wished she could share with her husband. Like the woman in a Parramatta shop who said the war could go on forever as far as she was concerned, profits were so great. Gladys had given her hell over that—much to the approval of several onlookers. Then there were their daughters. Marjorie was already married and Betty was planning to wed on Armistice Day that year.

As chance would have it, the Halls heard from Les again within a few days of his old friends' visit. A beaming postman delivered a card Les had written in Changi in 1942, more than two years previously! It was only twenty-five words long, but written in his own hand, and coming on top of news from Colin and Fred it was another bittersweet reassurance... perhaps an omen of better news to come. That brief card also brought glad tidings to the Israel family in Canberra, as it mentioned their son John, who was believed to have been killed in the Malayan Campaign. Gladys Hall sent a copy of the card to the Israels, who in their joy had it published in the Canberra Times.

On 11 November 1944 Betty Hall walked down the aisle in her sister's frock of purple and gold, the colours of Les's battalion. On that same day, 3,000 miles away at Brencassi in Thailand, Les was badly bashed up by a Jap guard and British planes bombed nearby marshalling yards. Ten Australians were killed and many more wounded.

The bombing of Brencassi had an unpleasant aftermath which, in this instance, did not involve Japanese or Korean guards.

It cannot be said that all the officers of 'A' Force spent their days spinebashing. They had a role to play in the management and protection of workers under their command and they acted as buffers between the guards and the unfortunate ORs whose task it was to complete the railway line. The guards took sadistic pleasure in causing the workers as much pain as possible, and that was where the kumicho (senior officer or NCO) came in. It was his job to protect his charges as best he could.

Nonetheless, many officers have been maligned, and deservedly so, for failing to act as ORs expected. Few of these officers were in 'A' Force, however. One of the main complaints concerned the distribution of rations. In many cases, the officers were better fed than those of lower rank. This became more common after the disbandment of 'A' Force and was particularly, particularly at Chungkai, in the latter part of 1944.

The rice issue was very low, though less so in the officers' quarters, and the ORs asked a senior NCO to demand a more equitable distribution of this basic staff of life. As he approached a group of officers seated beneath a palm tree he saw they were drinking rice coffee and enjoying rice cookies. Feeling outraged, he let fly at the assembly. They were living like country gentlemen, he told them, and just because they wore 'pips'.

The junior officers shuffled on their chairs, very much ill at ease, but the senior personnel (including a colonel) remained impassive, as if these 'delicacies' were their right regardless of the meagre rations being issued to the men they commanded.

The NCO turned on his bare heel—he had been bootless for months—and returned to the OR lines. But that was not the end of his frustrations. Shortly afterwards, he boarded a train heading north, destination unknown, in charge of ninety Australian POWs in association with 190 British troops. These British POWs were commanded by an English captain whose demeanour suggested immediate hostility which was soon borne out.

When Brencassi was bombed on 11 November and ten Australians were killed, another was diagnosed as fatally wounded by the MO. The Australian NCO approached the English captain to have the badly injured man moved back to Tamarkan by riverboat, but was told the victim was about to die and that no request for his hospitalisation would be made to the Japanese. The NCO then approached the Jap commandant, who agreed to the transfer in principle but could not spare a guard to accompany the wounded POW.

When the British officer discovered the Australian had gone over his head he went berserk, threatening the 'Colonial' with all kinds of punishment, including court martial. This outburst amused the Aussies, but not so the British lads, who resented their commander's acrimony and offered the beleaguered NCO their support.

The forthright 'Colonial' gave as good as he got, informing the captain that both he and the MO would be reported to the highest authority available in Tamarkan—Brigadier Varley—with a recommendation that they be court-martialled.

Fate then took a hand, as early the next morning all POWs were ordered to break camp prior to boarding a train that would transport them to Tamarkan.

When the train arrived at its destination ten hours later, the first to be detrained was the wounded Australian soldier. He was given the utmost care and attention by Lieutenant Colonel Coates, who quickly diagnosed superficial wounds, and within hours the lad had undergone surgery.

A Strange Romance

CHRISTMAS 1944 was not a time for universal rejoicing. Families worldwide worried about the welfare of friends and loved ones on active service or believed to be prisoners of war. And for Les Hall, in Thailand, thoughts turned to the home and homeland he had not seen for three years. Surprisingly, the lunch prepared by the cooks was a sumptuous one with greens, doovers and, for once, plenty of rice with real taste. There were even leftovers for those on the leggie line. Then, of all things, a dessert! Baked bananas with rice-flour custard? Well, that is what it was supposed to be. Even those whose appetites had all but deserted them ate lustily.

In the afternoon the Japanese permitted a concert which they too attended. On the make-do stage the artists strutted to a very receptive audience. It was truly a professional performance and it drew to a close with a beautiful tenor voice rendering 'The Bluebird of Happiness'. On his right wrist the singer had a mock-up blue and gold parrot which looked like the real thing from a distance and lent colour to the rendition.

The last line of the song brought down the 'house', which consisted of hundreds of near-naked bodies squatting on red earth. Even the Nips voiced their approval, though they clearly didn't understand the words as the lilting refrain ended with '*Keep alive... We will be home in '45!*'

That singer, name unknown, never sang truer words. Though the POWs were to endure eight more months in captivity, the men—even those amputees who could—rose to their feet to give this song a special ovation. Tears flowed copiously and the only dry faces to be found were those of the uncomprehending guards.

Christmas over, the new year came and the endless waiting became increasingly difficult to bear. Radio sets, especially those illegal ones hidden in the POW camps, were monitored in the hope that peace would soon be announced. In Europe the might of the German air force was slowly but inexorably being ground down. Allied fighters and bombers were now enjoying something close to freedom of the skies. And the same was beginning to apply to the Japanese forces in the Pacific, as the 'fried-egg' adorned planes became scarcer and scarcer. The pessimists began to waver and the optimists' attitudes prevailed.

When the Germans capitulated on 9 May, it was obvious that Tojo and his cohorts would have to rethink their position. Their 'co-prosperity sphere' was taking a beating and beginning to shrink as the Allied vice tightened. Rumour-mongers everywhere had a field day. Japan, however, was determined to fight on, and did so for a further three months and six days.

In the camps the Nipponese and Korean guards began to hint occasionally at an early finish to hostilities, although never admitting to what many of the

POWs already knew. However, scathing references to the alleged fighting abilities of the Germans and Italians meant but one thing—that they were no longer a threat. Even so, treatment of the prisoners of war remained as harsh as it had been for the previous year, and in some cases became worse.

Huge 'trenches', known as bunds, were built around most camps and the POWs felt a renewed unease and foreboding as they laboured long hours constructing what many of them imagined could end up as communal graves. The bund at Tamuan was completed in June, and its presence was ominous and unavoidable. Still, no-one could be sure of the Nips' intent.

One day in early August Max Nonmus expressed his concern to his adjutant, Les Hall, who was also responsible for operating the secret radio receiver that was in urgent need of new batteries. The 'speedo-speedo' approach used in digging the bund was alarmingly similar to the one employed on building the railway in 1943.

'It seems there's something sinister going on,' he said to Hall. 'The Japs are jittery and their hurry to complete the bund suggests to me we might end up as skeletons in it. It's twenty feet deep, just as wide, and the outer bank is forty feet high.'

'You think we might be driven into it and machine-gunned from the central tower?' Hall asked in response.

'I'm beginning to think so. We'd best have another go at getting batteries for your radio. What about putting it up to that lad they say is sweet on the river-boat owner's daughter?'

Hall knew the lad—Howard Hunter was his name—and knew a little of his supposed infatuation. In fact he'd spoken to Hunter on the subject, urging him to be cautious.

'I think she could probably get them,' he said, 'but there's one snag.'

'And what's that?'

'He tells me she's willing to help him, but that she really wants him to run away with her. She says there's a camp of British paratroopers only five kilometres from here.'

'Do you believe that?'

'No, I don't. It's more likely her dad's a bounty hunter. I've advised Howard to disregard her, but...'

'You think her interest in him is purely monetary?'

'I'm not sure. It's hard to know who to trust.'

'And you've questioned Howard about getting batteries?'

'No, not about batteries. I don't want too many of us knowing who's responsible for the radio.'

'Take the risk, Les. I feel we're on the verge of a massacre. If there are British troops nearby we may well need them. Give it a go.'

'What if she entices him away, only to hand him over for the blood money?'

'Then there'll be repercussions for all of us. Particularly for you and me, since we're responsible for all POWs in this camp. But we really need to do what we can to get outside news. Take this lad into your confidence as soon as you can and leave it up to him.'

That night Howard listened carefully as Les explained the risks involved. For a little while he remained silent and it looked as if he was not interested in taking so great a risk. But when he finally spoke the jumbled story that came tumbling out gave Les Hall one of the biggest shocks of his life.

'I'm madly in love with my Fawn,' Hunter said, using the name he used for Mouneen, the boat-owner's daughter. 'And I've already asked her to get me a radio. I had no idea you've got one here already. Sure, I'm certain she can help. I've had intercourse with her several times you know, before the bund was finished. Her father brought her up to within half a mile of the camp. I used to crawl out through the fence and meet her. I'll ask her tomorrow, batteries shouldn't be hard to conceal. She told me this morning that she's pregnant to me. When this is over I'm going to marry her and stay in Thailand.'

'Howard, are you off your head? What about your family back home?'

'What family? I was a foundling in England, then was sent to Australia where I was shunted from home to home and never spent long in any of them. Fawn told me her father will take me into business with him. He's a wealthy man.'

'You've knocked me for a sixer, Howard. How in blazes did you go outside and return without being spotted? And didn't you realise there was a big chance the girl and her dad were bounty hunters?'

'Yes, I considered everything before I was game enough to risk it. In fact I was still a bit on the windy side that first night, but as soon as it was dark I went through the wire where I'd loosened it beforehand. I waited until Goofy [a guard] had passed, then just rolled through. I'd only gone about fifty yards when I heard Fawn call me. We ran like mad for about a quarter of a mile to an empty hut.'

'You sure took great risks.' Les wasn't sure what amazed him more, Howard Hunter's daring or his stupidity. 'Didn't you feel a bit suspicious about entering a building where a guard could be waiting for you?'

'Never gave it a thought, really, not by then. Fawn kept kissing my hand and I felt quite safe. Once inside she just fell into my arms. I was burning up with desire, Fawn was too. What happened then was the most wonderful event of my life. I wanted to stay with her and not worry about returning to camp, but then there'd have been repercussions. I did get a bit of a shock when I realised the time, and a worse one when we got outside. Two young boys in saffron robes were there, waiting, but they spoke to Fawn, nodded, and led the way back. I just made it in time.'

'Did she give you any food?' Les wanted to know.

'Yes, plenty. I brought back nearly fifty boiled eggs and a hand of bananas. As well as the tucker, she gave me some iodoform powder which I gave to Major Hobbs.'

'Howard, are you telling me the truth or are you just romancing?'

'Ask the major. He will quick-smart prove my story... well the iodoform part of it anyway.'

'I hope you're being fair dinkum about this. It's pretty hard to believe you going out through the fence, meeting a Thai girl, and now you say she is pregnant to you. When did you last have intercourse with her?'

'Just before the bund was completed. I've only been able to exchange a few words with her since then, when we're unloading the boat. The guards watch us like hawks. I nearly did a flip this morning when she whispered, "Baby, yours". My mouth opened and I almost answered her, then a guard came close and went to touch her breast. Her father yelled at him and grabbed the long steering oar and made as if to whack him. He jumped off like a shot.'

'Do you mean to tell me the other Japs didn't interfere when her dad hit at one of them?'

'Yes, it sounds incredible but it's quite true. You can check with the other boys in the boat party. They'll back me up.'

'Frankly, I find it hard to accept any of this story. It's just so unbelievable. Still, I can't shake this feeling that you're telling the truth, except for one thing.'

'What's that?'

'Your refusal to escape and join the British troops if they are so close to the camp. Had I been in your situation that's exactly what I'd have wanted to do. And I would have too, unless...'

'Unless what?'

'Well, except for the executions that may have resulted here as the cost of my freedom.'

'That's the repercussion I mentioned earlier,' Howard said. 'Now tell me, have they called for a boat unloading party for tomorrow?'

'No, that's why you're on the water party. Why the question?'

'Well, Fawn can't get a radio, but she should be able to bring some batteries to get you back on the air. Please make certain I'm always on the boat group. It's hard getting someone to swap jobs when you list me for something else.'

'I certainly will. We need that radio working as a major priority. If your girlfriend can help us, then there's a real chance your dreams of a life on the river might be realised.'

Hall then hurried off to tell Max Nonmus Hunter's amazing story. Not surprisingly, Nonmus was both aghast and incredulous. There was no way, he said, that he could believe such a fairytale. 'Damned lot of rot. You're too impressionable, Les. Truth is he told you something he wanted to believe. Him and you both, most likely. Good God, I've never heard such a trumped-up yarn in my life, and I heard some beauties in my days as a publican.'

A couple of hours later, Max had changed his tune somewhat. Perhaps he'd done some preliminary checking; maybe he was clutching at straws.

'Jeez, Les,' he said, 'Hunter could be onto something after all. Tell you what, try to get Captain Cumming to go and have a look at this girl next trip. It's about ten weeks since the bund was finished and he might be able to see some telltale signs of pregnancy. Holy hell, though, what a yarn!'

THE END IS NIGH

SPECULATION HAD been rife for some time that the Nipponese were beaten, or all but, and were retreating on all fronts. Many Pacific islands were being bypassed despite the enemy garrisons known to be stationed on them. The only action taken against them was the occasional bombing raid—sufficient to keep the Nips on their toes, and in fear of seaborne invasion.

However, unknown to the general public, Japan had been seeking 'honourable' peace via neutral countries. Hirohito, Emperor of the Japanese, had no desire to lose face and was against unconditional surrender of the type he had demanded of the Allies after the battle for Singapore.

The collapse of the Axis partners in Europe had been a bitter blow to Hirohito, Tojo and his cohorts in the Japanese war cabinet. But as far as the Japanese people were concerned, their emperor was a god, invincible, and a loss of the Pacific war was unthinkable. The might and strength of his armed forces had been established over the previous decade. However, the real situation became all too apparent when U.S. Air Force bombers began unloading their deadly cargoes over Japanese cities. Prior to this, they had been told that American planes and naval vessels no longer existed, so successful had Nipponese pilots been in destroying them as fast as they could be put into action.

To the prisoners of war, it was obvious that the fighting in Burma was going against the previously all-powerful Japanese, and trainloads of their wounded were proof positive of this to the POWs on the 'puff-puff' (woodcutting) parties camped at various timber supply dumps along the line they had been forced to build. The Japs treated their wounded about as badly as they treated their prisoners and on more than one occasion the starving POWs offered succour to famished and dehydrated Nip soldiers as they lay wounded in crammed and unhygienic railway wagons. The sullen expressions on so many Nip faces were a further indication that all was not well up north. So great was the jubilation amongst the cutters that they managed, via the evergreen grapevine, to pass on the information to the off-line camps.

Tamuan was one such camp. At Tamuan, too, the commandant and guards were in time less severe—though still not humane—in their treatment of those under their 'care'. The work demands decreased and full bags of rice, of the correct weight rather than butts, were supplied. Something was in the wind. The bund, however, was still a grim reminder of the POWs' uncertain future.

As news filtered in from other centres it gave rise to much wishful thinking, and most of the homesick POWs could imagine return to Australia coming closer every day. The Dutch and English POWs still cast doubts on the veracity of the rumours and refused to accept the possibility of any sudden end to the conflict.

Max Nonmus and Les Hall were pinning their faith on the capacity of Howard Hunter to obtain batteries for Les's now-silent radio. However, things looked grim when they discovered that Hunter was down with a bad attack of malaria. If not controlled—and there were no appropriate drugs available—it could lead to the onset of blackwater fever. Many men in the camp already had it, some had already succumbed and were now statistics. Nonmus and Hall were disconsolate when they heard Major Alan Hobbs' diagnosis.

'Someone very important? To both of you?' the major enquired.

'Yes, very much so. He is the only man in this camp who can get us back on the air.'

'How on earth can he achieve that?'

For a moment there was complete silence. The Nonmus blurted out the complete story of Howard's and Fawn's romance.

'If you believe that...' Words temporarily failed the major. 'Obviously he was delirious when he spun you that one, Les.'

'He was completely normal when he spoke to me yesterday, Sir. The "bug" hit him later.'

'That girl... is she known to anyone else?'

'He seems to be the only one she speaks to, and only when the guards are out of earshot. She's been at him for some time to go with her to a British camp near here.'

'British camp! What tommy rot! All she is after is the 500 ticals bounty or blood money, whatever you want to call it.'

'I know it sounds like a tall tale,' Les Hall said. 'Max didn't believe me either, though he's less adamant now. But I feel he's telling the truth. One way to find out is for you or Captain Cumming to take a look at her... see if she really is pregnant.'

'Are you serious, Hall, or just stupid? Unless she's three or more months on the way only a physical examination can confirm her condition. Pregnant indeed! I gave you both credit for having more sense than to believe that.'

However, the persistence of the two men caused Hobbs to consult with Captain Gordon Cumming. When the major repeated what he'd just been told, Cumming surprised him by suggesting Hunter's story was worth checking out.

'Don't tell me you think the youngster is to be believed,' Hobbs replied. 'Good heavens, you'll be believing the war is already over if that's how you feel. Take my advice, forget the whole thing and let's get on with caring for the sick and injured.'

'Sorry, Alan, but I can't discount what Hunter told Les Hall. I've heard rumours, and there could be something in them. Where do you think he got the iodoform he gave you?'

From the look on his face, it seemed Major Hobbs thought his fellow Australians had gone quite mad. 'Les has always been a morale-builder,' he said at last, 'but he seems to have believed a fairytale fantasy this time.'

'Then again, he has had the opportunity to judge events when his "bird" is singing.'

'Think it will ever sing again?'

'Well, that's where the girl Fawn comes in,' Cumming replied. 'The most important thing right now is to get Hunter back on his feet and back onto the boat party.'

Day and night the medical officers fought to save the lives of Howard Hunter and the other patients suffering from malaria and Blackwater fever. Seven men had already passed on and it was something of a near-miracle that the MOs managed to more or less control the outbreak. Hunter was one of the survivors.

Unfortunately Hall was hospitalised on 12 August and Major Hobbs surgically corrected a bowel problem. He had been bedridden for a couple of days when Howard came to him in a very excited manner. His hands were trembling as he spilled out his information.

'I saw Fawn this morning. Her father kept the guards talking and I had a few minutes with her out of sight of the Nips. She told me the war is coming to an end, and that she will have the batteries for me next trip. I'm really worked up, Les. If Fawn is right we'll soon be man and wife and free of these Nip sadists. I'll come and see you as often as I can, and keep you posted. It shouldn't be long before I have what you want.'

After he had gone Glenn Campbell, two bed-spaces away, asked Les what 'the kid' was mumbling about. 'Do you know,' he said, 'he dead keen on that Thai boat girl; there's no doubt she is on him, too. I've been on the unloading party a few times and caught her looking for him. A couple of times the guard has almost caught them holding hands. If he's not onto a good thing I'll eat my hat. The trouble is finding the opportunities.'

'You really think so, Glenn?'

'Certainly. He was the one who brought us those eggs and bananas a while back. We all know where he got them from. He went out under the wire and she gave them to him. We had to cover for him at the first hourly hut check.'

'Was that the only time he went out to trade?'

'Crikey, no. He's done it a few times and we always had a good feed when he came back. A couple of times the guards nearly caught him, only we had a "cockatoo" to give him the signal. And another thing, Les, *Howard is no trader!* No-one in this camp has anything left to trade with anyway.'

'You think he's had sex with this girl?'

'Of course he has! We were all awake to that, envious too. I was a bit concerned at first—thought the Nips might have been using her and he might cop a load. When I told him that he nearly went through the roof; said she was a virgin and bled the first time. Did he tell you he has her up the duff?'

'Yes he did, but I thought he was having me on.'

'Well he isn't. I believe she is carrying his child. In fact she should be showing up a little by now. She's tiny, you know.'

'Did he tell you anything else—about the war, I mean?'

'Yes, according to what she told him it should be over any day now. Mind you, that was a few weeks ago.'

'Maybe she's just leading him up the garden path.'

'Garden path be damned. Both of them are fair dinkum and it's about time you, Nonmus and the rest took a bit of notice. Didn't he give Major Hobbs that "gold dust"? What more proof do you flaming well want? The kid has guts and plenty of it. Believe what he tells you, it is the truth.'

When Les told Max Nonmus this he became terribly excited. It was as if the Nips had tossed it in already.

'Just a moment, it's not done with yet,' Les had to remind him. 'Wait until Howard gets his hands on those batteries. Then I might be able to get some reliable up-to-date news. Is there a boat party required for tomorrow?'

'Yes, I've just come from the meeting. Don't worry, Hunter will be on it for certain. By the way, Doc Cumming will take a look at the girl tomorrow. He's as interested as we are, although Alan Hobbs is still a bit non-committal. See you in the morning.'

It was just on 2100 hours when Max hurried out of the hut. A little while later an excited Howard Hunter came in and told Les he had high hopes Fawn would have the batteries the next morning.

'I'm as anxious as anyone to find out how soon we'll be free,' he told Les. 'Perhaps even more so. The moment it's all over I'm heading for the river. I want my baby born in wedlock. I just wish I could get rid of this blasted toothache.'

'Toothache! You've got that?'

'Yes, bloomin' bad too. Why the question?'

'Howard, you just proved you *are* going to be a dad. That is the one sign your wife, girlfriend or whatever is pregnant. Congratulations! Hope it's twins.'

'Come on, don't wish that on me. One will be enough, first time anyhow. See you tomorrow.'

Les Hall spent an uncomfortable night, in pain after the operation but for another reason as well. He was troubled over the immediate future. If the war was going badly for Japan and an Allied landing was made nearby, then the bund around the camp could well become a mass grave.

There were four machine-guns mounted in the central tower above the parade ground. And the ill and crippled POWs in the huts would be easy prey for bayonet-wielding guards. As these thoughts raced through his mind Les imagined the awful carnage that could be so easily inflicted.

The first shots fired would result in a charge towards the tower to get below the elevation of the guns. No question of that. However, that first sweep would kill many before the tower could be toppled. Of course some of the guards would be targets too, and if they were withdrawn, leaving the POWs unguarded, that would be some sort of advance warning.

When Captain Cumming came to Hall on his rounds the next morning he was amazed at the sweat pouring from his body.

'What is it, Les?' he asked. 'A touch of malaria? You're burning up.'

'No, Doc, it's worry. The war seems to be drawing to a close very fast now, and I have a feeling that bund around the camp could be our last resting place. If we're ordered to form a hollow square at any time I reckon those machine-guns will start spitting hot lead into our ranks. You agree?'

'Well I'm not so sure about the progress of the hostilities, but I agree about our prospects if you're right.'

FREE IN '45

LES HALL WAS STILL listed as a bedpatient on 16 August 1945. Major Alan Hobbs had only just left him when there was a commotion at the end of the hospital building. Then Howard Hunter almost fell onto the bamboo platform beside Les. He was laughing loudly and in his hand he held a piece of paper which he tried to pass to Les without anyone else observing the act.

Sensing something unusual, Les feared the Jap guards had caught the excited lad communicating with his Thai girlfriend. Instead, he heard Howard say: 'Please read it... Go on, Les, read it! it's the truth, I swear it.'

'Hang on, laddie, what's the truth? Have the guards caught you and Fawn?'

'No... no, read what is written on the paper... Go on, *read it!*'

In perfect handwriting, Les read: 'JAPAN SURRENDERED YESTERDAY!'

Momentarily, he thought his eyes were playing tricks on him. The words danced as his hand quivered.

'Howard, can this really be true? Do you think it's a trick to get you to go away with her?'

'God no, Les, Fawn wouldn't do anything like that. We are all *free...* don't you understand? *Free at last!* That singer was right: "*Keep alive... We will be home in '45!*"'

'Steady on, Howard, keep your voice down or the whole camp will go mad. One false move and we could all go in a flash. The guard outside this hut has fixed his bayonet and is watching us. Take this to Max Nonmus and don't breathe a word of it to anyone until we know this is official. Go, for God's sake hurry.'

Within minutes Max was in close conversation with Les and they were discussing the advisability of questioning the Japanese camp interpreter, known to all as Turtle Neck. WO1 Eric Bailey was at that time in charge of all POWs and they were duty-bound to acquaint him with the information and suggest he seek a meeting with the Japanese commander.

An hour later Max was back and able to tell his friend the Nipponese colonel had agreed to see Bailey that evening. 'I think the Nip knows that it's all over, Les. He suggested to Eric that he organise a concert.'

'A concert? Then there's no question in my mind that it's finished. If it isn't then he'd have belted hell out of Eric, just for daring to ask for something. Max Nonmus, you beauty, we are as free as the birds that roam the sky, and I do not mean the bomber type.'

'I won't have time to see you again until after the evening tenko,' Max said, 'but keep your eyes on our hut. If you see Eric and me walk out and Eric waves a piece of paper above his head, it'll be confirmation of victory. We'll be free once again.'

As soon as the midday meal was served there was a concerted rush to erect a platform for the show the artists were already rehearsing—the first concert since last Christmas, it was to be a night of nights. There was an air of confidence everywhere except amongst the guards. No-one even bothered to salute them and no bashings resulted. That was another sure sign that the POW days had come to an end.

Throughout the afternoon many quizzed Les as to what was going on. Although his innards were doing somersaults and he wanted to yell out the good news, he had to retain an impassive countenance. The minutes passed slowly, so slowly it seemed as if the world had come to an end. Meanwhile, however, the workers erecting the stage whistled, chattered like monkeys, and some even sang old popular songs. All fears of the future seemed to be gone.

The wandering Korean guards kept as far away as possible from groups of POWs and practised none of their characteristic sadism. There were no 'currahs' or any attempts to interfere with what was going on. It was an extraordinary and unexpected, but wholesome, change.

About mid-afternoon young Howard Hunter came to see Les once again.

'You know what?' he said.'I've just come past the Nip commandant's office and I saw Turtle Neck and the boss squatting on the floor. They had their hands on their heads and they were muttering something in a singsong way. No-one took the slightest notice of me—not even Nasty, who was on guard.

'It looks as if I'll be spending the night with Fawn,' he went on.'But I ask you one favour, Les. Please cover for me until I return. I'll be a couple of days at least, but don't mark me AWL. You owe me that.'

'Howard, if all this is true I won't care if you're away for a month. Max and Eric are more likely to recommend you for a medal rather than punishment.'

'You fair dinkum, Les?'

'Never more so. You're worth your weight in gold and I'm going to see you're suitably rewarded. After tonight, provided your information is correct, you'll be the hero of this camp.'

'Oh come off it, I'm no flamin' hero. It's Fawn who should get a medal.'

Howard's modesty was as impressive as his bravery.

As evening drew nearer Les Hall was so excited he could hardly wait for the commencement of the concert. More than that, however, his eyes were glued on the hut from which he knew Eric Bailey and Max Nonmus would emerge at 1600 hours—Aussie time, *not* Tokyo!

With the meal and tenko over, everyone converged on the stage area. The bedpatients were carried out and given pride of place in front of the bamboo platform.

As if on a given signal, dead silence settled over the packed troops. Word of mouth had told them what they were all waiting for. But 1600 hours came and went, and hopeful spirits became tense and jittery.

At 1605, however, the two senior Australian NCOs emerged from the hut, but they walked about a hundred yards without giving the prearranged sign of victory.

It seemed more like a hundred miles to the assembled troops. Then up went Eric Bailey's hand. It was official! The war was over. Everyone was free at last.

Still, an eerie silence continued as Bailey made his way to the recently constructed concert stage. Then he raised his right hand once more and was heard to say: 'I have a message...'

That was enough! Pandemonium broke out. In seconds the Dutch flag went aloft, followed by the Union Jack, amid cheers, yells, the tossing of headgear. Sadly, no Australian flag was available. Many sang, a lot prayed. The noise must have scared the wits out of the Nip and Korean guards, and many of them shot through faster than a Bondi tram.

The scene that followed Bailey's brief announcement is totally indescribable on paper, canvas, or any other material. It was as if the whole world had gone berserk with pent-up emotions flowing everywhere ... something no serviceman present—none of them a POW any more—could ever forget.

After the few wild minutes a concerted rush was made for the Japanese stores. To the astonishment of the first to smash open the doors, they saw hundreds of Red Cross parcels stacked from floor to ceiling. Within a short time fires sprang up in every direction and 44-gallon drums of Nescafe soon came to the boil. With no immediate limit placed on who should eat and drink what, it was one wild, wonderful party.

In the midst of the celebrations Howard Hunter came to where Captain Gordon Cumming, Max Nonmus and Les Hall were grouped. His eyes were flashing as if they were neon lights and he whirled around in a queer gymnastic style, shook hands with each man and then ran like a deer in the direction of the river.

'Where in blazes is he going, Les?' someone asked.

'His paradise,' came the reply.

A number of the ex-POWs had built a roaring fire on the top of the river bank and were quaffing mugs of Nescafe and consuming Christmas cake and pudding, along with any other edibles found in the parcels they should have had as far back as 1943. In the midst of all the gaiety they caught the sound of a river-boat's diesel engine, a most unusual sound after dark. Their first thoughts were that it was probably full of Japs, not that it mattered any more.

They were surprised, however, as the vessel headed into the bank some 200 yards away. And instead of a Nip jumping to shore they saw what looked like a young girl. As she tied a rope to a stake they heard her laugh and could see her peering in the direction of the camp. At the same moment they heard someone slipping and sliding down the steep embankment. The observers were mystified until Reg Quinton recognised Howard Hunter, by now locked in an embrace with his darling Fawn.

As Howard boarded the sleek vessel, Fawn untied the mooring rope and joined him and, they presumed, her father at the helm. Seconds later they were out of sight, swallowed by the darkness as the swift-running waters carried the craft away into the night.

It had all happened so quickly the revellers were spellbound and silent. Then 'Darkie' Ryan called out, 'Good luck to you, Howie-boy. You deserve her.'

'He was as game as they come,' someone else observed. 'And but for that chit of a girl supplying medicines and whatever else she could lay her hands on, many of us wouldn't be here now.'

'All I hope is that he finds his bluebird of happiness,' Ryan said, 'and a family to call his own.'

Then the celebrations continued.

When the usual Lights Out call was sounded it was met with derision by all but a select few who felt they should try to set an example to the rest. However, no-one attempted to interfere with the enjoyment of the majority. In any case, who could sleep that night ... or wanted to?

Not all POWs received the news of the Japanese surrender so promptly—not even officers' camps.

Whilst associated with other ranks, officers in POW camps under the Japanese were not required to undertake manual labour. The situation was different, when they were taken to officer-only camps such as the one created at Kanburi. Despite all protests, the Nipponese demanded they either work or not be fed, it was as simple as that. So they laboured on many and varied tasks. Bert Parr was one who experienced the change towards the end of the war:

There were water-pump teams, wood carrying, camp maintenance, and teams carrying loads of dirt from point A to point B and then to point C for no apparent reason or purpose.

I recall one futile task...Around the camp was a moat-like trench [obviously, as was later discovered, intended as a mass grave] about ten feet deep. The rain had been very heavy and the sides of this trench were sliding down. So we were put to work standing in mud up to our knees, picking up handfuls of mud, tossing it onto the wall of the moat, only to watch it slide back to our feet. This went on for hours with Korean guards lording it over their white officer captives.

At this and earlier stages the extra hazard was the increasing frequency of air raids by our own Allied air forces, particularly at Tamarkan and Kanburi, as well as camps further up the line. Kanburi camp was controlled by a very nasty Japanese officer who handed out some vicious punishments.

From June '45 onwards prisoners were moved in groups from Kanburi. In August our group, after hanging about in the rain for a few hours, were put on a train of open cattle trucks with about thirty men to each. The train sat at Kanburi station for two hours. Some time later we were transferred to roofed cattle trucks in the railway yards, the floors of which were filthy, making it impossible to lie down.

A couple of days later we came to Nakom-Paton on the main Singapore-Bangkok line. After a precarious crossing on foot over a bridge badly damaged by the RAF we went on to the marshalling yards at Bangkok station. All the camp gear had to be unloaded and stacked into barges. We travelled downriver to a go-down which had been bombed and the rain poured through the holes in the roof.

On 13 August we were back onto more cattle trucks, thirty-two to each, and a Jap troop train pulled in beside us. I recall saying to my good friend and well-known journalist Rohan Rivett what a real picnic it would be if the bombers came over.

We were still travelling on 15 August [VP Day] until we arrived at Nakomnayok when we detrained and with packs on our backs trudged forty-eight kilometres in torrential rain. We marched for fifty minutes with a ten-minute rest.

The rain was incessant and it was not till the afternoon of 16 August we reached the camp. Here the rumours were strong about the war being over but we had heard it so often before and we were so exhausted we refused to believe it...

It was not until 17 August that Lt. Col. Toosey, the British Camp Commander, was able to confirm the Jap surrender.

The camp was now under our control!

The Japs released Red Cross parcels they had held for three months and mail dating back to 1942 came to light.

During our captivity there were many threats made of reprisals against our captors when peace came. What actually happened that momentous afternoon was that all now ex-POWs stood out on the parade ground and sang the National Anthem and hymns of thanksgiving.

As daylight dawned at Tamuan camp on 17 August, the remains of the overnight orgy were all too evident to Les Hall and his colleagues: paper wrappers, discarded condensed-milk tins (bedpans in what had passed for hospital huts and camps for the previous forty months), the embers of the many fires. There was also a long line of men awaiting their turn at the latrines, diarrhoea had resulted from gorging on those Red Cross parcels.

As daylight dawned on 17 August the remains of the overnight orgy were all too evident. Paper wrappers, discarded condensed-milk tins (bedpans in what had passed for hospital huts and camps for the previous forty months), the embers of the many fires. There was also a long line of men awaiting their turn at the latrines; diarrhoea had resulted from gorging on those Red Cross parcels.

Evident, too, were sullen Japanese guards manning their normal posts. Most of the Koreans had disappeared during the night. What really annoyed the ex-POWs was the fact the remaining guards still bore arms, but that situation was remedied when live ammunition was removed from every Nip on guard.

Goofy, who was on duty outside the hospital huts, cheerfully handed his rifle over. He had a grin from ear to ear as he said, 'Blurty war all over. Me go home, too.' He was without doubt the only Japanese national in Tamuan camp who was pleased freedom had come to the POWs he had been forced to guard. As was later disclosed, he and Howard Hunter had reached an agreement—

protection in return for fruit and eggs. If there were any good Japs, Goofy was one of them.

The most welcome event of the day was the arrival of a British officer and wireless operator. They came to take command and relieve Australian, British and Dutch NCOs from further responsibilities. Their uniforms were the envy of all—beautiful new jungle greens, boots and hats. But they were a sobering sight to Turtle Neck and the Nip commandant and guards. Servility instantly replaced sadism and swagger. It was sweet music to those listeners who heard the British officer read the riot act to men who had forded it over troops whose misfortune it had been to suffer under the iron fist of the Nipponese for such a long period.

On the morning of 19 August groups of local townspeople paid courtesy calls distributing fruit, cakes, sweets, toothbrushes and combs—luxuries all long since forgotten, but now very much appreciated. Thai women and children accompanied the men and caused some temporary embarrassment to the G-stringed ex-POWs. Still, chattering children, curious young maidens, their parents and saffron-robed boys were something the camp inmates had not seen for a very long time. Many spoke English quite well and questions and answers came thick and fast.

Mention of the atom bomb as the cause of the Japanese surrender intrigued the news-hungry lads, and their astonishment was so genuine the visitors were at pains to explain the lead-up to the war's end in as much detail as they could. The camp inmates were also informed that large numbers of POWs had been sent to Japan, including some 'A' Force members. They were told, too, that many lives had been lost when transport ships had been sunk by Allied submarines. Some survivors, it was believed, had been rescued and repatriated.

Les Hall was in conversation with a Thai gentleman who spoke perfect English, and he really opened Les's eyes when he spoke of the British parachutists who were in fact in a secret location about seven kilometres from Tamuan camp. The man told Les of their various underground activities. They had been prepared to attack the guards at three camps within a radius of fifty kilometres— Kanburi, Nakom-Paton and, of course, Tamuan, which was closest to UGH (underground headquarters).

Apparently they had also been monitoring all enemy military broadcasts and believed the Nipponese intended the execution of every prisoner under their control on the day Allied forces invaded Thailand or Malaya. They had been instructed to move to within rifle range of the three camps no later than 8 August, as Lord Mountbatten had ordered the invasion to take place on the 9th.

However, that plan was held over pending negotiations requested by the Japanese following the devastating success of the atom bombs dropped over Hiroshima on 6 August and Nagasaki three days later. Those bombs had saved the POWs' lives.

'The rest,' the Thai said, 'you know already.'

'I'm still a bit bewildered,' Les replied. 'We were completely in the dark, and hoping the girl on the river-boat could supply us with batteries for the radio I have secreted. But instead of batteries she gave us the message which ended the necessity. It was stunning news—a dream come true. We owe that girl a debt we will never be able to repay.'

'Oh yes you will, or your young soldier will. Preparations are now in hand for their marriage. In the eyes of every Thai, Mouneen is a heroine. Her interest in that Australian soldier helped the underground more than you will ever know. His reluctance to escape with her is well understood, but he too could have been of great use at UGH. However, that need no longer exists.'

Not long after the visitors departed a four-engine plane buzzed the camp, made a complete circle, and came in so low the men on the ground could see some crew standing at the open doors. They waved, then out came canisters of food, clothing, medicines, drugs and cigarettes. Unfortunately, quite a few of the drums and canisters burst open. But who cared? What spilled out was quickly gathered and taken to Q stores.

Arguments broke out when the Dutch troops claimed more than others thought was their due, but Eric Bailey and Max Nonmus soon intervened and equitable distribution was organised.

At various intervals throughout the day, and the two following, more supplies were dropped from the planes. As a direct result of the aerial drops, food once again became plentiful and a controlled diet was introduced. The leggie lines remained constant as the efects of years of starvation could not be wiped away in a few days.

What was remarkable and stood out was the almost immediate improvement in the health of those considered near death prior to 16 August. Colour returned to their features and they began to build up strength and bulk. Even those who had been too far gone to speak became communicative. Major Alan Hobbs and Captain Gordon Cumming were in their element once again—overwhelmed with the medical supplies that had been denied them for so long.

As the camp was open to visitors each day, villagers poured in to see for themselves the human wrecks who were the legacy of Nippon's push for supremacy throughout the Asia-Pacific area. They expressed amazement that any human beings could suffer so much and survive to tell of their experiences. Sadly, many of the POWs had not been so fortunate.

One vary talkative Thai gentleman was somewhat embarrassed when handing out gifts of soap. 'Bluey' Dingwall, when accepting a cake, asked him if any of the ex-POWs suffered from body odour. Momentarily taken aback, the kindly gentleman stumbled for a suitable answer, then burst out with, 'I'm afraid you all pong a little'.

After the fifth day enjoying a more or less balanced diet, everyone's thoughts were of mail from home and of how soon they could get out of the horrible hole they were in. The sight and sounds of children around the area excited the married men in particular, and their eyes turned longingly in the direction of the Southern Cross while their thoughts turned to wives, mothers and family members. Who could blame them after so long a period, during which their lives were at risk twenty-four hours a day?

The two WOs in charge of the Australians worked flat-out trying to arrange transport for their charges to Bangkok, sixty kilometres away. But as there were so many ex-POWs in various camps clamouring for the same consideration, all had to stand in line. Fretful as they may have been as prisoners or war, they were doubly so now. The sunny climes of Australia were constantly calling them and anxiety tested their patience sorely.

However, the happy day arrived after what seemed to many to have been an interminable waste of good time. But instead of Bangkok, they were debussed at Nakom-Paton, Holy City of Thailand. It was a large town, famous for its huge Pagoda with some 600 steps to the front entrance. However, no matter the beauty of the town's gardens, shops and streets, or the friendliness and generosity of its inhabitants, it was not Bangkok... the stepping stone to home.

Well over 10,000 troops were housed in huts which boasted timber floors and walls and atap roofing which, for a wonder, did not leak. The first few days were spent being rekitted in jungle greens, but sandshoes instead of leather footwear. At least and at last, all troops now sported something on their feet. The old style of bare feet was something to remember, but the memory was not a pleasant one, involving deaths of friends, and the frightful pain as medical officers gouged out ulcerated legs with spoons of all sorts.

Many were seriously jolted when they visited mates they had not seen for months. The ex-POWs sent from the camps deep in the Thai jungles had suffered the worst. Lieutenant Colonel Coates and his medical team and voluntary aids had worked near-miracles with rudimentary methods which all too frequently involved little more than water and encouragement. Now, however, with the aid of modern drugs, lives and limbs were being saved.

Les Hall received a particularly pleasant surprise when he met up with two of his best friends, Sonny Morris (2/15 Field Artillery) and Henry John Thomas Alexander Smith (2/20 Infantry Battalion), the latter a lucky, plucky boy who fought all odds to stay alive at Thanbyuzayat. How he had survived was something not even the medical officers could explain. They put it down to intestinal fortitude.

HOMECOMING

LEAVE WAS NO problem in that large encampment, but few wanted or sought day trips into Nakom-Paton as they settled in. They preferred letter writing, and in time reading and rereading their first batch of mail from home. Tears mixed with joyous announcements were daily occurrences and those who received no letters were deeply depressed. It was heartbreaking to witness the distress in their faces when the posties failed to call out their names.

In fact few of the Tamuan evacuees received a letter in the first week, but then three full mailbags arrived, and a queue formed immediately. The Morris, Smith and Hall trio held their breath as name after name was called out, but not theirs. Just as they were about to express their disappointment a mate of Harry Smith's came out of the room yelling: 'Smithy—Smith, H.J.T., I mean. Have a bundle for you.'

A few minutes later it was Sonny Morris' turn.

When all the mail seemed to have been distributed, Les still had none and his spirits hit an all-time low. He had been forgotten! As he walked away from his joyous colleagues, his eyes filled with tears, he thought he could hear someone saying, 'Hey Sonny, know where your mate Hall is? Got a heap for him here but he never answered his blasted name. Where in blazes is he?'

Les's heart beat a tattoo against his ribs as he ran, breathless, and as one lanky Londoner later said, 'Wiv water running down his blinkin' face like a Trafalgar Square fountain. 'Urt me a bit, too!' The happy Aussie soldier couldn't have cared less how he looked. He had letters, oodles of them, to read, read and read again until his peepers just about wore out.

It was not long before the three mates were swapping news items, though not the really private bits, they were just too personal for sharing. Excited in the extreme, Les held up a photo of his daughter Marjorie in her bridal gown, looking beautiful.

With the continued intake of good, wholesome food, and lots of it, the health of all who had left POW life behind them continued to improve—so much so one of the British Recovery Group said there was no way in the world anyone could make him believe they had suffered to the extent everyone made out... except...

'Except what, Limey?'

'Those near skeletons in the hospital huts. Blimey, I've seen some skinny chaps in my time, but absolutely nothing to compare with them. Just bleedin' scarecrows. But you blokes are saying even they look well. If that's true, how come any of you fellas are still alive?'

'Ever hear of fate, and patience, plus medical officer determination?'

'Yes, I suppose I have... but ain't you Orstralians pulling my leg a bit?'

'No, go and talk to some of your own blokes. Listen to what they tell you, and how thousands of their comrades now lie in jungle cemeteries up and down the line. Maybe you'll believe them.'

It was all true. The men still in hospital were on the improve, but to someone seeing them for the first time they were, to put it mildly, a frightful sight. Humans with skin still drawn tightly over their bones. They were, as Lady Mountbatten had said, unbelievably alive!

Although mail was still coming through at intervals, it was not fast enough to satisfy the the men who craved letters as they had once craved food. Worse than the seeming delay on mail deliveries was the monotony of daily life and uncertainty as to when any of them were going to return to Australia.

Major Bell, Camp Commandant, was moving heaven and earth in his determination to evacuate the impatient troops. Meanwhile, the locals were doing their utmost to welcome the hundreds who had taken to wandering around the town after sundown. Lasting friendships were made, and for some of the boys romance was in the air. Marriage, of course, seemed a taboo subject as religious and cultural differences between the troops and the Thais were too great. Commitment was easier for someone like Howard Hunter, who had no firm ties in Australia or England. Thailand could become his native country.

The days dragged on, but eventually orders were issued to prepare for the long-awaited journey to Bangkok. The excitement was contagious. At the same time many teary-eyed maidens tried to formalise their relationships with their 'temporary fiances' by claiming to be pregnant. Perhaps some, like Fawn, really were but none of the ex-POWs remained behind.

The first train pulled out of Nakom-Paton just after dark on 15 September, and cheers and shrill cries rent the air. To many, the train journey, short as it was (about five kilometres to the blown bridge) signified the real renewal of a life they had missed out on for almost four years.

Crossing the damaged bridge was a perilous undertaking as most of the troops were loaded down with their new equipment in addition to as many souvenirs as they could carry. There were a few near-mishaps, then everyone boarded a second train and enjoyed a trouble-free run to Bangkok.

After everyone had alighted and been counted, they were set off to the university where they were to be billeted until arrangements could be made for flights to Singapore. The supervising transport officer told the men that they would be selected for these flights by ballot. Les Hall found himself scheduled to be amongst the last to leave and there was nothing he could do about it. Or was there?

When the actual transit sheet was prepared the first name on the list was... Sergeant Leslie G. Hall! As he had approached no-one asking for any favours, he was completely dumbfounded. Who had intervened on his behalf? The question was never answered. Bombardier Sonny Morris was quite upset by this 'promotion' and pleaded with his mate to stay so they could fly out together, however long the wait. But when he saw the look on Les's face he flushed with embarrassment.

'Damn it, Les, I forgot you are not a single man. Of course you must go at once. See you in good old Aussie.'

The following morning the transport officer at the aerodrome apologised to the eighteen men in No. 6 party. 'Sorry lads, your plane is out of fuel.'

The would-be passengers were understandably upset and paced around wondering if anything could be done to remedy the situation. When Les Hall saw a British plane unloading what appeared to be petrol and oil and preparing a makeshift fuel dump, he called his group together and suggested they form an impromptu work party.

'Grab your gear,' he said. 'We're on our way.'

They marched briskly to the plane they had been allotted and Les asked the pilot how much fuel he needed. With a puzzled look he told them: 'At least 880 gallons of petrol and 132 of oil. Think you can get any?'

'Yes I do. How fast can you get it in the tanks?'

'As fast as you can get it here... but where are you going to find some?'

'From the Pommy bus unloading over there. It's only about a 200-yard roll. We get, you fill.'

The No. 6 party broke up into three groups and approached the dump from different directions. Les's group arrived first and he told the British guard they were to pick up urgently needed supplies of petrol and oil.

'OK, Sarge,' the guard said. 'Sign here.'

There was never a more willing lot of workers, and the drums were rolled at a run. Just as the last of the fuel was being pumped into their plane, the British guards woke up to the situation. 'You blasted Australians,' the NCO yelled. 'That's for our plane, not yours. We want it back.'

The pilot told the Australians to get aboard as fast as they could, and no-one questioned the command. In fact the last passenger boarded it as the plane was beginning to taxi down the runway. The radio was switched off and within minutes they were on their way. As they reached cruising height the number-one pilot came out into the cabin. Sweat was pouring down his face.

'Jeez, that was close,' he said. 'How much luggage have you boys got? You probably didn't notice in all the excitement, but we cleared the perimeter wire with just inches to spare. Doesn't matter now, we'll be in Singapore by mid-afternoon. Have a good trip. You darned near didn't.'

It was perfect weather for flying and eager eyes sought the various areas where they had fought—Gemas, Muar, Mersing and all the other battlefronts leading down to the Causeway. The touchdown at Singapore brought a further flood of memories, some good, most very bad. Then came another surprise... white women... the first most of them had seen for three and a half years. They were dispensing steaming cups of sweet white tea from a NAAFI wagon.

Blushes and smiles were worth all the money in the world, and how wealthy the men felt at that moment! They were reluctant to leave when an officer called to them to board a truck to take them, not to Selarang Barracks as they had hoped, but to tents erected at the beach front at Changi.

As the men were alighting, a long-forgotten smell assaulted their nostrils. Fresh bread. As one, they dropped all their possessions and headed for the bakery. When they told the bakers where they had just come from, loaves of hot bread were handed out at once. It was an image of home as most of the men remembered it, and as they tore the bread apart, someone pushed a number of one-pound packets of butter towards them. Good manners were abandoned and they stuffed the thickly buttered lumps into their mouths. The taste was beyond belief.

Soon, however, a voice yelled out: 'What in hell do you fellows think you are doing?'

The shouting man then grabbed at the beautiful, melt-in-the-mouth loaves. Les and his fellow 'gourmets' were astonished that anyone would want to deprive them of this simple yet deeply satisfying luxury.

'Sorry, boys, but I'm a medical officer,' the killjoy said. 'If I let you eat all that bread and butter you'll do yourselves an injury. We will give it to you, but in measured quantities. You have starved for too long for us to allow you a feeding frenzy now. Now come with me. You'll have to be examined to see what damage you've done already.'

The men followed the officer meekly, but each of them was inwardly cursing the MO's untimely arrival.

When the medical examination was over the orderly sergeant accompanied the new arrivals to the tents—'allotted for your stay under the best conditions possible', he told them with a smirk.

'Best on offer?' one of the men offered sarcastically. 'You have to be joking! Tents, with palliasses to sleep on. Are you housed in one, Sarge?'

'Well, no. We of the Recovery Group have huts, but we're packed in like sardines. At four to a tent you fellows are much better off than any of us. Anyhow, here's something to cheer you up—four bottles of Aussie beer. Enjoy them.'

A smile, a wave and he was gone.

The bottles of Dinner Ale were welcome indeed, but the fact that everyone was again under canvas left a nasty taste. It hurt their pride, and as someone observed, unless that orderly sergeant had worked on the Burma-Thailand railway he wouldn't know what a crowded hut looked like.

After the four men had aired their grievances, Les Hall suggested things could in fact be a lot worse, and that they were on the verge of getting much better. 'We're on the doorstep of Aussie,' he said, 'and living like this for a few days won't hurt any of us. The roof doesn't leak, and look down there,' he added, pointing, 'hot showers! Come on, boys, let's clean up.'

While Les had enjoyed an unconventional 'escape' from Bangkok and was settling in at Singapore, one of his POW colleagues, Lieutenant Johnny Kreckler, stayed behind a while longer in Thailand, where he made what he later called 'A Good Catch':

Captain Jack Carey was a great friend and I will always cherish our friendship. The war was over and we had but one wish: to go home. We didn't allow for the system. The army always had a great habit of ordering the unexpected, and did just that.

Colonel G.E. Ramsay was ordered to stay put until all POWs were repatriated and he was relieved by allied command. His duty was as military governor of Bangkok. He called for assistance. Jack and I volunteered, as we both had great respect for this gallant and heroic officer. We made an unlikely pair of provosts.

Jack was provost marshall, and I his assistant provost marshall. The reason for the extended stay was the communist army. The British had armed them and supplied them to fight the Japanese. Now that the war was over they decided to fight the British.

Our men were given leave in Bangkok, and the big attraction was the theatres, most of which were in the Chinese section of the city. We had time to ourselves for the first time in many years—a remarkable sense of freedom and joy after the experiences on the Burma railway and the various camps. I will always remember lessons in traditional Siamese dancing demonstrated by a young princess who became the Queen of Thailand.

One day our 'duties' took us to the American embassy, where we were to meet two young ladies. Jack was driving. As one we both saw him. We could not believe our eyes. Walking along the footpath in a well-cut suit, oblivious to those around him, was one of the more despicable and deadly of our former guards, the infamous Boy Bastard.

We stopped the car and crossed the street. Approaching him from behind, I drew my .45 and prodded him in the back. He did not give me a chance and submitted like a lamb. We took him back to headquarters, which previously had housed the Japanese Kempi-tai, or secret police. The lock-up was a barbarous place, made of steel mesh, and had to be entered through a small opening. The prisoner had to crawl on his stomach to enter the cage. In out best Japanese we told him to stand on one leg and count and not to stop! Just as they had done to us amidst other, more atrocious and barbaric behaviour.

Jack and I repaired to the bar. After a few hours we remembered our 'catch' and went back to check that it was all true. He was still standing on one leg and still counting. We didn't meet the ladies that day, and the Boy Bastard was executed after the subsequent war trials.

*

For the men who'd moved to the tents at Changi, memories and surprises crowded in on each other and continued to do so. When the mess call sounded at 1800 hours Les and his mates were directed to a hut fitted out like a big city restaurant. The meal they sat down to was of a type they had scarcely dared dream about for years. Three courses with all the trimmings. At the end of this veritable feast came coffee and cigarettes, the best brands only.

Smithy was elated. 'It never entered my mind the army could serve up such tucker. I feel really content. All I want now is a quick trip home.'

Everyone agreed, but shipping was at a premium and it could be weeks before any of them trod the deck of an Australia-bound boat. Meanwhile, hundreds of bags of mail were piled up in the make-do post office and the ex-POWs were invited to assist in the sorting. It was a good move, and they rushed the opportunity to find letters addressed to themselves. Men worked for hours, only stopping for lunch and for the almost daily medical examinations.

Again, the medical officers, fresh from various combat and POW areas, were amazed to find the former prisoners of the Japanese recovering their health so quickly.

After working in the post office for some time Les Hall had so many letters to pore over he gave up sorting. Of great concern for him was the lack of any word about his mother. Everyone who wrote to him avoided any reference to her and it worried him beyond belief. He had of course written to all his family as soon as he was able All had replied... except his beloved mum. Clearly, something was amiss.

On the seventh morning back at Singapore Les found himself sorting mail once more and came across a few more letters to himself. One of them seemed to stand out. It was from his sister Olive and he felt drawn to it like a magnet. Olive's letters were usually bulky, crammed with newspaper cuttings of possible interest, but this one was unusually thin. Deep in thought, Les wandered out of the building and sat down. His fingers trembled as he slowly opened the envelope and withdrew the brief letter.

It was as he had feared deep down, but had not allowed himself to contemplate. There would be no welcome from his mother when he arrived back in Australia. God had taken her Home.

Les went quite cold. He was not emotional as one might expect, just numb. And he had to get back to where he belonged as fast as he could. An emptiness pervaded his body and it was as if his mother's spirit guided him as he made his way to the orderly room. He gave Olive's letter to a sergeant, who read it, expressed his regret, and at once made a phone call. As if at a distance, Les thought he head a voice saying, 'Very sad. Put him on tomorrow's manifest.'

After that, a lot of things appeared to happen at once. Transport into Singapore, bedding down for the night, breakfast at dawn and making ready for the flight home, they all seemed to blend. Then a transport officer told Les that his plane had mechanical problems and would be delayed for at least twenty-four hours. A while later, however, a plane was cleared for take-off and Les Hall was on his way back to his family.

They had been airborne for only an hour or so when a signaller passenger conned his way into the cockpit. While there he translated a morse signal which shocked him deeply. 'Cannot fly above 8,000,' the message said. 'Hope to make Labuan, slowly losing height.' When the pilot noticed his passenger's horrified expression he realised he had understood the message. 'Don't say a word out there,' he cautioned. 'We've only got 500 miles to go and we'll make it. There's no need to panic.'

The distraught lad moved quietly back into the cabin and looked around for life jackets. There was none to be seen and the pilot's assurances suddenly had a hollow ring to them.

One of the other passengers on that flight was the legendary doctor, Lieutenant Colonel 'Weary' Dunlop, one of the heroes of the Burma-Thailand railway. 'You've gone as green as grass,' he told the young man, who was clearly incapable of putting on a happy face.

When he found out the reason, Dunlop strode into the cockpit and had a word with the crew. Then he returned and told his fellow passengers of the situation. There was no point in keeping them in the dark. 'But it's all right boys,' he added. 'We've been through worse. We'll make land.'

From that point on all eyes were trying to measure the plane's gradual but noticeable rate of fall as the ocean seemed to come closer and ever more closer. Still, the pilot was clearly doing a wonderful job nursing his injured plane along and eventually a dim outline of land mass began to take shape.

But it didn't seem to approach fast enough and already-taut nerves were dangerously close to fraying when the co-pilot told the passengers to move to the back of the plane. They'd probably have to make a crash landing on the beach, he said, and if the nose wheel is down it might dig into the sand.

The plane moved lower and lower until it was skimming over the water. They seemed to be surfing to shore. Then there was a horrid bump ... a lurch ... and a dead stop

A moment later the smiling pilot appeared, thanked his passengers for their cooperation and composure, and assured them once again that they had never been in real danger.

At this point a few of the ex-POWs exchanged nervous glances. It had been a nerve-racking time and they all knew that a plane that had left Singapore before theirs had crashed. Everyone on board had lived, but the mere thought of losing their lives on the way home, and after surviving all those years of captivity, was more than anyone could bear.

As for Les Hall's plane, when the petrol tanks were drained it was discovered they contained as much water as fuel. The young crewmen seemed to be unperturbed, it was as if they had no fears, and calmly prepared themselves for the last leg of the flight home.

At ten-twenty on a sunny Thursday morning the gleaming silver 'saviour' touched down at Sydney's Mascot Aerodrome. It was 18 October 1945, nine weeks to the day since the Japanese surrender.

When Les Hall stepped onto the tarmac he was surrounded at once by his loving, jubilant family. No greater welcome could have been extended to anyone as that proud man, happier than he had known it was possible to be, reached out his arms and clasped his wife, his daughters and other family members to his heaving breast. The dream that had sustained him for the best part of four years had finally come true. He was home, free, and overwhelmed with affection beyond belief.

Author's Comment

THE COMPILATION of the history of 'A' Force, Groups 3 and 5, has been long and painstaking. In addition to my own records I was very fortunate to have access to personal diaries and memoirs that filled in gaps I would otherwise never have bridged.

I was given an insight into the depths of feeling of men whose courage and fight to survive touched me deeply. Men on the very brink of death wrote of their determination to 'beat it', even when they knew the odds against such a possibility were immense.

How they survived is a miracle; they did it by sheer willpower, the doctors had nothing but hope and dedication with which to help them.

As prisoners of war they were at war against an implacable foe, one who treated them with contempt, who forced them to live on practically nothing yet expected them to work, at times, beyond thirty hours at a shift, when their health was at its lowest ebb.

They were flogged and bashed but never once was their spirit broken. No matter the circumstances, the halt and the lame helped one another. An invaluable bond of mateship was forged in those perilous times, one that cannot and will not ever be broken.

Those who survived that holocaust are a special race, held together by an unseen 'something' one knows is there but which cannot be seen. It will always be there, a kinship the value of which no-one can ever calculate.

Fate decreed not all would come home. Those who did not found peace of mind and body, a release from a horror no-one could ever have envisaged, and now rest in the serenity of hallowed ground in sight of the inhospitable jungles in which they laboured, suffered and lost.

They have gone but will never be forgotten, their memory will live forever.

> At the going down of the sun
> And in the morning
> We will remember them.

—L.G.H.

BIBLIOGRAPHY

AITKEN, E. F., and DICKSON, *The Story of the 2/2nd Australian Pioneer Battalion*, privately published, Melbourne, 1953.

ARNEIL, STAN, *One Man's War*, Sun Books, Melbourne, 1983.

BLAIR, JOAN, and BLAIR, CLAY, *Return From the River Kwai*, Vanguard, New York, 1954.

BOULLE, PIERRE, *The Bridge Over the River Kwai*, Vanguard, New York, 1954.

BOWDEN, TIM, *The Changi Photographer: George Aspinal's Record of Captivity*, William Collins, Sydney, 1984.

BRADDON, RUSSELL, *The Naked Island*, Werner Laurie, London, 1952.

CLARK, HUGH A., *A Life for Every Sleeper*, Allen & Unwin, Sydney, 1986.

DANDIE, ALEX, *The Story of J Force*, privately published, West Ryde, Sydney.

DUNLOP, E. E., *The War Diaries of Weary Dunlop*, Penguin, Ringwood, 1990.

GORDON, EMEST, *Miracle on the River Kwai*, William Collins, Glasgow, 1963.

HOLMES, LINDA GOETZ, *4,000 Bowls of Rice*, Allen & Unwin, Sydney, 1993.

HOMER, D. M., *High Command*, Allen & Unwin, Sydney, 1982.

LaFORTE, ROBERT, and MARCELLO, RONALD, *Building the Death Railway: The Ordeal of American POWs in Burma, 1942-45*, Scholarly Resources Inc., Wilmington, Delaware, 1992.

McLAGGAN, DOUGLAS, *The Will to Survive*, Kangaroo Press, Sydney, 1995.

NELSON, HANK, *Prisoners of War: Australians Under Nippon*, Australian Broadcasting Commission, Sydney, 1985.

RICHARDS, ROWLEY, and McEWAN, MARCIA, *The Survival Factor*, Kangaroo Press, Sydney, 1989.

RIVETT, ROWAN, *Behind Bamboo*, Angus & Robertson, Sydney, 1946.

LORD RUSSELL OF LIVERPOOL, *The Knights of Bushido: A Short History of Japanese War Crimes*, Cassell & Cassell, London, 1958.

SEARLE, RONALD, *To the Kwai—and Back: War Drawings, 1939-1945*, The Atlantic Monthly Press, New York, 1986.

SUMMONS, WALTER, *Twice Their Prisoner*, Oxford University Press, Melbourne, 1946.

WALL, DON, *Heroes at Sea*, privately published, 1991.

WARNER, LAVINIA, and SANDILANDS, J., *Women Beyond the Wire*. F.A. Thorpe, Leicester, 1982.

ROLLCALL

MEMBERS of the 2/30 Infantry Battalion who formed part of 1 Battalion, 'A' Force', which sailed from Singapore 15 May 1942 en route to Burma. Compiled by Lieutenant A. I. Farr.
'x' against a name denotes those who died in camps

NX46451 Pte Arnie M. Ainsworth
NX4516 Pte Fred J. Arnett
NX26670 Pte E.J.(Ted) Bahsen
NX47812 Pte J.H.(Jim) Baird
NX9869 Pte E.W. Biddle
NX50024 Pte C. Gordon Brewin
NX53156 Pte R.W.L. (Bill) Brownbill x
NX37577 Cpl J. (Stan) Bruce
NX56719 Pte Reg Burbury
NX29821 L/Cpl Clarrie J. Burgess
NX10272 Pte Phil F. Carey x
NX30470 Pte J.J. (Jack) Carley x
NX37304 Pte E.P. (Ted) Condie
NX33078 Pte R.A. (Bob) Cunningham
NX4333 Pte Alex (Ike) Denholm
NX31035 Sgt Merv C. Dixon
NX47640 Pte Laurie Drayton
NX51308 WO2 Harry A. Duprez
NX24909 Sgt Stan C.M. DuRoss
NX59028 Pte Ron Errington
NX70448 Lieut. A.I. (Bub) Farr
NX53170 Cpl Tom A. Fitzpatrick
NX51948 Pte Don W. Frith
NX6598 Pte O.C. (Lofty) Gersback
NX36271 Pte George Gough
NX57195 WO2 Syd G. Gratton
NX69322 Pte Fred W. (Pro) Griffiths
NX37566 Pte Jack R. Grossmith
NX37544 Pte Reg Guinton
NX55561 Sgt Les G. Hall
NX57453 Cpl J.A.R. (Ham) Hamilton
NX37281 Pte Vic P. Hamlin
NX25741 L/Cpl Ian G. (Horny) Hann
NX20247 Pte C.J. (Jack) Heatley

NX6920 Pte Con Hedwards
NX37360 Pte Doug A. Hicks
X57126 Pte George H. Holder
QX11044 Pte Glynn M. Holmes
NX37296 Pte Ashley C. Jones
NX42527 Pte Tom Kennedy
NX37305 Pte Ron (Pop Eye) Kentwell
NX46619 Cpl John Korsch
NX70447 Lieut. John F. (Bib) Kreckler
NX54051 Pte W. (Bill) Lamping
NX57812 Pte Jack (J.R.) Langley
NX31783 S/Sgt H.A. (Aub) Lansdown
NX17253 Pte Jack (Dinny)
NX35394 Pte S.J. Ledw
NX26885 Pte Vince Leonard
NX32474 Pte Arthur Lloyd
NX65297 Sgt Mick Lovell
NX20550 Pte Tom McCloud
NX42542 Pte Will R. McDonald
NX627 Pte Sydney R. McGovern
NX45789 L/Cpl J.M. (Jim) McGrath
NX41396 Pte Ron McLean
NX30302 L/Cpl Jim McNab
NX31777 Cpl W. (Bill) McNeil
NX7248 Pte Fred May
NX46367 Pte Ray (Joe Palooka) Marriott
NX34437 S/Sgt Jim Mitchell x
NX51725 L/Cpl R.W. (Dick) Morey
NX32703 Sgt W.J. (Bill) Moynihan
NX47353 Pte L.C. (Spearo) Nielson
NX37430 Pte Joe A. Noble
NX37637 Pte Jack North
NX52778 Pte Reg Nossiter
NX2561 Pte Tom Oliver

NX47292 L/Cpl George A. Osmond
NX2501 Pte Arthur G.M. Overett
NX913 Pte Watson Peck
NX72045 Pte Harold V. Perandis
NX36521 Pte Les G. Perry
NX55172 Pte C.J. (Tankie) Phillips **x**
NX37421 Pte Stuart H. Plowes
NX55420 Pte L.F. Pollard **x**
NX12548 Capt. J.A. Pryde (Gulah)
NX34599 Col. G.E. Ramsay (OIC, #1
Bn. 'A' Force)
NX47007 Pte Howard C. (Bill) Robinson
NX594 Pte Ron A. Sanson
NX37671 Pte Jim Saunderson
NX2567 Pte W.F. (Bill) Schberth **x**
NX37543 Pte Ossie V. Skinner

NX33384 Cpl E.F. (Ted) Skuse
NX51053 Pte W.F. (Bill) Slattery
NX47542 Pte M.L. (Jimmy) Small
NX37632 Pte W.R. Smedley **x**
NX68232 Pte J. (Ben) Templman
QX24188 Pte John H.S. Thomas
NX32743 Sgt Frank Tome
NX53104 Pte Elwin (Tim) Turner
QX15813 Pte V.D. (Tick) Wallace
NX71616 Pte I.F. Webber
NX41339 Pte Les H. Wharton
NX66840 Pte Dudley N. Wilkinson
NX596 Pte Leo Winters
NX41360 Cpl R.R. (Bob) Wright
★ Special entry: NX77799 S.H.T. Busine,
ex-Java Party #4, rejoined 2/30 Battalion.

Australian survivors of the sinking of the *Rakuyo Maru* rescued by the USS *Pampanito*.

VX.43376 Pte J.L. Boulter 2/2 MT Regt South Melbourne, Vic

NX.50497 Pte J.F.M. Browne 2/15 Fld Regt Parramatta, NSW

QX.9591 Pte R.C. Bullock 8 Div Provost Coy Brisbane, Qld

VX.26828 Pte H.C. Chivars 2/2 Pioneer Bn West Melbourne, Vic

WX.16369 Pte A.J. Cocking 2/2 MG Bn WA

NX.2111 Pte F.J. Coombes 3 Res MT Coy Sandringham, NSW

NX.44955 Pte R. Cornford 2/19 Bn Wollongong, NSW

VX.32993 Sgt D.W. Cunneen 4 A/Tk Regt Nagambie, Vic

NX.37529 Pte M.W. Curran 2/19 Bn Zetland, NSW

NX.35756 Cpl C.L. Farlow 2/19 Bn Hay, NSW

VX.60993 Pte. F.L. Farmer 2/10 Ord Wk Shps Black Rock, Vic

NX.36050 Cpl M.R. Farrands 2/19 Bn Ganmain, NSW

SX.10228 Dvr D.A. Flynn 2 Res MT Coy Adelaide, SA

VX.61502 Pte R.J. Gainger 2/10 Ord Wk Shps Geelong West, Vic

NX.44147 Pte R.G. Gollin MLFD Lismore, NSW

QX.9275 Gnr R.J. Harris 2/10 RAE Brisbane, Qld

VX.23586 Spr R.H. Hart 2/10 RAE Melbourne, Vic

VX.17768 Cpl J.R. Hocking 2/2 Pioneer Bn Castlemaine, Vic

QX.23670 Pte F. Holcroft 2/3 Ord Stores Coy Brisbane, Qld

VX.41958 Sig F.W. Jesse 2 Res MT Coy Blackburn, Vic

VX.65127 Gnr H.L. Kinleyside 4 A/Tk Rgt Mildura, Vic

QX.13551 Pte J.H. Lansdowne 2/26 Bn Murwillumbah, NSW

NX.72262 Desp Rdr C.T.S. Latham 3 MT Coy Merrylands, NSW

TX.4802 Pte C. Longey 2/40 Bn Hobart, Tas

QX.24156 Pte D.F. Lynch 2/2 Pioneer Bn Warwick, Qld

QX.22879 Pte C.W. Madden 8 Div HQ Tweed Heads, NSW

WX.204 Pte H.D. Martin 2/10 Ord Wk Shps Esperance, WA

VX.2064 Pte R.G. Mawby 2/2 Pioneer Bn Murumbeena, Vic

VX.36838 Cpl D. McArdle 2/29 Bn Rushworth, Vic

QX.14464 Bdr C. McKechnie 2/10 Fld Regt. Brisbane, Qld

NX.33414 Pte W.H. McKittrick 2/12 Fld. Coy RAE Woollahra, NSW

QX.13804 Gnr R.C. Miscamble 2/10 Fld Regt Brisbane, Qld

WX.7409 Dvr T.A. Pascoe 2/4 MG Bn Denmark, WA

WX.9055 Sig H. Pickett 2/4 MG Bn Midland Junction, WA

VX.22728 Pte K.C. Renton 2/2 Pioneer Bn Port Melbourne, Vic

NX.32726 Sgt J.O. Smith 2/19 Bn North Bondi, NSW

SX.11294 Cpl. C.G. Smith Ml Coy Goolwa, SA

NX.35359 Pte P. Smith 2/19 Bn Narrandera, NSW

VX.31123 Gnr R.S. Stewart 4 A/Tk Regt Malvern, Vic

SX.10112 Dvr J.W. Turner 2 Res MT Coy Adelaide, SA

VX.59658 Pte J.A. Vickers 27 Bde HQ Melbourne, Vic

VX.58797 Pte R.J. Wall 2 Res MT Bn Hopetown, Vic

NX.32373 Spr H.G. Weigand 2/12 RAE Katoomba, NSW

Pte S.McL. White 2/29 Bn Melbourne, Vic

SX.11200 Cpl K. Williams 27 Bde Army Ord Oak Bank, SA

WX.8110 Pte A.D. Winter 2/4 MG Bn Redcliffe, WA

WX.10373 Pte W.X. Winter 2/4 MG Bn South Perth, WA

INDEX